DEFINING DOCUMENTS IN WORLD HISTORY

The 17th Century (1601–1700)

DEFINING DOCUMENTS
IN WORLD HISTORY

The 17th Century (1601–1700)

Editor

David Simonelli, PhD

Volume 1

SALEM PRESS
A Division of EBSCO Information Services
Ipswich, Massachusetts

GREY HOUSE PUBLISHING

Cover image: Title page of *Sidereus nuncius*, 1610, by Galileo Galilei (1564-1642). Source: *IC6.G1333.610s, Houghton Library, Harvard University. (Public Domain, via Wikimedia Commons).

Copyright ©2017, by Schlager Group, Inc., and Grey House Publishing, Inc.

All rights reserved. No part of this work may be used or reproduced in any manner whatsoever or transmitted in any form or by any means, electronic or mechanical, including photocopy, recording, or any information storage and retrieval system, without written permission from the copyright owner.

∞ The paper used in these volumes conforms to the American National Standard for Permanence of Paper for Printed Library Materials, Z39.48 1992 (R2009).

Publisher's Cataloging-In-Publication Data
(Prepared by The Donohue Group, Inc.)

Names: Simonelli, David, editor.
Title: The 17th century (1601-1700) / editor, David Simonelli, PhD.
Other Titles: Defining documents in world history.
Description: [First edition]. | Ipswich, Massachusetts : Salem Press, a division of EBSCO Information Services ;
    [Amenia, New York] : Grey House Publishing, [2017] | Includes bibliographical references and index.
Identifiers: ISBN 978-1-68217-301-5 (set) | ISBN 978-1-68217-303-9 (v. 1) | ISBN 978-1-68217-304-6 (v. 2)
Subjects: LCSH: History, Modern--17th century--Sources. | Civilization, Modern--17th century--Sources. | Europe-
    -History--17th century--Sources. | Science--Europe--History--17th century--Sources. | Religions--History--17th
    century--Sources.
Classification: LCC D242 .A17 2017 | DDC 909.6--dc23

Table of Contents

Publisher's Note ix
Editor's Introduction. xi
Contributors xv

Volume 1

EUROPE: SCIENCE, RELIGION, AND LAW   1

Galileo Galilei: *Starry Messenger* 3
Letter of Cardinal Bellarmine to Paolo Antonio Foscarini concerning Galileo's Theories 13
Miguel de Cervantes: *Don Quixote* 19
Treaty of Westphalia. 28
Czar Alexis I: Great Muscovite Law Code 42
Louis XIV: Edict of Fontainebleau 54

ENGLAND: CIVIL WAR AND REVOLUTION   61

James I: Speech on the Divine Right of Kings 63
Westminster Confession 72
Charles I: Speech on the Scaffold 90
Thomas Hobbes: *Leviathan* 97
Habeas Corpus Act of the Restoration 106
John Bunyan: *The Pilgrim's Progress* 117
Isaac Newton: *The Mathematical Principles of Natural Philosophy* 133
English Bill of Rights 140
John Locke: *Second Treatise on Civil Government* 152

CHRISTIANITY AND SOCIETY IN THE EAST   167

Tokugawa Ieyasu: Laws Governing Military Households 169
Japan's Closed Country Edict 177
Matteo Ricci: "Religious Sects among the Chinese" 185
Li Yü: "On Being Happy Though Poor" 195
Regent Dorgon: Edict to the Board of War and Imperial Edict to the Board of Rites 200
Meritorious Deeds at No Cost 205

v

Yang Guangxian: *I Cannot Do Otherwise (Budeyi)* 210
Kangxi Emperor: Edict of Toleration 215

Volume 2

The Muslim World: Trade and Toleration   221

Raag Gond 223
Charles Davenant: An Essay on the East-India Trade 241
Jahangir: Twelve Decrees 250

European Colonies in the Americas: The English Mid-Atlantic   257

John Rolfe: Letter to Sir Edwin Sandys 259
Richard Frethorne: Letter to His Parents 269
John Smith: *The Generall Historie of Virginia* 274
Cecil Calvert: Maryland Toleration Act 284
Virginia's Act XII: Negro Women's Children to Serve according to the Condition of the Mother 290
Nathaniel Bacon: *Manifesto* 294
"A Minute against Slavery, Addressed to the Germantown Monthly Meeting" 301
Declaration of Protestant Subjects in Maryland 309

European Colonies in the Americas: New England   317

Letter of Edward Winslow to a Friend 319
John Winthrop: "A Model of Christian Charity" 324
Excerpts from the Massachusetts Bay Colony Trial against Anne Hutchinson 333
Roger Williams: *The Bloudy Tenent of Persecution* 341
Narrative of the Captivity and Restoration of Mrs. Mary Rowlandson 349
Declaration of the Gentlemen, Merchants and Inhabitants of Boston, and the Country Adjacent 359
Sir Edmund Andros: *Report of His Administration* 367

European Colonies in the Americas: Other Colonies — 375

Samuel de Champlain: *Voyages* 377
Charter of the Dutch West India Company 385
Father Paul Le Jeune: Brief Relation of the Journey to New France 393
Adriaen Van der Donck: *Description of the New-Netherlands* 403
António Vieira: "Children of God's Fire" 415

Appendixes — 425

Chronological List 427
Web Resources 429
Bibliography 435
Index 441

Publisher's Note

Defining Documents in World History series, produced by Salem Press, consists of a collection of essays on important historical documents by a diverse range of writers on a broad range of subjects in American history. This established series includes *Ancient World* (2700 BCE–c. 500 CE), *Middle Ages* (476–1500), and *Renaissance & Early Modern Era* (1308–1600) in addition to the latest title: *The 17th Century (1601–1700)*.

The 17th Century offers in-depth analysis of a broad range of historical documents and historic events that make up the story of a century marked by scientific discovery, codification of laws, the development of religious doctrine, civil war, colonization, and the expansion of trade on a global level. The set begins with the Galileo's writings about man's place in the universe and a denial of heliocentrism in *Starry Messenger* and concludes with a letter from Father António Vieira, a man who felt keenly the injustices of slavery but who called on the slaves themselves, not to revolt, but to await their heavenly reward for their sufferings on earth. The religious tracts, articles, essays, petitions, laws, and letters span the century to examine the way that the scholars, clerics, philosophers, kings, and revolutionaries of the time viewed the world and their place in it. The forty-nine articles in this volume are organized into seven sections:

- Europe: Science, Religion and Law
- England: Civil War and Revolution
- Christianity and Society in the East
- The Muslim World: Trade and Toleration
- European Colonies in the Americas: The English Mid-Atlantic
- European Colonies in the Americas: New England
- European Colonies in the Americas: Other Colonies

Historical documents provide a compelling view of the seventeenth century, an important aspect of world history. Designed for high school and college students, the aim of the series is to advance historical document studies as an important activity in learning about history.

Essay Format
The 17th Century contains forty-nine primary source documents—many in their entirety. Each document is supported by a critical essay, written by historians and teachers, that includes a Summary Overview, Defining Moment, Author Biography, Document Analysis, and Essential Themes. Readers will appreciate the diversity of the collected texts, including speeches, letters, political and religious sermons, laws, edicts, and charters among other genres. An important feature of each essay is a close reading of the primary source that develops evidence of broader themes, such as the author's rhetorical purpose, social or class position, point of view, and other relevant issues. In addition, essays are organized by section themes, listed above, highlighting major issues of the period, many of which extend across eras and continue to shape life as we know it around the world. Each section begins with a brief introduction that defines questions and problems underlying the subjects in the historical documents. Each essay also includes a Bibliography and Further Reading section for further research.

Appendixes
- **Chronological List** arranges all documents by year.
- **Web Resources** is an annotated list of websites that offer valuable supplemental resources.
- **Bibliography** lists helpful articles and books for further study.

Contributors
Salem Press would like to extend its appreciation to all involved in the development and production of this work. The essays have been written and signed by scholars of history, humanities, and other disciplines related to the essays' topics. Without these expert contributions, a project of this nature would not be possible. A full list of contributor's names appears in the front matter of this volume.

Editor's Introduction

In the western tradition, the seventeenth century is a turning point in the history of the world, marking a transition between the medieval and the modern age. In fact, the seventeenth century is often referred to as the "early modern age." The medieval era was a time when the world's great religions spread across continents, and empires perpetuated or established themselves at the expense of small nations. Medieval economies were simple and internal, inventions were few and far between, and science was still mostly rooted in the ancient era. In our modern era, some parts of the word are seeing religion lose its influence in government, the arts, and education, while in other areas, it remains a strong force that in some cases is extending its reach across continents and hemispheres. The idea of an empire is a mostly a relic of the past, replaced by today's nation-state, based on the idea that people's differences should determine who governs them. Democracy and capitalism have swept the globe, creating an intense international market where problems that arise in one place can have a destabilizing impact on the global economy. And inventions, innovations, science and technology are advancing by leaps and bounds, to the point where many people are uncomfortable with how quickly this is happening.

The early modern period in world history, then, was an era of transition between the medieval world and the one in which we find ourselves living. During that transition, some aspects of the old world gave way to newer, more modern ides, while others became more firmly entrenched, in seeming defiance of progress. In the seventeenth century, religions were carried across the oceans and trade routes to new sections of the world, and people began the process of learning to tolerate differing views regarding the forces they believed governed the universe. At the same time that a scientific revolution was opening up human minds to new ideas, efforts arose to wipe out heresies and stifle "alternative" religious concepts. Men who went to war found themselves fighting not only to defend their homes and property but also their right to hold ideas and beliefs that did not always square with the old, established order. While empires were still the preferred form of state management, colonization and rebellion were disrupting the old order. Meanwhile, the concept of monarchy was solidified and connected to religion—kings sat on thrones because God wanted them there. Worldwide trade connections made new and exotic products available to an emerging middle class; this growing trade meant that economies became increasing complex. At the same time that the world appeared to be opening up, those who saw these economic changes as a threat fought against them. While science made new revelations about the universe and how it worked, religious leaders worked diligently to prevent any challenges to a religious understanding of the universe.

Seventeenth-century Europe was the catalyst for much of this change. There were numerous reasons that Europeans were poised and motivated to reach out to a wider world. The Crusades had given them good reasons to build bigger and better ships that could carry armies to the Levant and bring imported goods home. One of these goods was gunpowder, invented in China and used in cannon; Europeans were the first people (along with the Japanese) to create a gun, essentially a handheld cannon. Europe's appetite for luxury goods from east and south Asia was whetted by the Crusades and fed by means of the comparatively open access to trade routes brought about by the success of the Mongol empires. Ever since the Renaissance opened up the Europeans' knowledge of geography, mapmakers were able to produce the maps that allowed explorers, conquerors, and merchants to travel the world. The Protestant Reformation unleashed competition between Catholics and Protestants and meant that priests and clerics also roamed the globe, looking for more and more souls to convert to their faith. Bigger ships and better maps meant that people could far more easily travel the oceans and seas that covered 80 percent of the planet to get to lands that were previously out of reach. Gunpowder and cannons meant that the new arrivals could not only defend themselves but also gain the wealth and power they sought, whether they were motivated by economic or religious purposes. The seventeenth century would prove to be an era when European adventurism reached its height.

It was also an era when crises throughout continental Europe reached a high point, due largely to disputes over religion. The Thirty Years' War exhausted all of the states involved, both Catholic and Protestant; an estimated one third of the people of Germany died either as casualties of war or from the famine, disease, and other hardships that came along with the war. Oddly, though, the state experiencing the most turmoil was

England, even though it remained largely removed from the war on the continent. The English had their own problems, including a brutal debate over the structure of the Church of England and the power of the reigning Stuart monarchs. Life in England was, as Thomas Hobbes famously formulated it, "nasty, brutish and short." When the Stuart king James I ascended to the throne, he brought with him a strong conviction about the divine right of kings, a concept which met strong resistance from his people, who believed they deserved to be consulted on matters of government and power, as they had when the Tudors were in power. Puritans in Parliament were especially aggravated over the king's insistence on maintaining a hierarchical structure in the Church of England that they found far too reminiscent of Catholicism for their liking. The situation deteriorated under Charles I, until finally he took up arms against Parliament in what became the English Civil War (1642-1649). Charles lost the war as well as his own head, leaving England's Puritans to rule simultaneously over all four nations of the British Isles— England, Wales, Scotland and Ireland—a rule which they managed very badly. By 1660, life had become so anarchic in Britain that the army invited Charles II to return to the throne to restore order. Yet Charles himself was repeatedly in conflict with his parliament. The situation only worsened under Charles's brother, James II, who was a converted Catholic. Parliament was offended both by James's religion and the fact that his wife gave birth to a Catholic son and heir. Members of Parliament found this intolerable enough to run James out of the country in favor of his Protestant daughter, Mary, and her Protestant husband, William. All of this turmoil ultimately resulted in a peaceable, representative, and religiously diverse state in the eighteenth century. The process of getting there, though, was as turbulent and momentous as any in European history.

There was an outlet for those who wanted to escape the turmoil in England, and indeed in all of Western Europe—the Americas. After the Spanish and Portuguese settled colonists in Central America, South America, and the Caribbean in the sixteenth century, the seventeenth century saw a regular stream of people gambling on a move across the Atlantic to expand their economic and religious opportunities in North America. The English were the most numerous—they had the most reason to leave. The colony of Virginia was established on the east coast of North America, centered around a town named for their monarch, Jamestown.

For years, the colonists struggled until they discovered a product that could be exported home at a profit— tobacco. The colonists still struggled against disease and hostile Indians throughout the century, but in general, Virginia prospered, especially once the colonists turned to a hardier labor force, in the form of African slaves. The inhumanity of slavery and its aftereffects would become a blight on the new nation's history for centuries to come.

Meantime, to the north, other colonists settled near Cape Cod in a colony they named after their home in England—Plymouth. The Plymouth "Pilgrims" had a different agenda from Jamestown's colonists. They intended to create a model Protestant religious community, a "city on a hill" as an example to the rest of the world of how to establish a proper Christian world. While profit was a necessity, it was distinctly secondary to living an upright and righteous life. Economic gains were understood to be the result of whether or not God smiled on the community. The colony proved successful enough to attract many Puritans who chose to leave England rather than stay and do battle against Charles I, and they started a second colony in Massachusetts Bay around the town they named Boston. Yet, as much as the colonists wished for their own religious freedom, they were also quite willing to suppress religious ideas they did not find suitable themselves. Colonists who wanted true religious tolerance moved to Maryland where they lived under the government of the Catholic Lord Baltimore. Later, Quakers settled in the colony of William Penn, called Pennsylvania.

The French and Dutch also set up colonies in North America—the French along the St. Lawrence River in the region they called New France (later Quebec) and the Dutch along the Hudson River in New Netherlands (modern day New York). Both sets of colonists maintained much better relations with the native Americans living in these areas than did the English, largely because the French and the Dutch relied on the native Americans for their help in securing the pelts that went into the lucrative fur trade. The Portuguese, meanwhile, supported their colonies, not by engaging with the indigenous peoples, but by bringing slaves from Africa to work their sugar plantations in Brazil.

In the climate of religious mayhem in Europe, it was vital to both Catholics and Protestants to acquire more souls to worship God in the appropriate manner. The Catholics were more ambitious. Jesuits traveled all over the world to teach the word of God, with their major goal being East Asia— Japan and China. The peoples there had different reactions to the coming of Christianity. In Japan, Christian missionaries arrived just after a vast civil war had come to an end. In this atmosphere of distrust and potential rebellion, the Tokugawa shoguns chose to ban Christianity altogether and cut Japan off from all but the most circumscribed European trade traffic. In China, Jesuits arrived during a period of economic prosperity so great that there was a dynastic turnover from the Ming to the Qing with few long-term economic consequences whatsoever. In this economically secure civilization, Jesuit missionaries were allowed to spread Christianity amongst elites in China, including the emperor Kangxi, who may have considered converting sometime during the 1690s.

The seventeenth-century Muslim world was divided into three empires of power and prosperity—the Safavids in Persia; the Ottomans in southern Europe, the Near East and North Africa; and the Mughals in south Asia. The Ottomans and Mughals in particular lived in multi-religious empires, celebrating their diversity and striving to treat all their subjects with Muslim compassion and responsibility. Internally, each empire was a paragon of stability, as we know from the contemporaneous reports from travelers to the region; externally, these empires sowed the seeds of their own decline by opening themselves up to European traders, whose economies often depended on their ability to distribute Turkish or Indian goods around the world.

The world of the seventeenth century may seem far removed from our own in terms of the level of its scientific understanding, material wealth, and its strict adherence to religious practices. Yet in many ways, the seventeenth century is much like the twenty-first. We can point to a growing decline in the numbers of those who count themselves as practicing members of a particular religion in more "Westernized" nations, at the same time that religious fundamentalists of all stripes plant their values like flags dotting the globe as a declaration of their rejection of the culture and mores of the decadent societies of the Western world. People who travel the planet today may well find themselves facing hostile populations when they arrive at a new destination. Democracy appears to be the most sought-after political system around the world, and yet even in democratic societies, many complain that economic elites have used lobbying and influence-peddling to subvert the system and bend it to their own ends. These elites work tirelessly for their interests, which are sometimes at odds with the interests of the majority. Science and technology are changing at an amazing pace, but while computers, microchips, and the internet are spurring advances on many fronts, they also carry the seeds that can grow into new harms to societies as they invade the private lives of those who embrace the brave new world. Yet those who lack the means or the education to be part of the technological revolution are being left behind. It can be argued that the twenty-first century, just like the seventeenth century, marks a period of transition between a modern and postmodern world. Viewed through that lens, the fundamental differences between the seventeenth century and ours do not appear so great.

David Simonelli
Department of History
Youngstown State University
Youngstown, Ohio

Contributors

Brian Bonhomme

William E. Burns

Lee Butler, PhD

Donald R. Franceschetti, PhD

Aaron Gulyas

Kirk R. MacGregor

Andrew Mansfield

Christopher Ohan

Michael J. O'Neal, PhD

Martha I. Pallante

Raymond A. Powell

Luca Prono, PhD

Peter Robinson

Peter Robinson

LaChelle E. M. Schilling

David Simonelli

Marcella Bush Treviño

Andrew J. Waskey

Europe: Science, Religion, and Law

Seventeenth-century Europe was a civilization on the verge of world domination. In the period following the dissolution of the Roman Empire in 1453, Europeans had neither the population nor the resources necessary to be a major regional power, let alone a civilization that could extend its reach around the planet. Yet numerous changes during the sixteenth century led to Europeans, both west and east, asserting their ambitions to build mercantile economies and colonial empires. All of those changes began at home.

The seventeenth century in Europe was the age of the scientific revolution. The Renaissance had revived interest in the ancient world and its scientific advances, and many Europeans were inspired to inquire about their universe and render it more understandable. In the past, the method of inquiry was simply to posit an answer to a problem and logically work it out, mostly in print— the quality of the logic one used determined whether the answer was considered true or not. The scientific revolution marked a different type of inquiry: men observed natural phenomena, created a hypothesis, and tested answers until one proved to be true. In this fashion, Robert Boyle discovered his laws on gases, Antonie van Leeuwenhoek invented the microscope, and Evangelista Torricelli used a barometer to measure air pressure and invent meteorology.

The field that attracted the most scientific inquiry, however, was astronomy, engaging the curiosity of the most famous scientist of the first half of the century, Galileo Galilei. In his work *Starry Messenger*, he asserted that the earth revolved around the sun, as opposed to the sun revolving around the earth. Publishing his ideas meant that Galileo ran headlong into opposition from the other major institution of seventeenth-century western civilization: the Roman Catholic church. The church established a group of institutions to combat heresy, know to us as the Inquisition. The Inquisition's "hammer," Cardinal Bellarmine, officially warned Galileo to back off on his claims, which contradicted Biblical "truth." When Galileo published his ideas in another work, *Dialogue Concerning the Two Chief World Systems* (1632), he was threatened with excommunication and forced to admit he was wrong. If science was forging the path forward into the European future, religion refused to ride along, determined instead to maintain medieval values of Christianity's primacy in European life.

This was also the era of the Thirty Years' War, concluded by the Treaty of Westphalia, which simply affirmed what had been true before the war started— people adopted the religion of their ruling prince. Even decades after the war was over, Louis XIV's revocation of the Edict of Nantes, which legalized toleration of Protestantism in France, meant that religious divisions still kept Europeans apart.

As a result of the changing economy in Europe, the feudal order and its tightly structured social order started to wither away. A growing mercantile order of traders, merchants, bankers, professionals, and successful farmers—what our capitalist world would call a middle class—began to challenge the aristocracies and monarchies. Lacking support from the larger proportion of the population, few of these challenges were successful in the long term. The English overthrew one monarch, then reinstated him, and then decided to run his grandson out of the country. The French aristocracy launched a rebellion, the Fronde, against the Bourbon Dynasty, but Louis XIV managed to survive it intact. The Thirty Years' War began as the effort to topple of the Holy Roman Emperor's administration in Prague in 1618. All of these events led to the restructuring of political and social hierarchies to keep the peace. In Russia, a period of disorder climaxed in a riot in Moscow against corruption, which led to the tsarist autocracy's issuing of the *Sobornoye Ulozhenie*, the great Muscovite Law Code. The *Ulozhenie* was an effort to reestablish the Romanov family's authority, in part by reinforcing feudalism and codifying what it meant to be a serf.

The function of all this turmoil was to inspire Europeans to expand—across the Atlantic, along the African coast, to India and East Asia, across Siberia. Some Europeans exploited the mercantile economy; others fought it and left it. Some Europeans were adventurers, inspired by science to explore the planet; others brought science with them to convince foreign peoples to adopt their religion. Some Europeans escaped religious conflict at home, often to set up further conflicts abroad. Some Europeans looked to exploit other peoples, particularly Africans whom they bought and sold, primarily in the Americas. All of these efforts and activities made the seventeenth century the first truly European century in world history.

■ Galileo Galilei: *Starry Messenger*

Date: 1610
Author: Galileo Galilei
Genre: Scientific treatise

Summary Overview

Published in 1610 in Venice, Galileo Galilei's *Sidereus Nuncius*, or *Starry Messenger*, reported the fascinating discoveries that Galileo had made thanks to his telescope observations. It was the first published astronomical treatise to be based on direct telescope observation. Galileo had been interested in astronomy for a few years when, in 1609, he began to build his own telescope. This new instrument enabled him to make detailed observations of the moon, the stars in the Milky Way, and Jupiter's moons. Galileo's observations of the Earth's moon allowed him to conclude that its topography was not too different from that of the earth. This conclusion challenged one of the basic principles of traditional Thomistic and Aristotelian cosmology, according to which celestial bodies were different on a quality level from the earth. Because of this challenge, the *Starry Messenger* caused some controversy. Yet, in 1611, the Jesuit Collegio Romano, the scientific authority of the Church, announced its support for all of Galileo's discoveries—thus contributing to the establishment of his scientific reputation. It was also enthusiastically received by the German mathematician and astronomer Johannes Kepler.

Defining Moment

In the seventeenth century, the religious wars that had engulfed Europe since the Protestant Reformation came to a climax in the Thirty Years' War between 1618 and 1648. Heresy and the loss of Christian followers made the Roman Catholic Church institutionally paranoid, always on the lookout for those who would disobey its doctrines or theology. This was especially the case with science. Since its inception, the Catholic Church had sponsored scientific inquiry as a way of finding out the workings of God's universe as revealed in the Bible and in church rhetoric. Yet with the Renaissance and the Scientific Revolution taking place in Europe – not to mention patrons outside the church for the first time who were willing to pay for scientists to manage their studies – there was a major challenge arising in defiance of the Roman Catholic Church's conception of the universe.

Since the time of the ancient Greeks, westerners had believed that the earth revolved around the sun, based largely on Aristotle's evidence of empirical observation: it just looked that way. The Roman Catholic Church adopted this view, and also sponsored the study of astronomy because understanding the stars was one means of trying to understand God. Calendars could be plotted against the stars and the moon's phases, and the heavens seemed the obvious place to find God Himself. The entire universe revolved around God's creation on earth, which coincided with the descriptions of the earth's creation in the Book of Genesis, and the story in the Book of Joshua where the Lord stops the sun from moving across the sky so the Hebrews can have more time to defeat their enemies.

Around the time of the Reformation in the early 1500s, a Polish priest, Nicolaus Copernicus, posited that the sun was at the center of the universe, because his mathematical calculations of orbits made more sense if that were the case. The sun seemed to move in the sky because the earth revolved once around its central axis once a day, therefore the sun crossed the sky during this period. Many astronomers considered these ideas a possibility, but the Roman Catholic Church condemned it right away. If the sun were at the center of the universe, the earth must revolve around it, and at an outrageous rate of speed (30 miles a second around the sun, 800 miles an hour around its axis). Without a conception of gravity, this seemed ludicrous – everything on the earth would fly off into space if it were true. Most of all, it conflicted with the vision set in Genesis of the creation, whereas Aristotle's model did not.

Seventy-five years later, Galileo Galilei began his studies of mathematics at the University of Padua. He studied mathematics because he considered it the key to understanding the universe as a function of the mind of God, an insight into his philosophical mindset. In 1609, he came upon a telescope, just invented in the Netherlands, and began toying with ideas for perfecting it as a tool. He learned how to grind spectacle lenses and reshape them to expand the telescope's magnifica-

Title page of *Sidereus nuncius*, 1610, by Galileo Galilei (1564-1642). Source: *IC6.G1333.610s, Houghton Library, Harvard University. [Public Domain]via Wikimedia Commons).

tion power, eventually by twenty times. At first he sold his improved telescopes to the Venetian navy, but eventually he spent eight weeks at his own home, pointing his telescope at the stars and sketching what he saw.

He observed the moon through all of its phases in that time and then made adaptations to the telescope to allow him to see even farther into the heavens. One week, he studied what he thought were three "fixed stars" near Jupiter; he eventually realized that there was a fourth one and that they were orbiting around Jupiter, and decided correctly that they were moons. These were the first heavenly bodies discovered by anyone on earth in a thousand years. Furthermore, when another planet appeared to have moons circulating around it, it was clear that not everything in the universe revolved around the earth.

Galileo hurried to get his ideas published, before someone else perfected a telescope too and came up with the same idea. *Sidereus Nuncius,* or *The Starry Messenger* was published in Venice in 1610 and sold out almost immediately. Galileo became the most famous natural philosopher in Europe almost overnight; he named the four moons after members of the Medici family and received the patronage he was searching for that would allow him to live and work without teaching. At the same time, he also came to the attention of the Roman Catholic Church.

Author Biography
Galileo Galilei was born in Pisa, Italy in 1564; his family moved to Florence when he was young. Italy at the time was divided into city-states and was in the midst of the Renaissance, a period of great cultural flowering in European history when the old Greco-Roman roots of western civilization were rediscovered. Thus, Galileo was surrounded by art, ideas, politics and science, and his life would reflect all of these things.

In 1581, Galileo started at the University of Pisa, where he studied pendulums and came up with the concept of the pendulum clock. He also tested the idea that objects of different densities fall at the same rate, a concept that would eventually lead to Newton's theory of gravity; he wrote his first book, *On Motion,* about the subject. Later, he moved to Padua to teach mathematics at the University of Padua. At the time, mathematicians were employed often as war machine engineers, and Galileo became a consultant to the Venetian navy, where he perfected the use of oars to power ships. He also created a military compass used to calculate distances for shipboard cannon.

While in Padua, Galileo learned about a comparatively new instrument, the telescope; its utility as a device that allowed a military host to see their enemy at a distance was obvious. At the same time, though, he was hoping to move out of working as a military engineer and step up in social rank to become a "natural philosopher", a scientist who used his skills to study nature, and thus God. Rather than training his telescopes on enemy soldiers, Galileo began to use them to study the stars.

He perfected the telescope, to improve its magnification from three times to twenty times. Using it, he could look at the skies, studying the moon, the stars, the moons of Jupiter, the other planets and the sun. Through his observations, he came to believe that the sun was at the center of the universe and that the earth revolved around it, rather than the other way around, reinforcing the ideas of the Polish astronomer Nicolaus Copernicus.

Galileo wanted to move back to Florence, the power seat of the Medici family, to get patronage that would allow him to quit teaching. He also wanted to stop inventing new war machines and study the stars, while still maintaining the patronage necessary to do his work. Galileo's answer was to tackle a major philosophical and physical question about the universe, and dedicate his answer to the Medicis who employed him, thus attaching their names to cutting-edge knowledge and technology. The subject he chose was heliocentrism, the theory that the earth revolved around the sun. It worked—in 1610 he received a stipend from the Medicis that would allow him to continue his studies.

Ideas such as that of gravity or heliocentrism were challenges to the science of physics as conceived by the Greek scientist and philosopher Aristotle, hardly a surprise after 2000 years. However, the Aristotelian system was the accepted way of knowing the universe within the Roman Catholic Church, and Copernicus' theories had been declared heresy already. This was a serious issue as Galileo considered himself a pious Catholic. Galileo was warned not to promote Copernicus' theories under order of Pope Paul V, that he should not discuss or defend Copernican theories.

In 1623, however, a new pope arrived, Urban VIII, who as a cardinal had talked at length to Galileo about his theories. Urban declared that Galileo could publicize Copernicus' heliocentrism so long as he did not treat it as an absolute truth of science. Galileo soon published *Dialogue Concerning the Two Chief World*

Systems (1633), believing he had followed this dictate—the church decided that he had not. Therefore Galileo was called to Rome, and on pain of excommunication, he was forced to renounce Copernican theory and accept house arrest for the remainder of his life. He returned to his home in Florence, where he gradually went blind before dying in 1642. He would be absolved by Pope John Paul II only in 1992.

HISTORICAL DOCUMENT

Excerpt from *Starry Messenger* by Galileo Galilei

In the present small treatise I set forth some matters of great interest for all observers of natural phenomena to look at and consider. They are of great interest, I think, first, from their intrinsic excellence; secondly, from their absolute novelty; and lastly, also on account of the instrument by the aid of which they have been presented to my apprehension.

The number of the Fixed Stars which observers have been able to see without artificial powers of sight up to this day can be counted. It is therefore decidedly a great feat to add to their number, and to set distinctly before the eyes other stars in myriads, which have never been seen before, and which surpass the old, previously known, stars in number more than ten times.

Again, it is a most beautiful and delightful sight to behold the body of the Moon, which is distant from us nearly sixty semi-diameters of the Earth, as near as if it was at a distance of only two of the same measures; so that the diameter of this same Moon appears about thirty times larger, its surface about nine hundred times, and its solid mass nearly 27,000 times larger than when it is viewed only with the naked eye; and consequently any one may know with the certainty that is due to the use of our senses, that the Moon certainly does not possess a smooth and polished surface, but one rough and uneven, and, just like the face of the Earth itself, is everywhere full of vast protuberances, deep chasms, and sinuosities.

Then to have got rid of disputes about the Galaxy or Milky Way, and to have made its nature clear to the very senses, not to say to the understanding, seems by no means a matter which ought to be considered of slight importance. In addition to this, to point out, as with one's finger, the nature of those stars which every one of the astronomers up to this time has called nebulous, and to demonstrate that it is very different from what has hitherto been believed, will be pleasant, and very fine. But that which will excite the greatest astonishment by far, and which indeed especially moved me to call the attention of all astronomers and philosophers, is this, namely, that I have discovered four planets, neither known nor observed by any one of the astronomers before my time, which have their orbits round a certain bright star, one of those previously known, like Venus and Mercury round the Sun, and are sometimes in front of it, sometimes behind it, though they never depart from it beyond certain limits. All which facts were discovered and observed a few days ago by the help of a telescope devised by me, through God's grace first enlightening my mind.

Perchance other discoveries still more excellent will be made from time to time by me or by other observers, with the assistance of a similar instrument, so I will first briefly record its shape and preparation, as well as the occasion of its being devised, and then I will give an account of the observations made by me. About ten months ago a report reached my ears that a Dutchman had constructed a telescope, by the aid of which visible objects, although at a great distance from the eye of the observer, were seen distinctly as if near; and some proofs of its most wonderful performances were reported, which some gave credence to, but others contradicted. A few days after, I received confirmation of the report in a letter written from Paris by a noble Frenchman, Jaques Badovere, which finally determined me to give myself up first to inquire into the principle of the telescope, and then to consider the means by which I might compass the invention of a similar instrument, which a little while after I succeeded in doing, through deep study of the theory of Refraction; and I prepared a tube, at first of lead, in the ends of which I fitted two glass lenses, both plane on one side, but on the other side one spherically convex, and the other concave. Then bringing my eye to the concave lens I saw objects satisfactorily large and near, for they appeared one-third of the distance off and nine times larger than when they are seen with the natural eye alone. I shortly afterwards constructed another telescope with more nicety, which magnified objects more than sixty times. At length, by sparing neither labour nor expense, I succeeded in constructing for myself an instrument so superior that objects seen through it appear magnified nearly a thousand times, and more than thirty times nearer than if viewed by the natural powers of sight alone.

It would be altogether a waste of time to enumerate the number and importance of the benefits which this instrument may be expected to confer, when used by land or sea. But without paying attention to its use for terrestrial objects, I betook myself to observations of the heavenly bodies; and first of all, I viewed the Moon as near as if it was scarcely two semi- diameters of the Earth distant. After the Moon, I frequently observed other heavenly bodies, both fixed stars and planets, with incredible delight; and, when I saw their very great number, I began to consider about a method by which I might be able to measure their distances apart, and at length I found one. And here it is fitting that all who intend to turn their attention to observations of this kind should receive certain cautions. For, in the first place, it is absolutely necessary for them to prepare a most perfect telescope, one which will show very bright objects distinct and free from any mistiness, and will magnify them at least 400 times, for then it will show them as if only one-twentieth of their distance off. For unless the instrument be of such power, it will be in vain to attempt to view all the things which have been seen by me in the heavens, or which will be enumerated hereafter. ...

Now let me review the observations made by me during the two months just past, again inviting the attention of all who are eager for true philosophy to the beginnings which led to the sight of most important phenomena.

The Moon. Let me speak first of the surface of the Moon, which is turned towards us. For the sake of being understood more easily, I distinguish two parts in it, which I call respectively the brighter and the darker. The brighter part seems to surround and pervade the whole hemisphere; but the darker part, like a sort of cloud, discolours the Moon's surface and makes it appear covered with spots. Now these spots, as they are somewhat dark and of considerable size, are plain to every one, and every age has seen them, wherefore I shall call them great or ancient spots, to distinguish them from other spots, smaller in size, but so thickly scattered that they sprinkle the whole surface of the Moon, but especially the brighter portion of it. These spots have never been observed by any one before me; and from my observations of them, often repeated, I have been led to that opinion which I have expressed, namely, that I feel sure that the surface of the Moon is not perfectly smooth, free from inequalities and exactly spherical, as a large school of philosophers considers with regard to the Moon and the other heavenly bodies, but that, on the contrary, it is full of inequalities, uneven, full of hollows and protuberances, just like the surface of the Earth itself, which is varied everywhere by lofty mountains and deep valleys.

The appearances from which we may gather these conclusions are of the following nature:—On the fourth or fifth day after new-moon, when the Moon presents itself to us with bright horns, the boundary which divides the part in shadow from the enlightened part does not extend continuously in an ellipse, as would happen in the case of a perfectly spherical body, but it is marked out by an irregular, uneven, and very wavy line, ... for several bright excrescences, as they may be called, extend beyond the boundary of light and shadow into the dark part, and on the other hand pieces of shadow encroach upon the light:—nay, even a great quantity of small blackish spots, altogether separated from the dark part, sprinkle everywhere almost the whole space which is at the time flooded with the Sun's light, with the exception of that part alone which is occupied by the great and ancient spots. I have noticed that the small spots just mentioned have this common characteristic always and in every case, that they have the dark part towards the Sun's position, and on the side away from the Sun they have brighter boundaries, as if they were crowned with shining summits. Now we have an appearance quite similar on the Earth about sunrise, when we behold the valleys, not yet flooded with light, but the mountains surrounding them on the side opposite to the Sun already ablaze with the splendour of his beams; and just as the shadows in the hollows of the Earth diminish in size as the Sun rises higher, so also these spots on the Moon lose their blackness as the illuminated part grows larger and larger. Again, not only are the boundaries of light and shadow in the Moon seen to be uneven and sinuous, but—and this produces still greater astonishment—there appear very many bright points within the darkened portion of the Moon, altogether divided and broken off from the illuminated tract, and separated from it by no inconsiderable interval, which, after a little while, gradually increase in size and brightness, and after an hour or two become joined on to the rest of the bright portion, now become somewhat larger; but in the meantime others, one here and another there, shooting up as if growing, are lighted up within the shaded portion, increase in size, and at last are linked on to the same luminous surface, now still more extended. ... Now, is it not the case on the Earth before sunrise, that while the level plain is still in shadow, the peaks of the most lofty mountains are illuminated by the Sun's rays? After a little while does not the light spread further, while the middle and larger parts of those mountains are becoming illuminated; and at length, when the Sun has risen, do not the illuminated parts of the plains and hills join together? The grandeur, however, of such prominences and depressions in the Moon seems to surpass both in magnitude and extent the ruggedness of the Earth's surface, as I shall hereafter show. And here I cannot refrain from mentioning what a remarkable spectacle I observed while the Moon was rapidly approaching her first quarter. ... A protuberance of the shadow, of great size, indented the illuminated part in the neighbourhood of the lower cusp; and when I had observed this indentation longer, and had seen that it was dark throughout, at length, after about two hours, a bright peak began to arise a little below the middle of the depression; this by degrees increased, and presented a triangular shape, but was as yet quite detached and separated from the illuminated surface. Soon around it three other small points began to shine, until, when the Moon was just about to set, that triangular figure, having now extended and widened, began to be connected with the rest of the illuminated part, and, still girt with the three bright peaks already mentioned, suddenly burst into the indentation of shadow like a vast promontory of light.

At the ends of the upper and lower cusps also certain bright points, quite away from the rest of the bright part, began to rise out of the shadow ... In both horns also, but especially in the lower one, there was a great quantity of dark spots, of which those which are nearer the boundary of light and shadow appear larger and darker, but those which are more remote less dark and more indistinct. In all cases, however, just as I have mentioned before, the dark portion of the spot faces the position of the Sun's illumination, and a brighter edge surrounds the darkened spot on the side away from the Sun, and towards the region of the Moon in shadow. This part of the surface of the Moon, where it is marked with spots like a peacock's tail with its azure eyes, is rendered like those glass vases which, through being plunged while still hot from the kiln into cold water, acquire a crackled and wavy surface, from which circumstance they are commonly called *frosted glasses*.

Now the great spots of the Moon observed at the same time are not seen to be at all similarly broken, or full of depressions and prominences, but rather to be even and uniform; for only here and there some spaces, rather brighter than the rest, crop up; so that if any one wishes to revive the old opinion of the Pythagoreans, that the Moon is another Earth, so to say, the brighter portion may very fitly represent the surface of the land, and the darker the expanse of water. Indeed, I have never doubted that if the sphere of the Earth were seen from a distance, when flooded with the Sun's rays, that part of the surface which is land would present itself to view as brighter, and that which is water as darker in comparison. Moreover, the great spots in the Moon are seen to be more depressed than the brighter tracts; for in the Moon, both when crescent and when waning, on the boundary between the light and shadow, which projects in some places round the great spots, the adjacent regions are always brighter, as I have noticed in drawing my illustrations, and the edges of the spots referred to are not only more depressed than the brighter parts, but are more even, and are not broken by ridges or ruggednesses. But the brighter part stands out most near the spots, so that both before the first quarter and about the third quarter also, around a certain spot in the upper part of the figure, that is, occupying the northern region of the Moon, some vast prominences on the upper and lower sides of it rise to an enormous elevation. ... This same spot before the third quarter is seen to be walled round with boundaries of a deeper shade, which just like very lofty mountain summits appear darker on the side away from the Sun, and brighter on the side where they face the Sun; but in the case of the cavities the opposite happens, for the part of them away from the Sun appears brilliant, and that part which lies nearer to the Sun dark and in shadow. After a time, when the enlightened portion of the Moon's surface has diminished in size, as soon as the whole or nearly so of the spot already mentioned is covered with shadow, the brighter ridges of the mountains mount high above the shade. ...

There is one other point which I must on no account forget, which I have noticed and rather wondered at. It is this:—The middle of the Moon, as it seems, is occupied by a certain cavity larger than all the rest, and in shape perfectly round. I have looked at this depression near both the first and third quarters. ... It produces the same appearance as to effects of light and shade as a tract like Bohemia would produce on the Earth, if it were shut in on all sides by very lofty mountains arranged on the circumference of a perfect circle; for the tract in the Moon is walled in with peaks of such enormous height that the furthest side adjacent to the dark portion of the Moon is seen bathed in sunlight before the boundary between light and shade reaches half-way across the circular space. But according to the characteristic property of the rest of the spots, the shaded portion of this too faces the Sun, and the bright part is towards the dark side of the Moon, which for the third time I advise to be carefully noticed as a most solid proof of the ruggednesses and unevennesses spread over the whole of the bright region of the Moon. Of these spots, moreover, the darkest are always those which are near to the boundary-line between the light and the shadow, but those further off appear both smaller in size and less decidedly dark; so that at length, when the Moon at opposition becomes full, the darkness of the cavities differs from the brightness of the prominences with a subdued and very slight difference.

These phenomena which we have reviewed are observed in the bright tracts of the Moon. In the great spots we do not see such differences of depressions and prominences as we are compelled to recognise in the brighter parts, owing to the change of their shapes under different degrees of illumination by the Sun's rays according to the manifold variety of the Sun's position with regard to the Moon. Still, in the great spots there do exist some spaces rather less dark than the rest, ... but these spaces always have the same appearance, and the depth of their shadow is neither intensified nor diminished; they do appear indeed sometimes a little more shaded, sometimes a little less, but the change of colour is very slight, according as the Sun's rays fall upon them more or less obliquely; and besides, they are joined to the adjacent parts of the spots with a very gradual connection, so that their boundaries mingle and melt into the surrounding region. But it is quite different with the spots which occupy the brighter parts of the Moon's surface, for, just as if they were precipitous crags with numerous rugged and jagged peaks, they have well-defined boundaries through the sharp contrast of light and shade. Moreover, inside those great spots certain other tracts are seen brighter than the surrounding region, and some of them very bright indeed, but the appearance of these, as well as of the darker parts, is always the same; there is no change of shape or brightness or depth of shadow, so that it becomes a matter of certainty and beyond doubt that their appearance is owing to real dissimilarity of parts, and not to unevennesses only in their configuration, changing in different ways the shadows of the same parts according to the variations of their illumination by the Sun, which really happens in the case of the other smaller spots occupying the brighter portion of the Moon, for day by day they change, increase, decrease, or disappear, inasmuch as they derive their origin only from the shadows of prominences. ...

**

Hitherto I have spoken of the observations which I have made concerning the Moon's body; now I will briefly announce the phenomena which have been, as yet, seen by me with reference to the *Fixed Stars*. And first of all the following fact is worthy of consideration:—The stars, fixed as well as erratic, when seen with a telescope, by no means appear to be increased in magnitude in the same proportion as other objects, and the Moon herself, gain increase of size; but in the case of the stars such increase appears much less, so that you may consider that a telescope, which (for the sake of illustration) is powerful enough to magnify other objects a hundred times, will scarcely render the stars magnified four or five times. But the reason of this is as follows:—When stars are viewed with our natural eyesight they do not present themselves to us of their bare, real size, but beaming with a certain vividness, and fringed with sparkling rays, especially when the night is far advanced; and from this circumstance they appear much larger than they would if they were stripped of those adventitious fringes, for the angle which they subtend at the eye is determined not by the primary disc of the star, but, by the brightness which so widely surrounds it. Perhaps you will understand this most clearly from the well-known circumstance that when stars rise just at sunset, in the beginning of twilight, they appear very small, although they may be stars of the first magnitude; and even the planet Venus itself, on any occasion when it may present itself to view in broad daylight, is so small to see that it scarcely seems to equal a star of the last magnitude. It is different in the case of other objects, and even of the Moon, which, whether viewed in the light of midday or in the depth of night, always appears of the same size. We conclude therefore that the stars are seen at midnight in uncurtailed glory, but their fringes are of such a nature that the daylight can cut them off, and not only daylight, but any slight cloud which may be interposed between a star and the eye of the observer. A dark veil or coloured glass has the same effect, for, upon placing them before the eye between it and the stars, all the blaze that surrounds them leaves them at once. A telescope also accomplishes the same result, for it removes from the stars their adventitious and accidental splendours before it enlarges their true discs (if indeed they are of that shape), and so they seem less magnified than other tobjects, for a star of the fifth or sixth magnitude seen through a telescope is shown as of the first magnitude only. …

***

The next object which I have observed is the essence or substance of the *Milky Way*. By the aid of a telescope, any one may behold this in a manner which so distinctly appeals to the senses that all the disputes which have tormented through so many ages are exploded at once by the irrefragable evidence of our eyes, and we are freed from wordy disputes upon this subject, for the Galaxy is nothing else but a mass of innumerable stars planted together in clusters. Upon whatever part of it you direct the telescope straightway a vast crowd of stars presents itself to view; many of them are tolerably large and extremely bright, but the number of small ones is quite beyond determination.

And whereas that milky brightness, like the brightness of a white cloud, is not only to be seen in Milky Way, but several spots of a similar colour shine faintly here and there in the heavens, if you turn the telescope upon any of them you will find a cluster of stars packed close together. Further—and you will be more surprised at this,—the stars which have been called by every one of the astronomers up to this day nebulous, are groups of small stars set thick together in a wonderful way, and although each one of them on account of its smallness, or its immense distance from us, escapes our sight, from the commingling of their rays there arises that brightness which has hitherto been believed to be the denser part of the heavens, able to reflect the rays of the stars or the Sun.

GLOSSARY

sinuosities: bends and curves

excrescences: bulges

Bohemia: a principality then in the Holy Roman Empire, today half of the Czech Republic; Galileo is describing Bohemia's shape on a map

Document Analysis

The text emphasizes the greatness of Galileo's discoveries and the amazement that they would provoke in the reader, particularly due to the instrument that made them possible. A cursory look at the first paragraphs immediately reveals this sense of wonder that the author wants to create in the reader thanks to the use of words such as "great" (repeated later in the text), "novelty," and "excellence." Employing a telescope, Galileo was able to discover a high number of fixed stars, mountains and valleys on the moon, the true nature of "nebulous" stars, and the "four wandering planets" around Jupiter. After summarizing the most important discoveries that constitute the topic of his treaty, the scientist goes on to explain how he constructed the instrument that made such discoveries possible: the telescope. Although he thinks that its application could be useful both on land and sea, he says that he has limited its use to celestial observations.

According to his report, Galileo first heard about the instrument ten months before the writing of the *Starry Messenger*. Although there was no consensus about the benefits of the instrument, the Italian scientists decided to construct one. This passage is typical of the Galilean scientific method in several respects. Galileo does not simply accept that the instrument is useful or useless because other people have said so. He proceeds to verify personally other people's opinions. This empirical validation is one of Galileo's major contributions to scientific enquiry. Following from this, Galileo thought that everyone should be able to replicate experiments made by other scientists, to prove them right or wrong. For this reason, he tells of the different steps that he took in the construction of the telescope, allowing everyone to try to construct one to observe the same things that he is writing about. Galileo is clearly speaking to those potential scientists ("to all who intend to turn their attention to observations of this kind") when he warns them that their telescope should be able to magnify the things they observe by at least four hundred times.

After explaining the construction and use of the telescope, Galileo delves into more details about his celestial observations. The majority of the document is devoted to his observations of the moon, while its concluding paragraphs focus on stars and the nature of the Milky Way. The Italian scientist addresses his description of the moon to "all who are eager for true philosophy," because the Aristotelian and medieval cosmology was predicated on the qualitative difference between the earth, rugged and irregular, with mountains, valleys, and caves, and perfect celestial bodies like the moon, "smooth, free from inequalities, and exactly spherical." This qualitative difference implied a moral superiority of the celestial bodies because of their perfection and the inferiority of the earth because of its imperfections. Yet Galileo was able to prove that this qualitative difference did not exist, as the moon, too, was "full of inequalities, uneven, full of hollows and protuberances, just like the surface of the Earth itself, which is varied everywhere by lofty mountains and deep valleys."

This conclusion is reinforced by Galileo's style, which draws parallels between what happens on the moon and terrestrial phenomena or uses everyday objects as metaphors to illustrate his conclusions. For example, when talking about the lunar spots, he recalls that "we have an appearance quite similar on Earth about sunrise." In a passage devoted to the moon's surface, he argues that "it is marked with spots like a peacock's tail with its azure eyes" and resembles "those glass vases which … acquire a crackled and wavy surface." These lexical choices show Galileo's aim to democratize the language of science, making it accessible not only to philosophers and highly educated theologians but also to those people who were genuinely interested in the subject.

Essential Themes

Galileo worked to demonstrate that the earth revolved around the sun. He found that, like the moon, Venus could only be seen as a crescent at certain times of the month based on its positioning between the sun and the earth. If one planet in the universe circled around the sun, likely they all did, otherwise they would all run into each other. Galileo had his proof – but he simultaneously gained a plethora of critics, starting with priests in Florence who accused him of being a heretic. Galileo argued that the priests had misinterpreted the Bible if they disagreed with the science that God had established for the universe's harmony; instead they accused him of the same thing. Galileo was called before the Inquisition, the church's court prosecuting heresy, with the possibility of receiving a death sentence. Instead, he received a warning, to stop promoting the ideas of the known heretic Copernicus until he had better proof. Galileo remained quiet, studying the stars for better proof.

In 1623, Pope Urban VIII came to the Vatican, the former Maffeo Cardinal Barberini, a patron of Galileo's.

Urban called Galileo to him six times to discuss his ideas, and he allowed Galileo to publish *Dialogue Concerning the Two Chief World Systems* (1632). Galileo believed this put an end to the matter – instead it was the beginning of his persecution. Urban may have been impressed with Galileo's ideas, but he would not allow Galileo to challenge the truth as received in the Bible – he was only to posit his ideas on heliocentrism as one possibility. The *Dialogue* sold out right away, but the Vatican ordered its publication to cease immediately. Pope Urban VIII accused Galileo of teaching Copernican theory and forced him to admit that he was wrong: the sun revolved around the earth. Galileo died under house arrest a decade later.

—Luca Prono, PhD

Bibliography and Further Reading

Dawes, Gregory W. *Galileo and the Conflict between Religion and Science*. New York: Routledge, 2016.

Drake, Stillman. *Galileo: A Very Short Introduction*. New York: Oxford University Press, 2001.

Mayer, Thomas F. *The Roman Inquisition: Trying Galileo*. Philadelphia: University of Pennsylvania Press, 2015.

Rowland, Wade. *Galileo's Mistake: A New Look at the Epic Confrontation between Galileo and the Church*. New York: Arcade Publishing, 2003.

Sobel, Dava. *Galileo's Daughter: A Historical Memoir of Science, Faith, and Love*. New York: Bloomsbury, 1999.

Steele, Philip. *Galileo: The Genius Who Faced the Inquisition*. Washington DC: National Geographic, 2005.

Websites

Helmann, Hal. "Two Views of the Universe: Galileo vs. the Pope". *Washington Post* (September 9, 1998) H01 http://www.washingtonpost.com/wp-srv/national/horizon/sept98/galileo.htm [accessed April 13, 2017].

Linder, Professor Douglas O. "Trial of Galileo (1633)". *Famous Trials*. University of Missouri-Kansas City School of Law http://www.famous-trials.com/galileo-trial [accessed April 13, 2017].

Smith, Sydney. "St. Robert Francis Romulus Bellarmine." *The Catholic Encyclopedia* Volume 2. New York: Robert Appleton Company, 1907 http://www.newadvent.org/cathen/02411d.htm [accessed April 11 2017].

Van Helden, Albert, and Elizabeth Burr. *The Galileo Project*. Rice University (1995) http://galileo.rice.edu/index.html [accessed April 13, 2017].

Letter of Cardinal Bellarmine to Paolo Antonio Foscarini concerning Galileo's Theories

Date: 1615
Author: Robert Cardinal Bellarmine
Genre: Correspondence

Summary Overview

In April 1615, Robert Cardinal Bellarmine wrote a letter to Paolo Antonio Foscarini, a priest and scientist, about the theories of another scientist, Galileo Galilei, on heliocentrism. The letter is an important document in the first phases of the conflict over Galileo's research. Eighteen years later, in 1633, the Roman Catholic Church put Galileo on trial, and he was convicted for teaching a Copernican view of the universe. The debate between supporters of the new heliocentric Copernican model, where the Earth and humankind lose their central place in the universe, and those who continued to defend the traditional Ptolemaic and Aristotelian system reveals the obstacles for science and scientists in gaining independence from religion and theologians. Aristotelian cosmology had become an integral part of Christian theology during the Middle Ages. Therefore, new physical and astronomical theories could be accepted only if they did not contradict Aristotelian cosmology and sacred scripture. Although Galileo himself had tried to prove that scientific discoveries and scripture were compatible in his famous letter to the Benedictine abbot and mathematician Benedetto Castelli (December 21, 1613), such contradiction was apparent in the case of the Copernican model. The Bible itself, in the Old Testament, contains explicit references to the Earth's immobility and the sun's movement around it.

Robert Bellarmine's letter to the Carmelite theologian Foscarini defended the authority of the Church to interpret sacred scripture and offered a possible compromise on Copernicus's theories. They could be accepted if they were treated as mere mathematical hypotheses to explain natural and physical phenomena, but they were to be condemned as heresy when treated as if they were absolutely true.

Defining Moment

The trial of Galileo Galilei, held in 1633, was one of the pivotal events in Western history. It marked a point where the Renaissance came to an end and the Scientific Revolution began to build momentum, when challenges to the authority of the Roman Catholic Church as an institution advanced beyond only politics or religion. Galileo would later be recognized as the founder of modern physics and astronomy.

Robert Cardinal Bellarmine, one of the central figures of the controversy surrounding Galileo, tried to steer through the rapids of Catholic ideology and scientific inquiry, and managed to clear neither.

In 1543, just before his own death, the Polish physicist Nicolaus Copernicus published *On the Revolutions of the Heavenly Spheres*, a work in which he posited that the Earth rotated around the sun once a year, as opposed to the sun orbiting the Earth. Copernicus also believed the Earth rotated on its own axis over the course of a day, explaining day and night as the sun appeared on different sides of the Earth at different times.

This theory was in direct contrast to the accepted notion of how the universe worked, as laid out by the Roman geographer Ptolemy in the year 150. Ptolemy believed the Earth was the center of the universe, and the moon, sun, planets, and stars orbited around it in concentric circles. Thomas Aquinas had translated Ptolemy into Catholic theology; the idea of the Earth at the center of the universe placed man at the center of the universe, too, which corresponded with Old Testament teachings.

Most scientists and intellectuals did not believe Copernicus; it seemed self-evident, and easily observable, that the Earth did not move at all, while the sun rotated through the sky every day. Yet over the course of the sixteenth century, more and more astronomers tested Copernicus's theories and came to the same conclusion. One was Galileo Galilei, mathematician and philosopher. Galileo kept his theories to himself, for fear of ridicule; he was a pious Catholic whose daughter had become a nun. Yet once he invented the telescope in 1609, he believed he had the tool available to prove the theory of heliocentrism—that the sun is the center of the universe—to a skeptical world, and to transform Catholic teachings and belief on the subject. He published *Letters on the Solar Spots* in 1613, defending Copernicus.

The *Index Librorum Prohibitorum*, a list of books banned by the Catholic Church. Following the Inquisition's 1616 judgment, the works of Copernicus, Galileo, Foscarini, Kepler and others advocating heliocentrism were banned. [Public domain], via Wikimedia Commons

The problem with heliocentrism was that it directly contradicted statements in the Bible's Old Testament. The Book of Joshua, 10:13, states that "the sun stood still in the midst of heaven." The Roman Catholic Church was likewise inclined to follow the Aristotelian conception of the universe, and Aristotle believed the sun revolved around the Earth. Galileo countered by arguing that new knowledge might allow the Bible to be interpreted more symbolically than literally; however, instead of calming the controversy, Galileo ended up having to answer to the Roman Inquisition.

Looking for character witnesses in his defense, Galileo turned to a cardinal he had met before, Robert Cardinal Bellarmine. Bellarmine had hosted Galileo in 1611, heard his ideas, and looked through a telescope. Yet while he was impressed, Bellarmine did not agree with Galileo's theories on the arrangement of the universe. Like most of the rest of the Catholic hierarchy, Bellarmine was largely concerned with the maintenance of the Church's predominant role in European education and society; if such a position either upheld scientific discovery or contradicted it, so be it.

To respond to Galileo, Bellarmine wrote a letter to a contemporary of Galileo's in the Church, Paolo Antonio Foscarini. Foscarini was an adherent of Copernicus's theory of heliocentrism, too; it is possible that he and Galileo were working together to publicize Copernican ideas. Foscarini had tried unsuccessfully to get the Church to recognize heliocentrism; for his trouble, Foscarini's works ended up on the Vatican's Index of Forbidden Books. He died soon afterward in 1616.

Author Biography

Robert Cardinal Bellarmine was one of the most influential Jesuit theologians of the seventeenth century and a major figure in the Inquisition. He joined the Society of Jesus in 1560 and was ordained in 1570 while he taught at Louvain in modern-day Belgium, a predominantly Protestant area. He became a reliable and thoughtful counter to the arguments of Protestants against Catholicism, writing a work called *De Controversiis* to address Protestant criticisms of Catholicism. In 1597 Bellarmine became the official theologian of Pope Clement VIII; he was made a cardinal in 1599 and spent his time in Rome after 1605. Bellarmine made his name in a long-term intellectual exchange with King James I of England over the power of the pope being superior to the divine right of kings. Pope Clement VIII made Bellarmine the point man in the arguments against the Copernican theory of heliocentrism and Paolo Antonio Foscarini. Bellarmine died in 1621.

HISTORICAL DOCUMENT

Letter from Cardinal Bellarmine to Paolo Antonio Foscarini Concerning Galileo's Theories

I have gladly read the letter in Italian and the treatise which Your Reverence sent me, and I thank you for both. And I confess that both are filled with ingenuity and learning, and since you ask for my opinion, I will give it to you very briefly, as you have little time for reading and I for writing:

First. I say that it seems to me that Your Reverence and Galileo did prudently to content yourself with speaking hypothetically, and not absolutely, as I have always believed that Copernicus spoke. For to say that, assuming the earth moves and the sun stands still, all the appearances are saved better than with eccentrics and epicycles, is to speak well; there is no danger in this, and it is sufficient for mathematicians. But to want to affirm that the sun really is fixed in the center of the heavens and only revolves around itself (i.e., turns upon its axis) without traveling from east to west, and that the earth is situated in the third sphere and revolves with great speed around the sun, is a very dangerous thing, not only by irritating all the philosophers and scholastic theologians, but also by injuring our holy faith and rendering the Holy Scriptures false. For Your Reverence has demonstrated many ways of explaining Holy Scripture, but you have not applied them in particular, and without a doubt you would have found it most difficult if you had attempted to explain all the passages which you yourself have cited.

Second. I say that, as you know, the Council prohibits expounding the Scriptures contrary to the common agreement of the holy Fathers. And if Your Reverence would read not only the Fathers but also the commentaries of modern writers on Genesis, Psalms, Ecclesiastes and Josue, you would find that all agree in explaining literally (*ad litteram*) that the sun is in the heavens and moves swiftly around the earth, and that the earth is far from the heavens and stands immobile in the center of the universe. Now consider whether in all prudence the Church could encourage giving to Scripture a sense contrary to the holy Fathers and all the Latin and Greek commentators. Nor may it be answered that this is not a matter of faith, for if it is not a matter of faith from the point of view of the subject matter, it is on the part of the ones who have spoken. It would be just as heretical to deny that Abraham had two sons and Jacob twelve, as it would be to deny the virgin birth of Christ, for both are declared by the Holy Ghost through the mouths of the prophets and apostles.

Third. I say that if there were a true demonstration that the sun was in the center of the universe and the earth in the third sphere, and that the sun did not travel around the earth but the earth circled the sun, then it would be necessary to proceed with great caution in explaining the passages of Scripture which seemed contrary, and we would rather have to say that we did not understand them than to say that something was false which has been demonstrated. But I do not believe that there is any such demonstration; none has been shown to me. It is not the same thing to show that the appearances are saved by assuming that the sun really is in the center and the earth in the heavens. I believe that the first demonstration might exist, but I have grave doubts about the second, and in a case of doubt, one may not depart from the Scriptures as explained by the holy Fathers. I add that the words "the sun also riseth and the sun goeth down, and hasteneth to the place where he ariseth, etc." were those of Solomon, who not only spoke by divine inspiration but was a man wise above all others and most learned in human sciences and in the knowledge of all created things, and his wisdom was from God. Thus it is not too likely that he would affirm something which was contrary to a truth either already demonstrated, or likely to be demonstrated. And if you tell me that Solomon spoke only according to the appearances, and that it seems to us that the sun goes around when actually it is the earth which moves, as it seems to one on a ship that the beach moves away from the ship, I shall answer that one who departs from the beach, though it looks to him as though the beach moves away, he knows that he is in error and corrects it, seeing clearly that the ship moves and not the beach. But with regard to the sun and the earth, no wise man is needed to correct the error, since he clearly experiences that the earth stands still and that his eye is not deceived when it judges that the moon and stars move. And that is enough for the present. I salute Your Reverence and ask God to grant you every happiness.

Document Analysis

Cardinal Bellarmine wrote this letter as a reply to a treatise by Foscarini, who, in a fashion similar to Galileo in his letter to Castelli, had argued for the compatibility of Copernican discoveries with scripture. However, Bellarmine makes it clear immediately that his remarks apply to Galileo, too. After the conventional greetings, in what has sometimes been interpreted as an ironic passage, Bellarmine praises Foscarini and Galileo in that they treated the Copernican system as a mathematical hypothesis, not as absolute truth. This, the Jesuit argues, is the spirit in which Copernicus himself made his heliocentric observations, which were not meant to describe the real condition of things but merely to find a better explanation for some phenomena ("all the appearances are saved better"). It is debatable whether Bellarmine really believed that Copernicus spoke hypothetically and did not regard his system as representing the real structure of the universe. Rhetorically, Bellarmine's opening remarks on the difference between a mathematical hypothesis and an absolute, true demonstration also serve as a warning to the two addressees to conform to the official Ptolemaic and Aristotelian view of the universe. In fact, speaking of Copernicus's ideas as if they were absolute truth would both irritate theologians and harm religious faith by making "the Holy Scriptures false."

In the second point of his argument, Bellarmine addresses Galileo and Foscarini's argument that scripture could be interpreted in ways that would not conflict with Copernican theories. The Jesuit recalls the Canons and Decrees of the Council of Trent, which, to counter the Reformation, prohibited new readings of the scriptures that went against those of the Holy Fathers. This proscription effectively limited the possibility of personal interpretations of the texts that could not benefit from the authority of the tradition. Bellarmine explicitly states that traditional exegeses clearly place the Earth at the center of the universe and conceives of the sun as moving around it. Therefore, to propose a heliocentric view of the universe would be just as heretical as challenging the dogma of "the virgin birth of Christ."

In his third and final point of the letter, Bellarmine makes recourse to the traditional Aristotelian hierarchy of knowledge, where astronomical laws proved through mathematical methods merely represent a possibility, while the principles of natural philosophy are absolute, and their truth does not need to be demonstrated. Bellarmine's concept of science, therefore, is radically different from the scientific practice embodied by Galileo. Galileo was a man of the Scientific Revolution and the scientific method as defined by Francis Bacon at the time. He observed phenomena, posited a hypothesis to explain what he observed, and then tested the hypothesis to find a general principle of explanation. On the contrary, Bellarmine's starting point must be an absolute principle that then leads to certain consequences. While the Aristotelian view of science started from the causes to explain the effects, the new Galilean and Copernican science would follow the opposite direction. On the specific matter of heliocentrism, Bellarmine added that common sense, too, goes against it, as we experience every day the fact that the Earth stands still. However, some historians have interpreted this third point as treating the heliocentric view as a possibility and thus as blurring the boundaries between absolute and possible truth. This is read as an attempt by Bellarmine and the Jesuits to keep the debate with Galileo open, despite the charges of heresy that were beginning to circulate.

Essential Themes

After Cardinal Bellarmine's warning, Galileo asked for a hearing from the Vatican on his ideas. Eleven theologians were asked to comment on two propositions: 1) that the sun is at the center of the universe and does not move, and 2) the Earth moves to orbit the sun. On February 23, 1616, the theologians unanimously ruled that both propositions were statements of heresy, and Copernicus's work was prohibited for Catholics to read. Bellarmine brought Galileo before Pope Paul V two days later and told Galileo to drop his heretical ideas and abandon teaching them. Galileo apparently acquiesced, according to Church records. Cardinal Bellarmine did leave open the possibility that Galileo might be correct, but he would have to find better proof that the Earth revolved around the sun. This kept Galileo busy enough to be quiet, and he dropped his advocacy of Copernican science.

Then in 1623, a new pope, Urban VIII, came to the Vatican. Galileo and Urban had known each other before—they were both from Florence. Before his appointment as pope, Urban VIII had been Maffeo Cardinal Barberini, and he had advocated for Galileo with the Inquisition back in 1616. Urban was a man of science, and called for six audiences with Galileo to discuss the latter's ideas. Galileo was urged to publish his findings on the universe, and he completed his masterwork, *Dialogue Concerning the Two Chief World Systems* (1632). The book was a narrative of an argument among three characters over the nature of the universe. The most persuasive character argued that Copernicus was right and that the Earth revolved around the sun. The pope agreed with these ideas, so long as Galileo put forward a hypothesis on the universe without positing it as the absolute scientific truth.

Wherein lay the problem: So far as Galileo was concerned, his theory had already been tested scientifically and found to be true; thus, there was nothing hypothetical about it. On the other hand, though, Galileo was a dedicated Catholic Christian. He considered himself loyal to the Church, and he believed his scientific findings would save the Church the embarrassment of error. He was certain the Church would not want to defend a false doctrine if there was proof it was false. In fact, in the *Dialogue*, he gave the old arguments for the Ptolemaic vision of the universe to a character called Simplicio, a simpleton. Unfortunately, these were also the beliefs of Urban VIII, and the depiction made the pope very angry.

When the *Dialogue* was in the manuscript stages, Church officials demanded that Galileo reword portions of it. It languished for a few years until finally being released to an avid intellectual public in 1632. The *Dialogue* sold out right away. The Vatican also demanded that publication cease immediately afterward. Pope Urban VIII turned from an enthusiastic supporter of Galileo to an angry and dangerous enemy, apparently believing that he had been deceived. In September 1632, the pope handed indictments over to the Roman

Inquisition, which accused Galileo of violating his conviction from 1616 by teaching the public about Copernican theory, about which he was supposed to remain silent.

In 1633, Galileo reported to the Vatican, where the Inquisition convicted him, and forced him to sign a deposition and admit that his defense of Copernican theory was incorrect: The sun revolved around the Earth. On June 22, 1633, under threat of torture and the possibility of being burned at the stake, Galileo Galilei was compelled to kneel before the pope and admit that his life's work was wrong. The *Dialogue* was prohibited for Catholics to read, and Galileo himself was imprisoned. He only served a few months before being sent home. He died in 1642, old and broken. Even then, Urban would not allow the grand duke of Tuscany, one of Galileo's patrons, to give Galileo a proper burial. The *Dialogue* would not be allowed off the Catholic list of prohibited books until 1822. And Galileo was not acquitted by the Church until Pope John Paul II looked over the evidence and reversed his conviction in 1992.

—*Luca Prono, PhD*

Bibliography and Further Reading

Dawes, Gregory W. *Galileo and the Conflict between Religion and Science*. Routledge, 2016.

Drake, Stillman. *Galileo: A Very Short Introduction*. Oxford University Press, 2001.

Mayer, Thomas F. *The Roman Inquisition: Trying Galileo*. University of Pennsylvania Press, 2015.

Rowland, Wade. *Galileo's Mistake: A New Look at the Epic Confrontation between Galileo and the Church*. Arcade Publishing, 2003.

Sobel, Dava. *Galileo's Daughter: A Historical Memoir of Science, Faith, and Love*. Bloomsbury, 1999.

Steele, Philip. *Galileo: The Genius Who Faced the Inquisition*. National Geographic, 2005.

Websites

Helmann, Hal. "Two Views of the Universe: Galileo vs. the Pope." *Washington Post*, 9 Sep. 1998, H01, http://www.washingtonpost.com/wp-srv/national/horizon/sept98/galileo.htm. Accessed 13 Apr. 2017.

Linder, Professor Douglas O. "Trial of Galileo (1633)." *Famous Trials*. University of Missouri-Kansas City School of Law, http://www.famous-trials.com/galileotrial. Accessed 13 Apr. 2017.

Smith, Sydney. "St. Robert Francis Romulus Bellarmine." *The Catholic Encyclopedia*, vol. 2. Robert Appleton Company, 1907, http://www.newadvent.org/cathen/02411d.htm. Accessed 11 Apr. 2017.

Van Helden, Albert, and Elizabeth Burr. *The Galileo Project*. Rice University, 1995, http://galileo.rice.edu/index.html. Accessed April 13, 2017.

Miguel de Cervantes: *Don Quixote*

Date: 1605–1615
Author: Miguel de Cervantes
Genre: Novel

Summary Overview

The novel referred to simply as *Don Quixote*, by Spanish author Miguel de Cervantes, was originally published in two volumes. The full title of the first, which appeared in 1605, is *El ingenioso hidalgo Don Quixote de la Mancha*, or, *The Ingenious Hidalgo Don Quixote de la Mancha*. (*Hidalgo* means "gentleman.") The second volume, published in 1615, was titled *Segunda parte del ingenioso cavallero Don Quixote de la Mancha*, or, *Second Part of the Ingenious Knight Don Quixote de la Mancha*.

Don Quixote is a satirical novel whose target was chivalric romances, which were very much in vogue in the sixteenth and early seventeenth centuries. It paints a portrait of an elderly knight who has become addled by reading too many of those romances and sets out on his old nag, Rocinante, along with his pragmatic, comic squire, Sancho Panza, in search of adventure. A knight is of no account without a ladylove, a role assigned to "Dulcinea," a beefy peasant girl whose real name is Aldonza Lorenzo. The imagination of the bemused knight, however, has transformed her into a lovely, golden-haired damsel. Like knights-errant before him, Don Quixote performs what he sees as feats of heroism as her champion. The novel has provided the English language with the word *quixotic,* referring to intentions or behaviors that reflect lofty ideals but that at bottom are impractical, hopeless, or unrealistic, and that often make matters worse.

Defining Moment

Don Quixote is a product of what is generally referred to as the Golden Age in Spain, a period that extended from the early sixteenth century into the seventeenth century. In 1492, Spain, during the reign of King Ferdinand and Queen Isabella, completed the *Reconquista* with the expulsion of Muslim Moors from the southern reaches of the country. That year, too, Christopher Columbus, under the monarchs' patronage, completed his historic voyage to the New World. Because of these events, followed by the political unification of Spain under the Spanish Habsburgs in 1516, Spain was primed to become a major world power, and its Golden Age (*El Siglo de Oro*) led to a cultural efflorescence in the visual arts, music, and literature, as well as to growing military might and extensive world exploration.

The names of the Spanish explorers who expanded the nation's empire in the Americas (and in Africa) throughout the sixteenth century and beyond are widely recognized: Francisco Vázquez de Coronado, Hernando de Soto, Hernán Cortés, Francisco Pizarro González, Vasco Núñez de Balboa, Hernando Pizarro, and numerous others. Major artists include Diego Velázquez and El Greco, while such figures as Tomás Luis de Victoria, Francisco Guerrero, and Alonso Lobo charted new courses in music. In literature, playwright, poet, and novelist Lope de Vega emerged as one of Spain's most prolific authors, alongside Miguel de Cervantes—both contemporaries of William Shakespeare in England.

During the Golden Age in Spain, interest in medieval and early Renaissance genres such as the chivalric and pastoral romance was beginning to wane, although these works continued to be written and read. They ultimately would be supplanted by the picaresque novel, which generally depicted the comic adventures of roguish characters. Among the practitioners of this form was the anonymous author of *The Life of Lazarillo de Tormes and of His Fortunes and Adversities* (1554), along with Mateo Alemán and *Francisco Gómez de Quevedo y Santibáñez Villegas*. For many readers, *Don Quixote* represents the acme of the Golden Age picaresque novel. In 1976, the Spanish Ministry of Culture awarded the first Cervantes Prize (*Premio de Literatura en Lengua Castellana Miguel de Cervantes*, or *Premio Cervantes*), the Spanish-speaking world's most prestigious literature award.

Author Biography

Much of Cervantes' life is shrouded in darkness. The exact date of his birth is unknown (possibly September 29, 1547), but it is known that he was born in the small Spanish town of Alcalá de Henares, near Madrid, and that he was baptized on October 9, 1547. His father was an apothecary-surgeon and a bit of a ne'er-do-well. His ancestry was highly respectable, but the family had

The Ingenious Gentleman Don Quixote de La Mancha. By Juan de la Cuesta (impresor); Miguel de Cervantes (autor) [Public domain], via Wikimedia Commons

fallen into debt and poverty. Throughout his life, Cervantes would suffer the fate of a penniless gentleman.

The first years of Cervantes' life are a blank. It is not even known where the family lived or where he went to school. The first reliable date is 1568, when he was a student at the City School of Madrid. He may have served in the army in Flanders before turning up in Rome as the chamberlain to a cardinal. He enlisted in the Spanish legion in Italy and in 1571 saw action in the campaign against the Turks, which culminated with the naval Battle of Lepanto. Cervantes' left hand was maimed in the campaign, and for the rest of his life it served the author as a reminder of the glory days of his military service. In 1573 he took part in the Tunis campaign, which resulted in the conquest of northern Africa by the Ottoman Empire. In 1575 he and his brother were captured by Algerian pirates, who held him for five years until his family ransomed him.

Cervantes turned to authorship and the theater in the early 1580s. His first published work was *La Galatea* (1585), a pastoral romance. In 1588, saddled with debt, he was relieved to take a post as a purveyor for the Spanish fleet. His travels throughout Spain in this position acquainted him with the speech and folk customs that would infuse *Don Quixote*. Throughout the 1590s he moved about (when he was not in prison for confiscating supplies and embezzlement) and launched his most famous work, *Don Quixote*, the first volume of which appeared in 1605. After 1608 he lived in Madrid, where he wrote the second volume of the novel, along with plays, a long poem titled *Journey to Parnassus,* and a romantic novel, *The Works of Persiles and Sigismunda*. Cervantes died of complications from edema on April 23, 1616. It is believed that he died on the exact same day as Shakespeare, but in fact he died ten days earlier, for Spain had adopted the Gregorian calendar, while England was still on the Julian calendar.

HISTORICAL DOCUMENT

Excerpt from Don Quixote by Miguel Cervantes
CHAPTER VIII: Of the Good Fortune Which the Valiant Don Quixote Had in the Terrible and Undreamt-of Adventure of the Windmills, with Other Occurrences Worthy to Be Fitly Recorded
At this point they came in sight of thirty or forty windmills that there are on plain, and as soon as Don Quixote saw them he said to his squire, "Fortune is arranging matters for us better than we could have shaped our desires ourselves, for look there, friend Sancho Panza, where thirty or more monstrous giants present themselves, all of whom I mean to engage in battle and slay, and with whose spoils we shall begin to make our fortunes; for this is righteous warfare, and it is God's good service to sweep so evil a breed from off the face of the earth."

"What giants?" said Sancho Panza.

"Those thou seest there," answered his master, "with the long arms, and some have them nearly two leagues long."

"Look, your worship," said Sancho; "what we see there are not giants but windmills, and what seem to be their arms are the sails that turned by the wind make the millstone go."

"It is easy to see," replied Don Quixote, "that thou art not used to this business of adventures; those are giants; and if thou art afraid, away with thee out of this and betake thyself to prayer while I engage them in fierce and unequal combat."

So saying, he gave the spur to his steed Rocinante, heedless of the cries his squire Sancho sent after him, warning him that most certainly they were windmills and not giants he was going to attack. He, however, was so positive they were giants that he neither heard the cries of Sancho, nor perceived, near as he was, what they were, but made at them shouting, "Fly not, cowards and vile beings, for a single knight attacks you."

A slight breeze at this moment sprang up, and the great sails began to move, seeing which Don Quixote exclaimed, "Though ye flourish more arms than the giant Briareus, ye have to reckon with me."

So saying, and commending himself with all his heart to his lady Dulcinea, imploring her to support him in such a peril, with lance in rest and covered by his buckler, he charged at Rocinante's fullest gallop and fell upon the first mill that stood in front of him; but as he drove his lance-point into the sail the wind whirled it round with such force that it shivered the lance to pieces, sweeping with it horse and rider, who went rolling over on the plain, in a sorry condition. Sancho hastened to his assistance as fast as his ass could go, and when he came up found him unable to move, with such a shock had Rocinante fallen with him.

"God bless me!" said Sancho, "did I not tell your worship to mind what you were about, for they were only windmills? and no one could have made any mistake about it but one who had something of the same kind in his head."

"Hush, friend Sancho," replied Don Quixote, "the fortunes of war more than any other are liable to frequent fluctuations; and moreover I think, and it is the truth, that that same sage Friston who carried off my study and books, has turned these giants into mills in order to rob me of the glory of vanquishing them, such is the enmity he bears me; but in the end his wicked arts will avail but little against my good sword."

"God order it as he may," said Sancho Panza, and helping him to rise got him up again on Rocinante, whose shoulder was half out; and then, discussing the late adventure, they followed the road to Puerto Lapice, for there, said Don Quixote, they could not fail to find adventures in abundance and variety, as it was a great thoroughfare. For all that, he was much grieved at the loss of his lance, and saying so to his squire, he added, "I remember having read how a Spanish knight, Diego Perez de Vargas by name, having broken his sword in battle, tore from an oak a ponderous bough or branch, and with it did such things that day, and pounded so many Moors, that he got the surname of Machuca, and he and his descendants from that day forth were called Vargas y Machuca. I mention this because from the first oak I see I mean to rend such another branch, large and stout like that, with which I am determined and resolved to do such deeds that thou mayest deem thyself very fortunate in being found worthy to come and see them, and be an eyewitness of things that will with difficulty be believed."

"Be that as God will," said Sancho, "I believe it all as your worship says it; but straighten yourself a little, for you seem all on one side, may be from the shaking of the fall."

"That is the truth," said Don Quixote, "and if I make no complaint of the pain it is because knights-errant are not permitted to complain of any wound, even though their bowels be coming out through it."

"If so," said Sancho, "I have nothing to say; but God knows I would rather your worship complained when anything ailed you. For my part, I confess I must complain however small the ache may be; unless this rule about not complaining extends to the squires of knights-errant also."

Don Quixote could not help laughing at his squire's simplicity, and he assured him he might complain whenever and however he chose, just as he liked, for, so far, he had never read of anything to the contrary in the order of knighthood.

Sancho bade him remember it was dinner-time, to which his master answered that he wanted nothing himself just then, but that he might eat when he had a mind. With this permission Sancho settled himself as comfortably as he could on his beast, and taking out of the alforjas [saddlebags] what he had stowed away in them, he jogged along behind his master munching deliberately, and from time to time taking a pull at the bota [leather container in which wine is kept] with a relish that the thirstiest tapster in Malaga might have envied; and while he went on in this way, gulping down draught after draught, he never gave a thought to any of the promises his master had made him, nor did he rate it as hardship but rather as recreation going in quest of adventures, however dangerous they might be. Finally they passed the night among some trees, from one of which Don Quixote plucked a dry branch to serve him after a fashion as a lance, and fixed on it the head he had removed from the broken one. All that night Don Quixote lay awake thinking of his lady Dulcinea, in order to conform to what he had read in his books, how many a night in the forests and deserts knights used to lie sleepless supported by the memory of their mistresses. Not so did Sancho Panza spend it, for having his stomach full of something stronger than chicory water he made but one sleep of it, and, if his master had not called him, neither the rays of the sun beating on his face nor all the cheery notes of the birds welcoming the approach of day would have had power to waken him.

On getting up he tried the bota and found it somewhat less full than the night before, which grieved his heart because they did not seem to be on the way to remedy the deficiency readily. Don Quixote did not care to break his fast, for, as has been already said, he confined himself to savoury recollections for nourishment.

They returned to the road they had set out with, leading to Puerto Lapice, and at three in the afternoon they came in sight of it. "Here, brother Sancho Panza," said Don Quixote when he saw it, "we may plunge our hands up to the elbows in what they call adventures; but observe, even shouldst thou see me in the greatest danger in the world, thou must not put a hand to thy sword in my defence, unless indeed thou perceives that those who assail me are rabble or base folk; for in that case thou mayest very properly aid me; but if they be knights it is on no account permitted or allowed thee by the laws of knighthood to help me until thou hast been dubbed a knight."

"Most certainly, senor," replied Sancho, "your worship shall be fully obeyed in this matter; all the more as of myself I am peaceful and no friend to mixing in strife and quarrels: it is true that as regards the defence of my own person I shall not give much heed to those laws, for laws human and divine allow each one to defend himself against any assailant whatever."

"That I grant," said Don Quixote, "but in this matter of aiding me against knights thou must put a restraint upon thy natural impetuosity."

"I will do so, I promise you," answered Sancho, "and will keep this precept as carefully as Sunday." While they were thus talking there appeared on the road two friars of the order of St. Benedict, mounted on two dromedaries, for not less tall were the two mules they rode on. They wore travelling spectacles and carried sunshades; and behind them came a coach attended by four or five persons on horseback and two muleteers on foot. In the coach there was, as afterwards appeared, a Biscay lady on her way to Seville, where her husband was about to take passage for the Indies with an appointment of high honour. The friars, though going the same road, were not in her company; but the moment Don Quixote perceived them he said to his squire, "Either I am mistaken, or this is going to be the most famous adventure that has ever been seen, for those black bodies we see there must be, and doubtless are, magicians who are carrying off some stolen princess in that coach, and with all my might I must undo this wrong."

"This will be worse than the windmills," said Sancho. "Look, senor; those are friars of St. Benedict, and the coach plainly belongs to some travellers: I tell you to mind well what you are about and don't let the devil mislead you."

"I have told thee already, Sancho," replied Don Quixote, "that on the subject of adventures thou knowest little. What I say is the truth, as thou shalt see presently."

So saying, he advanced and posted himself in the middle of the road along which the friars were coming, and as soon as he thought they had come near enough to hear what he said, he cried aloud, "Devilish and unnatural beings, release instantly the highborn princesses whom you are carrying off by force in this coach, else prepare to meet a speedy death as the just punishment of your evil deeds."

The friars drew rein and stood wondering at the appearance of Don Quixote as well as at his words, to which they replied, "Senor Caballero, we are not devilish or unnatural, but two brothers of St. Benedict following our road, nor do we know whether or not there are any captive princesses coming in this coach."

"No soft words with me, for I know you, lying rabble," said Don Quixote, and without waiting for a reply he spurred Rocinante and with levelled lance charged the first friar with such fury and determination, that, if the friar had not flung himself off the mule, he would have brought him to the ground against his will, and sore wounded, if not killed outright. The second brother, seeing how his comrade was treated, drove his heels into his castle of a mule and made off across the country faster than the wind.

Sancho Panza, when he saw the friar on the ground, dismounting briskly from his ass, rushed towards him and began to strip off his gown. At that instant the friars' muleteers came up and asked what he was stripping him for. Sancho answered them that this fell to him lawfully as spoil of the battle which his lord Don Quixote had won. The muleteers, who had no idea of a joke and did not understand all this about battles and spoils, seeing that Don Quixote was some distance off talking to the travellers in the coach, fell upon Sancho, knocked him down, and leaving hardly a hair in his beard, belaboured him with kicks and left him stretched breathless and senseless on the ground; and without any more delay helped the friar to mount, who, trembling, terrified, and pale, as soon as he found himself in the saddle, spurred after his companion, who was standing at a distance looking on, watching the result of the onslaught; then, not caring to wait for the end of the affair just begun, they pursued their journey making more crosses than if they had the devil after them.

Don Quixote was, as has been said, speaking to the lady in the coach: "Your beauty, lady mine," said he, "may now dispose of your person as may be most in accordance with your pleasure, for the pride of your ravishers lies prostrate on the ground through this strong arm of mine; and lest you should be pining to know the name of your deliverer, know that I am called Don Quixote of La Mancha, knight-errant and adventurer, and captive to the peerless and beautiful lady Dulcinea del Toboso: and in return for the service you have received of me I ask no more than that you should return to El Toboso, and on my behalf present yourself before that lady and tell her what I have done to set you free."

One of the squires in attendance upon the coach, a Biscayan, was listening to all Don Quixote was saying, and, perceiving that he would not allow the coach to go on, but was saying it must return at once to El Toboso, he made at him, and seizing his lance addressed him in bad Castilian and worse Biscayan after his fashion, "Begone, caballero, and I'll go with thee; by the God that made me, unless thou quittest coach, slayest thee as art here a Biscayan."

Don Quixote understood him quite well, and answered him very quietly, "If thou wert a knight, as thou art none, I should have already chastised thy folly and rashness, miserable creature." To which the Biscayan returned, "I no gentleman!—I swear to God thou liest as I am Christian: if thou droppest lance and drawest sword, soon shalt thou see thou art carrying water to the cat: Biscayan on land, hidalgo at sea, hidalgo at the devil, and look, if thou sayest otherwise thou liest."

"'You will see presently,' said Agrajes,'" replied Don Quixote; and throwing his lance on the ground he drew his sword, braced his buckler on his arm, and attacked the Biscayan, bent upon taking his life.

The Biscayan, when he saw him coming on, though he wished to dismount from his mule, in which, being one of those sorry ones let out for hire, he had no confidence, had no choice but to draw his sword; it was lucky for him, however, that he was near the coach, from which he was able to snatch a cushion that served him for a shield; and they went at one another as if they had been two mortal enemies. The others strove to make peace between them, but could not, for the Biscayan declared in his disjointed phrase that if they did not let him finish his battle he would kill his mistress and everyone that strove to prevent him. The lady in the coach, amazed and terrified at what she saw, ordered the coachman to draw aside a little, and set herself to watch this severe struggle, in the course of which the Biscayan smote Don Quixote a mighty stroke on the shoulder over the top of his buckler, which, given to one without armour, would have cleft him to the waist. Don Quixote, feeling the weight of this prodigious blow, cried aloud, saying, "O lady of my soul, Dulcinea, flower of beauty, come to the aid of this your knight, who, in fulfilling his obligations to your beauty, finds himself in this extreme peril." To say this, to lift his sword, to shelter himself well behind his buckler, and to assail the Biscayan was the work of an instant, determined as he was to venture all upon a single blow. The Biscayan, seeing him come on in this way, was convinced of his courage by his spirited bearing, and resolved to follow his example, so he waited for him keeping well under cover of his cushion, being unable to execute any sort of manoeuvre with his mule, which, dead tired and never meant for this kind of game, could not stir a step.

On, then, as aforesaid, came Don Quixote against the wary Biscayan, with uplifted sword and a firm intention of splitting him in half, while on his side the Biscayan waited for him sword in hand, and under the protection of his cushion; and all present stood trembling, waiting in suspense the result of blows such as threatened to fall, and the lady in the coach and the rest of her following were making a thousand vows and offerings to all the images and shrines of Spain, that God might deliver her squire and all of them from this great peril in which they found themselves. But it spoils all, that at this point and crisis the author of the history leaves this battle impending, giving as excuse that he could find nothing more written about these achievements of Don Quixote than what has been already set forth. It is true the second author of this work was unwilling to believe that a history so curious could have been allowed to fall under the sentence of oblivion, or that the wits of La Mancha could have been so undiscerning as not to preserve in their archives or registries some documents referring to this famous knight; and this being his persuasion, he did not despair of finding the conclusion of this pleasant history, which, heaven favouring him, he did find in a way that shall be related in the Second Part.

(Source: John Ormsby, trans. Don Quixote. New York: Smith and Elder, 1885.)

GLOSSARY

alforjas: saddlebags

bota: a leather container for wine

Briareus: in Greek mythology, a fifty-headed, hundred-armed storm giant

buckler: a small shield often worn on the forearm

dromedary: a camel with one hump

knight-errant: a wandering knight

league: roughly, the distance a person could walk in an hour

Document Analysis
Chapter VIII of the first volume of *Don Quixote* includes two of the novel's most well-known incidents. In the preceding chapters, he had himself dubbed a knight and made his first "sally" into the countryside. He donned his armor, along with his ill-fitting helmet, mounted his horse Rocinante, and set out to right wrongs, redress grievances, and stamp out abuses. The reader also learns the titles of many of the chivalric romances in the don's library; it is his immersion in these romances that has addled his mind and inflamed his imagination.

During his second sally in Chapter VIII, he encounters thirty or forty windmills on a plain. In his imagination, he sees the windmills as giants with long, massive arms and compares them to Briareus, the Greek mythological giant with a hundred arms. He resolves to do battle with the giants and slay them, and the spoils from the encounter will enable him to continue his mission. His squire, Sancho Panza, who serves as a foil to his master's romantic illusions, tries to convince his master that the windmills are windmills, but Don Quixote brushes Sancho's objections aside, arguing that he has no experience with adventures. The don commends himself to his ladylove, Dulcinea, and attacks the windmills at full gallop. The vanes of the windmills, however, are turning with such speed that they knock him and his horse to the ground and shatter his lance. The knight believes that his ill fortune is the work of the magician Friston, an imaginary character who, the knight believes, has enchanted the windmills. The phrase "tilting at windmills" survives as an indication that one is attacking imaginary enemies.

As Don Quixote and Sancho continue on their way, the knight laments the loss of his lance. He tells Sancho the story of Diego Pérez de Vargas, a historical Spanish knight who broke his sword in battle and replaced it with a heavy bough from an oak tree. The don acts in knightly fashion by refusing to complain about his aches and pains, and by going without sustenance while Sancho eats. Later, Sancho sleeps soundly while the don lies awake thinking of Dulcinea. On the road, he tells Sancho not to defend him if he is assaulted by knights, for he, Sancho, is not a knight, and to do so would violate the laws of knighthood; Sancho can come to his master's defense only if the attack comes from low-born rabble.

Their adventures continue when they meet a pair of Benedictine friars mounted on "camels" but in reality mounted on mules. Behind them is a coach with several attendants on horseback and on foot. Inside the coach is a lady from Biscay on her way to Seville, where she plans to join her husband, who has been assigned to a post in India. In the don's heated imagination, the black-clad friars are magicians, and they have abducted the "princess" in the coach. Once again, he sees a wrong that needs to be righted, so he resolves to come to the lady's rescue. He lowers his lance and charges the friars, knocking one to the ground while the other flees. As the knight talks to those in the coach, Sancho tries to seize the friar's habit as the spoils of war, but he is beaten and kicked by two of the mule drivers in the party.

Don Quixote then introduces himself to the lady in the coach, using the inflated language of chivalric romances: "'Your beauty, lady mine,' said he, 'may now dispose of your person as may be most in accordance with your pleasure, for the pride of your ravishers lies prostrate on the ground through this strong arm of mine; and lest you should be pining to know the name of your deliverer, know that I am called Don Quixote of La Mancha, knight-errant and adventurer, and captive to the peerless and beautiful lady Dulcinea del Toboso.'" One of coach's attendants confronts the don and insults him, leading to armed conflict; the scene is a comic one, for the attendant's mule is exhausted, and the attendant uses a cushion as his shield as the two men do battle. Just as the don is about to dispatch the attendant over the cries of distress coming from the lady in the coach, the narrative voice intervenes: "But it spoils all, that at this point and crisis the author of the history leaves this battle impending, giving as excuse that he could find nothing more written about these achievements of Don Quixote than what has been already set forth." This and similar statements maintain the pretense that the novel is a true history that is being passed down by a narrator.

Essential Themes

Don Quixote provides an example of the mock epic, a satirical literary form that adopted the conventions of epic literature but used them to make fun of trivial things. In Cervantes' novel, these conventions are readily apparent. The don is a knight. He has a trusty steed that carries him into battle. He has a squire who attends to his needs and who frequently becomes an audience for the knight's discourses. The knight has devoted himself to a beautiful damsel, and it is she who inspires him as he embarks on a quest to right wrongs and battle enemies. This is a pattern that extends back to Classical ages and has been used much more recently in such works as *The Adventures of Huckleberry Finn,* in which Huck is the knight and the escaped slave Jim is his trusted squire. The mock epic, however, parodies the chivalric romance for comic effect. Thus, the don does not battle giants; he battles windmills—windmills that defeat him but only because they are enchanted by an evil magician. He is determined to rescue a "damsel in distress," the lady in the coach. The lady, however, is merely on a journey accompanied by friars; her object is to join her husband, and she has not been abducted by magicians. The "battle" that ensues as Don Quixote rides to her rescue is absurd and comic, and has no culmination. The flow of ironic wit and parody continues throughout the novel.

Nevertheless, the comic misadventures of Don Quixote can also be read as a celebration of idealism. For all of his comic absurdity, Don Quixote is an admirable character. He operates out of noble motives. He wants to achieve good in the world. He longs to redress wrongs and save people from what he sees as dangers. Although his vivid imagination deludes him into seeing perils that do not exist—and thus leaving chaos in his wake—his motives remain pure. He is not acting out of a desire for personal gain, vengeance, greed, jealousy, or any of the other cardinal sins that give rise to tragic consequences. For this reason, perhaps, the figure of Don Quixote has survived as an emblem of nobility and that his adventures, comic as they are, have influenced numerous later authors—and inspired the hit musical *Man of La Mancha,* whose lead character, in one of the songs, dreams "the impossible dream."

—*Michael J. O'Neal, PhD*

Bibliography and Further Reading

Cervantes's Don Quixote. Edited by Harold Bloom, Chelsea House Publishers, 2000.

Duran, Manuel, and Fay R. Rogg. *Fighting Windmills: Encounters with Don Quixote.* Yale University Press, 2006.

Echevarria, Roberto Gonzalez. *Cervantes' Don Quixote: A Casebook.* Yale University Press, 2015.

Nabokov, Vladimir. *Lectures on Don Quixote.* Weidenfeld & Nicolson, 1983.

Schmidt, Rachel Lynn. *Forms of Modernity: Don Quixote and Modern Theories of the Novel.* University of Toronto Press, 2011.

Websites

Bloom, Harold. "The Knight in the Mirror." *Guardian*, 13 Dec. 2003, https://www.theguardian.com/books/2003/dec/13/classics.miguelcervantes.

Eisenberg, Daniel. "Romances of Chivalry in the Spanish Golden Age." *Biblioteca Virtual: Miguel de Cervantes*, http://www.cervantesvirtual.com/obra-visor/romances-of-chivalry-in-the-spanish-golden-age-0/html/ffcd58ce-82b1-11df-acc7-002185ce6064_37.html.

■ Treaty of Westphalia

Date: 1648
Authors: Various
Genre: International peace agreement

Summary Overview

The Treaty of Westphalia was actually a pair of treaties negotiated in the Westphalian towns of Münster and Osnabrück, and concluded on October 24, 1648, ending the Thirty Years' War (1618–1648). The Thirty Years' War, a period of violence and destruction unmatched in Europe until the twentieth century, had brought about a perspectival change in the way states dealt with one another. The medieval notion of universality, whereby rulers acted in the best interests of the Church, had given way to the brutal emergence of *raison d'état*, or the view that state interests trump all other concerns. The treaty was the European community's first attempt to reign in national aggression through fostering a balance of power and collective peace.

The Treaty of Westphalia set the year 1648 as the ultimate diplomatic and religious break between the medieval and early modern periods. The rupture, however, was neither simple nor accomplished by mutual consent, as demonstrated by the attitudes of two leaders of the time. The Habsburg Archduke Ferdinand, who in 1619 became Holy Roman Emperor, had declared in 1596 that he would sooner die than make any concessions to the sectarians on the topic of religion. His contemporary, Cardinal Richelieu of France, wrote: "The state has no immortality; its salvation is now or never." In twenty-first century terms, the former would be derided as a fanatic, while the latter would be considered a political realist.

Defining Moment

In the sixteenth century the Protestant Reformation had split much of Europe into opposing camps defined by religion. The rulers of Spain, France, and the Holy Roman Empire had initially pledged their support to the papacy against the then-heretical position of Martin Luther and his followers. Within a short time, however, many rulers—particularly German electors and princes from the northern states and principalities of the Holy Roman Empire as well as the kings of Sweden and Denmark—had decided to embrace Lutheranism, whether they were motivated by religious conviction, humanist inclinations, antipapal sentiment, or territorial greed.

The situation was most problematic for the Holy Roman Empire, since its Habsburg emperor, Charles V, was also King Charles I of staunchly Catholic Spain. In the early seventeenth century, the Holy Roman Empire encompassed modern-day Germany, Austria, the Czech Republic, Slovenia, Luxembourg, and parts of Poland, Slovakia, eastern France, and northern Italy. It also included the United Provinces, or the modern-day Netherlands; the Spanish Netherlands, or present-day Belgium; and the Swiss Confederation, or what was to become Switzerland. Charles V undertook a series of wars to root out Protestantism. Since the empire never enjoyed the political unity of other European states, the outcome of these conflicts was compromise. The most significant treaty resulting from Charles V's wars was the Peace of Augsburg (1555), in which the empire was effectively divided between Lutheran and Catholic principalities. The Peace of Augsburg established the principle of *cuius regio, eius religio*, which meant that the prince or elector of a certain territory would determine the religion for all of its inhabitants. This peace agreement, however, was more of a truce and demonstrated the weakness of the empire. Additionally, by 1555, the range of Protestant confessions had come to include not only Lutherans but also groups not permitted under the Peace of Augsburg: Calvinists, Anabaptists, and Unitarians.

Charles V's abdication shortly after the Peace of Augsburg temporarily settled religious controversy in the Holy Roman Empire. Other Habsburgs, though, saw themselves as defenders of Catholicism against the growing threats of both the Protestants and the Ottoman Turks. The tension between Protestants and Catholics in Europe, therefore, ought to be seen from the perspective of a wider threat to the Catholic faith, which was under attack on many fronts. In 1564 the imperial crown fell to Charles V's nephew, Maximilian II, who only added to the cauldron by preferring Lutheran to Catholic preachers and protecting Protestants from persecution. His son and successor, Rudolf II, believed that moderation and toleration served to undermine the unity of the empire.

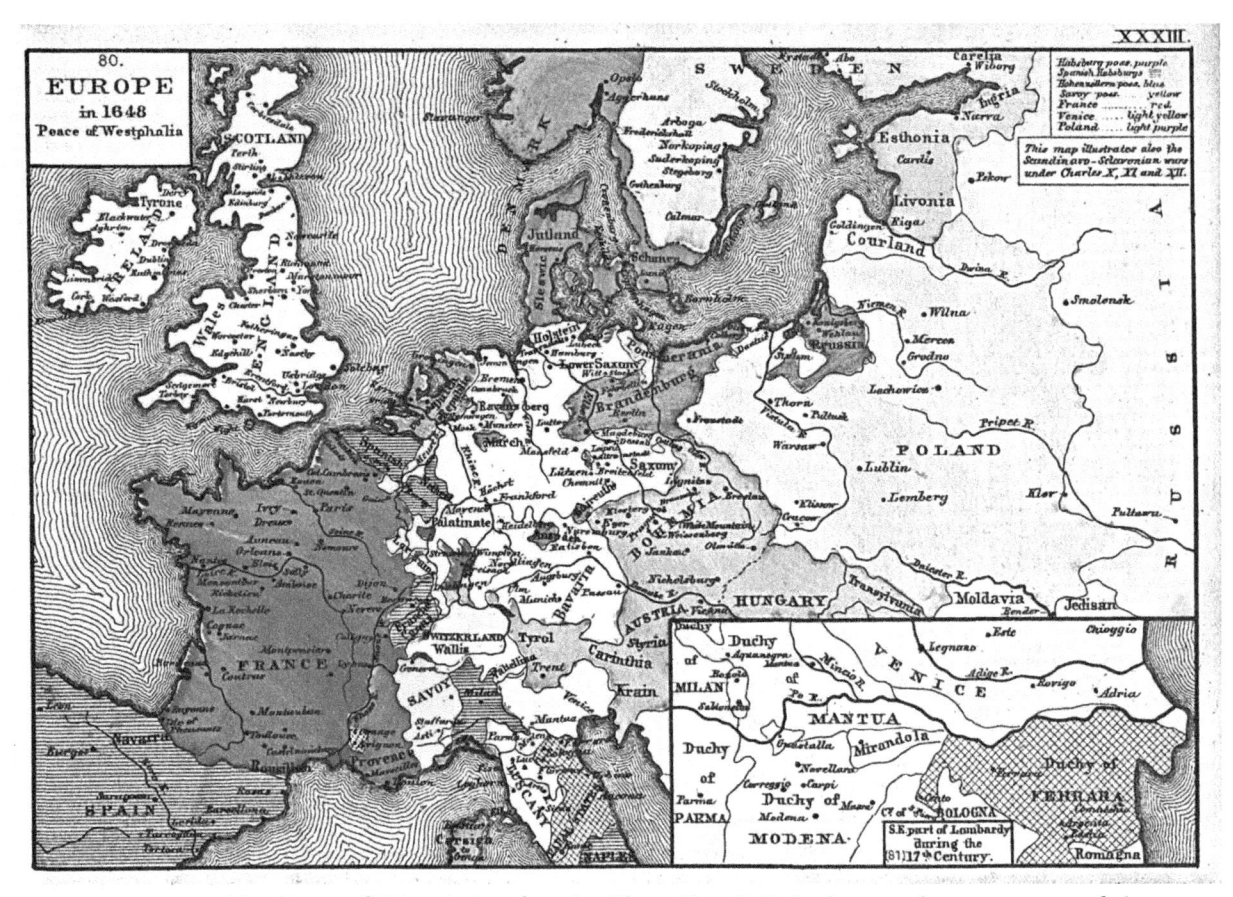

Europe in 1648 (the Peace of Westphalia after the Thirty Years' War), showing the possessions of the two branches of the house of Habsburg; the possessions of the house of Hohenzollern; the Swedish empire on both shores of the Baltic and in northern Germany; the Danish monarchy, Denmark, Norway, and Scania; the British isles, with the battlefields of the civil wars; France, with the battlefields of the civil wars; Germany with the battlefields of the Thirty Years' War; the republic of Poland at its greatest extent; the western boundary of Russia. Robert H. Labberton - University of Texas Library From "An Historical Atlas Containing a Chronological Series of One Hundred and Four Maps, at Successive Periods, from the Dawn of History to the Present Day." by Robert H. Labberton. Sixth Edition. 1884. [Public domain], via Wikimedia Commons

In addition, by the early seventeenth century, the economic prosperity once enjoyed by many German states had been undermined. The bulk of economic trade no longer flowed from the Mediterranean across the Alps and up through the German principalities but instead was being routed directly to northern Europe by sea. This was largely because England and the Netherlands, rather than Spain and Portugal, had come to dominate the Atlantic and many trade routes. Major German banking families were in steady decline. By 1600, the various currencies used within the empire were becoming unstable. As the economic situation worsened, the population continued to increase, which amplified the potential for unrest among the peasantry.

As is often typical during periods of economic instability, many tenaciously clung to religious beliefs. This served to rekindle strife over religious divisions. What formerly had been more of an academic debate between Catholics and Protestants was quickly becoming more heated. Protestant princes in the Holy Roman Empire formed the Protestant Union in 1608. In response, Catholic leaders formed the Catholic League the following year. Both had outside support; the French king, Henry IV, offered support to the Protestant Union, while the Spanish Habsburgs stood ready to help fellow Catholics.

In 1617 the Habsburg Archduke Ferdinand, a fervent Catholic, was made king of Bohemia, a mostly Protestant principality. On May 23, 1618, in Prague, the capital of Bohemia, a group of Protestant nobles, angry at the growing influence of Catholicism—and particularly the appointment of Archduke Ferdinand to the Bohemian throne—tossed two representatives of Holy Roman Emperor Matthias and their secretary out of a window. The three survived, but the action was an affront not only to the empire but also to Ferdinand and the Catholic League. Ferdinand immediately sent two armies into Bohemia. The Calvinist elector of the Palatinate, Frederick V, responded by organizing a counterforce. By the end of November 1618, Protestant forces had captured Pilsen, the Catholic stronghold in Bohemia. The following spring, Matthias was dead and Ferdinand had become his presumptive heir as Holy Roman Emperor. The Bohemian Diet declared that Ferdinand was deposed as king and offered the Bohemian crown to Frederick V, who accepted. There followed two years of war in central Europe, in which Ferdinand defended his claims to the thrones of the Empire and Bohemia, defeating Frederick at the Battle of White Mountain in November 1620. The Bohemian Protestants were defeated, and their land was confiscated. Ferdinand, who had become Holy Roman Emperor Ferdinand II by this time, was restored as Bohemian king, and he proceeded to sell former Protestant estates to Catholics, thereby creating a new Catholic nobility in Bohemia. The initial salvos of the Thirty Years' War in Bohemia were over, but many yearned for vengeance.

In the second phase of the conflict, the mantle of Protestant resistance was taken up by King Christian IV of Denmark. He intervened not so much to assist his fellow Protestants but primarily to acquire territory in northern Germany. Christian received nominal support from England, France, and the Netherlands, then known as the United Provinces, although none of these lands provided significant financial or military support. Unfortunately for Christian, the Holy Roman Empire found a brilliant general in Albrecht von Wallenstein, a Bohemian nobleman who sought to increase his own power by supporting Ferdinand II. In 1625 Wallenstein was commissioned to supply twenty thousand troops for the emperor's cause. By mid-1629, imperial forces had gained the upper hand, forcing Christian to renounce any claims to northern Germany. Ferdinand then confiscated the lands of those who had supported the Danish king and gave land to Wallenstein, including the North German duchy of Mecklenburg. Ferdinand also issued the Edict of Restitution in 1629, which prohibited Calvinist worship but, more important, restored all Catholic property that had been secularized since 1552, much of which had been bought and paid for. This edict convinced even Catholic princes that Ferdinand had overstretched his authority. Many had benefited economically from the decentralized structure of the empire, but Ferdinand's centralization of power, enforced by Wallenstein, was perceived as a threat.

Like Christian IV of Denmark, the Swedish king, Gustavus II Adolph, was primarily concerned about his state's political independence and economic development. For these reasons, in 1630 he positioned Sweden as the rescuer of Protestantism in the northern German states and a check against the power of the Habsburgs under Ferdinand II. While Gustavus, a Lutheran, prohibited forced conversions and tolerated Catholicism, the forces of the empire were brutal. For example, in 1631 an imperial army under Johann Tserclaes (also known as Count of Tilly) massacred twenty thousand in the Protestant archbishop city of Magdeburg and even destroyed its cathedral. After the first major Protestant victory in this phase of the war at Breitenfeld in Saxony in September 1631, many of Ferdinand's allies began entering the Swedish alliance. Gustavus moved into central and southern Germany, devastating the countryside as he marched, but he was mortally wounded in battle in 1632. Wallenstein was assassinated two years later, but thanks to the imperial army's reinforcement with Spanish troops, Sweden's military advance was halted at the South German town of Nördlingen in September 1634. In May 1635, Ferdinand II signed the Peace of Prague with the Saxons; this treaty also suspended the Edict of Restitution and prohibited German princes from forming military alliances with foreign powers.

The final phase of the Thirty Years' War came as a result of France's fear of being surrounded by powerful Habsburgs in both the Holy Roman Empire and Spain. The first minister of France, the Catholic Cardinal Richelieu, supported Lutheran Sweden and garnered the support of Pope Urban VIII, who feared that Habsburg power might threaten his holdings in Italy. Thus, leadership of the Protestant forces passed from Sweden to France, and the war became a wider European conflict. Since the entry of France meant the infusion of forces superior to those of the emperor, many Protestant leaders began to defect from their alliance with Ferdinand III, Ferdinand II's son who had become Holy Roman Emperor upon his father's death in 1637. At the Battle of Breitenfeld outside Vienna in 1642, the imperial army suffered a loss of ten thousand troops at the hands of the Swedes. In 1643 the French won a decisive victory at the Battle of Rocroi over the Spanish on the border of the Spanish Netherlands (modern-day Belgium). By 1646, Ferdinand III had sent representatives to Westphalia to seek peace negotiations.

The war had devastated most of central Europe. The six armies—of the Holy Roman Empire, Denmark, Sweden, Bohemia, Spain, and France—were made up primarily of mercenaries who had no attachment to the places where the fighting occurred; they would fight for any faith for a fee. These armies did not respect the right of surrender; they treated civilians as legitimate targets and made rape and torture general instruments of war. As armies traveled, so did disease. Typhus, dysentery, bubonic plague, and syphilis added to the demographic catastrophe. The war, the flight of refugees, and the ravages of disease brought about a drastic population decline. By the war's end in Germany and Austria, the population had fallen by nearly one-third, from an estimated 21 million to 13.5 million. Starvation was also a consequence of the long war. Farmers saw no reason to plant crops, since there was no assurance they would still be alive to harvest them. As at Versailles at the end of the First World War, diplomats gathered in Westphalia at the end of 1644 in the hope of creating a lasting peace.

Author Biographies

There is no solitary author of the treaty. However, since the treaty's original language was French, and considering France's advantageous position at the war's end, the French delegation perhaps had the most influence. It was headed by Henri II d'Orléans, the duke of Longueville, who, as a French prince, had previously served in the French military in both Italy and the Holy Roman Empire. Usually cast as a rebel of sorts, he used his role at Westphalia not only for the benefit of France but also to secure the independence of the Swiss Confederation. He was joined by the French diplomat Abel Servien, marquis de Sablé, and Claude de Mesmes, the count d'Avaux, a diplomat and public administrator.

While Sweden was in a rather advantageous position at war's end, the Swedish attempt to secure one of the electoral college votes within the empire was thwarted by the stronger influence of France at the conference. The Swedish representatives were Johan Adler Salvius and Count Bengt Gabrielsson Oxenstierna. The Holy Roman Empire's chief delegate was Count Maximilian von Trauttmansdorff. Trauttmansdorff had a long tenure in the service of the Habsburgs, securing both the Bohemian and the Hungarian crowns for the future Ferdinand II and, later, serving as the most influential minister to Ferdinand III.

The Spanish delegation was headed by Gaspar de Bracamonte y Guzmán. Many delegations were sent from the German principalities of the Holy Roman Empire. The representative of the Catholic Church, Fabio Chigi (later Pope Alexander VII), and the Venetian envoy, Alvise Contarini (who became the doge, or duke, of Venice), served as mediators. Many of the imperial states of the Holy Roman Empire also sent delegations. The most important was Brandenburg, which was represented by Count Johann von Sayn-Wittgenstein, the most prominent of the empire's Protestant representatives. He was able to increase the holdings of Brandenburg by obtaining eastern Pomerania as well as other, smaller territories.

HISTORICAL DOCUMENT

Excerpt from the Treaty of Westphalia

In the name of the most holy and individual Trinity: Be it known to all, and every one whom it may concern, or to whom in any manner it may belong, That for many Years past, Discords and Civil Divisions being stir'd up in the Roman Empire, which increas'd to such a degree, that not only all Germany, but also the neighbouring Kingdoms, and France particularly, have been involv'd in the Disorders of a long and cruel War: ... It has at last happen'd, by the effect of Divine Goodness, seconded by the Endeavours of the most Serene Republic of Venice, who in this sad time, when all Christendom is imbroil'd, has not ceas'd to contribute its Counsels for the publick Welfare and Tranquillity; so that on the side, and the other, they have form'd Thoughts of an universal Peace. ...

I. That there shall be a Christian and Universal Peace, and a perpetual, true, and sincere Amity, between his Sacred Imperial Majesty, and his most Christian Majesty; as also, between all and each of the Allies. ... That this Peace and Amity be observ'd and cultivated with such a Sincerity and Zeal, that each Party shall endeavour to procure the Benefit, Honour and Advantage of the other; that thus on all sides they may see this Peace and Friendship in the Roman Empire, and the Kingdom of France flourish, by entertaining a good and faithful Neighbourhood.

II. That there shall be on the one side and the other a perpetual Oblivion, Amnesty, or Pardon of all that has been committed since the beginning of these Troubles ...

VI. According to this foundation of reciprocal Amity, and a general Amnesty, all and every one of the Electors of the sacred Roman Empire, the Princes and States (therein comprehending the Nobility, which depend immediately on the Empire) their Vassals, Subjects, Citizens, Inhabitants (to whom on the account of the Bohemian or German Troubles or Alliances, contracted here and there, might have been done by the one Party or the other, any Prejudice or Damage in any manner, or under what pretence soever, as well in their Lordships, their fiefs, Underfiefs, Allodations, as in their Dignitys, Immunitys, Rights and Privileges) shall be fully re-establish'd on the one side and the other, in the Ecclesiastick or Laick State, which they enjoy'd, or could lawfully enjoy, notwithstanding any Alterations, which have been made in the mean time to the contrary. ...

VII. It shall also be free for the Elector of Treves, as well in the Quality of Bishop of Spires as Bishop of Worms, to sue before competent Judges for the Rights he pretends to certain Ecclesiastical Lands, situated in the Territorys of the Lower Palatinate, if so be those Princes make not a friendly Agreement among themselves. ...

XXVIII. That those of the Confession of Augsburg, and particularly the Inhabitants of Oppenheim, shall be put in possession again of their Churches, and Ecclesiastical Estates, as they were in the Year 1624. as also that all others of the said Confession of Augsburg, who shall demand it, shall have the free Exercise of their Religion, as well in publick Churches at the appointed Hours, as in private in their own Houses, or in others chosen for this purpose by their Ministers, or by those of their Neighbours, preaching the Word of God. ...

XXXIX. That the Debts either by Purchase, Sale, Revenues, or by what other name they may be call'd, if they have been violently extorted by one of the Partys in War, and if the Debtors alledge and offer to prove there has been a real Payment, they shall be no more prosecuted, before these Exceptions be first adjusted. That the Debtors shall be oblig'd to produce their Exceptions within the term of two years after the Publication of the Peace, upon pain of being afterwards condemn'd to perpetual Silence.

XL. That Processes which have been hitherto enter'd on this Account, together with the Transactions and Promises made for the Restitution of Debts, shall be look'd upon as void; and yet the Sums of Money, which during the War have been exacted bona fide, and with a good intent, by way of Contributions, to prevent greater Evils by the Contributors, are not comprehended herein.

XLI. That Sentences pronounc'd during the War about Matters purely Secular, if the Defect in the Proceedings be not fully manifest, or cannot be immediately demonstrated, shall not be esteem'd wholly void; but that the Effect shall be suspended until the Acts of Justice (if one of the Partys demand the space of six months after the Publication of the Peace, for the reviewing of his Process) be review'd and weigh'd in a proper Court, and according to the ordinary or extraordinary Forms us'd in the Empire: to the end that the former Judgments may be confirm'd, amended, or quite eras'd, in case of Nullity.

XLII. In the like manner, if any Royal, or particular Fiefs, have not been renew'd since the Year 1618.

nor Homage paid to whom it belongs; the same shall bring no prejudice, and the Investiture shall be renew'd the day the Peace shall be concluded.

XLIII. Finally, That all and each of the Officers, as well Military Men as Counsellors and Gownmen, and Ecclesiasticks of what degree they may be, who have serv'd the one or other Party among the Allies, or among their Adherents, let it be in the Gown, or with the Sword, from the highest to the lowest, without any distinction or exception ... shall be restor'd by all Partys in the State of Life, Honour, Renown, Liberty of Conscience, Rights and Privileges, which they enjoy'd before the abovesaid Disorders; that no prejudice shall be done to their Effects and Persons, that no Action or accusation shall be enter'd against them; and that further, no Punishment be inflicted on them, or they to bear any damage under what pretence soever: And all this shall have its full effect in respect to those who are not Subjects or Vassals of his Imperial Majesty, or of the House of Austria.

XLIV. But for those who are Subjects and Hereditary Vassals of the Emperor, and of the House of Austria, they shall really have the benefit of the Amnesty, as for their Persons, Life, Reputation, Honours: and they may return with Safety to their former Country; but they shall be oblig'd to conform, and submit themselves to the Laws of the Realms, or particular Provinces they shall belong to.

XLV. As to their Estates that have been lost by Confiscation or otherways, before they took the part of the Crown of France, or of Swedeland, notwithstanding the Plenipotentiarys of Swedeland have made long instances they may be also restor'd. Nevertheless his Imperial Majesty being to receive Law from none, and the Imperialists sticking close thereto, it has not been thought convenient by the States of the Empire, that for such a Subject the War should be continu'd: And that thus those who have lost their Effects as aforesaid, cannot recover them to the prejudice of their last Masters and Possessors. But the Estates, which have been taken away by reason of Arms taken for France or Swedeland, against the Emperor and the House of Austria, they shall be restor'd in the State they are found, and that without any Compensation for Profit or Damage.

XLIX. And since for the greater Tranquillity of the Empire, in its general Assemblys of Peace, a certain Agreement has been made between the Emperor, Princes and States of the Empire, which has been inserted in the Instrument and Treaty of Peace, ... touching the Differences about Ecclesiastical Lands, and the Liberty of the Exercise of Religion; it has been found expedient to confirm, and ratify it by this present Treaty, in the same manner as the abovesaid Agreement has been made with the said Crown of Swedeland; also with those call'd the Reformed, in the same manner, as if the words of the abovesaid Instrument were reported here verbatim. ...

LVI. ... That if within the term of nine Months, the whole Sum be not paid to Madam the Landgravine, not only Cuesfeldt and Newhaus shall remain in her Hands till the full Payment, but also for the remainder, she shall be paid Interest at Five per Cent. and the Treasurers and Collectors of the Bayliwicks appertaining to the abovesaid Arch-bishopricks, Bishopricks and Abby, bordering on the Principality of Hesse, ... they shall yearly pay the Interest of the remaining Sum notwithstanding the Prohibitions of their Masters. If the Treasurers and Collectors delay the Payment, or alienate the Revenues, Madam the Landgravine shall have liberty to constrain them to pay, by all sorts of means, always saving the Right of the Lord Proprietor of the Territory. ...

LVIII. ... The Fortifications and Ramparts, rais'd during the Possession of the Places, shall be destroy'd and demolish'd as much as possible, without exposing the Towns, Borroughs, Castles and Fortresses, to Invasions and Robberys. ...

LXIII. And as His Imperial Majesty, upon Complaints made in the name of the City of Basle, and of all Switzerland, in the presence of their Plenipotentiarys deputed to the present Assembly, touching some Procedures and Executions proceeding from the Imperial Chamber against the said City, and the other united Cantons of the Swiss Country, and their Citizens and Subjects having demanded the Advice of the States of the Empire and their Council; these have, by a Decree of the 14th of May of the last Year, declared the said City of Basle, and the other Swiss-Cantons, to be as it were in possession of their full Liberty and Exemption of the Empire; so that they are no ways subject to the Judicatures, or Judgments of the Empire, and it was thought convenient to insert the same in this Treaty of Peace, and confirm it, and thereby to make void and annul all such Procedures and Arrests given on this Account in what form soever.

LXIV. And to prevent for the future any Differences arising in the Politick State, all and every one of the Electors, Princes and States of the Roman Empire, are so establish'd and confirm'd in their antient Rights, Prerogatives, Libertys, Privileges, free exercise of Territorial Right, as well Ecclesiastick, as Politick Lordships, Regales, by virtue of this present Transaction: that they never can or ought to be molested therein by any whomsoever upon any manner of pretence.

LXV. They shall enjoy without contradiction, the Right of Suffrage in all Deliberations touching the Affairs of the Empire; but above all, when the Business in hand shall be the making or interpreting of Laws, the declaring of Wars, imposing of Taxes, levying or quartering of Soldiers, erecting new Fortifications in the Territorys of the States, or reinforcing the old Garisons; as also when a Peace of Alliance is to be concluded, and treated about, or the like, none of these, or the like things shall be acted for the future, without the Suffrage and Consent of the Free Assembly of all the States of the Empire: Above all, it shall be free perpetually to each of the States of the Empire, to make Alliances with Strangers for their Preservation and Safety; provided, nevertheless, such Alliances be not against the Emperor, and the Empire, nor against the Publick Peace, and this Treaty, and without prejudice to the Oath by which every one is bound to the Emperor and the Empire.

LXVI. That the Diets of the Empire shall be held within six Months after the Ratification of the Peace; and after that time as often as the Publick Utility, or Necessity requires. That in the first Diet the Defects of precedent Assemblys be chiefly remedy'd; and that then also be treated and settled by common Consent of the States, the Form and Election of the Kings of the Romans, by a Form, and certain Imperial Resolution; the Manner and Order which is to be observ'd for declaring one or more States, to be within the Territorys of the Empire, besides the Manner otherways describ'd in the Constitutions of the Empire; that they consider also of re-establishing the Circles, the renewing the Matricular-Book, the re-establishing suppress'd States, the moderating and lessening the Collects of the Empire, Reformation of Justice and Policy, the taxing of Fees in the Chamber of Justice, the Due and requisite instructing of ordinary Deputys for the Advantage of the Publick, the true Office of Directors in the Colleges of the Empire, and such other Business as could not be here expedited.

LXVII. That as well as general as particular Diets, the free Towns, and other States of the Empire, shall have decisive Votes; they shall, without molestation, keep their Regales, Customs, annual Revenues, Libertys, Privileges to confiscate, to raise Taxes, and other Rights, lawfully obtain'd from the Emperor and Empire, or enjoy'd long before these Commotions, with a full Jurisdiction within the inclosure of their Walls, and their Territorys: making void at the same time, annulling and for the future prohibiting all Things, which by Reprisals, Arrests, stopping of Passages, and other prejudicial Acts, either during the War, under what pretext soever they have been done and attempted hitherto by private Authority, or may hereafter without any preceding formality of Right be enterpris'd. As for the rest, all laudable Customs of the sacred Roman Empire, the fundamental Constitutions and Laws, shall for the future be strictly observ'd, all the Confusions which time of War have, or could introduce, being remov'd and laid aside. ...

LXX. The Rights and Privileges of Territorys, water'd by Rivers or otherways, as Customs granted by the Emperor, with the Consent of the Electors, and among others, to the Count of Oldenburg on the Viserg, and introduc'd by a long Usage, shall remain in their Vigour and Execution. There shall be a full Liberty of Commerce, a secure Passage by Sea and Land: and after this manner all and every one of the Vassals, Subjects, Inhabitants and Servants of the Allys, on the one side and the other, shall have full power to go and come, to trade and return back, by Virtue of this present Article, after the same manner as was allowed before the Troubles of Germany; the Magistrates, on the one side and on the other, shall be oblig'd to protect and defend them against all sorts of Oppressions, equally with their own Subjects, without prejudice to the other Articles of this Convention, and the particular laws and Rights of each place. And that the said Peace and Amity between the Emperor and the Most Christian King, may be the more corroborated, and the publick Safety provided for, it has been agreed with the Consent, Advice and Will of the Electors, Princes and States of the Empire, for the Benefit of Peace. ...

LXXII. That Monsieur Francis, Duke of Lorain, shall be restor'd to the possession of the Bishoprick of Verdun, as being the lawful Bishop thereof; and shall be left in the peaceable Administration of this Bishoprick and its Abbys (saving the Right of the King and of particular Persons) and shall enjoy his Patrimonial Estates, and his other Rights, wherever they may be situated (and as far as they do not contradict the present Resignation) his Privileges, Revenues and Incomes; having previously taken the Oath of Fidelity to the King, and provided he undertakes nothing against the Good of the State and the Service of his Majesty.

LXXIII. In the second place, the Emperor and Empire resign and transfer to the most Christian King, and his Successors, the Right of direct Lordship and Sovereignty, and all that has belong'd, or might hitherto belong to him, or the sacred Roman Empire, upon Pignerol. ...

LXXVI. Item, All the Vassals, Subjects, People, Towns, Boroughs, Castles, Houses, Fortresses, Woods, Coppices, Gold or Silver Mines, Minerals, Rivers, Brooks, Pastures; and in a word, all the Rights, Regales and Appurtenances, without any reserve, shall belong to the most Christian King, and shall be for ever incorporated with the Kingdom France, with all manner of Jurisdiction and Sovereignty, without any contradiction from the Emperor, the Empire, House of Austria, or any other: so that no Emperor, or any Prince of the House of Austria, shall, or ever ought to usurp, nor so much as pretend any Right and Power over the said Countrys, as well on this, as the other side the Rhine.

LXXVII. The most Christian King shall, nevertheless, be oblig'd to preserve in all and every one of these Countrys the Catholick Religion, as maintain'd under the Princes of Austria, and to abolish all Innovations crept in during the War. ...

LXXXI. For the greater Validity of the said Cessions and Alienations, the Emperor and Empire, by virtue of this present Treaty, abolish all and every one of the Decrees, Constitutions, Statutes and Customs of their Predecessors, Emperors of the sacred Roman Empire, tho they have been confirm'd by Oath, or shall be confirm'd for the future; particularly this Article of the Imperial Capitulation, by which all or any Alienation of the Appurtenances and Rights of the Empire is prohibited: and by the same means they exclude for ever all Exceptions hereunto, on what Right and Titles soever they may be grounded.

LXXXII. Further it has been agreed, That besides the Ratification promis'd hereafter in the next Diet by the Emperor and the States of the Empire, they shall ratify anew the Alienations of the said Lordships and Rights: insomuch, that if it shou'd be agreed in the Imperial Capitulation, or if there shou'd be a Proposal made for the future, in the Diet, to recover the Lands and Rights of the Empire, the abovenam'd things shall not be comprehended therein, as having been legally transfer'd to another's Dominion, with the common Consent of the States, for the benefit of the publick Tranquillity; for which reason it has been found expedient the said Seigniorys shou'd be ras'd out of the Matricular-Book of the Empire. ...

LXXXIX. ... No King of France can or ought ever to pretend to or usurp any Right or Power over the said Countrys situated on this and the other side the Rhine: ...

XCII. That the most Christian King shall be bound to leave not only the Bishops of Strasburg and Basle, with the City of Strasburg, but also the other States or Orders, ... so that he cannot pretend any Royal Superiority over them, but shall rest contented with the Rights which appertain'd to the House of Austria, and which by this present Treaty of Pacification, are yielded to the Crown of France. In such a manner, nevertheless, that by the present Declaration, nothing is intended that shall derogate from the Sovereign Dominion already hereabove agreed to. ...

XCIX. Who hereafter, with the Authority and Consent of their Imperial and most Christian Majestys, by virtue of this solemn Treaty of Peace, shall have no Action for this account against the Duke of Savoy, or his Heirs and Successors. ...

CIV. As soon as the Treaty of Peace shall be sign'd and seal'd by the Plenipotentiarys and Ambassadors, all Hostilitys shall cease, and all Partys shall study immediately to put in execution what has been agreed to; ... That when it shall be known that the signing has been made in these two Places, divers Couriers shall presently be sent to the Generals of the Armys, to acquaint them that the Peace is concluded, and take care that the Generals chuse a Day, on which shall be made on all sides a Cessation of Arms and Hostilitys for the publishing of the Peace in the Army; and that command be given to all and each of the chief Officers Military and Civil, and to the Governors of Fortresses, to abstain for the future from all Acts of Hostility: and if it happen that any thing be attempted, or actually innovated after the said Publication, the same shall be forthwith repair'd and restor'd to its former State.

CV. The Plenipotentiarys on all sides shall agree among themselves, between the Conclusion and the Ratification of the Peace, upon the Ways, Time, and Securitys which are to be taken for the Restitution of Places, and for the Disbanding of Troops; of that both Partys may be assur'd, that all things agreed to shall be sincerely accomplish'd.

CVI. The Emperor above all things shall publish an Edict thro'out the Empire, and strictly enjoin all, who by these Articles of Pacification are oblig'd to restore or do any thing else, to obey it promptly and without tergi-versation, between the signing and the ratifying of this present Treaty; commanding as well the Directors as Governors of the Militia of the Circles, to hasten and finish the Restitution to be made to every one, in conformity to those Conventions, when the same are demanded. ...

CVII. If any of those who are to have something restor'd to them, suppose that the Emperor's Commissarys are necessary to be present at the Execution of some Restitution (which is left to their Choice) they shall have them. In which case, that the effect of the things agreed on may be the less hinder'd, it shall be permitted as well to those who restore, as to those to whom Restitution is to be made, to nominate two or three Commissarys immediately after the signing of the Peace, of whom his Imperial Majesty shall chuse two, one of each Religion, and one of each Party, whom he shall injoin to accomplish without delay all that which ought to be done by virtue of this present Treaty. ...

CVIII. Finally, That all and every one either States, Commonaltys, or private Men, either Ecclesiastical or Secular, who by virtue of this Transaction and its general Articles, or by the express and special Disposition of any of them, are oblig'd to restore, transfer, give, do, or execute any thing, shall be bound forthwith after the Publication of the Emperor's Edicts, and after Notification given, to restore, transfer, give, do, or execute the same, without any Delay or Exception, or evading Clause either general or particular, contain'd in the precedent Amnesty, and without any Exception and Fraud as to what they are oblig'd unto. ...

CXII. That the very Places, Citys, Towns, Boroughs, Villages, Castles, Fortresses and Forts ... shall be restor'd without delay to their former and lawful

Possessors and Lords, whether they be mediately or immediately States of the Empire, Ecclesiastical or Secular, comprehending therein also the free Nobility of the Empire: and they shall be left at their own free disposal, either according to Right and Custom, or according to the Force this present Treaty. ...

CXIII. And that this Restitution of possess'd Places, as well by his Imperial Majesty as the most Christian King, and the Allys and Adherents of the one and the other Party, shall be reciprocally and bona fide executed.

CXIV. That the Records, Writings and Documents, and other Moveables, be also restor'd. ...

CXV. That the Inhabitants of each Place shall be oblig'd, when the Soldiers and Garisons draw out, to furnish them without Money the necessary Waggons, Horses, Boats and Provisions, to carry off all things to the appointed Places in the Empire. ...

CXVII. That it shall not for the future, or at present, prove to the damage and prejudice of any Town, that has been taken and kept by the one or other Party; but that all and every one of them, with their Citizens and Inhabitants, shall enjoy as well the general Benefit of the Amnesty, as the rest of this Pacification. And for the Remainder of their Rights and Privileges, Ecclesiastical and Secular, which they enjoy'd before these Troubles, they shall be maintain'd therein; save, nevertheless the Rights of Sovereignty, and what depends thereon, for the Lords to whom they belong.

CXVIII. Finally, that the Troops and Armys of all those who are making War in the Empire, shall be disbanded and discharg'd; only each Party shall send to and keep up as many Men in his own Dominion, as he shall judge necessary for his Security.

CXIX. The Ambassadors and Plenipotentiarys of the Emperor, of the King, and the States of the Empire, promise respectively and the one to the other, to cause the Emperor, the most Christian King, the Electors of the Sacred Roman Empire, the Princes and States, to agree and ratify the Peace which has been concluded in this manner, and by general Consent; and so infallibly to order it, that the solemn Acts of Ratification be presented at Munster, and mutually and in good form exchang'd in the term of eight weeks, to reckon from the day of signing. ...

CXXI. That it never shall be alledg'd, allow'd, or admitted, that any Canonical or Civil Law, any general or particular Decrees of Councils, any Privileges, any Indulgences, any Edicts, any Commissions, Inhibitions, Mandates, Decrees, Rescripts, Suspensions of Law, Judgments pronounc'd at any time, Adjudications, Capitulations of the Emperor, and other Rules and Exceptions of Religious Orders, past or future Protestations, Contradictions, Appeals, Investitures, Transactions, Oaths, Renunciations, Contracts, and much less the Edict of 1629 or the Transaction of Prague, with its Appendixes, or the Concordates with the Popes, or the Interims of the Year 1548. or any other politick Statutes, or Ecclesiastical Decrees, Dispensations, Absolutions, or any other Exceptions, under what pretence or colour they can be invented; shall take place against this Convention, or any of its Clauses and Articles neither shall any inhibitory or other Processes or Commissions be ever allow'd to the Plaintiff or Defendant.

CXXXII. That he who by his Assistance or Counsel shall contravene this Transaction or Publick Peace, or shall oppose its Execution and the abovesaid Restitution, or who shall have endeavour'd, after the Restitution has been lawfully made, and without exceeding the manner agreed on before, without a lawful Cognizance of the Cause, and without the ordinary Course of Justice, to molest those that have been restor'd, whether Ecclesiasticks or Laymen; he shall incur the Punishment of being an Infringer of the publick Peace, and Sentence given against him according to the Constitutions of the Empire, so that the Restitution and Reparation may have its full effect.

CXXIII. That nevertheless the concluded Peace shall remain in force, and all Partys in this Transaction shall be oblig'd to defend and protect all and every Article of this Peace against any one, without distinction of Religion; and if it happens any point shall be violated, the Offended shall before all things exhort the Offender not to come to any Hostility, submitting the Cause to a friendly Composition, or the ordinary Proceedings of Justice. ...

CXXVI. And as often as any would march Troops thro' the other Territorys, this Passage shall be done at the charge of him whom the Troops belong to, and that without burdening or doing any harm or damage to those whole Countrys they march thro'. In a word, all that the Imperial Constitutions determine and ordain touching the Preservation of the publick Peace, shall be strictly observ'd. ...

CXXVIII. In Testimony of all and each of these things, and for their greater Validity, the Ambassadors of their Imperial and most Christian Majestys, and the Deputys, in the name of all the Electors, Princes, and States of the Empire, sent particularly for this end (by virtue of what has been concluded the 13th of October, in the Year hereafter mention'd, and has been deliver'd. ...

And that on condition that by the Subscription of the abovesaid Ambassadors and Deputys, all and every one of the other States who shall abstain from signing and ratifying the present Treaty, shall be no less oblig'd to maintain and observe what is contain'd in this present Treaty of Pacification, than if they had subscrib'd and ratify'd it; and no Protestation or Contradiction of the Council of Direction in the Roman Empire shall be valid, or receiv'd in respect to the Subscription and said Deputys have made.

Done, pass'd and concluded at Munster in Westphalia, the 24th Day of October, 1648.

GLOSSARY

allodations: lands or estates held outright, with no ties of feudal obligation

cessions and alienations: territories ceded or otherwise conveyed to other parties

Diets of the Empire: qualified legislative bodies of the participating states

his most Christian Majesty: Louis XIV, king of France

his Sacred Imperial Majesty: Ferdinand III, ruler of the Holy Roman Empire and eldest son of Emperor Ferdinand II

Imperial Capitulation: approval of the treaty, a statement saying that the emperor will have to capitulate to the dictates of Westphalia

laick: secular

renewing the Matricular-Book: renewal of imperial allegiance within the Holy Roman Empire

moveables: personal property

regales: royal prerogatives

Document Analysis

The Treaty of Westphalia is named for the northern German region where the negotiations were conducted. Representatives did not gather at one location, however. At the town of Münster, the delegates from France and the Holy Roman Empire met under the mediation of the papacy and the republic of Venice. A mere fifty kilometers away in Osnabrück, the delegates of France, the Holy Roman Empire, and Sweden gathered with Christian IV of Denmark as mediator. This segregation of powers was necessary, since Sweden refused to be mediated by a representative of the papacy and the papal representative refused to sit in the same room with a "heretic."

The Congress of Westphalia opened in December 1644 and concluded with much fanfare on October 24, 1648. The comprehensive treaty's introduction declares a "universal Peace," which, according to Article I, is to be founded not on a common religion or dictated by religious authority but is to occur "between all and each of the Allies ... that each Party shall endeavour to procure the Benefit, Honour and Advantage of the other." In other words, abiding by the principles of the treaty was intended to benefit all parties. In order to halt the cycle of violence, Article II and Article VI provided for amnesty and pardon for all offenses committed since the beginning of the war while avoiding the rhetoric typical of an imposed peace.

The language of the treaty was new to diplomatic discourse in that it is conciliatory toward different religious sects. This was clearly an effort to remove religious difference as a cause of conflict. To this end, Article XLV proclaims "the Liberty of the Exercise of Religion" throughout the Holy Roman Empire, thus strengthening the position of the Protestants. Article XXVIII specifically granted religious freedom to Lutherans (called "those of the Confession of Augsburg" in the document) and restored ecclesiastical property to them based on their holdings as of 1624. Articles XXII, XXV, and XXVI offered an olive branch to Charles I Louis of the Lower Palatinate, who was the son of Frederick V, the Calvinist elector whom the Protestants had selected as Bohemian king in 1619 in their attempted rebellion against Ferdinand II.

The monetary cost of the war had been significant, and the treaty attempted to anticipate and address economic concerns. Article XXXIX gave all parties a period of two years to show claim, after which debts were to be considered settled. Since economic conditions had worsened throughout the Holy Roman Empire during the war, the signatories wanted to ensure that indemnities either would be paid quickly or would be forgiven to avoid future strife and acts of vengeance. For similar reasons, Article XLI upheld secular judicial pronouncements issued during the war.

The latter half of the treaty dealt, in particular, with the Holy Roman Emperor and his subjects. Article XLIV repeated the earlier proclamation of general amnesty, and Article XLV provided for the return of some royal land but without compensation for damages. Herein the overriding influence of France and Sweden in drafting the document is evident; while the emperor and Austria, whom the delegates wanted to conciliate, could regain lost property, these provisions implied that others within the empire who lost property might not have it returned. Article XLIX restated the principle regarding religious liberty and the return of Church land. It refers to an agreement among those powers that were meeting at Münster and extended it to apply to the Swedish delegation at Osnabrück.

Specific regions and allies are mentioned in the treaty. For example, Article LVI stipulated the repayment of a sum to "Madam the Landgravine," whose family had been a long-term supporter of the Protestant cause in the state of Hesse. Article XCIX absolved the House of Savoy, which assisted in the French cause, of any retribution on the part of the empire. Article LVIII stipulated that fortresses of war throughout the empire were to be dismantled as long as they did not leave an area lacking in security. Article LXXXII called upon each prince of the empire to respect the traditions and rights of other states, participate in the empire's assemblies, and regard the authority of the Holy Roman Emperor.

Territorial realignments were recognized in the treaty. For example, the United Provinces of the Netherlands were pronounced independent of Spain. Article LXXVI recognized France's right to the towns of Metz, Toul, and Verdun on the western border of the empire, as well as most of Alsace, although article LXXXIX required France to renounce further claims to territory in the vicinity of the Rhine. Article LXXVII stipulates that the French king is obligated to "preserve" Catholicism in areas where it is dominant. Contrary to the Edict of Restitution, only territory that the empire had conquered by 1624 was to be returned to the Catholic Church. French territorial gains were small, but the treaty assured that France, while being obliged to respect religious traditions, could achieve its security goals by maintaining a buffer between itself and the Holy Roman Empire.

Articles CIV through CXIX provided for the implementation of peace. Specifically, Articles CIV and CV spelled out the time and method for cessation of hostilities, CVI the publication of the peace, CVII through CXIV the restoration or transfer of property, CXV the responsibilities of local inhabitants toward departing soldiers, and CXVIII the demobilization of troops and the maintenance of those necessary for security.

With respect to the treaties and covenants established during the course of the war, such as the Edict of Restitution and Peace of Prague, Article CXXI made clear that the Treaty of Westphalia superseded all other provisions, treaties, and agreements. Article CXXXII warned anyone who might infringe on what the treaty termed "Publick Peace." While no specific punishment was given, Article CXXIII enjoined all signatories to "defend and protect all and every Article of this Peace." This provision gave France and Sweden the ability to frustrate the Habsburgs. France and Sweden thus became the guarantors of the new imperial constitution with the obligation to protect the rights of princes against the Holy Roman Emperor. They became the counterbalance to ensure that future conflict over or within the empire would be quelled.

Essential Themes

The significance of the Treaty of Westphalia is often underestimated. It would serve as a model for resolving future European conflicts. Six armies had participated in the conflict. Those six states as well as many princes of the empire participated in a gathering that brought together more than one hundred delegations. For the first time, a congress with representatives from all parties involved in a multinational conflict not only addressed international disputes but also agreed to abide by the resulting settlement.

France and Sweden gained the most from the treaty. Ultimately, France would replace Spain as the dominant power on the continent (and the two countries would not officially cease hostilities until 1659). Sweden emerged as the major power in the Baltic, a position it would enjoy for a half-century until military defeat by Czar Peter I of Russia. The Habsburgs lost the most. The Austrian branch, the traditional rulers of the Holy Roman Empire, agreed to the independence of the Swiss Confederation. In addition, German princes were not only recognized as independent but also were given the right to establish Lutheranism, Catholicism, or Calvinism within their territories. The treaty also required the Spanish Habsburgs to recognize the independence of a Dutch Republic, which included two provinces taken from the Spanish Netherlands (present-day Belgium).

These territorial and political realignments were significant, and many would last well into the nineteenth century. The treaty also determined religious distribution within the empire by confirming the Peace of Augsburg, which had first established the principle that the prince's religion would determine the religion of his people and expanded it to include Calvinism. As a result, the northern parts of the empire remained largely Lutheran and the area along the Rhine Calvinist, and Catholicism prevailed in the south.

With the catastrophic decline in agriculture, many farmers lacked the capital to remain independent and were forced to become day laborers. In parts of central Europe, especially areas east of the Elbe River, the loss of peasant holdings resulted in the consolidation of large estates and the expansion of serfdom.

The treaty also brought about a formal break between German principalities and territories controlled by the Austrian Habsburgs. Princely power demonstrated during the war and guaranteed by the treaty revealed how little most German states and principalities had to offer the Habsburgs. After 1648, the Austrian Habsburgs increasingly focused attention on their own territories, both inside and outside the empire, and expanded farther into southeastern Europe. This absence of Habsburg influence coupled with the religious and territorial provisions of the treaty enabled a formerly weak principality, such as Brandenburg-Prussia, to begin the process of state building, especially under the Calvinist Frederick William, who was both the elector of Brandenburg and the duke of Prussia.

Finally, the Treaty of Westphalia signaled the loss of power of the papacy. Since late antiquity, the Church had battled for supremacy over European princes and kings, in particular, the Holy Roman Emperor. Even though the Holy Roman Empire had fought on behalf of the Catholic religion in the Thirty Years' War, its loss and the emergence of Richelieu's version of statecraft left little room for the Catholic Church as a power player after 1648.

In the broadest sense, the Treaty of Westphalia may be considered the culmination of the European medieval experience. The significance of this ambitious document is often neglected, since it cannot be read simply as the treaty that ended the Thirty Years' War. It addressed social, political, economic, and religious trends, as well as other issues arising from domestic and international perspectives, in order to create a collective and enduring peace.

—*Christopher Ohan*

Bibliography and Further Reading

Asch, Robert G. *The Thirty Years War: The Holy Roman Empire and Europe, 1618-1648.* St. Martin's Press, 1997.

Bireley, Robert. *Ferdinand II, Counter-Reformation Emperor, 1578-1637.* Cambridge University Press, 2014.

Ingrao, Charles W. *The Habsburg Monarchy, 1618–1815.* Cambridge University Press, 1994.

Wedgwood, C.V. *The Thirty Years War.* New York Review Books, 2005.

Wilson, Peter H. *The Thirty Years War: Europe's Tragedy.* Belknap Press, 2011.

Websites

Cavendish, Richard. "The Treaty of Westphalia." *History Today,* vol. 48, no. 10, Nov. 1998, http://www.historytoday.com/richard-cavendish/treaty-westphalia. Accessed 21 Feb. 2017.

P.C. "The Economist Explains—What Happened in the Thirty Years War?" *The Economist,* 17 Jan. 2016, http://www.economist.com/blogs/economist-explains/2016/01/economist-explains-5. Accessed 21 Feb. 2017.

"The Thirty Years' War." *New Advent: Catholic Encyclopedia,* http://www.newadvent.org/cathen/14648b.htm. Accessed 21 Feb. 2017.

Czar Alexis I: Great Muscovite Law Code

Date: 1649
Author: Czar Alexis I
Genre: Law code

Summary Overview

The *Ulozhenie*, or Great Muscovite Law Code, was Muscovite Russia's main legal code, issued by Alexis I Mikhaylovich ("Alexei Mikhailovich" in the document) in 1649. Its full title, *Sobornoye Ulozhenie*, literally means "Collected Code of Laws." It replaced the Sudebniki (law codes) of Ivan III Vasilyevich (1497) and Ivan IV Vasilyevich (1550). These codes had promoted state centralization and the rise of state and legal bureaucracies. The *Ulozhenie*—a complex document running well over two hundred pages in modern printings—continued this process. It is primarily known, however, for its passages on serfdom, which take up only a few pages. In this, the code represented the legal climax of a long historical process whereby Russia's once-free peasants (about 90 percent of the total population) had been reduced to a form of serfdom often compared to slavery. The new code terminated the few remaining rights of movement left to serfs from earlier legislation; ended time limitations on the return of runaways; eroded the differences between serf and slave classes (the two categories remained legally distinct until 1723, however); and pronounced the resulting system hereditary, permanent, and irrevocable. More generally, the *Ulozhenie* was a striking statement of political authority and social hierarchy, covering topics that included the relation of various social classes to the state and questions of authority within families.

Defining Moment

The *Ulozhenie* was an effort to bring order to a corpus of law that, owing to the issuance of numerous edicts over the previous two centuries, had become confusing, contradictory, and ineffective. A specific trigger was a major riot that shook Moscow in 1648. The riot was in response to an unpopular salt tax and perceived corruption and abuses among state officials. More generally, the *Ulozhenie* was intended as a means of enforcing authority, order, and social hierarchy in a state that had suffered numerous major upheavals in the preceding decades, including foreign invasions, civil war, peasant uprisings, "false" czars, and mass migrations, many of them connected with the difficult interregnum of 1598 to 1613 known as the Time of Troubles. This traumatic period followed the death in 1598 of Fyodor I Ivanovich, son of Ivan IV (known as Ivan the Terrible). Fyodor was the last member of the seven-century-old Rurik dynasty of Russian rulers. The Time of Troubles almost led to the complete collapse of Russia and the establishment of Polish Catholic rule in Moscow. Ultimately, however, it instead spawned a broad-based national movement for the regeneration of Muscovite and Orthodox Christian Russia as well as a deeply ingrained sense of the need for strong, central rule and clear lines of authority. The *Ulozhenie* addressed all these concerns.

In the early summer of 1648, Alexis consulted with Patriarch Joseph of Moscow, Church officials, boyars (nobles), and other prominent advisers. Then, on July 16, he appointed a five-person commission headed by the talented and prominent state servant Nikita Odoevsky and ordered them to compile a draft law. This was done by October 3. Odoevsky, a favorite also of the previous czar, was a minor noble who had already carved out successful careers for himself as a diplomat and military commander. Before being recruited for work on the *Ulozhenie*, he had proved himself in legal affairs, running the chancelleries of Kazan and Siberia. His commission drew on a wide body of existing legislation, including past legal cases, earlier Russian secular law codes, Orthodox ecclesiastical law, and Byzantine and Lithuanian codes. The draft was then amended and expanded by an "Assembly of the Land," comprising men from every rank of society (except the peasant masses) and two noblemen from each town. All these men were required to read and sign the finished product. The *Ulozhenie* was essentially a compilation and codification of existing laws, rather than an original composition. Nonetheless, it is considered one of the great achievements of Russian literature prior to the nineteenth century.

Author Biography

The *Ulozhenie* was established at the order of Czar Alexis I. Alexis was born in March 1629 and took the throne at the age of sixteen. His father and royal predecessor,

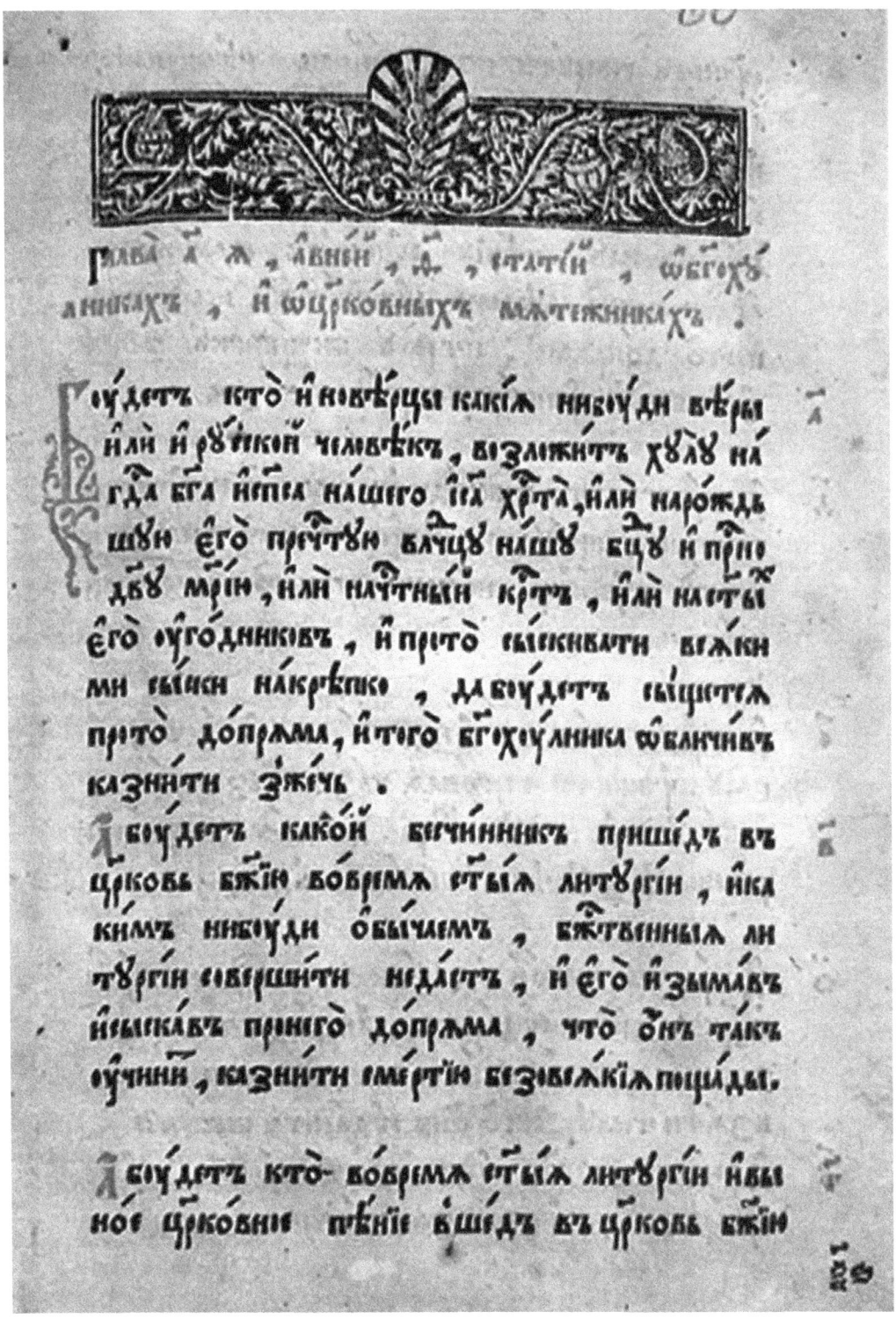

First chapter of the code. By. Alex1709 at ru.wikipedia [Public domain], via Wikimedia Commons

Mikhail, was the founder of the Romanov dynasty. Most historians consider Alexis to have been a pious and fairly effective ruler. Conservative rather than reactionary, he was cautiously favorable to reforms that appeared likely to strengthen or preserve tradition and authority, such as a new and more comprehensive law code. He was also distinguished by an ability to choose wise and talented advisers and to give them sufficient freedom of action. This last trait is also clearly exemplified by the *Ulozhenie*, which Alexis authorized but did not compose. He died in 1676.

HISTORICAL DOCUMENT

Excerpt from the Great Muscovite Law Code of Czar Alexis I
Chapter 10.—The Judicial Process. In It Are 287 Articles.

1. The judicial process of the Sovereign, Tsar, and Grand Prince of all Russia Aleksei Mikhailovich shall be directed by boyars, and *okol'nichie*, and counselors, and state secretaries, and various chancellery officials, and judges. All justice shall be meted out to all people of the Muscovite state, from the highest to the lowest rank, according to the law. Moreover, arriving foreigners and various people from elsewhere who are in the Muscovite state shall be tried by that same judicial process and rendered justice by the sovereign's decree according to the law. No one on his own initiative shall out of friendship or out of enmity add anything to or remove anything from judicial records. No one shall favor a friend nor wreak vengeance on an enemy in any matter. No one shall favor anyone in any matter for any reason. All of the sovereign's cases shall be processed without diffidence to the powerful. Deliver the wronged from the hand of the unjust.

2. Disputed cases which for any reason cannot be resolved in the chancelleries shall be transferred from the chancelleries in a report to the Sovereign, Tsar, and Grand Prince of all Russia Aleksei Mikhailovich and to his royal boyars, and *okol'nichie*, and counselors. The boyars, and *okol'nichie*, and counselors shall sit in the Palace [of Facets], and by the sovereign's decree shall handle the sovereign's various cases all together.

3. If a judge is an enemy of the plaintiff and a friend, or relative, of the defendant, and the plaintiff proceeds to petition the sovereign about that prior to the trial, [saying] that he is unable to bring a suit before that judge; or if a defendant proceeds to petition prior to a trial that the judge is a friend, or relative, or his plaintiff, and that he is unable to defend himself before that judge: that judge against whom there is such a petition shall not try that plaintiff and defendant. Another judge, whom the sovereign will appoint, shall try them.

4. But if a plaintiff or defendant proceeds to petition against a judge after a trial on grounds that the latter is a relative [of the opposing litigant], or was hostile: do not believe that petition, and do not transfer the case from chancellery to chancellery so that there will be no excessive delay for the plaintiff and defendant in this matter.

5. If a boyar, or *okol'nichii*, or counselor, or state secretary, or any other judge, in response to bribes of the plaintiff or defendant, or out of friendship or enmity convicts an innocent party and exculpates the guilty party, and that is established conclusively: collect from such judges the plaintiff's claim three-fold, and give it to the plaintiff. Collect the legal fees, and the judicial transaction fee, and the legal tenth for the sovereign from them as well. For that offense a boyar, and *okol'nichii*, and counselor shall be deprived of his rank. If a judge not of counselor rank commits such an injustice: inflict on those people a beating with the knout in the market place, and henceforth they shall not try judicial cases [i.e., they shall be deprived of their offices].

6. In the provincial towns, apply that same decree to governors, and state secretaries, and various chancellery officials for such injustices. . . .

Chapter 11.—The Judicial Process for Peasants. In It Are 34 Articles.

1. Concerning the sovereign's peasants and landless peasants of court villages and rural taxpaying districts who, having fled from the sovereign's court villages and from the rural taxpaying districts, are now living under the patriarch, or under the metropolitans, and under the archbishops, and the bishop [sic]; or under monasteries; or under boyars, or under *okol'nichie*, and under counselors, and under chamberlains, and under *stol'niki*, and under *striapchie*, and under Moscow *dvoriane*, and under state secretaries, and under *zhil'tsy*, and under provincial *dvoriane* and *deti boiarskie*, and under foreigners, and under all hereditary estate owners and service landholders; and in the cadastral books, which books the census takers submitted to the Service Land Chancellery and to other chancelleries after the Moscow fire of the past year 1626, those fugitive peasants or their fathers were registered [as living] under the sovereign: having hunted down those fugitive peasants and landless peasants of the sovereign, cart them [back] to the sovereign's court villages and to the rural taxpaying districts, to their old allotments as [registered in] the cadastral books, with their wives, and with their children, and with all their movable peasant property, without any statute of limitations.

2. Similarly, if hereditary estate owners and service landholders proceed to petition the sovereign about their fugitive peasants and about landless peasants; and they testify that their peasants and landless peasants, having fled from them, are living in the sovereign's court villages, and in rural taxpaying districts, or as townsmen in the urban taxpaying districts, or as musketeers, or as cossacks, or as gunners, or as any other type of servicemen in the trans-Moscow or in the frontier towns; or under the patriarch, or under the metropolitans, or under the archbishops and bishops; or under monasteries; or under boyars, and under *okol'nichie*, and under counselors, and under chamberlains, and under *stol'niki*, and under *striapchie*, and under Moscow *dvoriane*, and under state secretaries, and under *zhil'tsy*, and under provincial *dvoriane* and *deti boiarskie*, and under foreigners, and under any hereditary estate owners and service landholders: return such peasants and landless peasants after trial and investigation on the basis of the cadastral books, which books the census takers submitted to the Service Land Chancellery after the Moscow fire of the past year 1626, if those fugitive peasants of theirs, or the fathers of those peasants of theirs, were recorded [as living] under them in those cadastral books, or [if] after those cadastral books [were compiled] those peasants, or their children, were recorded in new grants [as living] under someone in books allotting lands or in books registering land transfers. Return fugitive peasants and landless peasants from flight on the basis of the cadastral books to people of all ranks, without any statute of limitations.

3. If it becomes necessary to return fugitive peasants and landless peasants to someone after trial and investigation: return those peasants with their wives, and with their children, and with all their movable property, with their standing grain and with their threshed grain. Do not impose a fine for those peasants [on their current lords] for the years prior to this present Law Code.

    Concerning peasants who, while fugitives, married off their unmarried daughters, or sisters, or kinswomen to peasants of those estate owners and service landholders under whom they were living, or elsewhere in another village or hamlet: do not fault that person and, on the basis of the status of those unmarried women, do not hand over the husbands to their former estate owners and service landholders because until the present sovereign's decree there was no rule by the sovereign that no one could receive peasants [to live] under him. [Only] statutes of limitations [on the recovery of] fugitive peasants were decreed and, moreover, in many years after the census takers [did their work], the hereditary estates and service landholdings of many hereditary estate owners and service landholders changed hands.

4. If fugitive peasants and landless peasants are returned to someone: chancellery officials of the sovereign's court villages and the rural taxpaying districts, and estate owners, and service landholders shall get from those people [to whom the fugitives are returned] inventory receipts, signed by them, for those peasants and landless peasants of theirs and their movable property in case of dispute in the future.

   Order the town public square scribes to write the inventory receipts in Moscow and in the provincial towns; in villages and hamlets where there are no public square scribes, order the civil administration or church scribes of other villages to write such inventories. They shall issue such inventory receipts signed by their own hand.

   Concerning people who are illiterate: those people shall order their own spiritual fathers, or people of the vicinity whom they trust, to sign those inventory receipts in their stead. No one shall order his own priests, and scribes, and slaves to write such inventories so that henceforth there will be no dispute by anybody or with anybody over such inventories.

5. Concerning the vacant houses of peasants and landless peasants, or [their] house lots, registered in the cadastral books with certain estate owners and service landholders; and in the cadastral books it is written about the peasants and landless peasants of those houses that those peasants and landless peasants fled from them in the years prior to [the compilation of] those cadastral books, but there was no petition from them against anyone about those peasants throughout this time: do not grant a trial for those peasants and landless peasants on the basis of those vacant houses and vacant lots because for many years they did not petition the sovereign against anyone about those peasants of theirs.

6. If fugitive peasants and landless peasants are returned from someone to plaintiffs after trial and investigation, and according to the cadastral books; or if someone returns [fugitives] without trial according to [this] Law Code: on the petition of those people under whom they had lived while fugitives, register those peasants in the Service Land Chancellery [as living] under those people to whom they are returned.

   Concerning those people from whom they are taken: do not collect any of the sovereign's levies [due from the peasants] from such service landholders and hereditary estate owners on the basis of the census books. Collect all of the sovereign's levies from those estate owners and service landholders under whom they proceed to live as peasants upon their return.

7. If, after trial and investigation, and according to the cadastral books, peasants are taken away from any hereditary estate owners and returned to plaintiffs from their purchased estates; and they purchased those estates from estate owners with those peasants [living on them] after [the compilation of] the cadastres; and those peasants are registered on their lands in the purchase documents: those estate owners, in the stead of those returned peasants, shall take from the sellers similar peasants with all [their] movable property, and with [their] standing grain and with [their] threshed grain, from their other estates.

8. Concerning those estate owners and service landholders who in the past years had a trial about fugitive peasants and landless peasants; and at trial someone's [claims] to such fugitive peasants were rejected, prior to this decree of the sovereign, on the basis of the statute of limitations on the recovery of fugitive peasants in the prior decree of the great Sovereign, Tsar, and Grand Prince of all Russia Mikhail Fedorovich of blessed memory; and those fugitive peasants and landless peasants were ordered to live under those people under whom they lived out the years [of the] statute of limitations; or certain service landholders and hereditary estate owners arranged an amicable agreement in past years, prior to this decree of the sovereign, about fugitive peasants and landless peasants, and according to the amicable agreement someone ceded his peasants to some-

one else, and they confirmed it with registered documents, or they submitted reconciliation petitions [to settle court suits]: all those cases shall remain as those cases were resolved prior to this decree of the sovereign. Do not consider those cases anew and do not renegotiate [them].

9. Concerning peasants and landless peasants registered under someone in the census books of the past years 1645/46 and 1646/47; and after [the compilation of] those census books they fled from those people under whom they were registered in the census books, or they proceed to flee in the future: return those fugitive peasants and landless peasants, and their brothers, and children, and kinsmen, and grandchildren with [their] wives and with [their] children and with all [their] movable property, and with [their] standing grain and with threshed grain, from flight to those people from whom they fled, on the basis of the census books, without any statute of limitations. Henceforth no one ever shall receive others' peasants and shall not retain them under himself.

10. If someone after this royal Law Code proceeds to receive and retain under himself fugitive peasants, and landless peasants, and their children, and brothers, and kinsmen; and hereditary estate owners and service landholders demand those fugitive peasants of theirs from them [in a trial]: after trial and investigation, and according to the census books, return those fugitive peasants and landless peasants of theirs to them with [their] wives and with [their] children, and with all their movable property, and with [their] standing grain, and with [their] threshed grain, and with [their] grain still in the ground, without any statute of limitations.

    Concerning the length of the time they live under someone as fugitives after this royal Law Code: collect from those under whom they proceed to live 10 rubles each for any peasant per year for the sovereign's taxes and the service landholder's incomes. Give [the money] to the plaintiffs whose peasants and landless peasants they are.

11. If someone proceeds to petition the sovereign against someone about such fugitive peasants and landless peasants; and those peasants and their fathers are not registered in the cadastral books under either the plaintiff or the defendant, but those peasants are registered under the plaintiff or the defendant in the census books of the past years 1645/46 and 1646/47: on the basis of the census books, return those peasants and landless peasants to that person under whom they are registered in the census books. ...

12. If any people come to someone on [his] hereditary estate and service landholding and say about themselves that they are free; and those people desire to live under them as peasants or landless peasants: those people whom they approach shall interrogate them—what kind of free people are they? And where is their birth place? And under whom did they live? And whence did they come? And are they not someone's fugitive slaves, and peasants, and landless peasants? And do they have manumission documents?

    If they say that they do not have manumission documents on their person: service landholders and hereditary estate owners shall find out about such people accurately, whether they really are free people. Having investigated accurately, bring them in the same year for registration to the Service Land Chancellery in Moscow; Kazan'-area residents and residents of Kazan' by-towns shall bring them to Kazan'; Novgorodians and residents of the Novgorodian by-towns shall bring them to Novgorod; Pskovians and residents of the Pskov by-towns shall bring them to Pskov. [Chancellery officials] in the Service Land Chancellery and governors in the provincial towns shall interrogate such free people on that subject and shall record their testimonies accurately.

    If it becomes necessary to give those people who are brought in for registration, on the basis of their testimony under interrogation, as peasants to those people who brought them in for registration: order those people to whom they will be given as peasants to affix their signatures to the testimonies of those people after they have been taken.

13. If an estate owner or a service landholder brings in for registration the person who approached him without having checked accurately, and they proceed to take such people in as peasants: return such people as peasants to plaintiffs after trial and investigation, and according to the census book, along with [their] wives, and with [their] children, and with [their] movable property.

Concerning [what shall be exacted] from those people who take in someone else's peasant or landless peasant without checking accurately: collect for those years, however many [the peasant] lived under someone, 10 rubles per year for the sovereign's taxes and for the incomes of the hereditary estate owner and service landholder because [of this rule]: without checking accurately, do not receive someone else's [peasant]. ...

Chapter 19.—Townsmen. In It Are 40 Articles.

1. Concerning the [tax-exempt] settlements in Moscow belonging to the patriarch, and metropolitans, and other high church officials, and monasteries, and boyars, and *okol'nichie*, and counselors, and [tsar's] intimates, and people of all ranks; and in those settlements are living merchants and artisans who pursue various trading enterprises and own shops, but are not paying the sovereign's taxes and are not rendering service: confiscate all of those settlements, with all the people who are living in those settlements, for the sovereign [and place them] all on the tax rolls [and force them to render] service without any statute of limitations and irrevocably, except for limited service contract slaves.

   If it is said in an inquiry that the limited service contract slaves are their perpetual slaves, return them to those people to whom they belong. Order them moved back to their houses. Concerning those limited service contract slaves whose fathers and whose clan ancestors were townsmen, or from the sovereign's rural districts: take those [people] to live in the urban taxpaying districts.

Henceforth, except for the sovereign's settlements, no one shall have [tax-exempt] settlements in Moscow or in the provincial towns.

Confiscate the patriarch's settlements completely, excepting those palace court officials who for a long time lived under former patriarchs in their patriarchal ranks as *deti boiarskie*, singers, secretaries, scribes, furnace tenders, guards, cooks and bakers, grooms, and as his palace court officials of other ranks who are given an annual salary and grain. ...

Chapter 22.—Decree: For Which Offenses the Death Penalty Should Be Inflicted on Someone, and for Which Offenses the Penalty Should Not Be Death, but [Another] Punishment Should Be Imposed. In It Are 26 Articles.

1. If any son or daughter kills his father or mother: for patricide or matricide, punish them also with death, without the slightest mercy.

2. If any son or daughter kills his or her father or mother with some other people, and that is established conclusively: after investigation, also punish with death, without the slightest mercy, those who committed such a deed with them.

3. If a father or mother kills a son or daughter: imprison them for a year after that. After having sat in prison for a year, they shall go to God's church, and in God's church they shall declare aloud that sin of theirs to all the people. Do not punish a father or mother with death for [killing] a son or daughter.

4. If someone, a son or a daughter, forgetting Christian law, proceeds to utter coarse speeches to a father or mother, or out of impudence strikes a father or mother, and the father or mother proceeds to petition against them for that: beat such forgetters of Christian law with the knout for the father and mother.

5. If any son or daughter plunder[s] a father's or mother's movable property by force; or not honoring the father and mother and [attempting] to drive

them out, proceed[s] to denounce them for some evil deeds; or a son or daughter does not proceed to respect and feed a father and mother in their old age, does not proceed to support them materially in any way, and the father or mother proceed[s] to petition the sovereign against him or her about that: inflict a severe punishment on such children for such deeds of theirs, beat them mercilessly with the knout, and command them to attend to their father and mother in all obedience without any back-talk. Do not believe their denunciation.

6. If any son or daughter proceed[s] to petition for a trial against a father or mother: do not grant them a trial in any matter against a father or mother. Beat them with the knout for such a petition and return them to the father and mother. ...

7. If a wife kills her husband, or feeds him poison, and that is established conclusively: punish her for that, bury her alive in the ground and punish her with that punishment without any mercy, even if the children of the killed [husband], or any other close relatives of his, do not desire that she be executed. Do not show her the slightest mercy, and keep her in the ground until that time when she dies.

8. If a woman is sentenced to the death penalty and she is pregnant at that time: do not punish that woman with death until she gives birth, and execute her at the time when she has given birth. Until that time, keep her in prison, or in the custody of reliable bailiffs, so that she will not depart.

9. If someone with felonious intent comes into someone's house, and desires to do something shameful to the mistress of that house, or desires to carry her away somewhere out of that house; and her slaves do not defend her against that felon, and proceed to assist those people who have come for her in the commission [of the crime]; and subsequently such a deed of theirs is discovered: punish with death all those felons who with such intent come into another's house and those slaves who assist them in the commission of such a felony. ...

10. If someone shoot[s] from a handgun or from a bow at a wild animal, or at a bird, or at a target; and the arrow or bullet goes astray and kills someone over a hill or beyond a fence; or if someone by any chance kills someone with a piece of wood, or a rock, or anything else in a non-deliberate act; and previously there was no enmity or other animosity between that person who killed and that [person] he killed; and it is established about that conclusively that such a homicide occurred without deliberation and without intent: do not punish anyone with death for such a homicide and do not incarcerate anyone in prison because that event occurred accidently, without intent. ...

11. If a Muslim by any means whatsoever, by force or by deceit, compels a Russian [to convert] to his Islamic faith; and he circumcises that Russian according to his Islamic faith; and that is established conclusively: punish that Muslim after investigation, burn him with fire without any mercy.

    Concerning the Russian whom he converted to Islam: send that Russian to the patriarch, or to another high ecclesiastical figure, and order him to compile a decree according to the canons of the Holy Apostles and the Holy Fathers.

12. If someone of the male gender, or the female gender, having forgotten the wrath of God and Christian law, proceeds to procure adult women and mature girls for fornication, and that is established conclusively: inflict a severe punishment on them for such a lawless and vile business, beat them with the knout.

13. If a woman proceeds to live in fornication and vileness, and in fornication begets children with someone; and she herself, or someone else at her command, destroys those children; and that is established conclusively: punish with death without any mercy such lawless women and that person who destroyed her children at her order so that others looking on will not commit such a lawless and vile deed and will refrain from fornication.

> **GLOSSARY**
>
> **knout:** a barbed whip used for state-ordered physical punishments in czarist Russia
>
> **manumission documents:** official papers stating that the bearer, a former slave, has been freed
>
> **Mikhail Fedorovich:** Mikhail Fedorovich Romanov (1596–1645)
>
> **service landholding:** rented land whose tenant was required to serve the state lifelong or until too infirm to continue his duties (that is, until superannuated)
>
> **spiritual fathers:** Orthodox clergy and other personnel
>
> ***stol'niki*, ..., *striapchie*, ..., *dvoriane*, ... *zhil'tsy*:** specific ranks or titles within the service gentry, with *dvoriane* referring to nobles and gentry in state service

Document Analysis

The complete *Ulozhenie* is divided into twenty-five chapters, each dealing with a different general topic or legislative area. They are presented in a specific order, corresponding to the importance or status accorded to each at the time, from the highest to the lowest. Thus, chapter 1 considers the honor and authority of God and his Church, the second chapter treats the personal honor of the czar, the third looks at matters of conduct in the czar's court, and so on. The final chapter (the "lowest") treats unlawful taverns. The chapters between consider a wealth of issues, including the mint and currency, travel and foreigners, various ranks of service personnel, tolls and fees, the judicial process at various social levels, monasteries, different categories of landholding, social and political estates, slaves and serfs, robbery and theft, the death penalty, and palace musketeers. Some chapters are short—the one on palace musketeers has only three articles. Others are much longer. There are, for instance, 104 articles on robbery and theft and 119 on the judicial process regarding slaves. The longest of all, at 287 articles, considers the judicial process in general.

Chapter 10.—The Judicial Process

This chapter speaks to a basic goal of the *Ulozhenie*: the creation of a state of law, with all the apparatuses, offices, and procedures that might require. Alexis's concept of a state of law should not be misunderstood, however. In the *Ulozhenie* there is no concept of people as individuals, imbued with natural rights or equal before the law. Instead, the assumptions are that the law exists to serve the interests of the state (largely synonymous with the person and authority of the czar) and that persons will be treated collectively according to social order, religion, nationality, and other factors. As evidence of the high level of concern for creating a state of law, the chapter contains 287 articles, the most by far of any in the code. Only the first six are reproduced here; but they suggest the basic parameters of the overall system.

The czar emphasizes his own authority. The *Ulozhenie* and the legal system more generally are *his* possessions and expressions of *his* will—even if specific and important tasks must be delegated to boyars, *okol'nichie*, and others. Boyars were hereditary nobles in state service and held the highest rank in the Muscovite social hierarchy; *okol'nichie* were second in rank. There were at least eighteen different service ranks at the time. Beyond this initial statement, however, the czar calls for impartiality, honesty, and adherence to the principles and rulings of his code, both by the Muscovite court and in the provinces.

Chapter 11.—The Judicial Process for Peasants

This chapter includes thirty-four articles; about two-thirds of them are reproduced here. It is in this chapter that we find the legal basis for the full-fledged system of serfdom with which the social history of Russia from the seventeenth to nineteenth centuries is nearly synonymous.

Article 1 establishes the tone of the chapter. It takes as a reference point the cadastral books of 1626, which showed the place of registration of peasant families at that time. In some cases, a later census of 1646–1647 provided the reference point. The article calls for all runaway peasants and their descendants—along with their wives, children, and "movable property"—to be returned to their original estates "without any statute of limitations" regardless of where they currently reside. Article 1 deals specifically with peasants originally registered on crown lands (the "sovereign's peasants"); article 2 extends the ruling to all categories of landowners. According to the law, a peasant originally registered with a member of the service gentry (such as a *stol'nik* or *striapchii*) but now living elsewhere must also be returned to his place of registration as of 1626. Note that this rule applied even to peasants who had moved onto lands belonging directly to the czar. Thus, the first two articles establish a basic and draconian principle: Peasants have only one rightful and lawful place to live, the place at which they were properly and originally registered. They and their descendants were to be returned there no matter how long they had lived at some other place.

Article 3 establishes that the law would not be used to punish landlords who have previously held runaway peasants, only those landlords who would do so henceforth. This surely suggests the scale of the issue. No doubt "runaways" were extremely common. More generally, this article and numerous others throughout the code deal with the many problems, disputes, and uncertainties bound to arise as soon as efforts began to establish the "rightful" place of residence of any given peasant or peasant family. What should one do, for example, when marriages have been made among peasants not registered on the same estate in 1626? To which estate should the resulting family and any descendants properly belong? Should the larger family be broken up? And what about the "vacant houses" of runaway peasants (article 5)? On these and other similar issues, the *Ulozhenie* generally calls for proper investigations and trials, and it establishes that complications based on actions taken before passage of the law should be treated with some sympathy. Future actions, by contrast, are to be dealt with more legalistically. Article 10, for example, specifically calls for a fine of ten rubles per peasant per year to be levied against any landlord under whom fugitive peasants are living.

The law greatly affected not only peasants but also landowners. For the most part, the idea was to help them secure and retain labor for their landholdings. But the code could also cause them problems. Article 7, for example, treats the case of a landowner whose peasants are found after investigation to be the lawful property of another and therefore subject to removal. Articles 20 and 21 place upon landowners the responsibility of properly ascertaining the current legal status of persons wishing to settle on their estates. No doubt this would have presented a burden to landowners, and there was always the chance that a landlord, even one who intended to follow the law properly, might make a mistake or be deceived by his peasants. That landlord would still risk being levied a hefty fine.

Chapter 19.—Townsmen

This chapter establishes yet another social category: the "townsmen." Only the first article of a total of forty is reproduced here. It shows the czar's intent to exert his will, centralize control, and improve the collection of taxes from people and places either previously exempt under the authority of other high-ranking persons, such as the Russian Orthodox patriarch, or from whom it had otherwise been hard to collect taxes. By the seventeenth century, towns had become the loci of significant commercial activity and thus also of potential taxable wealth. When townsmen moved, those taxes, which generally were levied collectively rather than individually, often went uncollected. Beginning with the official approval of the *Ulozhenie* in 1649, townsmen were required to remain where they were, and they could, like serfs, be forcibly returned if they moved elsewhere without authorization. In return, they obtained certain monopolies on trade and commercial activities. In this article, a "limited service contract slave" is distinguished by possession of a contract stipulating the duration and nature of servitude. "*Deti boiarskie*" refers to a middle rank within the provincial, as opposed to the Muscovite, service class.

Chapter 22.—Decree: For Which Offenses the Death Penalty Should Be Inflicted on Someone, and for Which Offenses the Penalty Should Not Be Death, but [Another] Punishment Should Be Imposed

This chapter contains twenty-six articles, half of which are reproduced here. Many of these articles exemplify the *Ulozhenie's* emphasis on clear hierarchy, unquestionable authority, and strict punishment. They are largely untempered by concerns for mitigating circumstances and possible exceptions. When reading the first articles, dealing with murders within families, it should be kept in mind that the law's authors imagined the nuclear family as a microcosm of the larger "state family." The authority given to parents, especially fathers, as heads of families mirrors that assumed by the czar over his larger "family"—the population of the Muscovite state. Similarly, the lack of power given to children represents in microcosm the subordination of all subjects to their social superiors and ultimately to the czar. Thus, crimes committed by children against their parents are considered extremely serious, while crimes committed by parents against their children are reckoned to be minor. Following articles 5 and 6, any complaints made by children against their parents are to be ignored and even punished, but their responsibility to care for and feed their parents in old age is sacrosanct. Of course, one can also see in these articles the influence of some of the Ten Commandments, rather strictly and literally applied.

Returning to family themes, articles 14 to 16 reflect the harsh patriarchal culture of the time. A man's authority over his wife is considered absolute and sacred. A woman who violates this order by murdering her husband has committed a terrible crime. Whereas clauses treating the murder of a master by his slave (not reproduced here) simply call for the slave's death, article 14 goes so far as to prescribe the manner of the offending wife's execution. The seriousness of her action, as viewed by Muscovite culture, is further emphasized in the same article by the refusal to contemplate any mitigating circumstances or calls for leniency made by the children or other relatives. This stands in stark contrast to some other parts of the code, where a clear concern is indeed shown for mitigating circumstances and intent (see, for example, article 20 in this chapter).

Note, however, that article 15 stipulates that the wife's crime, though unpardonable, is not to be paid for by the death of any innocent unborn child. The concern shown in article 16 for a woman's honor echoes the patriarchal tone of article 14 in that it seeks primarily to protect the exclusive ownership of the wife by her husband. The use of the term "mistress of that house" speaks to the fact that the law had in mind primarily elite women and not the ordinary peasant, whose affairs were largely regulated by this time by their landlords. Articles 24 to 26 return to religious themes and freely mix elements of harsh legalism with Christian compassion.

Essential Themes

As a general statement of state authority and social hierarchy, the *Ulozhenie* was intended ultimately for the entire Russian populace. It would, however, have been directly read or encountered only by a small literate minority, especially members of the service gentry, court officials, and the Church hierarchy. Twelve hundred copies were made in the spring of 1649, and a further twelve hundred in the winter. Both quickly sold out, with the majority of copies probably going to courts and other government offices in Moscow and throughout provincial towns, where it henceforth provided the framework for legal cases and procedures (the main exception being cases coming under Church jurisdiction).

Some of the *Ulozhenie*'s most important articles involve serfdom, specifically its transformation into virtual slavery. Muscovite Russia's aristocrats received land grants from the czarist state as a function of inheritance or as a reward for service to the czar. The value of a land grant was determined almost entirely by the presence of peasants, who provided income in the form of labor and crops—the primary and often the only sources of revenue for the landlord. Until the late fifteenth century, it had remained common for landlords to negotiate terms of labor with peasants residing upon their lands. The two groups often had opposite interests, however. The landlords wanted permanent and reliable workers and ever-higher incomes. The peasants valued their freedom and independence, and they resented encroaching authority and rising taxation. Often, they simply moved on, leaving their landlords to face untended fields and economic hardship. The absence of natural boundaries and the lure of seemingly endless horizons to the east and south compounded the problem. Flight was especially common during the dislocations of the Time of Troubles.

Among landlords, however, the service gentry were especially vulnerable, since they faced the additional threat of having their peasants seized and transferred wholesale to the estates of higher-ranking and more powerful nobles. Thus, it was the service gentry who most actively pressured the state for help. Since Muscovy relied heavily on them for services and loyalty, as well as on military recruits from their lands, their pleas were taken to heart. Continued peasant flight spurred ever-more repressive countermeasures. In 1570 in parts of the province of Novgorod, Ivan IV declared a one-off "prohibited year," during which peasants would not be able to move for any reason, regardless of their ability to pay all debts and release fees. Thereafter, the concept was applied more widely. By the 1580s prohibited years had become the norm throughout Muscovite Russia. Instead, the state designated occasional "free years."

The last one was in 1602. Around the same time, the statute of limitations on recovery of a runaway peasant was increased, reaching fifteen years in the first part of the sixteenth century. The *Ulozhenie* abolished the limitation altogether, and subsequent legislation criminalized peasant flight.

All classes of persons were affected by the *Ulozhenie*. The law's most enduring and significant consequences centered on its codification of serfdom, however. This system became the backbone of the economy and a fundamental determinant of the historical trajectory of the Russian state. Although serfdom had long provided both elites and the state with more or less stable sources of income, labor, and conscripts, it also fostered diverse and huge challenges that ultimately hampered the country's development. Under conditions of serf labor, for example, there was little incentive for investment in more productive or efficient farming methods and technologies, with the result that agriculture in Russia remained less efficient and productive than in many Western European regions. Russia's industrial and military development also lagged for similar reasons. Not surprisingly, the peasants themselves chafed under the burden of serfdom. After 1649, rebellions grew in frequency and scale. Peasant unrest, along with Russia's humiliating defeat in the Crimean War (1853–1856), which also could be traced to serfdom, eventually persuaded Alexander II to abolish the system "from above" in 1861, before the peasants abolished it themselves "from below." By 1861 serfdom was widely blamed for a stifling backwardness in many aspects of Russian society, whether in agriculture, industry, military effectiveness, or public morality.

—Brian Bonhomme

Bibliography and Further Reading

Longworth, Philip. *Alexis, Tsar of All the Russias.* Franklin Watts, 1984.

Pipes, Richard. *Russia under the Old Regime.* 2nd ed. Penguin, 1995.

Poe, Marshall T. *The Russian Elite in the Seventeenth Century. Vol. 2: A Quantitative Analysis of the "Duma Ranks," 1613–1713.* Finnish Academy of Science and Letters, 2004.

"Russian Law from Oleg to Peter the Great." Foreword to *The Laws of Rus': Tenth to Fifteenth Centuries.* Translated and edited by Daniel H. Kaiser, Charles Schlacks, Jr., 1992.

The Muscovite Law Code (Ulozhenie) of 1649. Translated and edited by Richard Hellie, Charles Schlacks, Jr., 1988.

Wirtschafter, Elise Kimerling. *Russia's Age of Serfdom 1649–1861.* Blackwell Publishers, 2008.

Louis XIV: Edict of Fontainebleau

Date: 1685
Author: Louis XIV, king of France
Genre: Edict

Summary Overview

Under the pretense that no Protestants remained in France, in 1685 King Louis XIV issued the Edict of Fontainebleau, his revocation of the Edict of Nantes, which had preserved a tentative peace between the nation's Catholic majority and the Calvinist Protestant minority, called Huguenots. Issued by Louis' grandfather Henry IV, the Edict of Nantes had guaranteed Huguenots the right to worship without the interference of Catholics since 1598. The revocation came as the culmination of the king's twenty-five-year program to eradicate French Calvinists through policies of ecclesiastical, financial, and personal harassment. With the revocation, French Protestants finally lost all freedom of worship, forcing them either to leave the nation or to practice their faith clandestinely in the Cévennes of southeastern France.

The Edict of Fontainebleau proved to be a turning point in Louis' reign. The Huguenots were a prosperous and taxpaying proportion of French society, and many of them left France for the United Provinces of the Netherlands and England. They took with them money and artisanal skills, reducing the profitable middle sector of the French economy. The Protestant powers of western Europe, particularly the United Provinces and England, were already at war with French expansionist armies, and now they had a further religious excuse to resist the French monarch's advance. Furthermore, Louis' intolerance shocked educated society in France itself; many aristocrats and educated figures began meeting regularly to discuss how to change the French state, and so the revocation is often seen as one of the events that sparked the Enlightenment.

Defining Moment

During the Protestant Reformation, one of the geographical meeting points between Catholics and Protestants was France, which experienced fierce religious violence between the majority Catholic population and the smaller but richer Protestant Calvinist population, called Huguenots. Only about a fifth of the French population was Huguenot, but they were concentrated in small, fortified towns, and since Catholics often would not sell them land to farm, many were wealthy due to the artisanal skills they learned in order to make a living. This only built more resentment between the two populations. The worst incident was the St Bartholomew's Day Massacre in Paris and the countryside in 1572, when an estimated eight thousand Huguenots were slaughtered.

Religious wars between Catholics and Protestants continued through the reign of the Catholic King Henry III until he was assassinated in 1589, ending the Valois dynasty. His successor was Henry IV, the Huguenot king of a tiny kingdom on the Spanish Pyrenees border named Navarre, was the first monarch of the Bourbon dynasty. A shrewd politician, Henry converted to Catholicism in 1593, famously declaring that "Paris is worth a mass." As such, this made him of the same religion as most of his subjects, but also sympathetic to the powerful minority of which he had once been a part.

To bring the brutal religious violence to an end, Catholic and Huguenot negotiators hammered out an agreement in 1598, which Henry IV signed into law as the Edict of Nantes. Huguenots were allowed to worship publicly in some two hundred designated Protestant towns and on the estates of Protestant landowners, and could worship everywhere privately. They were to be treated as any other French subject in property, economy, education, and medicine, and a general amnesty was declared for the atrocities committed during the religious wars.

The Edict of Nantes was a success; peace settled in over French religious issues. Henry IV became a popular monarch, though he was assassinated by an unhinged Catholic zealot in 1610. Catholics and Huguenots lived peaceably with each other for a century, even as France became involved in the Thirty Years' War. However, while Catholics could count on a Catholic Bourbon monarch to protect their interests in France, Huguenots had fewer and fewer patrons, and adherence to Protestantism went into decline over the course of the seventeenth century. Henry's successors, Louis XIII and Louis XIV, both had powerful Catholic cardinals as their chief ministers, Cardinal Richelieu and Cardinal Mazarin. Each of them worked diligently to reduce Protestant economic, political, and military power in France, largely without going to war with the Huguenots.

In 1660, upon Mazarin's death, Louis XIV became his own chief minister. Louis was a staunch Catholic and determined to undermine Protestantism and create religious unity in his state in any way possible. This was not an uncommon sentiment at the time—many monarchs wanted to avoid exactly the sort of religious unrest that had unsettled France in the sixteenth century. Louis had the means to effect his wishes, however. He first legislated repressive laws against Huguenots, but when this proved inadequate, he decided to revoke the Edict of Nantes in the Edict of Fontainebleau (1685). This law claimed that Protestantism was nearly dead in France, and therefore, for the purposes of social harmony, France would henceforth forbid Protestant religious practice, destroy Protestant churches, and force any Protestant who wanted to stay in France to convert to Catholicism.

Author Biography

Louis XIV (ruled 1643-1715) was the central monarch in the French Bourbon dynasty, the longest reigning monarch in European history, and the defining figure of his age. Born on September 5, 1638, he inherited the French throne when he was only four years old; his regents were his mother, Anne of Austria, and a cardinal of the Roman Catholic Church, Cardinal Mazarin. At age ten, a number of aristocrats and Parisian magistrates inspired many of the people of Paris to join them in trying to overthrow the Bourbons in a coup d'etat; Louis and his family fled Paris twice, were captured, and risked being executed by the rebels. The rebellion, called the Fronde, lasted for a few years and left a lasting impression on young Louis—his people were not to be trusted, and he would have to keep them in thrall to his rulership ever after.

In 1660, at age twenty-two, Louis married the Spanish Princess Maria Theresa to end a war with Spain, and a year later, when Mazarin died, Louis decided to take control of his own state, declaring himself to be his own chief minister, famously declaring *l'état c'est moi*: I am the state. Louis XIV was an absolute monarch—he believed himself to be appointed by God to sit on the French throne and do what was best for the French people. He believed their destinies to be one with his—despite the fact that they were untrustworthy—and used Biblical verses to cite as evidence. And he was popular as king; he was hardworking, physically imposing, competent, and inclined to appoint people who were newer, lower-level aristocrats to important state jobs, since he did not trust his aristocracy. Such people were grateful for their positions and therefore loyal to Louis as tax collectors, governors, soldiers, and legal officers. They competed with the aristocracy for power and position, and gave the French people a sense that there was social mobility in Louis' state.

France maintained the second biggest population in Europe and therefore collected a great deal of money in taxes. Concordantly, Louis was the richest man in Europe. France expanded its colonial and missionary concerns in North America, the Caribbean, Southeast Asia, and India. Under Louis' chief minister, his Controller-General Jean-Baptiste Colbert, the state promoted full male employment at home, overseas trade, the development of the colonies, and strategically placed tariffs on foreign goods, all with an eye on increasingly Louis' treasury through taxation. Louis considered it important to subsidize the arts and architecture to leave behind a glorious legacy; his reign saw the building of the Louvre, the royal palace at Versailles, and French academies dedicated to science, astronomy, music, painting, and sculpture. Louis patronized artists and playwrights, and his court was renowned as the most fabulous and fashionable in Europe.

With so much money on hand, Louis was also inclined to throw his military weight around. He became obsessed with expansion to fill France's "natural boundaries," as he saw them, bordering on the Rhine River. Not coincidentally, the area he wished to occupy, consisting of the modern-day Rhineland, Belgium, and the Netherlands, was predominantly Protestant, and Louis was a staunch Catholic. Between 1667 and 1697, French armies were at war with most of Protestant Europe; it was in this context, with Louis recognizing himself as Catholic Europe's top champion, that the revocation of the Edict of Nantes took place.

The Edict of Fontainebleau is generally taken to be a dividing point in Louis's reign—he was powerful and dynamic before it, challenged and compromised afterward. His European wars climaxed with the War of the Spanish Succession (1701-14), in which Louis tried to hang onto his grandson's claim to the Spanish throne. Too much of Europe was opposed to a single monarch ruling both France and Spain, and the effort to defeat so many enemies depleted the French treasury. Though French victories were considerable, Louis was forced to agree that the crowns of France and Spain would remain separate. He died a year later in 1715, having outlived most of his heirs; his throne was occupied by his great-grandson, Louis XV.

HISTORICAL DOCUMENT

Excerpts from the Edict of Fontainebleau

Louis, by the grace of God king of France and Navarre, to all present and to come, greeting:

King Henry the Great, our grandfather of glorious memory, being desirous that the peace which he had procured for his subjects after the grievous losses they had sustained in the course of domestic and foreign wars, should not be troubled on account of the RPR [*religion pretendu réformée*, or "pretended Reformed religion"], as had happened in the reigns of the kings, his predecessors, by his edict, granted at Nantes in the month of April, 1598, regulated the procedure to be adopted with regard to those of the said religion, and the places in which they might meet for public worship, established extraordinary judges to administer justice to them, and, in fine, provided in particular articles for whatever could be thought necessary for maintaining the tranquility of his kingdom and for diminishing mutual aversion between the members of the two religions, so as to put himself in a better position to labor, as he had resolved to do, for the reunion to the Church of those who had so lightly withdrawn from it.

As the intention of the king, our grandfather, was frustrated by his sudden death, and as the execution of the said edict was interrupted during the minority of the late king, our most honored lord and father of glorious memory, by new encroachments on the part of the adherents of the said RPR, which gave occasion for their being deprived of divers advantages accorded to them by the said edict; nevertheless the king, our late lord and father, in the exercise of his usual clemency, granted them yet another edict at Nîmes, in July, 1629, by means of which, tranquility being established anew, the said late king, animated by the same spirit and the same zeal for religion as the king, our said grandfather, had resolved to take advantage of this repose to attempt to put his said pious design into execution. But foreign wars having supervened soon after, so that the kingdom was seldom tranquil from 1635 to the truce concluded in 1684 with the powers of Europe, nothing more could be done for the advantage of religion beyond diminishing the number of places for the public exercise of the RPR, interdicting such places as were found established to the prejudice of the dispositions made by the edicts, and suppressing of the bi-partisan courts, these having been appointed provisionally only.

God having at last permitted that our people should enjoy perfect peace, we, no longer absorbed in protecting them from our enemies, are able to profit by this truce (which we have ourselves facilitated), and devote our whole attention to the means of accomplishing the designs of our said grandfather and father, which we have consistently kept before us since our succession to the crown.

And now we perceive, with thankful acknowledgment of God's aid, that our endeavors have attained their proposed end, inasmuch as the better and the greater part of our subjects of the said RPR have embraced the Catholic faith. And since by this fact the execution of the Edict of Nantes and of all that has ever been ordained in favor of the said RPR has been rendered nugatory, we have determined that we can do nothing better, in order wholly to obliterate the memory of the troubles, the confusion, and the evils which the progress of this false religion has caused in this kingdom, and which furnished occasion for the said edict and for so many previous and subsequent edicts and declarations, than entirely to revoke the said Edict of Nantes, with the special articles granted as a sequel to it, as well as all that has since been done in favor of the said religion.

I. Be it known that for these causes and others us hereunto moving, and of our certain knowledge, full power, and royal authority, we have, by this present perpetual and irrevocable edict, suppressed and revoked, and do suppress and revoke, the edict of our said grandfather, given at Nantes in April, 1598, in its whole extent, together with the particular articles agreed upon in the month of May following, and the letters patent issued upon the same date; and also the edict given at Nîmes in July, 1629; we declare them null and void, together with all concessions, of whatever nature they may be, made by them as well as by other edicts, declarations, and orders, in favor of the said persons of the RPR, the which shall remain in like manner as if they had never been granted; and in consequence we desire, and it is our pleasure, that all the temples of those of the said RPR situate in our kingdom, countries, territories, and the lordships under our crown, shall be demolished without delay.

II. We forbid our subjects of the RPR to meet any more for the exercise of the said religion in any place or private house, under any pretext whatever. ...

III. We likewise forbid all noblemen, of what condition soever, to hold such religious exercises in their houses or fiefs, under penalty to be inflicted upon all our said subjects who shall engage in the said exercises, of imprisonment and confiscation.

IV. We enjoin all ministers of the said RPR, who do not choose to become converts and to embrace the Catholic, apostolic, and Roman religion, to leave our kingdom and the territories subject to us within a fortnight of the publication of our present edict, without leave to reside therein beyond that period, or, during the said fortnight, to engage in any preaching, exhortation, or any other function, on pain of being sent to the galleys. ...

V. We forbid private schools for the instruction of children of the said RPR, and in general all things whatever which can be regarded as a concession of any kind in favor of the said religion.

VI. As for children who may be born of persons of the said RPR, we desire that from henceforth they be baptized by the parish priests. We enjoin parents to send them to the churches for that purpose, under penalty of five hundred livres fine, to be increased as circumstances may demand; and thereafter the children shall be brought up in the Catholic, apostolic, and Roman religion, which we expressly enjoin the local magistrates to see done.

VII. And in the exercise of our clemency towards our subjects of the said RPR who have emigrated from our kingdom, lands, and territories subject to us, previous to the publication of our present edict, it is our will and pleasure that in case of their returning within the period of four months from the day of the said publication, they may, and it shall be lawful for them to, again take possession of their property, and to enjoy the same as if they had all along remained there: on the contrary, the property abandoned by those who, during the specified period of four months, shall not have returned into our kingdom, lands, and territories subject to us, shall remain and be confiscated in consequence of our declaration of the 20th of August last.

VIII. We repeat our most express prohibition to all our subjects of the said RPR, together with their wives and children, against leaving our kingdom, lands, and territories subject to us, or transporting their goods and effects therefrom under penalty, as respects the men, of being sent to the galleys, and as respects the women, of imprisonment and confiscation.

IX. It is our will and intention that the declarations rendered against the relapsed shall be executed according to their form and tenor.

X. As for the rest, liberty is granted to the said persons of the RPR, pending the time when it shall please God to enlighten them as well as others, to remain in the cities and places of our kingdom, lands, and territories subject to us, and there to continue their commerce, and to enjoy their possessions, without being subjected to molestation or hindrance on account of the said RPR, on condition of not engaging in the exercise of the said religion, or of meeting under pretext of prayers or religious services, of whatever nature these may be, under the penalties above mentioned of imprisonment and confiscation. This do we give in charge to our trusty and well-beloved counselors, etc.

Given at Fontainebleau in the month of October, in the year of grace 1685, and of our reign the forty-third.

GLOSSARY

nugatory: of no value or importance

RPR [*religion pretendu réformée*, or "pretended Reformed religion"]: Protestantism

Document Analysis

The preamble classifies the Edict of Nantes as a temporary measure taken by Henry IV to protect the peace he had secured for his subjects from being threatened by the *religion pretendu réformée* (RPR, or "pretended Reformed religion"). It then argues that Henry and his successors mercifully enacted policies favorable to the Huguenots in order to reduce Catholic-Protestant hostility and, it was hoped, win the Huguenots back to the Roman Church. Although this strategy was successful in restoring most French Calvinists to Catholicism, an obstinate few Huguenots took advantage of France's involvement in foreign wars from 1635 to 1684 by engaging in a pattern of illegal activities. The preamble claims that, at the present time, the Reformed faith could be eliminated without undermining national tranquility; it also claims that failure to crush the false religion endangered the commonweal. Under such circumstances, the edict ceased to be valid, a judgment with which the preamble asserts monarchs from Henry on would have agreed.

Article I formally repeals all French legislation beneficial to the Huguenots. As a result, all Calvinist temples in France were to be pulled down summarily. Article II forbids all public and private Protestant worship on pain of property confiscation plus banishment or death. Significantly, the article is so worded as to turn the singing of Psalms, a Calvinist hallmark, into a capital crime. Article III explicitly extends the prohibition of Reformed worship to the houses and lands of nobles.

Articles IV, V, and VI concern Reformed pastors. Pastors who refused to embrace Catholicism were commanded to leave France no more than fifteen days after the publication of the Revocation. In the meantime, they were not to preach or execute any other ministerial function, with enslavement to the galleys as punishment for noncompliance. But to those who chose to quit the pastorate and convert to the Roman faith, the Revocation offers an attractive package of benefits, including exemption from taxes and the obligation to lodge soldiers, an annual stipend one-third greater than their ministerial salary, and a sizable pension for their widows upon their passing. It even allows former pastors to take examinations for law degrees at half the normal cost and without the requisite three years of university study.

Article VII abolishes all Protestant schools, in particular, and everything in general that might imply compromise with Calvinism. Article VIII prescribes that all children born of Protestant parents be baptized by the parish priests and brought up in the Roman Church. In practical terms, this article entailed that all children five years and older at the time of its promulgation be removed from their Reformed families and placed in Jesuit schools or nunneries. Parents with children younger than five who refused to procure Catholic baptism for their children would be fined a minimum of five hundred livres.

Article IX gives Huguenots who fled France four months to return, as Catholics, and reclaim their property; if they failed to return, however, their property would be seized by the crown. Contrary to the option of flight afforded their pastors, Article X prohibits Protestant laypeople from leaving France or exporting their goods overseas, on penalty of the galleys for men and loss of property and life for women. Article XI makes all Huguenot converts to Catholicism who later revert to Protestantism or on their deathbeds decline the Catholic sacrament of extreme unction liable to the death penalty pronounced on those who relapse into heresy. Article XII disingenuously grants all Huguenots who keep their religious convictions totally private (by definition an impossible feat) full protection of the law. In this way, the Revocation shrewdly keeps the letter of the tolerance statutes in the 1648 Peace of Westphalia while denying their substance.

Essential Themes

The Edict of Fontainebleau surprised the literate public throughout Europe. While Catholics in France largely approved of it, even French intellectuals were shocked at the intolerance of the law, in particular the ban on emigration. Huguenots were forced to stay in France and at least declare their conversion to Catholicism, and anyone caught practicing the Calvinist ceremony would be sold into slavery as a rower on a warship. "Dragonnades," basically impromptu army groups, stole through Huguenot towns to force conversions or capture anyone who disobeyed. Even Protestant children could be taken from their families and given over to Catholic foster parents.

Of course, a ban on emigration did not mean people did not leave. Thousands of Huguenots left France over the next two decades, moving to England, Switzerland, the United Provinces, and the German principalities. A select few even moved to the English colonies in North America and the Dutch colony in South Africa. Many of them worked in finance and industry, besides those with artisanal skills. Their loss to the French economy was immediately apparent, and their moves to Protestant states against which Louis fought wars only added to the difficulty.

In general, the Edict of Fontainebleau marked a turning point in Louis XIV's reign. Previously to 1685 he had the hearts of his people and the power to impose his will on Europe; after that year, however, the French intellectual classes no longer trusted him or his absolutist style of rulership, and his armies faced the resolve of the Protestant states of northwest Europe which now had tangible proof of his intolerance. Louis would die in 1715 as a comparatively bitter man, never having achieved his territorial aims in Europe. As well, efforts to describe what a more tolerant state in France should look like resulted in the discussions and writings that would eventually spawn the Enlightenment in Europe, with Paris at its center.

—Kirk R. MacGregor

Bibliography and Further Reading

Levi, Anthony. *Louis XIV.* Carroll & Graf, 2004.
McCullough, Roy L. *Coercion, Conversion and Counterinsurgency in Louis XIV's France.* Brill, 2007.
Prest, Julia and Guy Rowlands, editors. *The Third Reign of Louis XIV, c.1682-1715.* Routledge, 2017.
Sutherland, N. M. *The Huguenot Struggle for Recognition.* Yale University Press, 1980.

Websites

"The Edict of Fontainebleau or the Revocation (1685)." *Virtual Museum of Protestantism*, https://www.museeprotestant.org/en/notice/the-edict-of-fontainebleau-or-the-revocation-1685/. Accessed 27 Apr. 2017.

England: Civil War and Revolution

No country on earth experienced as much turmoil in the seventeenth century as England. A series of factors, both medieval and modern in origin, came together at one time, in one place, to bring about overwhelming political trauma and violence. England, and later Britain, made its reputation in the world for establishing the principles of representative government and carrying them around the world through the building of a vast empire. The trouble with building such a reputation was getting there.

England had long been a country of subjects who expected to be consulted on matters of government. Since the time of the Magna Carta, English parliaments had sat regularly, though not every year, and advised the English monarch on what his or her people would consider reasonable state measures to achieve the monarch's goals. This had reached a degree of regularity under the Tudor Dynasty (1485-1603), where, at the behest of Henry VIII and Elizabeth I, the English people had even converted hesitantly to a Protestant church as a majority, and came to see the church as a symbol of English nationalism. In fact, the Church of England became so revered by the end of the sixteenth century, a group of Anglicans began working to purge the Church of England of all of its Catholic elements. Their efforts at purification earned them the name Puritans.

Following Henry VIII, the English throne was inherited by James Stuart, king of Scotland and an adherent to the concept of the "divine right of kings," James I, and his son Charles I, both believed that they had been chosen by God to rule over the English people and that they had a divinely-inspired conception of what was best for the English people. This did not sit well with a people who were used to being consulted by their monarchs about governmental matters. To make matters worse, James and Charles wanted to establish a strict hierarchical order throughout all of the institutions they managed, including the Church of England—choosing virtually the same hierarchical order as that of the Roman Catholic Church.

Tensions flared over these issues; some Puritans left England for North America to found colonies where they could realize their religious dreams. Others stayed, challenged their monarchs, and eventually ended up at war in a battle to determine the future of English souls. The English Civil War (1642-1649) saw the Puritans define their principles in the Westminster Confession, win the war, and chop off the head of Charles I, who defended himself on the scaffold before his execution. English armies then conquered Scotland and Ireland to found the British Commonwealth, dedicated to Protestant perfection. The chaos following Charles' death and the religious state that emerged was too much for political figures like Thomas Hobbes, who believed people needed a strong monarchy if only to keep them from setting upon one another. Eventually, Charles' son, Charles II, was asked to return to the throne in 1660 and the Stuart monarchy resumed.

Emotions ran hot during Charles II's reign, a period know as the Restoration. Charles II did not believe he had been restored to the throne simply to turn the government of his state over to the hysterical Puritans. In part to keep Charles' power in check, the Habeas Corpus Act was passed. His younger brother, James II, proved even more adamant with regard to his prerogatives as monarch. James converted to Catholicism while in exile, and, while historians differ as to his motives, he obviously wanted to privilege Catholicism in the English state, if not convert its subjects altogether.

Once again, the English people decided that they had no patience for the notion that kings ruled by divine right. They turned to James' Protestant son-in-law and daughter, William and Mary, encouraging them to drive their father off the throne. When they succeeded, Parliament took action to prevent the turbulence of the Restoration. They drew up a petition of rights, the English Bill of Rights, that specified the kind of regime they wanted and made William and Mary sign it as a condition of their accession to the English throne. A former state official of Charles and James, John Locke, wrote about the need for this changeover in his *Second Treatise of Civil Government*.

By the end of the seventeenth century, England was rapidly evolving into one of the richest, most civil, and cooperative societies of any country in the world. The seventeenth century proved to be its crucible. The values of the civil war and revolution were carried to colonies overseas in America and Asia and eventually spread throughout the world.

James I: Speech on the Divine Right of Kings

Date: 1609
Author: King James I of England
Genre: Declarative speech

Summary Overview

James I gave his Speech on the Divine Right of Kings to Parliament, asserting his stance that a monarch is not subject to earthly authority and derives his right to rule directly from the will of God. James VI of Scotland became James I of England in 1603 upon the death of Queen Elizabeth I, passing the English throne from the Tudor to the Stuart house. He expounded his belief in the divine right of kings through a series of speeches delivered to Parliament in 1609. As the result of his lavish spending habits and challenges to parliamentary authority, James I frequently came into conflict with Parliament and its increasingly powerful House of Commons after ascending the throne. He also faced opposition from the gentry seeking political influence, and Puritans and Roman Catholics seeking religious reform.

The questions of the extent of power of secular monarchs in relation to the papacy, the limits of monarchical control over the Church, and the right of the people to challenge heretical or tyrannical monarchs had been debated since the Middle Ages. The theory of the divine right of kings developed to justify the political obligation of subjects to their rulers. The Divine Right was based on the hereditary right to rule granted by God's law and nature. Monarchs were therefore answerable only to God and were the only makers of law. They were not answerable to their subjects, who had a religious obligation to be dutiful.

Defining Moment

The Protestant Reformation began in 1517; it prompted a Catholic Counter-Reformation of equal fervor in the sixteenth century. All over Europe religious revolts took shape, challenging the authority of monarchs everywhere for supposedly not being representative of God's will. As monarchs discovered, very little could be done to control a people who had decided to assert their interests and beliefs en masse. This was in addition to the numerous and routine intrigues taking place in royal courts across Europe at the same time.

The result was the further refining and promotion of a political concept, the divine right of kings. The goal of its proponents was to connect monarchy to religion, to assert that God wanted certain individuals and families on the throne, and therefore any unrest beyond the monarch's control was circumscribed by heaven. In turn, monarchs and the philosophers who supported them hoped to drum up support from the same upper classes who might otherwise challenge the monarch's legitimacy. At a time when the vast majority of Europeans believed that the Christian God had created the Earth and everything in it, and that man was created in God's image, it made logical sense that such a God would favor certain families and people as rulers. The same idea had supported the Sunni Muslim caliphate in Islam, the position of the raja in the caste system in India, and the concept of the mandate of heaven in China.

The best philosopher of the divine right of kings was the Frenchman Jean Bodin. Bodin lived in an era of turmoil in France; Catholics persecuted French Protestants, or Huguenots, while different provincial aristocrats used religion to intrigue and plot against the throne in anticipation of replacing the monarch as king of France. In his *Six Books of the Commonweal* (1576), Bodin stated that the only way to stop such dissension was to establish the royals' connection to God. Kings were not accountable to their people; rather, they had been placed on their thrones by God to understand their peoples' interests, often better than the people themselves. Aristocrats were too self-interested, peasants too uneducated to run the state's affairs from a parliamentary seat. Only a king could or should make decisions on aspects of government, and anyone else in the state was—by necessity of stability and peace—beholden to the king's decisions.

Bodin was perhaps the first writer to articulate these ideas in print, but they were by no means new. Since the foundation of the Holy Roman Empire in the ninth century, monarchs had challenged the pope's authority, claiming a similar divinely appointed status within their own states. The Protestant Reformation had placed the English monarch at the head of the Church of England, adding a religious aspect to monarchical power.

Charles I of England, with a divine hand moving his crown. [Public domain], via Wikimedia Commons

The Catholic Mary I's attainment of the English throne had challenged this arrangement—Protestants in England began arguing that resistance to the exercise of a monarch's will might sometimes be legitimate, if that monarch was religiously tyrannical. Later, in the 1560s, Scottish Presbyterians would argue the same thing as justification for the removal of James I's mother, Mary, Queen of Scots, from the Scottish throne. So James, in some respects, owed his Scottish throne to the concept of popular legitimacy.

James's tutor as a child was George Buchanan, the same politician who had supported Mary's removal from the throne with pamphlets and essays. From 1570—when James was king, but only four years old—until 1578, Buchanan ran a strict teaching regimen and schooled James to believe in the sharing of power with the Scottish Parliament. James hated this teaching, which included brutal whippings. Not surprisingly, James reacted strongly against anything his former tutor believed; therefore, he was temperamentally inclined to believe in the divine right of kings. By his mid-twenties, James was publishing works about the defense of royal power, *Basilikon Doron* (1599) and *The Trew Law of Free Monarchies* (1603), arguing that kings are accountable to God alone.

James succeeded to the English throne in 1603, and while he found many people in Parliament willing to support his power in the state, more wanted to maintain the traditions established by the Tudors of consulting Parliament over major decisions. Restlessness grew as James tried to raise money through extra-parliamentary levies on exports and imports, ignoring Parliament to do so. In this speech, James explained his philosophy on monarchy—and obviously expected his subjects to agree with it.

Author Biography

James Charles Stuart was born on June 19, 1566, the heir to the throne of Scotland. His mother was Mary Stuart, daughter of King James V of Scotland, and grand-niece of King Henry VIII of England. One year after his birth, James's father, the Earl of Darnley, was killed in a mysterious explosion; his mother was suspected of complicity by the Scottish aristocracy. Mary abdicated and ran off to England, where Queen Elizabeth I had her thrown in prison. Thus, her son inherited the Scottish throne as James VI and grew up under several regencies until he came of age and formally became the proper ruler of Scotland in 1581. He ruled a nation divided between lowland Presbyterians and highland Catholics, and as an absolutist, did a credible job of keeping his people united and calm.

James's mother Mary, Queen of Scots, was an ambitious embarrassment to both her son and her cousin, Elizabeth I. As a Catholic and from the Tudor bloodline, Mary inspired many English Catholics to believe she might overthrow the Protestant Elizabeth I; when she consorted with one of the people conspiring against Elizabeth, Elizabeth had her executed in 1586. In the same year, she signed an alliance with James, and he became recognized as Elizabeth's likely heir. Soon after, James married Princess Anne of Denmark in 1589; they had three children who survived into adulthood. In March 1603, Elizabeth died and James VI of Scotland also became King James I of England, Wales and Ireland.

As the new monarch of a much larger and more internationally consequential kingdom, James largely abandoned his duties in Scotland, but not for a happier occupation. He was irascible, disliking the public demands of his job. Worse, he arrived to expectations by both Puritans and Catholics who hoped he would sympathize with their interests and enact religious reforms in England. He disappointed both; he preferred a hierarchical structure to his Church that resembled Catholicism, but he also did nothing to relax discrimination against Catholics in England. In response, several Catholics led by Guy Fawkes tried to blow up the houses of Parliament with gunpowder. Meanwhile, Puritans in the House of Commons were increasingly irritated with James's haughty assertion of his monarchical privileges and his massive expense account.

Still, James proved an accomplished king in his time on the throne. His name has become famous as the sponsor of the King James Bible, produced in 1611, and which has become the standard text of the Bible in English. He ended the long-running war with Spain, gave his blessing to the Virginia Company, which settled in Jamestown in Virginia in 1607, and expanded contacts with the Mughal Empire in India to advance the spice trade. One of his daughters married the elector of the Palatinate in the Holy Roman Empire; a hundred years later, his daughter's grandson would inaugurate the Hanover dynasty in Britain.

James died on March 27, 1625, and was succeeded by his second son, who eventually became Charles I.

HISTORICAL DOCUMENT

James I: Speech on the Divine Right of Kings

I will reduce to three general and main grounds, the principal things that have been agitated in this Parliament, and whereof I will now speak.

First, the Errand for which you were called by me; And that was, for supporting of my state, and necessities.

The second is, that which the people are to move unto the King: To represent unto him such things, whereby the Subjects are vexed, or wherein the state of the Commonwealth is to be redressed: And that is the thing which you call grievances.

The third ground that hath been handled amongst you, and not only in talk amongst you in the Parliament, but even in many other peoples' mouths, as well within, as without the Parliament, is of a higher nature then any of the former, though it be but an Incident; and the reason is, because it concerns a higher point: And this is a doubt, which hath been in the heads of some, of my Intention in two things.

First, whether I was resolved in the general, to continue still my government according to the ancient form of this State, and the Laws of this Kingdom: Or if I had an intention not to limit myself within those bounds, but to alter the same when I thought convenient, by the absolute power of a King. …

The State of MONARCHY is the supremest thing upon earth: For Kings are not only GOD'S Lieutenants upon earth, and sit upon GOD'S throne, but even by GOD himself they are called Gods. There be three principal similitudes that illustrates the state of MONARCHY: One taken out of the word of GOD; and the two other out of the grounds of Policy and Philosophy. In the Scriptures Kings are called Gods, and so their power after a certain relation compared to the Divine power. Kings are also compared to Fathers of families: for a King is truly *Parens patriae*, the politic father of his people. And lastly, Kings are compared to the head of this Microcosm of the body of man.

Kings are justly called Gods, for that they exercise a manner or resemblance of Divine power upon earth: For if you will consider the Attributes to God, you shall see how they agree in the person of a King. God hath power to create, or destroy, make, or unmake at his pleasure, to give life, or send death, to judge all, and to be judged nor acco[un]table to none: To raise low things, and to make high things low at his -pleasure, and to God are both soul and body due. And the like power have Kings: they make and unmake their subjects: they have power of raising, and casting down: of life, and of death: Judges over all their subjects, and in all causes, and yet acco[un]table to none but God only. They have power to exalt low things, and abase high things, and make of their subjects like men at the Chess; A pawn to take a Bishop or a Knight, and to cry up, or down any of their subjects, as they do their money. And to the King is due both the affection of the soul, and the service of the body of his subjects: …

As for the Father of a family, they had of old under the Law of Nature *Patriam potestatem*, which was *Potestatem vitæ & necis*, over their children or family (I mean such Fathers of families as were the lineal heirs of those families whereof Kings did originally come): For Kings had their first original from them, who planted and spread themselves in *Colonies* through the world. Now a Father may dispose of his Inheritance to his children, at his pleasure: yea, even disinherit the eldest upon just occasions, and prefer the youngest, according to his liking; make them beggars, or rich at his pleasure; restrain, or banish out of his presence, as he finds them give cause of offence, or restore them in favour again with the penitent sinner: So may the King deal with his Subjects.

And lastly, as for the head of the natural body, the head hath the power of directing all the members of the body to that use which the judgment in the head thinks most convenient. It may apply sharp cures, or cut off corrupt members, let blood in what proportion it thinks fit, and as the body may spare, but yet is all this power ordained by God *Ad ædificationem, non ad destructionem*. For although God have power as well of destruction, as of creation or maintenance; yet will it not agree with the wisdom of God, to exercise his power in the destruction of nature, and overturning the whole frame of things, since his creatures were made, that his glory might thereby be the better expressed: So were he a foolish father that would disinherit or destroy his children without a cause, or leave off the careful education of them; And it were an idle head that would in place of physick so poison or phlebotomize the body as might breed a dangerous distemper or destruction thereof. ...

I conclude then this point touching the power of Kings, with this Axiom of Divinity, That as to dispute what God may do, is Blasphemy; but *quid vult Deus*, that Divines may lawfully, and do ordinarily dispute and discuss; for to dispute *A Posse ad Esse* is both against Logic and Divinity: So is it sedition in Subjects, to dispute what a King may do in the height of his power: But just Kings will ever be willing to declare what they will do, if they will not incur the curse of God. I will not be content that my power be disputed upon: but I shall ever be willing to make the reason appear of all my doings, and rule my actions according to my Laws.

The other branch of this incident is concerning the Common Law, being conceived by some, that I con[d]emned it, and preferred the Civil Law thereunto. As I have already said, Kings' Actions (even in the secretest places) are as the actions of those that are set upon the Stages, or on the tops of houses: and I hope never to speak that in private, which I shall not avow in public, and Print it if need be. ...For it is true, that within these few days I spake freely my mind touching the Common Law in my Privy Chamber, at the time of my dinner, which is come to all your ears; and the same was likewise related unto you by my Treasurer, and now I will again repeat and confirm the same myself unto you. First, as a King I have least cause of any man to dislike the Common Law: For no Law can be more favourable and advantageous for a King, and extendeth further his Prerogative, than it doth: And for a King of England to despise the Common Law, it is to neglect his own Crown. It is true, that I do greatly esteem the Civil Law, the profession thereof serving more for general learning and being most necessary for matters of Treaty with all foreign Nations: And I think that if it should be taken away, it would make an entry to Barbarism in this Kingdom, and would blemish the honour of England. ...My meaning therefore is not to prefer the Civil Law before the Common Law; but only that it should not be extinguished, and yet so bounded, (I mean to such Courts and Causes) as have been in ancient use. ... Nay, I am so far from disallowing the Common Law, as I protest, that if it were in my hand to choose a new Law for this Kingdom, I would not only prefer it before any other National Law, but even before the very Judicial Law of Moses: and yet I speak no blasphemy in preferring it for conveniency to this Kingdom, and at this time, to the very Law of God. ...Now the second general ground whereof I am to speak, concerns the matter of Grievances. ...I would wish you to be careful to avoid three things in the matter of Grievances.

First, that you do not meddle with the main points of Government; that is my craft: *tractent fabrilia fabri*; to meddle with that, were to lessen me: I am now an old King; for six and thirty years have I governed in *Scotland* personally, and now have I accomplished my apprenticeship of seven years here; and seven years is a great time for a King's experience in Government: Therefore there would not be too many *Phormios* to teach *Hannibal*: I must not be taught my Office.

Secondly, I would not have you meddle with such ancient Rights of mine, as I have received from my Predecessors, possessing them, *More Maiorum*: such things I would be sorry should be accounted for *Grievances*. All novelties are dangerous as well in a politic as in a natural Body: And therefore I would be loath to be quarreled in my ancient Rights and possessions: for that were to judge me unworthily of that which my Predecessors had and left me.

And lastly, I pray you beware to exhibit for Grievance any thing that is established by a settled Law, and whereunto (as you have already had a proof) you know I will never give a plausible answer: For it is an undutiful part in Subjects to press their King, wherein they know beforehand he will refuse them. Now, if any Law or Statute be not convenient, let it be amended by Parliament, but in the meantime term it not a *Grievance*: for to be grieved with the Law, is to be grieved with the King, who is sworn to be the Patron and maintainer thereof. But as all men are flesh, and may err in the execution of Laws; So may ye justly make a *Grievance* of any abuse of the Law, distinguishing wisely between the faults of the person, and the thing itself. As for example, Complaints may be made unto you of the high

Commissioners: If so be, try the abuse, and spare not to complain upon it, but say not there shall be no Commission; For that were to abridge the power that is in me: and I will plainly tell you, That something I have with myself resolved anent that point, which I mean ever to keep, except I see other great cause: which is, That in regard the high Commission is of so high a nature, from which there is no appellation to any other Court, I have thought good to restrain it only to the two Archbishops, where before it was common amongst a great part of the Bishops in England. This Law I have set to myself, and therefore you may be assured, that I will never find fault with any man, nor think him the more Puritan, that will complain to me out of Parliament, as well as in Parliament, of any error in execution thereof, so that he prove it; Otherwise it were but a calumny. Only I would be loath that any man should grieve at the Commission itself, as I have already said. Ye have heard (I am sure) of the pains I took both in the causes of the Admiralty, and of the Prohibitions: If any man therefore will bring me any just complaints upon any matters of so high a nature as this is, ye may assure yourselves that I will not spare my labour in hearing it. In faith you never had a more painful King, or that will be readier in his person to determine causes that are fit for his hearing. And whenever any of you shall make experience of me in this point, ye may be sure never to want access, nor ye shall never come wrong to me, in, or out of Parliament.

AND now the third point remains to be spoken of; which is the cause of my calling of this Parliament. And in this I have done but as I use to do in all my life, which is to leave mine own errand hindmost. …

I am not now… to dispute of a King's power, but to tell you what I may justly crave, and expect with your good wills. I was ever against all extremes; and in this case I will likewise wish you to avoid them on both sides. For if you fail in the one, I might have great cause to blame you as Parliament men, being called by me for my Errands: And if you fall into the other extreme, by supply of my necessities without respective care to avoid oppression or partiality in the Levy, both I and the Country will have cause to blame you. …

First, ye all know, that by the accession of more Crowns, which in my Person I have brought unto you, my charge must be the greater in all reason: For the greater your King be, both in his dominion and number of Subjects, he cannot but be forced thereby to be at the more charge, and it is the more your honour, so to have it.

Next, that posterity and issue which it hath pleased God to send me for your use, cannot but bring necessarily with it a greater proportion of charge. You all know that the late Queen of famous memory (notwithstanding her orbity) had much given unto her, and more than ever any of her predecessors had before her.

Thirdly, the time of creation of my Son doth now draw near, which I choose for the greater honour to be done in this time of Parliament. As for him I say no more; the sight of himself here speaks for him.

Fourthly, it is true I have spent much; but yet if I had spared any of those things, which caused a great part of my expense, I should have dishonored the kingdom, myself, and the late Queen. …But I hope you will never mislike me for my liberality, since I can look very few of you this day in the face, that have not made suits to me, at least for something, either of honour or profit. It is true, a Kings liberality must never be dried up altogether: for then he can never maintain nor oblige his servants and well deserving Subjects. …For to conclude this point anent expenses, I hold that a King's expense must always be honourable, though not wasteful, and the charges of your King in maintaining those ancient honourable forms of living that the former Kings of England my Predecessors have done, and his living to be ruled according to the proportion of his greatness, is as well for the honour of your Kingdom, as of your King. Now this cannot be supplied out of the a[ir]or liquid elements, but must come from the people. … For I hope there are no good Subjects either within, or out of the Parliament House, that would not be content for setting straight once and settling the Honourable State of their King, to spare so much every one of them out of their purses, which per adventure they would in one night throw away at Dice or Cards, or bestow upon a horse for their fancies, that might break his neck or his leg the next morning: Nay I am sure every good Subject would rather choose to live more sparingly upon his own, than that his King's State should be in want. …

And now in the end of all this fashious Speech, I must conclude like a Grey Friar, in speaking for myself at last. At the beginning of this Session of Parliament, when the Treasurer opened my necessities unto you, then my Purse only laboured; But now that word is spread both at home and abroad of the demands I have made unto you; my Reputation laboureth as well as my Purse: For if you part without the repairing of my State in some reasonable sort, what can the world think, but that the evil will my Subjects bear unto me, hath bred a refuse? And ye can never part so, without apprehending that I am distasted with your behaviour, and yet to be in fear of my displeasure. But I assure and promise myself far otherwise. …

To conclude then: As all these three days of *Jubilee* have fallen in the midst of this season of penitence, wherein you have presented your thanks to me, and I the like again to you: So do I wish and hope, that the end of this Parliament will be such, as we may all have cause (both I your Head, and ye the Body) to join in Eucharistic Thanks and Praises unto God, for our so good and happy an End.

GLOSSARY

similitudes: similarities

anent: about

Patriam potestatem, … Potestatem vitæ & necis: power of life and death

Ad ædificationem, non ad destructionem: for their betterment, not their destruction

quid vult Deus: that which God does

A Posse ad Esse: literally, that which gathers being; meaning, deductive reasoning

tractent fabrilia fabri: literally, carpenter's tools were treated with; meaning, you meddle with my tools

Phormio: according to Roman legend, a Greco-Persian philosopher who tried to lecture Hannibal about the merits of good generalship—in short, a foolish know-it-all

More Maiorum: moreover from women; meaning, from birth

the late Queen of famous memory: Queen Elizabeth I, James's predecessor on the English throne

orbity: mourning a lost parent or child, in Elizabeth's case, her mother Anne Boleyn, beheaded by her father King Henry VIII's order, for unsubstantiated charges

fashious: annoying; even James is tired of hearing himself speak

Grey Friar: a Franciscan monk; the Franciscans were famous for their poverty—James is saying he is "impoverished of words" and will conclude briefly

Document Analysis

James I addressed Parliament to resolve three crucial issues: parliamentary monetary support for his estate, grievances of his subjects, and uncertainties surrounding his intention to rule according to the country's ancient customs (common law). James I first sought to establish the king's absolute prerogative to rule, reiterating his belief in the divine right of kings. The power of kings, he believed, is derived directly from God rather than their subjects and is similar to God's power. Kings are God's representatives and therefore are accountable only to God and not to their subjects. All other political figures or institutions are subordinate and accountable to the king, as are his subjects.

Questions of law were at the center of the debate over divine right. James I's speeches espoused the proponents' view that the law was the king's instrument, and kings were above the law, while opponents countered that the king was instead bound by the law. Opponents relied on common law courts, as they felt they had no effective voice in Parliament and that divine right challenged their ability as subjects to appeal to the law for redress of grievances. Most English critics wanted to limit, not eliminate, the king's prerogative to rule. James I answered charges that he favored civil law over common law by stating that common law was not antithetical to the divine right.

A key goal of the divine right of kings was to ensure the submissive obedience of a monarch's subjects. All subjects, regardless of their social class, held a religious as well as a moral obligation to obey and serve their monarchs in both body and soul. James I thus emphasized both Parliament members' roles as subjects and the king's right to deal with his subjects as a father would his children and heirs. The divine right of kings also held that active resistance against kings was never acceptable, even in the face of tyrannical or heretical behavior. James I acknowledged that kings should not violate the laws of God or nature and should show just cause for disciplining a subject.

James I concedes that subjects have the right to bring grievances before their monarch, but he names three issues that Parliament should consider before bringing grievances to his attention. First, he warns that it is the king's prerogative alone to change the main points of government. Second, he cautions against interference with his ancient rights and possessions. Last, he counsels against pressing grievances with the law itself, for which the king is responsible, rather than with persons carrying out the law, who are fallible. He states his openness to addressing grievances that involve errors of execution of the law that can be proved.

James I warns Parliament to avoid extremes in carrying out their duty to provide for the king's expenses, whether by failing to adequately support those needs or by oppressing or favoring certain subjects in raising money to meet those expenses. He also justifies his need for expenses through reminders of monies delivered to his predecessor, Elizabeth I; the need to honor the custom of meeting expenses; and considerations of the honor and future of the country. Here, he returns to his point that common law as well as divine right supports the duty of subjects to provide for their monarch. He warns that failure will result in his assumption of ill will on the part of his subjects, who will risk the possible consequences of his displeasure, providing him with just cause for discipline.

Essential Themes

James maintained a steadily poor relationship with his Puritan-dominated parliament until his death in 1625. His son, Charles I, also believed in the divine rights of kings; on the other hand, he had little of his father's philosophical conception of the subject. At least James had ideological underpinnings behind his actions as monarch; Charles had no such basis for being profligate, religiously challenging, and politically authoritarian. For eleven years, he ruled without calling a parliament, and tried to levy his own taxes and fees on his subjects without obtaining their consent. In other European states and world empires, such actions were the norm; in England, the state the Stuarts had inherited, it was a challenge to the Magna Carta itself, and built Charles a very bad reputation with his people.

In 1639, Charles's Scottish charges rebelled against his insistence that they adopt the Anglican Book of Common Prayer for their Presbyterian religious ceremonies. Charles was forced to call Parliament into session in order to get funding for an army to put down the rebellion. The Irish followed up with their own rebellion in 1641; when Parliament balked at providing Charles with another army that he might use on them, Charles called on Loyal Englishmen to support him in his own army, effectively declaring war on his Parliament. In the following Civil War, Charles lost the war and lost his head to an execution in 1649. Far from being an absolute monarchy, England became the location of a single republic governing over all four nations in the British Isles.

By 1660, the republic had failed and James's grandson, Charles II, was restored to the English and Scottish thrones. Charles II and his supporters also claimed divine right, but the king was smart enough never to test his principles with a parliament that had executed his father. His brother, James II, was not so smart. A converted Catholic, James was a threat even to his biggest supporters, as he wanted to bring England—

a 150-year-old Protestant state—back to the Roman Catholic Church. No one in Parliament defended James when his daughter and son-in-law, Mary Henrietta Stuart and William of Orange, ran him off the throne in 1688. With his flight from England went any significant English support for a divine right of kings. The concept would last in Europe until the French Revolution made it obvious that monarchs had no connection to any god which would allow them to have their heads cut off by their people.

—*Marcella Bush Treviño*

Bibliography and Further Reading

Asch, Ronald G. *Sacral Kingship between Disenchantment and Re-enchantment: The French and English Monarchies 1587-1688*. Berghahn Books, 2014.

Bodin, Jean. *On Sovereignty: Four Chapters from the Six Books of the Commonwealth*. Edited and translated by Julian H. Franklin. Cambridge University Press, 1992.

Harris, Tim. *Rebellion: Britain's First Stuart Kings, 1567-1642*. Oxford University Press, 2014.

Lyon, Thomas. *The Theory of Religious Liberty in England, 1603-39*. Octagon Books, 1976.

Websites

"James I and VI (1566 - 1625)." *BBC History*, 2014, http://www.bbc.co.uk/history/historic_figures/james_i_vi.shtml. Accessed 11 Apr. 2017.

Sommerville, J.P. "The Divine Right of Kings." University of Wisconsin History Department, https://faculty.history.wisc.edu/sommerville/367/367-04.htm. Accessed 11 Apr. 2017.

Westminster Confession

Date: 1646
Authors: John Calvin and the Westminster Assembly of the Divines
Genre: Statement

Summary Overview

The Westminster Confession, written in 1646, is a statement of Christian faith in the tradition of Calvinist, or "Reformed," Protestantism. Its thirty-three chapters were meant to cover all the major issues of Christian theology as they existed in the mid-seventeenth century. The Westminster Confession was created by a group of ministers and theological experts from England and Scotland, mostly Presbyterian in faith, during the English Civil War (1642–1651). The group had originally been summoned by the English Parliament to reform the Church of England.

Along with the Westminster Larger and Shorter Catechisms that summarize its doctrines, the Westminster Confession is the most influential statement of faith in the English-speaking Calvinist tradition, and remains the theological foundation of most Presbyterian churches as well as strongly influencing Churches outside that tradition, including Congregationalist and Baptist bodies.

Defining Moment

Reformed theology developed from the Protestant Reformation of the sixteenth century as a mixture whose strongest component was the thought of the French theologian John Calvin (1509–1564). The major issues that distinguished the Reformed tradition from other branches of Protestantism included the Eucharist and infant baptism, which Reformed theologians supported. The issues most identified with a distinctive Reformed tradition, however, were those concerning salvation. As was true of Protestants generally, the Reformed supported the idea of justification by faith alone, not through works. However, Reformed theology was particularly associated with predestination, the theory that God had determined, solely of his own will, who was to be saved (a minority known as the "elect") and who was damned (the rest of humanity, known as the "reprobate.") This was accompanied by the doctrine of "Total Depravity," the belief that human beings, since the fall of Adam, were by their nature utterly corrupt. Only divine grace, which God was completely free to bestow or withhold, could exempt a human from damnation. Jesus Christ had not died to save all, but the elect only—"Limited Atonement." The systematization of these beliefs is often associated with the Synod of Dort, a meeting of Reformed male divines from all over Western Europe held at the Dutch city of Dort (or Dordrecht) in 1618 and 1619 that put forward *The Decision of the Synod of Dort on the Five Main Points of Doctrine in Dispute in the Netherlands*. The "Five Points" are Total Depravity; Unconditional Election, not predicated on any quality of saved individuals but solely on God's grace; Irresistible Grace, which cannot be rejected by a human; Limited Atonement; and the Perseverance of the Saints, or the doctrine that grace once given will never be withdrawn. Although the term *Five Points* is not found there, the Westminster Confession follows this model.

The "covenantal" element of Reformed theology was not principally derived from Calvin, although there are elements of Calvin's thought that point to it. Its original sources include the theology of the Swiss minister Heinrich Bullinger (1504–1575). Covenantal theology placed the relationship between God and the saved individual on a contractual basis. By entering into an agreement binding on both sides, God voluntarily limited his absolute power. God's first covenant, the covenant of works made with Adam, was no longer in effect. In the covenant of works, salvation would be granted in return for obedience to the law of God. Adam himself had destroyed the covenant of works by yielding to temptation and violating God's commands. The covenant of grace, as originally offered to Abraham, replaced the covenant of works. In the covenant of grace, God bound himself to save those who took up their side of the covenant by having faith and striving to follow the moral law, even though they would inevitably fail to live lives of absolute perfection. Covenant theologians sometimes moved far away from Calvin's emphasis on the unknowability and mystery of God's decrees toward a legalistic interpretation of the relationship of God and humanity, although they never viewed the covenant as abrogating the doctrine of predestination.

Title page of a 1647 printing of the *Confession*. Westminster Assembly [Public domain], via Wikimedia Commons

Reformed doctrine since the sixteenth century had been put forth in a series of creeds and confessions produced primarily on the European continent. The necessity of establishing a common theological basis for the numerous Reformed Churches led to a demand for relatively simple, portable statements of Reformed belief.

Reformed theology had a strong influence on the Church of England when it was formed in the mid-sixteenth century. However, the Church was not a theologically rigid organization. Some leaned toward Arminianism or opposed Calvinism without being very clear what they supported. In the Church of Scotland, however, Reformed theology was combined with a widespread belief in the government of the Church by ministers and elders rather than bishops—"Presbyterianism." In 1603 the accession of James VI of Scotland (1566–1625) to the English throne as James I brought the two countries under one royal dynasty, the House of Stuart. James, and far more openly his son Charles I (1600–1649), opposed Presbyterian organization in both kingdoms.

In the years immediately preceding the Westminster Assembly, the principal conflict within the Church of England was between the "Arminians," led by Archbishop of Canterbury William Laud (1573–1645) with the support of King Charles, and "Puritans," most of whom leaned toward Calvinist theology. Arminianism is the doctrine associated with the Dutch theologian Jacobus Arminius (1560–1609) that rejects the doctrine of predestination to hold that Christ died for all, not just the elect, and that all are potentially, if not actually, saved. The Arminianism of Laud, sometimes referred to as "English Arminianism," however, was based less on Arminius's doctrinal positions and more on a view of Christianity that emphasized ritual and the "beauty of holiness" over the Calvinist practice of emphasizing doctrine and the sermon.

The conflict between Arminians and Puritans led many Puritans to oppose the institutions of bishops—"Episcopacy"—altogether, in favor of either Presbyterianism or "Congregationalism," built on the supremacy of individual congregations. A similar conflict was raging in Scotland. The outbreak, first of the Scottish rebellion (known as the First Bishops' War) in 1639 and then of the English Civil War in 1642, involved political as well as religious issues. However, Arminians in both kingdoms usually supported the king, while many English Puritans along with the Scottish "Covenanters" (so-called for their support of the Scottish National Covenant of 1638) supported the rebellions. By 1642 there was a full-scale civil war in England as well, between the king and the English Parliament. The cause of "further Reformation," purging the Church of Catholic and Arminian elements, was popular in Parliament. It voted to reform the Church of England and convoked a meeting at the Henry VII Chapel at Westminster to do so. The gathering was composed of some of England's leading theologians and religious scholars, nearly all Presbyterian or Congregationalist with a small minority of Anglicans.

Shortly afterward, Scottish Covenanters and English Parliamentarians made an alliance, the "Solemn League and Covenant," in 1643. One goal of the Solemn League and Covenant was to reform the Churches in both kingdoms, which to the signers meant moving their theology closer to the Reformed tradition. It was followed by the incorporation of Scottish delegates into the Westminster Assembly.

Author Biographies

The Westminster Assembly of Divines was originally a group of English clergy and lay commissioners assigned to revise the doctrine and practices of the Church of England further away from Catholicism. In addition to drawing up a statement of faith, they were charged with reforming Church government and public worship. They initially drew from a diversity of factions in the Church, including Anglicans, but as the proceedings continued, they were dominated by Reformed Presbyterian and Congregational divines. Many members came from the universities, and three ministers of French Reformed churches in London were members. The English members were joined by Scottish lay and clerical delegates following the adoption of the Solemn League and Covenant. The English members were chosen by Parliament and the Scots by the General Assembly of the Church of Scotland. Leaders of the Assembly included the prolocutor, or president, of the Assembly, the philosopher and theologian William Twisse (1578–1646); John Selden (1584–1654), a layman and England's leading Hebrew scholar; and Stephen Marshall (ca. 1594–1655), one of the greatest preachers of the day. The Scottish commissioners included the eminent theologian Samuel Rutherford (ca. 1600–1661), the Presbyterian leader Alexander Henderson (ca. 1583–1646), and the brilliant polemicist George Gillespie (1613–1648). One of the Scottish commissioners, Robert Baille (1602–1662), was only a minor actor in the Assembly, but his gossipy letters are one of our principal historical sources for the making of the Westminster Confession. Despite disagreements over particular points, the Assembly had a broadly Reformed consensus, and there were no openly expressed disagreements over fundamentals.

The Assembly did not follow a rigid set of procedures. Much of its work, including the drafting of parts of the Westminster Confession, was entrusted to committees, but some sections were presented to the whole by men who were not members of the relevant or, indeed, any committee.

HISTORICAL DOCUMENT

Excerpts from Westminster Confession by John Calvin
CHAPTER I.
Of the holy Scripture.

I. Although the light of nature, and the works of creation and providence, do so far manifest the goodness, wisdom, and power of God, as to leave men inexcusable; yet are they not sufficient to give that knowledge of God, and of his will, which is necessary unto salvation; therefore it pleased the Lord, at sundry times, and in divers manners, to reveal himself, and to declare that his will unto his Church; and afterwards for the better preserving and propagating of the truth, and for the more sure establishment and comfort of the Church against the corruption of the flesh, and the malice of Satan and of the world, to commit the same wholly unto writing; which maketh the holy Scripture to be most necessary; those former ways of God's revealing his will unto his people being now ceased.

II. Under the name of holy Scripture, or the Word of God written, are now contained all the Books of the Old and New Testament, which are these:

Of the Old Testament:

Genesis
Exodus
Leviticus
Numbers
Deuteronomy
Joshua
Judges
Ruth
I Samuel
II Samuel
I Kings
II Kings
I Chronicles
II Chronicles
Ezra
Nehemiah
Esther
Job
Psalms
Proverbs
Ecclesiastes
The Song of Songs
Isaiah
Jeremiah
Lamentations
Ezekiel
Daniel
Hosea
Joel
Amos
Obadiah
Jonah
Micah
Nahum
Habakkuk
Zephaniah
Haggai
Zechariah
Malachi

Of the New Testament:
The Gospels according to

Matthew
Mark
Luke
John

The Acts of the Apostles
Paul's Epistles to the Romans
Corinthians I
Corinthians II
Galatians
Ephesians
Philippians
Colossians
Thessalonians I
Thessalonians II
Timothy I
Timothy II
Titus
Philemon
The Epistle to the Hebrews
The Epistle of James
The First and Second Epistles of Peter
The First, Second, and Third Epistles of John
The Epistle of Jude
The Revelation

All which are given by inspiration of God, to be the rule of faith and life.

III. The books commonly called Apocrypha, not being of divine inspiration, are no part of the Canon of Scripture; and therefore are of no authority in the Church of God, nor to be any otherwise approved, or made use of, than other human writings.

IV. The authority of the holy Scripture, for which it ought to be believed and obeyed, dependeth not upon the testimony of any man or Church, but wholly upon God (who is truth itself), the Author thereof; and therefore it is to be received, because it is the Word of God.

V. We may be moved and induced by the testimony of the Church to an high and reverent esteem of the holy Scripture; and the heavenliness of the matter, the efficacy of the doctrine, the majesty of the style, the consent of all the parts, the scope of the whole (which is to give all glory to God), the full discovery it makes of the only way of man's salvation, the many other incomparable excellencies, and the entire perfection thereof, are arguments whereby it doth abundantly evidence itself to be the Word of God; yet, notwithstanding, our full persuasion and assurance of the infallible truth and divine authority thereof, is from the inward work of the Holy Spirit, bearing witness by and with the Word in our hearts.

VI. The whole counsel of God, concerning all things necessary for his own glory, man's salvation, faith, and life, is either expressly set down in Scripture, or by good and necessary consequence may be deduced from Scripture: unto which nothing at any time is to be added, whether by new revelations of the Spirit, or traditions of men. Nevertheless we acknowledge the inward illumination of the Spirit of God to be necessary for the saving understanding of such things as are revealed in the Word; and that there are some circumstances concerning the worship of God, and the government of the Church, common to human actions and societies, which are to be ordered by the light of nature and Christian prudence, according to the general rules of the Word, which are always to be observed.

VII. All things in Scripture are not alike plain in themselves, nor alike clear unto all; yet those things which are necessary to be known, believed, and observed, for salvation, are so clearly propounded and opened in some place of Scripture or other, that not only the learned, but the unlearned, in a due use of the ordinary means, may attain unto a sufficient understanding of them.

VIII. The Old Testament in Hebrew (which was the native language of the people of God of old), and the New Testament in Greek (which at the time of the writing of it was most generally known to the nations), being immediately inspired by God, and by his singular care and providence kept pure in all ages, are therefore authentical; so as in all controversies of religion the Church is finally to appeal unto them. But because these original tongues are not known to all the people of God who have right unto, and interest in, the Scriptures, and are commanded, in the fear of God, to read and search them, therefore they are to be translated into the vulgar language of every nation unto which they come, that the Word of God dwelling plentifully in all, they may worship him in an acceptable manner, and, through patience and comfort of the Scriptures, may have hope.

IX. The infallible rule of interpretation of Scripture, is the Scripture itself; and therefore, when there is a question about the true and full sense of any scripture (which is not manifold, but one), it may be searched and known by other places that speak more clearly.

X. The Supreme Judge, by which all controversies of religion are to be determined, and all decrees of councils, opinions of ancient writers, doctrines of men, and private spirits, are to be examined, and in whose sentence we are to rest, can be no other but the Holy Spirit speaking in the Scripture.

CHAPTER II.
Of God, and of the Holy Trinity.

I. There is but one only living and true God, who is infinite in being and perfection, a most pure spirit, invisible, without body, parts, or passions, immutable, immense, eternal, incomprehensible, almighty, most wise, most holy, most free, most absolute, working all things according to the counsel of his own immutable and most righteous will, for his own glory, most loving, gracious, merciful, long-suffering, abundant in goodness and truth, forgiving iniquity, transgression, and sin; the rewarder of them that diligently seek him; and withal most just and terrible in his judgments; hating all sin; and who will by no means clear the guilty.

II. God hath all life, glory, goodness, blessedness, in and of himself; and is alone in and unto himself all-sufficient, not standing in need of any creatures which he hath made, nor deriving any glory from them, but only manifesting his own glory in, by, unto, and upon them; he is the alone foundation of all being, of whom, through whom, and to whom, are all things; and hath most sovereign dominion over them, to do by them, for them, or upon them, whatsoever himself pleaseth. In his sight all things are open and manifest; his knowledge is infinite, infallible, and independent upon the creature; so as nothing is to him contingent or uncertain. He is most holy in all his counsels, in all his works, and in all his commands. To him is due from angels and men, and every other creature, whatsoever worship, service, or obedience he is pleased to require of them.

III. In the unity of the Godhead there be three Persons of one substance, power, and eternity: God the Father, God the Son, and God the Holy Ghost. The Father is of none, neither begotten nor proceeding; the Son is eternally begotten of the Father; the Holy Ghost eternally proceeding from the Father and the Son.

CHAPTER III.
Of God's Eternal Decree.

I. God from all eternity did by the most wise and holy counsel of his own will, freely and unchangeably ordain whatsoever comes to pass; yet so as thereby neither is God the author of sin; nor is violence offered to the will of the creatures, nor is the liberty or contingency of second causes taken away, but rather established.

II. Although God knows whatsoever may or can come to pass, upon all supposed conditions; yet hath he not decreed any thing because he foresaw it as future, as that which would come to pass, upon such conditions.

III. By the decree of God, for the manifestation of his glory, some men and angels are predestinated unto everlasting life, and others foreordained to everlasting death.

IV. These angels and men, thus predestinated and foreordained, are particularly and unchangeably designed; and their number is so certain and definite that it can not be either increased or diminished.

V. Those of mankind that are predestinated unto life, God, before the foundation of the world was laid, according to his eternal and immutable purpose, and the secret counsel and good pleasure of his will, hath chosen in Christ, unto everlasting glory, out of his free grace and love alone, without any foresight of faith or good works, or perseverance in either of them, or any other thing in the creature, as conditions, or causes moving him thereunto; and all to the praise of his glorious grace.

VI. As God hath appointed the elect unto glory, so hath he, by the eternal and most free purpose of his will, foreordained all the means thereunto. Wherefore they who are elected being fallen in Adam are redeemed by Christ, are effectually called unto faith in Christ by his Spirit working in due season; are justified, adopted, sanctified, and kept by his power through faith unto salvation. Neither are any other redeemed by Christ, effectually called, justified, adopted, sanctified, and saved, but the elect only.

VII. The rest of mankind, God was pleased, according to the unsearchable counsel of his own will, whereby he extendeth or withholdeth mercy as he pleaseth, for the glory of his sovereign power over his creatures, to pass by, and to ordain them to dishonor and wrath for their sin, to the praise of his glorious justice.

VIII. The doctrine of this high mystery of predestination is to be handled with special prudence and care, that men attending to the will of God revealed in his Word, and yielding obedience thereunto, may, from the certainty of their effectual vocation, be assured of their eternal election. So shall this doctrine afford matter of praise, reverence, and admiration of God; and of humility, diligence, and abundant consolation to all that sincerely obey the gospel.

CHAPTER IV.
Of Creation.

I. It pleased God the Father, Son, and Holy Ghost, for the manifestation of the glory of his eternal power, wisdom, and goodness, in the beginning, to create or make of nothing the world, and all things therein, whether visible or invisible, in the space of six days, and all very good.

II. After God had made all other creatures, he created man, male and female, with reasonable and immortal souls, endued with knowledge, righteousness, and true holiness after his own image, having the law of God written in their hearts, and power to fulfill it; and yet under a possibility of transgressing, being left to the liberty of their own will, which was subject unto change. Besides this law written in their hearts, they received a command not to eat of the tree of the knowledge of good and evil; which while they kept were happy in their communion with God, and had dominion over the creatures.

CHAPTER V.
Of Providence.

I. God, the great Creator of all things, doth uphold, direct dispose, and govern all creatures, actions, and things, from the greatest even to the least, by his most wise and holy providence, according to his infallible foreknowledge, and the free and immutable counsel of his own will, to the praise of the glory of his wisdom, power, justice, goodness, and mercy.

II. Although in relation to the foreknowledge and decree of God, the first cause, all things come to pass immutably and infallibly, yet, by the same providence, he ordereth them to fall out according to the nature of second causes, either necessarily, freely, or contingently.

III. God, in his ordinary providence, maketh use of means, yet is free to work without, above, and against them, at his pleasure.

IV. The almighty power, unsearchable wisdom, and infinite goodness of God, so far manifest themselves in his providence, that it extendeth itself even to the first Fall, and all other sins of angels and men, and that not by a bare permission, but such as hath joined with it a most wise and powerful bounding, and otherwise ordering and governing of them, in a manifold dispensation, to his own holy ends; yet so, as the sinfulness thereof proceedeth only from the creature, and not from God; who being most holy and righteous, neither is nor can be the author or approver of sin.

V. The most wise, righteous, and gracious God, doth oftentimes leave for a season his own children to manifold temptations and the corruption of their own hearts, to chastise them for their former sins, or to discover unto them the hidden strength of corruption and deceitfulness of their hearts, that they may be humbled; and to raise them to a more close and constant dependence for their support upon himself, and to make them more watchful against all future occasions of sin, and for sundry other just and holy ends.

VI. As for those wicked and ungodly men whom God, as a righteous judge, for former sins, doth blind and harden; from them he not only withholdeth his grace, whereby they might have been enlightened in their understandings, and wrought upon their hearts; but sometimes also withdraweth the gifts which they had; and exposeth them to such objects as their corruption makes occasion of sin; and withal, gives them over to their own lusts, the temptations of the world, and the power of Satan; whereby it comes to pass that they harden themselves, even under those means which God useth for the softening of others.

VII. As the providence of God doth, in general, reach to all creatures, so, after a most special manner, it taketh care of his Church, and disposeth all things to the good thereof.

CHAPTER VI.
Of the Fall of Man, of Sin, and of the Punishment thereof.

I. Our first parents, begin seduced by the subtlety and temptations of Satan, sinned in eating the forbidden fruit. This their sin God was pleased, according to his wise and holy counsel, to permit, having purposed to order it to his own glory.

II. By this sin they fell from their original righteousness and communion with God, and so became dead in sin, and wholly defiled in all the faculties and parts of soul and body.

III. They being the root of mankind, the guilt of this sin was imputed, and the same death in sin and corrupted nature conveyed to all their posterity, descending from them by original generation.

IV. From this original corruption, whereby we are utterly indisposed, disabled, and made opposite to all good, and wholly inclined to all evil, do proceed all actual transgressions.

V. This corruption of nature, during this life, doth remain in those that are regenerated; and although it be through Christ pardoned and mortified, yet both itself, and all the motions thereof, are truly and properly sin.

VI. Every sin, both original and actual, being a transgression of the righteous law of God, and contrary thereunto, doth, in its own nature, bring guilt upon the sinner, whereby he is bound over to the wrath of God, and curse of the law, and so made subject to death, with all miseries spiritual, temporal, and eternal.

CHAPTER VII.
Of God's Covenant with Man.

I. The distance between God and the creature is so great, that although reasonable creatures do owe obedience unto him as their Creator, yet they could never have any fruition of him, as their blessedness and reward, but by some voluntary condescension on God's part, which he hath been pleased to express by way of covenant.

II. The first covenant made with man was a covenant of works, wherein life was promised to Adam, and in him to his posterity, upon condition of perfect and personal obedience.

III. Man by his fall having made himself incapable of life by that covenant, the Lord was pleased to make a second, commonly called the covenant of grace: wherein he freely offered unto sinners life and salvation by Jesus Christ, requiring of them faith in him, that they may be saved, and promising to give unto all those that are ordained unto life, his Holy Spirit, to make them willing and able to believe.

IV. This covenant of grace is frequently set forth in the Scripture by the name of a testament, in reference to the death of Jesus Christ, the testator, and to the everlasting inheritance, with all things belonging to it, therein bequeathed.

V. This covenant was differently administered in the time of the law, and in the time of the gospel: under the law it was administered by promises, prophecies, sacrifices, circumcision, the paschal lamb, and other types and ordinances delivered to the people of the Jews, all fore-signifying Christ to come, which were for that time sufficient and efficacious, through the operation of the Spirit, to instruct and build up the elect in faith in the promised Messiah, by whom they had full remission of sins, and eternal salvation, and is called the Old Testament.

VI. Under the gospel, when Christ the substance was exhibited, the ordinances in which this covenant is dispensed, are the preaching of the Word, and the administration of the sacraments of Baptism and the Lord's Supper; which, though fewer in number, and administered with more simplicity and less outward glory, yet in them it is held forth in more fullness, evidence, and spiritual efficacy, to all nations, both Jews and Gentiles; and is called the New Testament. There are not, therefore, two covenants of grace differing in substance, but one and the same under various dispensations.

CHAPTER VIII.
Of Christ the Mediator.

I. It pleased God, in his eternal purpose, to choose and ordain the Lord Jesus, his only-begotten Son, to be the Mediator between God and men, the prophet, priest, and king; the head and Savior of the Church, the heir or all things, and judge of the world; unto whom he did, from all eternity, give a people to be his seed, and to be by him in time redeemed, called, justified, sanctified, and glorified.

II. The Son of God, the second Person in the Trinity, being very and eternal God, of one substance, and equal with the Father, did, when the fullness of time was come, take upon him man's nature, with all the essential properties and common infirmities thereof; yet without sin: being conceived by he power of the Holy Ghost, in the womb of the Virgin Mary, of her substance. So that two whole, perfect, and distinct natures, the Godhead and the manhood, were inseparably joined together in one person, without conversion, composition, or confusion. Which person is very God and very man, yet one Christ, the only Mediator between God and man.

III. The Lord Jesus in his human nature thus united to the divine, was sanctified and anointed with the Holy Spirit above measure; having in him all the treasures of wisdom and knowledge, in whom it pleased the Father that all fullness should dwell: to the end that being holy, harmless, undefiled, and full of grace and truth, he might be thoroughly furnished to execute the office of a Mediator and Surety. Which office he took not unto himself, but was thereunto called by his Father; who put all power and judgment into his hand, and gave him commandment to execute the same.

IV. This office the Lord Jesus did most willingly undertake, which, that he might discharge, he was made under the law, and did perfectly fulfill it; endured most grievous torments immediately in his soul, and most painful sufferings in his body; was crucified and died; was buried, and remained under the power of death, yet saw no corruption. On the third day he arose from the dead, with the same body in which he suffered; with which also he ascended into heaven, and there sitteth at the right hand of his Father, making intercession; and shall return to judge men and angels, at the end of the world.

V. The Lord Jesus, by his perfect obedience and sacrifice of himself, which he through the eternal Spirit once offered up unto God, hath fully satisfied the justice of his Father; and purchased not only reconciliation, but an everlasting inheritance in the kingdom of heaven, for all those whom the Father hath given unto him.

VI. Although the work of redemption was not actually wrought by Christ till after his incarnation, yet the virtue, efficacy, and benefits thereof were communicated into the elect, in all ages successively from the beginning of the world, in and by those promises, types, and sacrifices wherein he was revealed, and signified to be the seed of the woman, which should bruise the serpent's head, and the Lamb slain from the beginning of the world, being yesterday and today the same and for ever.

VII. Christ, in the work of mediation, acteth according to both natures; by each nature doing that which is proper to itself; yet by reason of the unity of the person, that which is proper to one nature is sometimes, in Scripture, attributed to the person denominated by the other nature.

VIII. To all those for whom Christ hath purchased redemption, he doth certainly and effectually apply and communicate the same; making intercession for them, and revealing unto them, in and by the Word, the mysteries of salvation; effectually persuading them by his Spirit to believe and obey; and governing their hearts by his Word and Spirit; overcoming all their enemies by his almighty power and wisdom, in such manner and ways as are most consonant to his wonderful and unsearchable dispensation.

CHAPTER IX.
Of Free Will.

I. God hath endued the will of man with that natural liberty, that is neither forced, nor by any absolute necessity of nature determined to good or evil.

II. Man, in his state of innocency, had freedom and power to will and to do that which is good and well-pleasing to God; but yet mutably, so that he might fall from it.

III. Man, by his fall into a state of sin, hath wholly lost all ability of will to any spiritual good accompanying salvation; so as a natural man, being altogether averse from that good, and dead in sin, is not able, by his own strength, to convert himself, or to prepare himself thereunto.

IV. When God converts a sinner and translates him into the state of grace, he freeth him from his natural bondage under sin, and, by his grace alone, enables him freely to will and to do that which is spiritually good; yet so as that, by reason of his remaining corruption, he doth not perfectly, nor only, will that which is good, but doth also will that which is evil.

V. The will of man is made perfectly and immutable free to good alone, in the state of glory only.

CHAPTER X.
Of Effectual Calling.

I. All those whom God hath predestinated unto life, and those only, he is pleased, in his appointed and accepted time, effectually to call, by his Word and Spirit, out of that state of sin and death in which they are by nature, to grace and salvation by Jesus Christ: enlightening their minds, spiritually and savingly, to understand the things of God, taking away their heart of stone, and giving unto them an heart of flesh; renewing their wills, and by his almighty power determining them to that which is good; and effectually drawing them to Jesus Christ; yet so as they come most freely, being made willing by his grace.

II. This effectual call is of God's free and special grace alone, not from any thing at all foreseen in man, who is altogether passive therein, until, being quickened and renewed by the Holy Spirit, he is thereby enabled to answer this call, and to embrace the grace offered and conveyed in it.

III. Elect infants, dying in infancy, are regenerated and saved by Christ through the Spirit, who worketh when, and where, and how he pleaseth. So also are all other elect persons who are incapable of being outwardly called by the ministry of the Word.

IV. Others, not elected, although they may be called by the ministry of the Word, and may have some common operations of the Spirit, yet they never truly come to Christ, and therefore can not be saved: much less can men, not professing the Christian religion, be saved in any other way whatsoever, be they never so diligent to frame their lives according to the light of nature, and the law of that religion they do profess; and to assert and maintain that they may is without warrant of the Word of God.

CHAPTER XI.
Of Justification.

I. Those whom God effectually calleth, he also freely justifieth: not by infusing righteousness into them, but by pardoning their sins, and by accounting and accepting their persons as righteous; not for any thing wrought in them, or done by them, but for Christ's sake alone; not by imputing faith itself, the act of believing, or any other evangelical obedience to them, as their righteousness; but by imputing the obedience and satisfaction of Christ unto them, they receiving and resting on him and his righteousness by faith; which faith they have not of themselves, it is the gift of God.

II. Faith, thus receiving and resting on Christ and his righteousness, is the alone instrument of justification; yet is it not alone in the person justified, but is ever accompanied with all other saving graces, and is no dead faith, but worketh by love.

III. Christ, by his obedience and death, did fully discharge the debt of all those that are thus justified, and did make a proper, real, and full satisfaction of his Father's justice in their behalf. Yet inasmuch as he was given by the Father for them, and his obedience and satisfaction accepted in their stead, and both freely, not for any thing in them, their justification is only of free grace, that both the exact justice and rich grace of God might be glorified in the justification of sinners.

IV. God did, from all eternity, decree to justify the elect; and Christ did, in the fullness of time, die for their sins and rise again for their justification; nevertheless they are not justified until the Holy Spirit doth, in due time, actually apply Christ unto them.

V. God doth continue to forgive the sins of those that are justified; and although they can never fall from the state of justification, yet they may by their sins fall under God's Fatherly displeasure, and not have the light of his countenance restored unto them, until they humble themselves, confess their sins, beg pardon, and renew their faith and repentance.

VI. The justification of believers under the Old Testament was, in all these respect, one and the same with the justification of believers under the New Testament.

CHAPTER XII.
Of Adoption.

All those that are justified, God vouchsafeth, in and for his only Son Jesus Christ, to make partakers of the grace of adoption: by which they are taken into the number, and enjoy the liberties and privileges of the children of God; have his name put upon them; receive the Spirit of adoption; have access to the throne of grace with boldness; are enabled to cry, Abba, Father; are pitied, protected, provided for, and chastened by his as by a father; yet never cast off, but sealed to the day of redemption, and inherit the promises, as heirs of everlasting salvation.

CHAPTER XIII.
Of Sanctification.

I. They who are effectually called and regenerated, having a new heart and a new spirit created in them, are further sanctified, really and personally, through the virtue of Christ's death and resurrection, by his Word and Spirit dwelling in them; the dominion of the whole body of sin is destroyed, and the several lusts thereof are more and more weakened and mortified, and they more and more quickened and strengthened, in all saving graces, to the practice of true holiness, without which no man shall see the Lord.

II. This sanctification is throughout in the whole man, yet imperfect in this life: there abideth still some remnants of corruption in every part, whence ariseth a continual and irreconcilable war, the flesh lusting against the Spirit, and the Spirit against the flesh.

III. In which war, although the remaining corruption for a time may much prevail, yet, through the continual supply of strength from the sanctifying Spirit of Christ, the regenerate part doth overcome: and so the saints grow in grace, perfecting holiness in the fear of God.

CHAPTER XIV.
Of Saving Faith.

I. The grace of faith, whereby the elect are enabled to believe to the saving of their souls, is the work of the Spirit of Christ in their hearts; and is ordinarily wrought by the ministry of the Word: by which also, and by the administration of the sacraments, and prayer, it is increased and strengthened.

II. By this faith, a Christian believeth to be true whatsoever is revealed in the Word, for the authority of God himself speaking therein; and acteth differently, upon that which each particular passage thereof containeth; yielding obedience to the commands, trembling at the threatenings, and embracing the promises of God for this life, and that which is to come. But the principle acts of saving faith are, accepting, receiving, and resting upon Christ alone for justification, sanctification, and eternal life, by virtue of the covenant of grace.

III. This faith is different in degrees, weak or strong; may be often and many ways assailed and weakened, but gets the victory; growing up in many to the attainment of a full assurance through Christ, who is both the author and finisher of our faith.

CHAPTER XV.
Of Repentance unto Life.

I. Repentance unto life is an evangelical grace, the doctrine whereof is to be preached by every minister of the gospel, as well as that of faith in Christ.

II. By it a sinner, out of the sight and sense, not only of the danger, but also of the filthiness and odiousness of his sins, as contrary to the holy nature and righteous law of God, and upon the apprehension of his mercy in Christ to such as are penitent, so grieves for, and hates his sins, as to turn from them all unto God, purposing and endeavoring to walk with him in all the ways of his commandments.

III. Although repentance be not to be rested in as any satisfaction for sin, or any cause of the pardon thereof, which is the act of God's free grace in Christ; yet is it of such necessity to all sinners, that none may expect pardon without it.

IV. As there is no sin so small but it deserves damnation; so there is no sin so great that it can bring damnation upon those who truly repent.

V. Men ought not to content themselves with a general repentance, but it is every man's duty to endeavor to repent of his particular sins, particularly.

VI. As every man is bound to make private confession of his sins to God, praying for the pardon thereof, upon which, and the forsaking of them, he shall find mercy: so he that scandalizeth his brother, or the Church of Christ, ought to be willing, by a private or public confession and sorrow for his sin, to declare his repentance to those that are offended; who are thereupon to be reconciled to him, and in love to receive him.

CHAPTER XVI.
Of Good Works.

I. Good works are only such as God hath commanded in his holy Word, and not such as, without the warrant thereof, are devised by men out of blind zeal, or upon any pretense of good intention.

II. These good works, done in obedience to God's commandments, are the fruits and evidences of a true and lively faith: and by them believers manifest their thankfulness, strengthen their assurance, edify their brethren, adorn the profession of the gospel, stop the mouths of the adversaries, and glorify God, whose workmanship they are, created in Christ Jesus thereunto, that, having their fruit unto holiness, they may have the end, eternal life.

III. Their ability to do good works is not at all of themselves, but wholly from the Spirit of Christ. And that they may be enabled thereunto, besides the graces they have already received, there is required an actual influence of the same Holy Spirit to work in them to will and to do of his good pleasure; yet are they not hereupon to grow negligent, as if they were not bound to perform any duty unless upon a special motion of the Spirit; but they ought to be diligent in stirring up the grace of God that is in them.

IV. They, who in their obedience, attain to the greatest height which is possible in this life, are so far from being able to supererogate and to do more than God requires, that they fall short of much which in duty they are bound to do.

V. We can not, by our best works, merit pardon of sin, or eternal life, at the hand of God, because of the great disproportion that is between them and the glory to come, and the infinite distance that is between us and God, whom by them we can neither profit, nor satisfy for the debt of our former sins; but when we have done all we can, we have done but our duty, and are unprofitable servants: and because, as they are good, they proceed from his Spirit; and as they are wrought by us, they are defiled and mixed with so much weakness and imperfection that they can not endure the severity of God's judgment.

VI. Yet notwithstanding, the persons of believers being accepted through Christ, their good works also are accepted in him, not as though they were in this life wholly unblamable and unreprovable in God's sight; but that he, looking upon them in his Son, is pleased to accept and reward that which is sincere, although accompanied with many weaknesses and imperfections.

VII. Works done by unregenerate men, although for the matter of them they may be things which God commands, and of good use both to themselves and others; yet, because they proceed not from a heart purified by faith; nor are done in a right manner, according to the Word; nor to a right end, the glory of God; they are therefore sinful and can not please God, or make a man meet to receive grace from God. And yet their neglect of them is more sinful, and displeasing unto God.

CHAPTER XVII.
Of The Perseverance of the Saints.

I. They whom God hath accepted in his Beloved, effectually called and sanctified by his Spirit, can neither totally nor finally fall away from the state of grace; but shall certainly persevere therein to the end, and be eternally saved.

II. This perseverance of the saints depends, not upon their own free-will, but upon the immutability of the decree of election, flowing from the free and unchangeable love of God the Father; upon the efficacy of the merit and intercession of Jesus Christ; the abiding of the Spirit and of the seed of God within them; and the nature of the covenant of grace; from all which ariseth also the certainty and infallibility thereof.

III. Nevertheless they may, through the temptations of Satan and of the world, the prevalancy of corruption remaining in them, and the neglect of the means of their perseverance, fall into grievous sins; ad for a time continue therein: whereby they incur God's displeasure, and grieve his Holy Spirit; come to be deprived of some measure of their graces and comforts; have their hearts hardened, and their consciences wounded; hurt and prevalancy others, and bring temporal judgments upon themselves.

CHAPTER XVIII.
Of the Assurance of Grace and Salvation.

I. Although hypocrites, and other unregenerate men, may vainly deceive themselves with false hopes and carnal presumptions: of being in the favor of God and estate of salvation; which hope of theirs shall perish: yet such as truly believe in the Lord Jesus, and love him in sincerity, endeavoring to walk in all good conscience before him, may in this life be certainly assured that they are in a state of grace, and may rejoice in the hope of the glory of God: which hope shall never make them ashamed.

II. This certainty is not a bare conjectural and probably persuasion, grounded upon a fallible hope; but an infallible assurance of faith, founded upon the divine truth of the promises of salvation, the inward evidence of those graces unto which these promises are made, the testimony of the Spirit of adoption witnessing with our spirits that we are the children of God; which Spirit is the earnest of our inheritance, whereby we are sealed to the day of redemption.

III. This infallible assurance doth not so belong to the essence of faith but that a true believer may wait long and conflict with many difficulties before he be partaker of it: yet, being enabled by the Spirit to know the things which are freely given him of God, he may, without extraordinary revelation, in the right use of ordinary means, attain thereunto. And therefore it is the duty of everyone to give all diligence to make his calling and election sure; that thereby his heart may be enlarged in peace and joy in the Holy Ghost, in love and thankfulness to God, and in strength and cheerfulness in the duties of obedience, the proper fruits of this assurance: so far is it from inclining men to looseness.

IV. True believers may have the assurance of their salvation divers ways shaken, diminished, and intermitted; as, by negligence in preserving of it; by falling into some special sin, which woundeth the conscience, and grieveth the Spirit; by some sudden or vehement temptation; by God's withdrawing the light of his countenance and suffering even such as fear him to walk in darkness and to have no light: yet are they never utterly destitute of that seed of God, and life of faith, that love of Christ and the brethren, that sincerity of heart and conscience of duty, out of which, by the operation of the Spirit, this assurance may in due time be revived, and by the which, in the meantime, they are supported from utter despair.

> **GLOSSARY**
>
> **Abba:** a name infrequently used in the Bible to refer to God the Father
>
> **Apocrypha:** any of the various Bible-like books that, for various reasons, are not accepted as scriptural
>
> **divers:** diverse, assorted
>
> **justification:** in Christian theology, God's act of declaring or making a sinner righteous before God
>
> **Lamb:** Christ
>
> **paschal lamb:** a lamb the Israelites were to eat with particular rites as part of the Passover celebration; generally regarded as a prefiguration of Christ
>
> **supererogate:** to perform more than a required duty or more than is asked for
>
> **Surety:** guarantor; in Christian theology, the concept that Christ functioned as a surety for undeserving sinners by dying for their sins
>
> **vouchsafeth:** to grant a right, benefit, or outcome

Document Analysis

The Westminster Confession was meant to be a complete treatment of the major issues of Christian theology. The authors strove for clarity and logic, as befits what was meant to be a definitive doctrinal statement, not a piece of speculative theology.

Chapter I.
One of the fundamental principles of the Protestant Reformation was *sola scriptura*—the Bible as the sole source of Christian truth. This principle denied the Catholic belief that the "tradition of the church," independent of the Bible, supplemented it as a source of truth. The Westminster Confession supports this principle by dealing with the Bible first of all, even before God. The first chapter also defines exactly what the Bible is by listing the canonical books of the Old and New Testaments, and explicitly excluding the Apocrypha, which Catholics viewed as divinely inspired but to a lesser degree than the canonical books.

Chapter II.
The definition of God was one of the most difficult issues with which the Westminster Assembly grappled. What resulted emphasizes—as the Reformed tradition tends to generally emphasize—God's absoluteness, sovereignty, and utter independence of the created. The doctrine of the Trinity, central to Christian theology, appears almost as an afterthought in this chapter. The Westminster Confession's trinitarianism is in the Western Christian mainstream, endorsing the "double procession" of the Holy Spirit from both the Father and the Son, as opposed to the belief of the Eastern Orthodox Churches that the Spirit proceeds from the Father alone.

Chapter III.
Predestination is the subject of Chapter III. God chose those people and angels who are to be saved and those who are to be damned in eternity, not at a specific moment in time but "before the foundation of the world was laid." This chapter's placement before the chapter on Creation dramatically exemplifies "supralapsarianism," the doctrine that God chose the saved and the damned preceding the Fall of Man in the Garden of Eden. (The idea that God chose the saved and the damned as a logical consequence of the Fall is called "sublapsarianism.") Its early appearance in the Confession also indicates its overall importance to the writers.

Chapter IV.
In Chapter IV, Creation is described as a means of expressing God's glory. The first humans were made with the law of God "written on their hearts," meaning that

they needed no Bible or other external source for the law. Unlike later humans, the first humans had the power to obey God's law but also the freedom of will to choose not to obey.

Chapter V.
Chapter V deals with God's providence, or government of the universe. The concept of providence was central to seventeenth-century Puritan thinking, and the smallest events could be treated as the evidence of God's divine care. The Westminster Confession emphasizes that God's providence can work both within and without what we ordinarily think of as cause and effect. Even the Fall of Man was a working out of God's providence, although this in no way transfers the blame from Adam and Eve to God. The idea that God's omnipotence made him the creator or "author of sin" is one the Westminster writers are very concerned to reject. God's providence is exemplified in exposing both the elect and the regenerated to the temptation of sin, the former to teach them humility and their utter dependence on his grace, the latter to render them still more worthy of damnation. The Confession also points out that the Church is the object of God's particular care.

Chapter VI.
After addressing the subject tangentially in the preceding chapters, the Confession here comes to grips with the Fall of the human being and human bondage to sin. The Fall was caused by the temptation of Satan (one of the devil's few appearances in the Confession) but was ultimately ordained to God's glory. In line with Reformed thinking, the Confession emphasizes humanity's utter bondage to sin following the Fall, as we all inherited the "Original Sin" of our first ancestors, completely unable to do that which is good by our own efforts. Everyone, even the elect, remains subject to sin, and each sin, however trivial it seems, is justly punished by eternal death—the Reformed tradition knows nothing of the Catholic distinction between venial sins (which do not alienate the sinner from God completely) and mortal sins (which deprive the sinner of all grace, figuratively "killing" the soul).

Chapter VII.
This chapter introduces a key concept of Reformed theology as it developed—the Covenant. There are two Covenants governing the relation between God and humanity. With the original Covenant of Works, humans could be granted salvation by their obedience and conformity with God's will. The Covenant of Works was abrogated by Adam's sin. In its place stands another Covenant, the Covenant of Grace, divided into two dispensations, one between God and the Jews in the pre-Christian era and one between God and the Christian Church. In the Covenant of Grace, God offers salvation to those who have faith in Christ. However, salvation is still utterly dependent on God's grace—only the elect, predestined by God, will receive the grace to have faith.

The Covenant of Grace worked differently in the time of the Old Testament and before Christ's coming to Earth—the "time of the law." The elect among the ancient Jews were saved not through explicit faith in the historical figure of Jesus Christ, of whom they knew nothing, but through faith in Jewish ritual practices, all of which prefigured the Messiah, Christ. However, this does not mean that there was a separate covenant operating before Christ; there was one covenant working in two different ways. The coming of Christ ended the earlier operation of the Covenant of Grace. (Chapter X deals with practitioners of religions other than Christianity in the present time, implicitly including the Jews, and states that it is impossible for them to be saved.)

Chapter VIII.
This chapter deals with the central tenet of Christianity—the redemptive mission of Jesus Christ. The Confession's Christology again is in the Western mainstream, describing Jesus as fully man and fully God in the position established by the Council of Chalcedon in 451. Christ's mission on Earth is viewed as a redemptive sacrifice in satisfaction of God's justice, although the Confession avoids the legalism of some interpretations of Christ's redemptive work, such as that of the eleventh-century theologian Anselm's *Cur Deus Homo?* ("Why God Became Man"). Christ's sacrifice applies not to all humankind but only to the elect, "those whom the Father hath given unto him."

Chapter IX.
The Westminster Assembly here endorsed a fundamental Calvinist tenet, the inability of the fallen human being to will anything spiritually good. This does not mean that human beings are unable by their own efforts to will anything "ethically" good, but that these things are irrelevant to salvation. The ability to will the spiritually good, lost by the Fall of Adam and Eve, can be restored only by the grace of God. This is one benefit

God gives, but only to his elect. Although their ability to will the spiritually good is restored, even the elect retain the corruption inherent to all humanity and will continue to will evil as well as good. Only in heaven will the saved will only good.

Chapter X.
A common Reformed belief was in a calling—a time when God made an elect person's status known to him or her. The moment of "calling" was central to the spiritual autobiographies of many Puritans. Calling comes only to the elect, and even for them it comes only at the time of God's choosing—there is nothing the elect can do to prepare themselves for the calling. Even the ability to respond to the calling is a gift of the Holy Spirit. The chapter also speaks of persons who die in infancy (an important issue in early modern societies with a high infant mortality rate), the elect among whom God will save in a way of his choosing. The discussion of infant deaths contains no mention of the sacrament of baptism, in line with the generally secondary role the sacraments play in Reformed theology. (A discussion of the sacraments does not occur until Chapter XXVII.) This chapter also answers the question of whether virtuous persons who are non-Christian can be saved with a firm "no."

Chapter XI.
Chapter XI reaffirms the fundamental Reformation doctrine of justification by faith. There are several important qualifications. Faith is a gift from God to the elect for Christ's sake and not something that can ever be attained by a person's own efforts. Faith is accompanied by other graces, even though these graces are irrelevant to salvation. Once they are saved, the elect can never lose that salvation, but God might still punish them for particular sins.

Chapter XII.
This chapter describes the glory of the elect in heaven through the metaphor of "adoption," which had a long Christian history. The idea of the elect becoming children of God and his love for them helps soften the stern and arbitrary image of God that is common in Reformed theology.

Chapter XIII.
Although the Reformed tradition proclaims that works do not matter in salvation, that does not mean that there is no distinction between the saved and unsaved in terms of their behavior. "Sanctification" is the process whereby the elect are changed in this life through the infusion of God's goodness and holiness in them. Although grace frees the elect from the bondage of sin, in this life they are never entirely freed. The ability to struggle against sinful nature and sometimes to win comes not from one's own strength or virtue but solely from the power of God.

Chapter XIV.
This chapter discusses the origin and impact of saving faith. The Confession is careful not to limit the ways in which faith comes into the hearts of the saved but emphasizes the most common routes by which it enters and is strengthened—preaching (the "Ministry of the Word"), prayer, and sacraments. True faith is followed by obedience to God, though not all the saved are obedient to the same degree. "Strong" and "weak" faith, however, are both saving faith.

Chapter XV.
Saving faith is also followed by repentance. Since everyone is a vile and filthy sinner, everyone with faith should also be struck by horror at the sins they have committed. The article suggests that while in itself repentance cannot save, it should be felt by every saved person. Confessing one's sins is appropriate, but the article is careful not to follow the Catholic model of treating confession to a priest as a sacrament of Penance. Confession should be made to God or to the person or community offended, or to the Church at large, but the ministry is not mentioned as playing any role in hearing people's confessions.

Chapter XVI.
This chapter deals with the complicated topic of good works. The Westminster Assembly, like other Reformed Christians, had to thread a narrow passage between the "Catholic" idea that good works contribute to salvation and the "antinomian" idea that good works are completely irrelevant to the saved. The writers emphasize the importance of good works in glorifying Christ while insisting that the ability to do good works does not come out of our own strength but is instead a gift from God. Once again, they declare that good works are irrelevant to salvation. However, only the saved can do truly good works; even what seem to be the virtuous deeds of the unsaved are not inspired by the right motives or done in the right way, and are therefore not truly good works at all.

Chapter XVII.
The "Perseverance of the Saints," one of the Five Points of Calvinism, is the belief that God's decree of election will never be undone—that the saved person is saved forever. This doctrine could be a powerful source of spiritual comfort for those who thought themselves children of God. However, saved people could still sin grievously, thereby meriting some kind of chastisement from God delivered in this world.

Chapter XVIII.
The assurance of salvation was often a difficult problem for Puritans, who wanted to be assured of their own salvation but also wanted it to be the right kind of assurance, caused by knowledge of God's grace rather than vain hope or overconfidence. In fact, being too certain of one's own salvation could be viewed as evidence that one was not truly saved. The Westminster Confession describes the process by which the elect come to be convinced of their salvation while assuring its readers that doubts and occasional weakening of one's assurance do not mean that one has "lost" it.

Essential Themes
Although the Westminster Confession was designed for the reformation of the Church of England, it ultimately had little impact on that body. After the fall of the parliamentary regime and the restoration of the monarchy and the bishops of the Church of England in 1660, the Church moved steadily away from the Calvinism of the Confession. The Westminster Confession's principal impact was on the Church of Scotland, other Scottish Presbyterian churches, and English Dissenting churches, particularly the Presbyterians. Congregationalists and Particular Baptists also accepted many aspects of Reformed theology, if not Presbyterian Church order; although the specifically Presbyterian components of the Westminster Confession prevented them from adopting it in toto, statements of faith such as the Congregationalist Savoy Declaration of Faith and Order (1658) and the Particular Baptist Confession of Faith (1689) drew heavily from the Westminster Confession.

From the seventeenth to the nineteenth centuries, the reach of the Westminster Confession grew along with that of the British Empire, as Presbyterian, Congregational, and other Reformed churches in the English-speaking world adopted it in whole or in part as a statement of their faith, including churches in Canada, Australia, and New Zealand. As the former British colonies in North America became independent, the Westminster Confession, like many aspects of the British religious tradition, remained a powerful force in shaping the new nation's religion and has been adopted by many American churches. The Presbyterian Synod of Philadelphia adopted it in 1729, followed by the first official Presbyterian denomination in the newly independent United States, the Presbyterian Church of the United States, in 1788. However, the document has been substantially modified to weaken the power of the state over religious belief in the direction of liberty of conscience. A clause denouncing the pope as Antichrist (not reproduced in this excerpt) is also omitted or repudiated by most modern Presbyterians. For America's largest Presbyterian denomination, the Presbyterian Church (USA), the Westminster Confession has been supplanted by the Confession of 1967, although the Westminster Confession, along with the Westminster Larger and Shorter Catechisms, is included in the Church's Book of Confessions. The Presbyterian Church in America, which broke off from the Presbyterian Church (USA) in part as a response to the theological liberalism it identified in the Confession of 1967, continues to use the Westminster Confession with modifications as its standard, as do many other more conservative Presbyterian bodies.

—*William E. Burns*

Bibliography and Further Reading
Coffey, John. *Politics, Religion and the British Revolutions: The Mind of Samuel Rutherford*. Cambridge University Press, 1997.
Leith, John H. *Assembly at Westminster: Reformed Theology in the Making*. John Knox Press, 1973.
Letham, Robert. *The Westminster Assembly: Reading Its Theology in Historical Context*. P & R Publications, 2009.
Rolston, Holmes. *John Calvin versus the Westminster Confession*. John Knox Press, 1972.

Website
Center for Reformed Theology and Apologetics, http://www.reformed.org/index.html.

Charles I: Speech on the Scaffold

Date: 1649
Author: King Charles I
Genre: Declarative speech

Summary Overview

In 1642, long-simmering tensions finally boiled over into war in England, as King Charles I raised an army against his own Parliament in order to re-establish his authority in his kingdom. The division between them was largely religious, as Charles was inclined toward tolerance of all Christian religions, while his parliament was full of Protestant "Puritans" who wanted to purge England of any Catholic elements.

In the resulting English Civil War, Charles's forces were eventually routed, and the king was captured by Puritan forces. However, Charles escaped once and rallied his forces to take on the parliamentary army a second time. Since Charles had proven that he would fight for his kingdom so long as he was alive, the Puritans in Parliament appointed a special court to try Charles for treason. He was convicted and sentenced to death by beheading, the sentence carried out on January 30, 1649.

As was the custom, the king was allowed to make a speech before his execution, although his executioners took steps to keep the crowds too distant to actually hear it. He was accompanied by the clergyman of his choice, Bishop William Juxon of London, a member of the "high church" faction that the king had always supported. Few of the large crowd gathered to witness the execution (which included both supporters and opponents of the king) would have been able to hear him, but his speech on the scaffold was printed shortly afterward and had a major impact in creating the myth of Charles I as a martyr-king.

Defining Moment

When King Charles I began his reign in England, he was greeted as a breath of fresh air, as his father, James I, had died very unpopular. Within a single year, circumstances conspired to make Charles just as unpopular as his father, and set him on the road to civil war with the English Parliament and its contingent of Puritans.

To start, Charles was, as royals go, broke. James had lived extravagantly and depleted the treasury, and not surprisingly, as James's son, Charles was trained and inclined to do the same. Worse, relations had broken down with Parliament over James's spending and his attitude toward monarchy. James and Charles both believed in the "divine right of kings"—that they were the Christian God's representatives on Earth to the kingdoms and peoples of the British Isles, that they were divinely inspired to work in their peoples' interests, and therefore entitled to have their bidding obeyed without question. Such was not the way the English Parliament had operated with the previous century's Tudor monarchs, who had consulted with their parliaments regularly. The Tudors and King Henry VIII had brought the English people out of the Catholic Church to make them members of a new Church of England (called Anglicans) with Henry, and future monarchs, as their religious leader. After the defeat of the Catholic Spanish Armada's invasion force in 1588, to be Protestant in England was to be patriotic: God was clearly Protestant, and liked the English. Part of what made England favored by God amongst all nations was the positive and consultative relationship between the English monarch and the people, through Parliament. James, and now Charles, threatened to destroy that relationship.

Worse, Charles threatened to destroy the Church of England altogether, in the opinion of a number of radical Anglicans who were inspired by Calvinism to purify the Church of England of all its Catholic elements. These "Puritans" feared Charles right away. He was married to the Catholic Henrietta Maria of France, and in deference to her, Charles relaxed penalties against practicing Catholics in England. Since the 1550s, Catholics had persecuted Protestants in England under Queen Mary I, tried to invade with the Spanish Armada, tried to blow up James in the Gunpowder Plot of 1605, and were at that time warring with Protestants on the European continent in the Thirty Years' War. It would hardly be a surprise that any concessions to Catholicism would be viewed warily. In such a climate, the simple wearing of purple robes, the stained-glass windows in churches, the practices in the Church's mass, and the hierarchy of the Church were all actionable issues that angered Puritans with their king, who prized deference and obeisance to his will above all things.

Contemporary German print of Charles I's beheading. Unknown artist.-National Portrait Gallery: NPG D1306. [Public domain], via Wikimedia Commons

The relationship broke down over money. Charles needed tax money to maintain his priorities and his lifestyle; the Puritan-dominated Parliament did not wish to grant him the money he wanted without religious reforms. For eleven years, from 1629 to 1640, Charles refused to call Parliament into session, trying to raise money on his own without consultation from his people's representatives—a tradition dating back to the Magna Carta in 1215. Charles imposed fees on his aristocracy for the use of their lands, sold monopolies to merchants in England and the colonies, and demanded that all counties in England pay for the building and maintenance of the navy. In the meantime, Charles appointed church leaders who maintained his priorities in the Church of England, such as statues and incense in church ceremonies, to the fury of the Puritans, who despised such "popery."

In 1637, Charles's archbishop, William Laud, drew up a new Book of Common Prayer for the Anglican mass ceremony, and Charles decreed that one of his other kingdoms, Presbyterian Scotland, would be forced to use it. In response, Scottish leaders drew up a covenant in which they affirmed their loyalty to Charles as their king but swore they would also defend their Calvinist faith from any encroachment. Charles saw this as a challenge to his authority and sent an army to impose the use of the Book of Common Prayer. The Scots defeated the English army easily, and Charles needed another army and the money to pay it—which he could only attain by calling Parliament into session. Thus, in 1640 Parliament met for the first time in eleven years.

Since they had been out of government for so long, the members of Parliament came to Westminster with a long list of grievances and laws they expected to be addressed before they would grant Charles the money he wanted for any army. Charles was aggravated and dismissed Parliament in a month—but he still needed the money to defeat the Scots, whose army sat on English soil. Charles thus had to call Parliament back into session and listen to their grievances. At the Puritans' insistence, Archbishop William Laud was imprisoned for treason; he would be executed five years later. Charles's top advisor, Thomas Wentworth, lord deputy of Ireland and Earl of Strafford, was executed for suggesting that Charles had an army in Ireland which he might use to subdue Parliament at home in England.

Finally, a Catholic rebellion broke out in Ireland in 1641. Now Charles needed an army to put down yet another challenge to his rule—but the Puritans in Parliament would not grant it to him for fear he would turn it on them. Enraged, Charles entered the House of Commons with soldiers to arrest five members of Parliament on charges of treason. Tipped off, none of the five were there, but Charles had committed an unpardonable violation of the governing traditions that the English people held dear. After some negotiations, both sides raised armies in the summer of 1642, and England descended into civil war.

The English Civil War was a stop-start affair, with battles coming together and armies falling away as the two sides negotiated for peace in between. More than once, Charles agreed to a tentative peace; each time, Charles continued the march of his armies, violating the principle of any future peace. He negotiated peace with the Irish Catholic rebels, thus undermining his reputation in Protestant England, especially with the Puritans. When the Scottish army in the north joined with the parliamentary army to chase down Charles's armies, the tide began to turn against him. In 1646, he surrendered to the Scots at the town of Southwell.

Negotiations opened for a new relationship between king and parliament, this one defined in print. Charles was handed over to Parliament in 1647. While parliamentarians, Puritans, and soldiers argued over what the new constitution would look like, Charles escaped from his house arrest at Hampton Court. He was arrested again on the Isle of Wight, but he negotiated secretly with the Scots to have them switch sides and allow him to retake his throne. The civil war began again as royalists were newly inspired to fight for their monarch, but the parliamentary army easily put down all of the king's supporters.

Since it had become obvious that Charles could not be trusted under any capacity to abide by any agreement he made for peace, religion, or political power, the House of Commons put him on trial before a specially appointed High Court of Justice in January 1649. Charles was convicted of treason and sentenced to be executed on January 30, 1649.

Author Biography

Charles I, king of England, Wales, Scotland, and Ireland, was a member of the Scottish Stuart family, first cousins of the Tudor Queen Elizabeth I of England. His father, then James VI of Scotland, inherited the English throne when Elizabeth died in 1603, bringing the two nations and their states together under one monarch. Territorially the most powerful family in the history of the British Isles to that time, the Stuarts were also the most ill-fated clan in British history, and Charles was the most star-crossed of them all, if his difficulties proved largely to be of his own making.

Charles was born in Scotland on November 19, 1600, James's second son. His older brother Henry was expected to inherit the throne, but he died of typhus in 1612, leaving the preteen Charles as his father's heir. When James died, Charles ascended to the thrones of the four nations at the age of 25. He married Queen Henrietta Maria of Portugal, and the marriage was comparatively positive in nature, but the queen was always suspect to the English people for her Catholicism. Charles himself was personally imposing, of a tall and haughty bearing, which did not help in his relations with his subjects or his court. One of his few friends, the Duke of Buckingham, was so brazen in his insistence that Parliament obey its monarch that he was assassinated in 1628. Buckingham's death only soured Charles's relationship with his people all the more. He got along badly with Parliament already, and a year later, he dismissed them altogether to attempt to run England all by himself.

At first, Charles's dismissal of the religious concerns of the Puritans and other Protestant sects led many of them to sail to America. It says something for his equal opportunity offensiveness that many Catholics fled England, too, for the colony of Lord Baltimore in North America, later Maryland, named for Henrietta Maria. As the 1630s continued without a Parliament, however, more of the Puritans stayed home in England to challenge their monarch and save what they considered to be their Protestant church. The Scottish Presbyterian uprising against the Book of Common Prayer had the sympathy of the Puritans against Charles; the Catholic Irish rebellion inspired only fear that Charles would use any army sent to suppress it to march on Parliament itself. These negative opinions of Charles's bearing and reign should have been signs to him of the need to improve his relations with his charges—instead, they only reinforced his need to subdue his subjects to his own divinely inspired will.

The English Civil War brought out the worst in Charles. Typical of his aloofness was the fact that he sent only a single statement to all of his colonists in North America, demanding their support; the Puritans in Parliament, on the other hand, expanded trade with the northern colonies and blockaded Virginia against the king's receiving any supplies from overseas to help in the war. Charles's defeat brought out his duplicity, assuring his enemies that he could never be trusted to sit on the throne ever again. He was tried for treason, found guilty, and beheaded on January 30, 1649. He left behind his wife, Henrietta Maria, and six of his children, one of whom, Charles, would try to establish himself on the Scottish throne after his father's death; he would eventually become the restored Charles II. Another son, the future James II, moved to France and converted to the Catholicism of his French patron, Louis XIV; he would also end up being run off the throne in 1688, this time to keep his head, however.

HISTORICAL DOCUMENT

Charles I: Speech on the Scaffold

I shall be very little heard of anybody here; I shall therefore speak a word unto you here.

Indeed I could hold my peace very well, if I did not think that holding my peace would make some men think that I did submit to the guilt as well as to the punishment. But I think it is my duty to God first and to my country for to clear myself both as an honest man and a good King, and a good Christian.

I shall begin first with my innocence.

In troth I think it not very needful for me to insist long upon this, for all the world knows that I never did begin a war with the two Houses of Parliament. And I call God to witness, to whom I must shortly make an account, that I never did intend for to encroach upon their privileges. They began upon me. It is the Militia they began upon; they confest that the Militia was mine, but they thought it fit for to have it from me. And, to be short, if anybody will look to the dates of Commissions, of their commissions and mine, and likewise to the Declarations, [they] will see clearly that they began these unhappy troubles, not I. So that as the guilt of these enormous crimes that are laid against me I hope in God that God will clear me of it.

I will not. I am in charity. God forbid that I should lay it upon the two Houses of Parliament; there is no necessity of either. I hope that they are free of this guilt. For I do believe that ill instruments between them and me has been the chief cause of all this bloodshed. So that, by way of speaking, as I find myself clear of this, I hope (and pray God) that they may too. Yet, for all this, God forbid that I should be so ill a Christian as not to say God's judgments are just upon me. Many times he does pay justice by an unjust sentence; that is ordinary. I will only say this, that an unjust sentence that I suffered for to take effect, is punished now by an unjust sentence upon me. That is, so far as I have said, to show you that I am an innocent man.

Now for to show you that I am a good Christian. I hope there is [pointing to Dr. Juxon] a good man that will bear me witness that I have forgiven all the world, and even those in particular that have been the chief causes of my death. Who they are, God knows. I do not desire to know. God forgive them.

But this is not all; my charity must go further. I wish that they may repent, for indeed they have committed a great sin in that particular. I pray God, with St. Stephen, that this be not laid to their charge. Nay, not only so, but that they may take the right way to the peace of the kingdom, for my charity commands me not only to forgive particular men, but my charity commands me to endeavour to the last gasp the Peace of the Kingdom. So, Sirs, I do wish with all my soul, and I do hope there is some here [turning to some gentlemen that wrote] that will carry it further, that they may endeavour the peace of the Kingdom.

Now, Sirs, I must show you both how you are out of the way and will put you in a way. First, you are out of the way, for certainly all the way you have ever had yet, as I could find by anything, is by way of conquest. Certainly this is an ill way, for conquest, Sir, in my opinion, is never just, except that there be a good just cause, either for matter of wrong or just title. And then if you go beyond it, the first quarrel that you have to it, that makes it unjust at the end that was just at the first. But if it be only matter of conquest, there is a great robbery; as a Pirate said to Alexander that he was the great robber, he was but a petty robber; and so, Sir, I do think the way that you are in is much out of the way. Now, Sir, for to put you in the way. Believe it you will never do right, nor God will never prosper you, until you give God his due, the King his due (that is, my successors) and the People their due; I am as much for them as any of you. You must give God his due by regulating rightly His Church (according to the Scripture) which is now out of order. For to set you in a way particularly now I cannot, but only this. A national synod freely called, freely debating among themselves, must settle this, when that every opinion is freely and clearly heard.

For the King, indeed I will not … (then turning to a gentleman that touched the Ax, said, "Hurt not the ax, that may hurt me," meaning if he did blunt the edge). For the King, the laws of the land will clearly instruct you for that. Therefore because it concerns my own particular, I only give you a touch of it.

For the people. And truly I desire their liberty and freedom as much as anybody whomsoever. But I must tell you that their liberty and freedom consists in having of government those laws by which their life and their goods may be most their own. It is not for having share in government, Sir; that is nothing pertaining to them. A subject and a sovereign are clean different things; and therefore until they do that, I mean, that you do put the people in that liberty as I say, certainly they will never enjoy themselves.

Sirs, it was for this that now I am come here. If I would have given way to an arbitrary way, for to have all laws changed according to the power of the sword I needed not to have come here. And, therefore, I tell you, and I pray God it be not laid to your charge, that I am the martyr of the people.

In troth, Sirs, I shall not hold you much longer, for I will only say thus to you. That in truth I could have desired some little time longer, because I would have put then that I have said in a little more order, and a little better digested than I have done. And, therefore, I hope that you will excuse me.

I have delivered my conscience. I pray God that you do take those courses that are best for the good of the Kingdom and your own salvations.

Dr. Juxon: Will Your Majesty, though it may be very well known Your Majesty's affections to religion, yet it may be expected that you should say somewhat for the world's satisfaction.

King: I thank you very heartily, my lord, for that I had almost forgotten it. In truth, sirs, my conscience in religion, I think is very well known to all the world. And therefore I declare before you all that I die a Christian according to the profession of the Church of England as I found it left me by my father. And this honest man (pointing to Dr. Juxon) I think will witness it.

Then turning to the officers, the King said: Sirs, excuse me for this same. I have a good cause, and I have a gracious God. I will say no more. … I go from a corruptible to an incorruptible crown, where no disturbance can be, no disturbance in the world.

Document Analysis

Charles's goals in his speech on the scaffold were twofold: to demonstrate a proper attitude for a Christian facing death and to vindicate his conduct in the English Civil War, perhaps laying the ground for a restoration of his children. Charles puts himself in the Christian tradition of martyrdom, even referring to himself as "the martyr of the people." He links himself with Saint Stephen, the "proto-martyr," the first, according to Christian legend, to die for the faith of Jesus. As a Christian, it was vitally important for Charles to forgive his enemies. Rather than blaming his judges, he claims that the true cause of the dissensions of the realm was neither himself nor Parliament but unnamed and unknown "ill instruments." He even forgives these persons, whose identities neither he nor his hearers knew, and he prays for their repentance.

Repentance was also important for the dying person, and Charles's protestations of innocence might be taken as showing a proud and unrepentant disposition. Charles deals with this potential line of criticism by being careful to distinguish between the unjust earthly authorities who passed judgment on him and the justice of God. He claims that his unjust execution is a punishment for his having previously allowed the execution of Thomas Wentworth, Earl of Strafford. Strafford is unnamed (in the words "an unjust sentence that I suffered for to take effect"), but the reference was clear.

Charles denies any responsibility for the Civil War, presenting himself as one who defended himself in a war that Parliament had begun. He claims that the dates on the commissions that both he and Parliament had sent to raise troops show that Parliament, not the king, had begun the war. He uses an anecdote he probably read in a medieval English poem to describe the relationship between himself and Parliament: Alexander the Great admonishing a pirate for stealing at sea, with the pirate retorting that, because Alexander was an emperor, Alexander got to steal from the whole world. Charles wanted to deny the charge frequently made against him, that he wished to govern without law. He does not claim that as king he was not bound by law, but he argues that he always respected it. The trouble was not caused by Charles's encroachment on the bounds of law but by evil men who had usurped a royal authority that was not theirs. He presents himself as a defender of the freedom of the subject, but this freedom did not extend to having a share in government. "A subject and a sovereign are clean different things."

Although the king accepted his own death, he did not view the Royalist cause as lost, and part of the speech is devoted to pleading with his people to restore the proper form of government. Charles paints a portrait of contemporary England—his other kingdoms, Ireland and Scotland, are not referred to in the speech—as a kingdom "out of the way," in which his own legitimate authority has been overthrown by authority based on naked power—"conquest" which is only a "great robbery." To remedy this situation, England must restore Charles's son, his "successor," the boy Prince Charles, then safely in exile with his mother, Queen Henrietta Maria. England must also restore the right "order" of the Church. Charles supported the traditional Church of England with its hierarchy of bishops, but this form of church organization, strongly identified with the Royalist cause, had been overthrown in the Civil War. Charles concludes his speech by claiming the assurance of salvation, the "incorruptible crown."

Essential Themes

Unlike with the French Revolution a century and a half later, the death of the monarch in England was met with dismay by the crowd of observers around the scaffold. A wail went up from the audience; nations did not go around executing the monarchs who allegedly represented their interests before God. Nevertheless, the Puritans in Parliament—always representing a minority of Anglicans in England—settled in to govern without a king. The four British nations would now be united as a republic, or as the Puritans styled it, the "Commonwealth."

The popular hero of the English Civil War was Oliver Cromwell, the general in command of Parliament's New Model Army when the war ended. Cromwell organized the court to try Charles, and he became the de facto leader of the Commonwealth, later taking the title "Lord Protector." From 1649 to 1652, he led armies to subdue the Irish and the Scots to his rule. He renewed an old series of medieval laws called the Navigation Acts to ensure that the colonies in North America and the Caribbean traded only with England. Yet he was unable to subdue the religious radicals in the House of Commons, who squabbled incessantly over how to turn the Commonwealth into a godly state. In 1653 he dismissed the government, and his army officers chose 144 of the most saintly men in England to sit in the Commons. These men wrote up a constitution, the Instrument of Government, to unite the governments of

England, Wales, Scotland, and Ireland under Cromwell as the Lord Protector for life. When the new parliament was called, it squabbled as much as the old one, now over the meaning of the terms in the Instrument of Government. Cromwell gave up and divided England amongst his Puritan generals.

The new government of the generals imposed Puritan moral standards on the people of England, whether they agreed with those standards or not. Sundays were to be observed as the Lord's Day, but all other religious holidays such as Christmas and Easter were abandoned as being too Catholic. Plays, drunkenness, swearing, arguing, and gambling were all banned. Adultery was a death sentence. Swearing and cursing brought fines. Blasphemy—however the Puritans defined it—was punished with imprisonment. People despised these laws, and longed for an end to the rule of the generals and a return to the normality of monarchy. A new constitution was written, but the same men served in it and argued as much as they ever had, now over land redistribution. Cromwell was offered the crown but refused it.

Finally, Cromwell died in September 1658. His son Richard succeeded him as Lord Protector but had none of the support from the army that his father had as a general. As parliament and the army fell into arguing about the godly future of the British state, the four nations lapsed into anarchy, and Richard Cromwell resigned. No one succeeded him. Finally, in 1660, General George Monck took control and called for a new election to Parliament; when it met, Monck called for its members to ask for the restoration of the Stuart monarchy. In the Declaration of Breda, Charles I's son, also named Charles, promised general pardons and religious freedom, and allowed that parliamentary laws would be obeyed. In May 1660, Parliament invited Charles II to reclaim the throne. The British monarchy has remained in place ever since.

—William E. Burns

Bibliography and Further Reading

Clarendon, Edward Hyde, Earl of. *History of the Rebellion and Civil Wars in England Begun in the Year 1641.* Oxford University Press, 2009.

Cressy, David. *Charles I and the People of England.* Oxford University Press, 2015.

Hunt, Tristram. *The English Civil War at First Hand.* Penguin, 2011.

Spencer, Charles Spencer, Earl. *Killers of the King: The Men Who Dared to Execute Charles I.* Bloomsbury Press, 2014.

White, Peter O.G. *Predestination, Policy and Polemic: Conflict and Consensus in the English Church from the Reformation to the Civil War.* Cambridge University Press, 1992.

Websites

"Charles I (r. 1625-1649)." *The Royal Encyclopedia—The British Monarchy,* https://www.royal.uk/charles-i-r-1625-1649. Accessed 4 Apr. 2017.

"Civil War and Revolution." *BBC—History,* http://www.bbc.co.uk/history/british/civil_war_revolution/. Accessed 4 Apr. 2017.

■ Thomas Hobbes: *Leviathan*

Date: 1651
Author: Thomas Hobbes
Genre: Philosophical tract

Summary Overview

Thomas Hobbes (1588–1679) was a hugely influential and controversial philosopher and political theorist. His *Leviathan* (1651) is frequently deemed to be the greatest work of political theory written in the English language. Its impact on global political thought has been immeasurable, influencing many subsequent philosophers as well as the American Declaration of Independence (1776) and the French Declaration of the Rights of Man and of the Citizen (1789). The work's discussion of society and the creation and nature of government was a response to the destructive division experienced during the English Civil War (1642–1651). Hobbes's response was to imagine the creation of an absolute government that would prevent such damaging internal state conflict while shaping government and society under the power of one sovereign.

Defining Moment

The English Civil War began in 1642, the climax of the most turbulent era in English history. Charles I conflicted with his own parliament over political rights and traditions, constitutional policy, religion, and social distinctions. He was opposed by religious radicals like the Puritans, who were not in a majority in the population but dominated the House of Commons. Most people instead were irritated with the religious hysteria of the day, disliking both the haughty hierarchical dictation coming from Charles and his ecclesiastical order, and the wild-eyed Protestant communitarianism issuing from Parliament and its allies. Thomas Hobbes—in temperament a royalist but also a religious moderate—was the voice of these people.

After attending Oxford, Hobbes worked for William Cavendish, the Earl of Devonshire, a devoted royal servant; he would work on and off for the Cavendish family for most of his life. While looking for tutorial work, he translated the great Athenian general Thucydides' *History of the Peloponnesian Wars*. Athens lost the Peloponnesian Wars with Sparta; Thucydides blamed democracy for producing demagogues and allowing the average uneducated citizen to have a say in governmental decisions of which they knew only the direction in which the political wind blew. Thucydides' work seems to have had a major impact on Hobbes's thinking.

In 1640, Charles I was forced to call Parliament into session to get the money to put down a rebellion in Scotland. Hobbes ran for office in the Commons, but lost. Instead, he wrote up a political defense of the king's position in *The Elements of Law, Natural and Politic*. The supporters of Charles in Parliament used its arguments often and thus gained a great deal of notoriety for Hobbes. On the other hand, Charles himself hesitated to assert his power in the English state, which was much of what Hobbes's argument was dedicated to in the book. When the next Parliament began searching for writers in support of the king's prerogatives in the state, Hobbes fled to France with the royal family and their supporters.

While he was in France, Hobbes secured a position as the mathematics tutor for the Stuart heir to the English throne, the eventual Charles II. In 1649, Charles I was executed; his son was offered the throne of Scotland soon after, so long as he converted to the predominant Presbyterian religion. This would alienate the heir from his supporters in England, especially the bishops in the Church of England for whom Charles was their leader. Charles still agreed, desperate for a throne; he went to war in Scotland to attain his throne there and lost to Oliver Cromwell's New Model Army. Those advisors whom Charles had listened to in his failed campaign to take the Scottish throne were immediately on the wrong side of the royals—including Hobbes. Despite Charles's fondness for his former math tutor, Hobbes had recently written his most famous work, *Leviathan: or The Matter, Forme and Power of a Common Wealth Ecclesiasticall and Civil* (1651), in which he asserted that a monarch must not be beholden to anyone's sanction, including religious figures such as Anglican bishops. Hobbes believed that the Church of England's hierarchy should rather be subordinated to the monarch.

Banished from Charles's court in France for these views after the Scottish escapade, Hobbes returned quietly to England and kept a low profile.

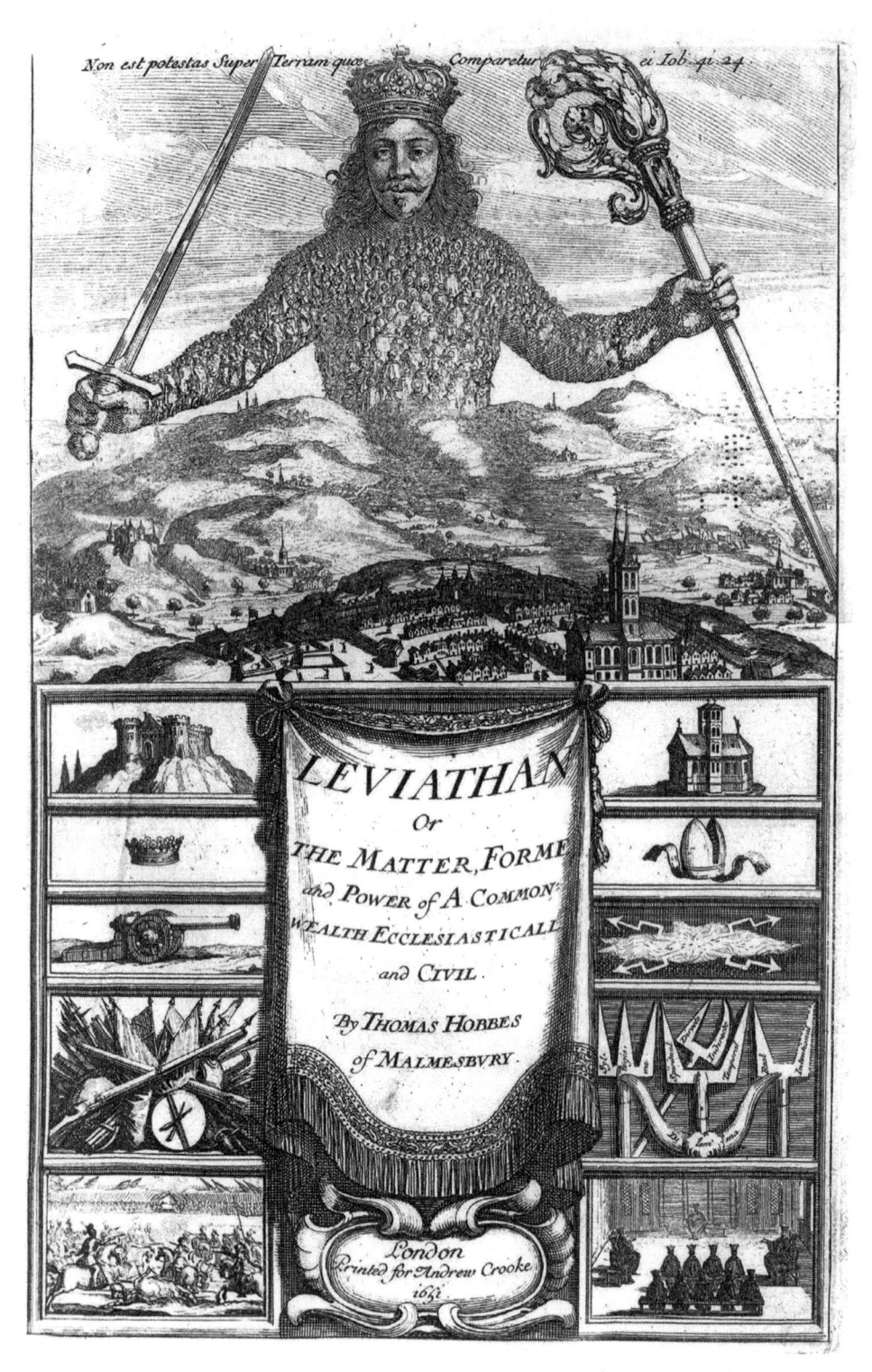

The frontispiece of the book *Leviathan* by Thomas Hobbes; engraving by Abraham Bosse. [Public domain], via Wikimedia Commons

Author Biography

Thomas Hobbes was one of the most accomplished political philosophers of the seventeenth century, and is still widely read and influential today. He was born in 1588, the son of the vicar of Westport who lost his position for getting into a fight in front of his own church. Thomas was raised largely by his paternal uncle, who paid for his education all the way through Magdalen College at Oxford. Through Oxford connections, he became tutor to the son of Lord Cavendish of Hardwick, later the Earl of Devonshire. Devonshire was an active member of Parliament in an era when English politics were highly volatile. Hobbes traveled with the Cavendish family on the continent, and also met many of the major political and philosophical figures of the day in England, including King James I.

Hobbes sat in on a number of parliamentary debates, in an era when such debates were literally the difference between peace and war. He was a royalist when conflict began between the Puritans in Parliament and the Stuart king Charles I, and he wrote a tract defending the king's prerogative in the state in 1640. Many royalists read it and used arguments in it during debates. For fear of arrest by the House of Commons, Hobbes left England later in the year; he eventually became a math tutor for the king's grandson, the future Charles II. After Charles I's loss in the civil war, indictment, and execution, Hobbes returned in 1651, the same year he produced his masterwork, *Leviathan: or The Matter, Forme and Power of a Common Wealth Ecclesiasticall and Civil*. His time in France led him to correspond with some of the other major intellectual figures of his day, notably René Descartes.

Hobbes's return must have been occasioned with a certain fear he would be punished for his royal associations—instead he became one of the most widely read philosophers of his day, especially as the British Puritan republic descended into anarchy. England was riven with politically radical groups, calling for any number of major social, political, and religious changes in English society, all of them fighting with one another for a say in the remaking of the English state. This gave Hobbes a lifelong fear of anarchy; *Leviathan* is effectively a description of what Hobbes saw as necessary politics based on men's often irascible natures.

Living in the era between the Renaissance and the Enlightenment, Hobbes life had much in common with the lives of accomplished men in both those eras. He studied optics, mathematics, Latin and Greek, law, metaphysics, and epistemology. Like any of his age living in England at the time, he wrote much on religion and politics. He lived to the age of 91, dying in 1679.

HISTORICAL DOCUMENT

Excerpt from Leviathan by Thomas Hobbes
Chapter XIII: Of the Natural Condition of Mankind as Concerning Their Felicity and Misery

Nature hath made men so equal in the faculties of body and mind as that, though there be found one man sometimes manifestly stronger in body or of quicker mind than another, yet when all is reckoned together the difference between man and man is not so considerable as that one man can thereupon claim to himself any benefit to which another may not pretend as well as he. For as to the strength of body, the weakest has strength enough to kill the strongest, either by secret machination or by confederacy with others that are in the same danger with himself.

And as to the faculties of the mind, …I find yet a greater equality amongst men than that of strength. For prudence is but experience, which equal time equally bestows on all men in those things they equally apply themselves unto. That which may perhaps make such equality incredible is but a vain conceit of one's own wisdom, which almost all men think they have in a greater degree than the vulgar; that is, than all men but themselves, and a few others, whom by fame, or for concurring with themselves, they approve. For such is the nature of men that howsoever they may acknowledge many others to be more witty, or more eloquent or more learned, yet they will hardly believe there be many so wise as themselves; for they see their own wit at hand, and other men's at a distance. But this proveth rather that men are in that point equal, than unequal. For there is not ordinarily a greater sign of the equal distribution of anything than that every man is contented with his share.

From this equality of ability ariseth equality of hope in the attaining of our ends. And therefore if any two men desire the same thing, which nevertheless they cannot both enjoy, they become enemies; and in the way to their end (which is principally their own conservation, and sometimes their delectation only) endeavour to destroy or subdue one another. And from hence it comes to pass that where an invader hath no more to fear than another man's single power, if one plant, sow, build, or possess a convenient seat, others may probably be expected to come prepared with forces united to dispossess and deprive him, not only of the fruit of his labour, but also of his life or liberty. And the invader again is in the like danger of another.

And from this diffidence of one another, there is no way for any man to secure himself so reasonable as anticipation; that is, by force, or wiles, to master the persons of all men he can, so long till he see no other power great enough to endanger him: and this is no more than his own conservation requireth, and is generally allowed. Also, because there be some that, taking pleasure in contemplating their own power in the acts of conquest, which they pursue farther than their security requires, if others, that otherwise would be glad to be at ease within modest bounds, should not by invasion increase their power, they would not be able, long time, by standing only on their defence, to subsist. And by consequence, such augmentation of dominion over men being necessary to a man's conservation, it ought to be allowed him. …

So that in the nature of man, we find three principal causes of quarrel. First, competition; secondly, diffidence; thirdly, glory.

The first maketh men invade for gain; the second, for safety; and the third, for reputation. The first use violence, to make themselves masters of other men's persons, wives, children, and cattle; the second, to defend them; the third, for trifles, as a word, a smile, a different opinion, and any other sign of undervalue, either direct in their persons or by reflection in their kindred, their friends, their nation, their profession, or their name.

Hereby it is manifest that during the time men live without a common power to keep them all in awe, they are in that condition which is called war; and such a war as is of every man against every man. For war consisteth not in battle only, or the act of fighting, but in a tract of time, wherein the will to contend by battle is sufficiently known: and therefore the notion of time is to be considered in the nature of war, as it is in the nature of weather. For as the nature of foul weather lieth not in a shower or two of rain, but in an inclination thereto of many days together: so the nature of war consisteth not in actual fighting, but in the known disposition thereto during all the time there is no assurance to the contrary. All other time is peace.

Whatsoever therefore is consequent to a time of war, where every man is enemy to every man, the same consequent to the time wherein men live without other security than what their own strength and their own invention shall furnish them withal. In such condition there is no place for industry, because the fruit thereof is uncertain: and consequently no culture of the earth; no navigation, nor use of the commodities that may be imported by sea; no commodious building; no instruments of moving and removing such things as require much force; no knowledge of the face of the earth; no account of time; no arts; no letters; no society; and which is worst of all, continual fear, and danger of violent death; and the life of man, solitary, poor, nasty, brutish, and short.

It may seem strange to some man that has not well weighed these things that Nature should thus dissociate and render men apt to invade and destroy one another: and he may therefore, not trusting to this inference, made from the passions, desire perhaps to have the same confirmed by experience. Let him therefore consider with himself: when taking a journey, he arms himself and seeks to go well accompanied; when going to sleep, he locks his doors; when even in his house he locks his chests; and this when he knows there be laws and public officers, armed, to revenge all injuries shall be done him; what opinion he has of his fellow subjects, when he rides armed; of his fellow citizens, when he locks his doors; and of his children, and servants, when he locks his chests. Does he not there as much accuse mankind by his actions as I do by my words? But neither of us accuse man's nature in it. The desires, and other passions of man, are in themselves no sin. No more are the actions that proceed from those passions till they know a law that forbids them; which till laws be made they cannot know, nor can any law be made till they have agreed upon the person that shall make it. ...

To this war of every man against every man, this also is consequent; that nothing can be unjust. The notions of right and wrong, justice and injustice, have there no place. Where there is no common power, there is no law; where no law, no injustice. Force and fraud are in war the two cardinal virtues. Justice and injustice are none of the faculties neither of the body nor mind. If they were, they might be in a man that were alone in the world, as well as his senses and passions. They are qualities that relate to men in society, not in solitude. It is consequent also to the same condition that there be no propriety, no dominion, no mine and thine distinct; but only that to be every man's that he can get, and for so long as he can keep it. And thus much for the ill condition which man by mere nature is actually placed in; though with a possibility to come out of it, consisting partly in the passions, partly in his reason.

The passions that incline men to peace are: fear of death; desire of such things as are necessary to commodious living; and a hope by their industry to obtain them. And reason suggesteth convenient articles of peace upon which men may be drawn to agreement. These articles are they which otherwise are called the laws of nature. ...

Chapter XVII: Of the Causes, Generation, and Definition of a Commonwealth

The final cause, end, or design of men (who naturally love liberty, and dominion over others) in the introduction of that restraint upon themselves, in which we see them live in Commonwealths, is the foresight of their own preservation, and of a more contented life thereby; that is to say, of getting themselves out from that miserable condition of war which is necessarily consequent, as hath been shown, to the natural passions of men when there is no visible power to keep them in awe, and tie them by fear of punishment to the performance of their covenants, and observation of those laws of nature set down in the fourteenth and fifteenth chapters.

For the laws of nature, as justice, equity, modesty, mercy, and, in sum, doing to others as we would be done to, of themselves, without the terror of some power to cause them to be observed, are contrary to our natural passions, that carry us to partiality, pride, revenge, and the like. And covenants, without the sword, are but words and of no strength to secure a man at all. Therefore, notwithstanding the laws of nature (which every one hath then kept, when he has the will to keep them, when he can do it safely), if there be no power erected, or not great enough for our security, every man will and may lawfully rely on his own strength and art for caution against all other men. And in all places, where men have lived by small families, to rob and spoil one another has been a trade, and so far from being reputed against the law of nature that the greater spoils they gained, the greater was their honour; and men observed no other laws therein but the laws of honour; that is, to abstain from cruelty, leaving to men their lives and instruments of husbandry. And as small families did then; so now do cities and kingdoms, which are but greater families (for their own security), enlarge their dominions upon all pretences of danger, and fear of invasion, or assistance that may be given to invaders; endeavour as much as they can to subdue or weaken their neighbours by open force, and secret arts, for want of other caution, justly; and are remembered for it in after ages with honour. ...[W]hen there is no common enemy, they make war upon each other for their particular interests. For if we could suppose a great multitude of men to consent in the observation of justice, and other laws of nature, without a common power to keep them all in awe, we might as well suppose all mankind to do the same; and then there neither would be, nor need to be, any civil government or Commonwealth at all, because there would be peace without subjection. ...

The only way to erect such a common power, as may be able to defend them from the invasion of foreigners, and the injuries of one another, and thereby to secure them in such sort as that by their own industry and by the fruits of the earth they may nourish themselves and live contentedly, is to confer all their power and strength upon one man, or upon one assembly of men, that may reduce all their wills, by plurality of voices, unto one will: which is as much as to say, to appoint one man, or assembly of men, to bear their person; and every one to own and acknowledge himself to be author of whatsoever he that so beareth their person shall act, or cause to be acted, in those things which concern the common peace and safety; and therein to submit their wills, every one to his will, and their judgments to his judgment. This is more than consent, or concord; it is a real unity of them all in one and the same person, made by covenant of every man with every man, in such manner as if every man should say to every man: I authorise and give up my right of governing myself to this man, or to this assembly of men, on this condition; that thou give up, thy right to him, and authorise all his actions in like manner. This done, the multitude so united in one person is called a COMMONWEALTH; in Latin, CIVITAS. This is the generation of that great LEVIATHAN, or rather, to speak more reverently, of that mortal god to which we owe, under the immortal God, our peace and defence. For by this authority, given him by every particular man in the Commonwealth, he hath the use of so much power and strength conferred on him that, by terror thereof, he is enabled to form the wills of them all, to peace at home, and mutual aid against their enemies abroad. And in him consisteth the essence of the Commonwealth; which, to define it, is: one person, of whose acts a great multitude, by mutual covenants one with another, have made themselves every one the author, to the end he may use the strength and means of them all as he shall think expedient for their peace and common defence.

And he that carryeth this person is called sovereign, and said to have sovereign power; and every one besides, his subject. ...

A Review and Conclusion

From the contrariety of some of the natural faculties of the mind, one to another, as also of one passion to another, and from their reference to conversation, there has been an argument taken to infer an impossibility that any one man should be sufficiently disposed to all sorts of civil duty. The severity of judgment, they say, makes men censorious and unapt to pardon the errors and infirmities of other men: and on the other side, celerity of fancy makes the thoughts less steady than is necessary to discern exactly between right and wrong. Again, in all deliberations, and in all pleadings, the faculty of solid reasoning is necessary: for without it, the resolutions of men are rash, and their sentences unjust: and yet if there be not powerful eloquence, which procureth attention and consent, the effect of reason will be little. But these are contrary faculties; the former being grounded upon principles of truth; the other upon opinions already received, true or false; and upon the passions and interests of men, which are different and mutable.

And amongst the passions, courage (by which I mean the contempt of wounds and violent death) inclineth men to private revenges, and sometimes to endeavour the unsettling of the public peace: and timorousness many times disposeth to the desertion of the public defence. Both these, they say, cannot stand together in the same person.

And to consider the contrariety of men's opinions and manners in general, it is, they say, impossible to entertain a constant civil amity with all those with whom the business of the world constrains us to converse: which business consisteth almost in nothing else but a perpetual contention for honour, riches, and authority.

To which I answer that these are indeed great difficulties, but not impossibilities: for by education and discipline, they may be, and are sometimes, reconciled. Judgment and fancy may have place in the same man; but by turns; as the end which he aimeth at requireth. As the Israelites in Egypt were sometimes fastened to their labour of making bricks, and other times were ranging abroad to gather straw: so also may the judgment sometimes be fixed upon one certain consideration, and the fancy at another time wandering about the world. So also reason and eloquence (though not perhaps in the natural sciences, yet in the moral) may stand very well together. For wheresoever there is place for adorning and preferring of error, there is much more place for adorning and preferring of truth, if they have it to adorn. Nor is there any repugnancy between fearing the laws, and not fearing a public enemy; nor between abstaining from injury, and pardoning it in others. There is therefore no such inconsistence of human nature with civil duties, as some think. ...

And because the name of tyranny signifieth nothing more nor less than the name of sovereignty, be it in one or many men, saving that they that use the former word are understood to be angry with them they call tyrants; I think the toleration of a professed hatred of tyranny is a toleration of hatred to Commonwealth in general, and another evil seed, not differing much from the former. For to the justification of the cause of a conqueror, the reproach of the cause of the conquered is for the most part necessary: but neither of them necessary for the obligation of the conquered. ...

I ground the civil right of sovereigns, and both the duty and liberty of subjects, upon the known natural inclinations of mankind, and upon the articles of the law of nature; of which no man, that pretends but reason enough to govern his private family, ought to be ignorant. And for the power ecclesiastical of the same sovereigns, I ground it on such texts as are both evident in themselves and consonant to the scope of the whole Scripture, and therefore am persuaded that he that shall read it with a purpose only to be informed, shall be informed by it. But for those that by writing or public discourse, or by their eminent actions, have already engaged themselves to the maintaining of contrary opinions, they will not be so easily satisfied. For in such cases, it is natural for men, at one and the same time, both to proceed in reading and to lose their attention in the search of objections to that they had read before: of which, in a time wherein the interests of men are changed (seeing much of that doctrine which serveth to the establishing of a new government must needs be contrary to that which conduced to the dissolution of the old), there cannot choose but be very many. ...

And thus I have brought to an end my discourse of civil and ecclesiastical government, occasioned by the disorders of the present time, without partiality, without application, and without other design than to set before men's eyes the mutual relation between protection and obedience; of which the condition of human nature, and the laws divine, both natural and positive, require an inviolable observation. And though in the revolution of states there can be no very good constellation for truths of this nature to be born under (as having an angry aspect from the dissolvers of an old government, and seeing but the backs of them that erect a new); yet I cannot think it will be condemned at this time, either by the public judge of doctrine, or by any that desires the continuance of public peace. And in this hope I return to my interrupted speculation of bodies natural; wherein, if God give me health to finish it, I hope the novelty will as much please as in the doctrine of this artificial body it useth to offend. For such truth as opposeth no man's profit nor pleasure is to all men welcome.

GLOSSARY

celerity: speed; in this context, the quickness with which thoughts turn from one to another

Commonwealth: in this context, government

delectation: pleasure

diffidence: fear

Document Analysis

In *Leviathan*, Hobbes argues that "Nature hath made men ... equal in the faculties of body and mind." While some men may be marginally superior in strength or intelligence to their fellows, the ability of the weakest to kill the strongest either "by secret machination or by confederacy with others" ensures that each man is, in terms of the mortal danger he represents, equal to the next. As a consequence of this "equality of ability," there arises an "equality of hope" in the "attaining of our ends." The result of the common abilities to attain these shared hopes and "ends" is the creation of "fear" between men, who see their others as "enemies" competing against them. Fear ("diffidence") of one another and a need for each man to preserve himself in a world of natural equality lead men to progress from the need to protect themselves to a desire to exert their "own power" through "acts of conquest." Hobbes argues that within this natural state there are three principal causes of quarrel: "competition," "diffidence," and "glory." Competition makes "men invade for gain," diffidence makes men attack "for safety," and glory makes men attack for recognition of their power by their fellows (that is, they fight for status).

Man's need to dominate others places him in a state of war, "such a war as is of every man against every man." In this state of existence there is no civil government or law, no civilization, and no industry; nor do the concepts of right and wrong or just or unjust exist. All action is acceptable within the laws of nature, as it is dependent upon self-preservation. Such a state of war would continue until law is created to restrict man's selfish (passion-driven) behavior. For Hobbes, the answer is to appeal to the "passions that incline men to peace"; these are "fear of death; desire of such things as are necessary for commodious living; and a hope by their industry to obtain them."

Hobbes finds the mechanism for achieving peace and security: "Commonwealth" (government). If humankind possessed the ability to live peaceably, there would be no need for government; yet owing to humankind's fears, passions, competitiveness, and the desire to dominate one another, this is not possible. He argues that the final end or "design of men" in creating a "Commonwealth" (sovereign body) is man's "own preservation" and "a more contented life." To end the state of war, a "common power" must be erected over all to secure each individual through the agreement ("concord") of all men. In consenting to obey such a sovereign body, each individual cedes the rights to govern and kill in return for protection from the "Commonwealth." This "Commonwealth" would be ruled by one person, the sovereign, who would exercise all "sovereign power" on behalf of the people.

Hobbes argues that reason enables man to overcome his passions and differences with other men in order to live civilly together. Other differences and points of antagonism could be further combated through education and discipline for the good of a unified Commonwealth. To truly achieve this, government must be absolute and its power undivided under one sovereign—for if sovereignty were divided, the sovereign's power would become impaired, and this would limit his power and ability to act. A sovereign must rule alone and exercise power alone for the Commonwealth, even if sovereignty could be seen as "tyranny." Furthermore, the kingdom of God is civil in Hobbes's opinion, and the power of sovereignty given to the Jewish people by God is exercised by the sovereign. This ensures that the authority of the Commonwealth is not only civil in nature but also divine. The aim of *Leviathan* was, therefore, to "set before men's eyes the mutual relation between protection and obedience; of which the condition of human nature, and the laws divine, both natural and positive, require an inviolable observation."

Essential Themes

In 1660, Charles II was restored to his thrones in England and Scotland; when he returned, Hobbes's security was assured. He received a small pension from the king so he could continue writing, completing a history of the Civil War he tellingly named *Behemoth*. He was an unpopular figure with Restoration politicians, seen as an opponent of a church hierarchy of which Charles II approved. Charles himself knew better—Hobbes disliked religious intolerance, whether it came from Puritans and religious radicals or from the Church of England itself.

Charles was similarly inclined, but just as disinclined to overrule his parliament in the interest of keeping his head. Over the course of Charles's reign during the Restoration, many of Hobbes's fears about the over-officious nature of the bishops in the Church of England turned out to be true. Upon being restored to power, religious leaders pushed a series of acts through Parliament to discriminate against "dissenters," meaning any non-Anglican Protestant living in England. These included Scottish Presbyterians, Dutch Reformed Calvinists, "separatists" or Congregationalists, Baptists, Quakers, and others. For 150 years following, dissenting Protestants would be excluded from politics but would succeed in any number of other trades during the Industrial Revolution.

Thus, despite Hobbes's theories, which have been highly influential in the centuries to follow, the kings he wished most to influence gained little from his ideas in *Leviathan*. Hobbes died in 1679; Charles II died in 1685.

—*Andrew Mansfield*

Bibliography and Further Reading

A Restoration Reader. Edited by James Holly Hanford. Kennikat Press, 1971.

Democracy in Britain: A Reader. Edited by Jack Lively and Adam Lively. Blackwell Publishers, 1994.

Hobbes, Thomas. *Leviathan*. Edited by Noel Malcolm. Clarendon Press, 2012.

Websites

Lloyd, Sharon A. and Susanne Sreedhar. "Hobbes's Moral and Political Philosophy." *The Stanford Encyclopedia of Philosophy*, 2014. Stanford University, https://plato.stanford.edu/entries/hobbes-moral/. Accessed 15 Apr. 2017.

Somerville, Johann P. "Thomas Hobbes: 1588-1679." University of Wisconsin, http://faculty.history.wisc.Edu/sommerville/367/367-091.htm. Accessed 15 Apr. 2017.

"The Significations of His Words." *The Economist*, 6 Oct. 2012, http://www.economist.com /node/21564180. Accessed 15 Apr. 2017.

"Thomas Hobbes (1588-1679)." *BBC History*, 2014. BBC.com, http://www.bbc.co.uk/history /historic_figures/hobbes_thomas.shtml. Accessed 15 Apr. 2017.

Williams, Garrath. "Thomas Hobbes: Moral and Political Philosophy." *Internet Encyclopedia of Philosophy*. University of Tennessee at Martin, http://www.iep.utm.edu/hobmoral/. Accessed 15 Apr. 2017.

Habeas Corpus Act of the Restoration

Date: 1679
Authors: Charles Paulet, First Duke of Bolton; Anthony Ashley Cooper, First Earl of Shaftesbury
Genres: Law, legal act

Summary Overview

The Habeas Corpus Act of the Restoration, based on the common-law writ of *habeas corpus ad subjiciendum* (Latin for "you shall have the body for submitting"), was enacted in England on May 27, 1679. The Habeas Corpus Act of the Restoration was, and with amendments continues to be a key piece of legislation that protects the rights of individuals against arbitrary and unlawful detention by the king or the executive and against abuses of procedure by the judiciary and state custodians. The concept of habeas corpus was not born with the 1679 act, having origins predating the Magna Carta. A cornerstone of the English constitution, the Magna Carta, or Great Charter, which was written in Latin and first issued in 1215, established that the will of the monarch, King John, was bound by the law. It specifically set out particular rights to be enjoyed by all subjects, whether free or imprisoned, which supported appeals against unlawful detention. The Habeas Corpus Act of 1679 is held to be of similar constitutional importance to the U.S. Bill of Rights and even the Magna Carta itself.

The Habeas Corpus Act outlines in concrete terms the duties of judges and custodians, including the legally binding procedures to be followed, details of the time frames within which to work, and remedies and punishments for failure to comply with these terms. Above all, it confirms that every English subject has the legal right to be presented before a judge, even when the courts are not in session; to obtain the reason for detention; and to ascertain whether the custodian has legal authority to detain him or her.

Following the act, English subjects were safeguarded from lengthy unlawful detention and intermittent periods of incarceration without trial (excluding under treason and felony charges). As directed toward the originators of detention, the act made clear that in all criminal cases except treason and felony (which carried longer periods of detention but not total exemption from the principle of habeas corpus), clear charges substantiated with evidence would have to be brought before the detainee in a timely manner. This was not necessarily expected to reduce the number of detainees, but it was expected to reduce their arbitrary and uncertain nature. Finally, from the procedural point of view, those responsible for the execution of justice were given clear duties and responsibilities, which went a long way toward standardizing the way habeas corpus writs were handled.

Defining Moment

The Habeas Corpus Act did not emerge and crystallize overnight. Versions of the bill containing all the key elements of the 1679 act passed through the House of Commons with little difficulty in 1668, 1674, 1675, and 1677 before stalling in the House of Lords. The pre-existence of the common-law writ, a well-established legal principle, raised questions about why an act securing it was really necessary. The foremost reason was that the early years of the Restoration—which commenced when Charles II's enthronement reinstated the monarchies of England, Scotland, and Ireland in 1660—were years in which the Stuart monarchs sought to re-establish the royal prerogative, including the detention of people for seditious libel under the king's name, simply on the grounds of suspicion. Thus, protecting the basic rights of individuals under these conditions came to be considered of fundamental importance by many members of Parliament. There already existed statute legislation from the reign of Charles I that, to some extent, protected the subject's right to habeas corpus, but it was ineffective because it did not provide full guidance regarding the duties and responsibilities of the judges or custodians, nor did it set out punishment for breaches.

Throughout the 1660s, there were vast disparities concerning the duration of a prisoner's detention without trial. However, a wait of a year was not considered uncommon. In addition, during this decade there was a substantial increase in the number of unlawful detentions of subjects even after a writ of habeas corpus had been served. Four famous cases in 1666 and 1667 offer real evidence of the prevailing and often ambivalent attitude of judges and custodians toward the writ before enactment of the act securing it. The case of William

Taylor, surveyor of Windsor Castle, who was unlawfully detained by John Mordaunt, First Viscount Mordaunt of Avalon, and whose appeal for issue of a writ of habeas corpus was turned down on arbitrary grounds (while his daughter was allegedly raped by Mordaunt) is often cited as one of the more notorious infractions. The case of Samuel Moyer, who was imprisoned for five years without trial, caused a scandal when his five hundred-pound bribe to his two jailers to obtain his release became the subject of a quarrel between them. The third case involved Edward Hyde, First Earl of Clarendon, who was alleged to have advocated that prisoners should be sent to outlying dominions to avoid the serving of a writ of habeas corpus. Finally, Lord Chief Justice Sir John Kelynge was charged with refusing to issue a writ of habeas corpus and forcing the detainee concerned to appeal directly to the king.

These four cases contributed to the persuading of some in the House of Lords that a habeas corpus act was really necessary. In addition, it became apparent that even if a writ was speedily issued, executing the writ was still sometimes problematic. Under the common law as it stood, jailers or custodians were under no legal obligation to accept the first or second (*alias*) writs, and only on the third (*pluries*) writ were they obligated to take action. This could mean a delay of weeks or even months before a writ would be enforced. The Whig-inclined Sir Henry Care, in his much cited work *English Liberties; or, The Free-Born Subject's Inheritance* (1680), attributed the bill primarily to the abuses of jailers whose efforts to extort money to accept the writ, or in many cases simple negligence, caused the common law to be ineffective. Custodial and judicial indiscretion alike therefore contributed greatly to the need for a statute.

Yet abuse of the common law was not the only motive force behind the habeas corpus bill. Alongside the high-profile cases of abuse, the bill was very much influenced by the politics of Anthony Ashley Cooper, First Earl of Shaftesbury, and his coterie of followers, who sought to weaken the royal prerogative and bolster parliamentary sovereignty. Individual liberties, they argued, could not be guaranteed under existing laws. The habeas corpus bill was framed at the height of Shaftesbury's politically incendiary "exclusion bill" campaign, which sought to prevent James, Charles II's Catholic brother, from acceding to the throne upon Charles's death. It was popularly believed that James would use the royal prerogative much more widely and arbitrarily. However, despite significant support in the House of Commons, many in the House of Lords and among Country Whigs felt that the habeas corpus bill encroached too far on the royal prerogative, which was the basis of the Lords' continued rejection of the bill as passed by the Commons on four separate occasions. In turn, the bill was very unfavorably received by the king himself.

After so many readings of the bill over several years, the need to buttress the broad principle of habeas corpus with statutory force was largely ingrained within members of the House of Commons. To gain more traction in the House of Lords, members of the Commons saw fit to redraft the bill. The long Shaftesburian preamble, which many lords found offensive, was dropped, making the bill much leaner and more palatable. Throughout the mid-1670s there had already been two proposed bills relating to detainees' rights: the habeas corpus bill and the transportation bill. The latter was proposed as a specific remedy to prevent those detained without trial from being deported to the colonies, at a time when deportations to Jamaica were at their peak. The decision to make this a separate bill was based on the political calculation that it would overload the habeas corpus bill and potentially jeopardize it. However, those in the Commons opted to amalgamate the two for the bill of 1679.

In April 1679, the redrafted habeas corpus bill passed through the Commons and up to the House of Lords. After two readings to the House, the bill was read to the whole House sitting in committee, a procedure that allowed greater scrutiny and the opportunity for individual members to pass comment before the bill was subjected to examination by a smaller select committee. The select committee made several important amendments before sending it back to the Commons on May 2. These amendments were finally accepted by the House of Commons, more or less verbatim, in a compromise to ensure that the bill became law before the end of the parliamentary session. The amendments by the Lords appear in the final act as clauses IV, VIII, XIII, XVIII, XX, and XXI. The Commons did add its own amendment to one of the Lords' amendments—Clause XIX—and the bill finally became law on May 27, 1679, although the provisions of the act would not take force until June 1 and were not retroactive.

There have been persistent rumors, first attributed to the historian Gilbert Burnet soon after the passage of the act, that it was not legally passed into law owing to a deliberate miscount of votes by Ford Grey, Third Baron Grey of Warke, who counted in a very fat member of Parliament as ten votes—a jest not picked up by the second teller, James Bertie, First Earl of Abingdon (Lord Norreys), and allowed to stand. Fueling this rumor, the minutes of the session state that 112 votes were cast in total, while the official attendance list records only 107 House of Lords members present. However, recent scholarship has explained this discrepancy and shown that attendance lists of this period were notoriously unreliable. There is now broad consent that the story has no foundation in fact.

The cause of the favorable change of attitude toward the habeas corpus legislation by members of the House of Lords has been the subject of some debate. Helen A. Nutting has attributed the shift to the lessening of post-Restoration paranoia and, more important, has suggested that the courts, especially the King's Bench Division—where the common-law writ of habeas corpus was most applied for—had made significant improvements to the efficiency of the judicial system and records, such that there was less resistance on the part of justices. In fact, in the years immediately prior to the passing of the act, the long pretrial detentions typical of the 1660s were uncommon.

Author Biographies
The initiator of the legislation was Charles Paulet, First Duke of Bolton (Lord St. John), who was first granted permission to introduce a bill in April 1668. Lord St. John (1631–1699) began his parliamentary career as a supporter of Charles II, but during the 1670s moved to the ranks of the opposition. He participated in various important parliamentary committees, most notably investigating the conduct of Thomas Osborne, known as the Earl of Danby, who was impeached on charges of high treason for negotiating with France on matters of peace and war without the knowledge of the Privy Council. He also participated in an inquiry concerning the "Popish plot," a supposed (but fictitious) Catholic conspiracy to murder Charles II.

Anthony Ashley Cooper, First Earl of Shaftesbury, a prominent Whig, had significant input into the bill, although the extent of his role has been called into question in recent years. Shaftesbury (1621–1683) had a rich and varied career, and became one of the most influential politicians of his generation. At the beginning of the English Civil War in 1641, he supported the Royalist cause but defected to the Parliamentarians in 1644. Never completely supportive of Oliver Cromwell's Protectorate (the period after the Civil War during which England was ruled by a Lord Protector), by 1660 his political sentiments placed him on the commission to recall Charles II to the throne. During the 1670s his previously tolerant position toward Catholics hardened, and this attitude placed him at odds with the Crown. His vehement attacks against the administration for what he perceived as tolerance to Catholics led to his imprisonment in 1677. He was released in 1678 and continued to play a leading role in Whig circles.

Significant alterations and additions to the bill were made during its final passage through Parliament, and the work of Francis North, First Baron of Guilford, relating to the six amendments made by the House of Lords are worthy of particular note. Lord North and the Earl of Shaftesbury had clashed on the issue of the impeachment of Thomas Osborne, Lord Danby. The Earl of Shaftesbury had long been in opposition to Danby's strict interpretation of penal laws against Catholics and what he suspected was his support for absolute monarchy. In some sense, the act was therefore a remarkable compromise between two men who had long been fiercely opposed to each other. Lord North (1637–1685) had a long career as a judge, having been called to the bar in 1661. A prodigious early legal career culminated in his appointment as solicitor-general in 1671, from which point his focus turned to politics. In 1673, he became attorney-general and in 1675 lord chief justice. In 1679, he became a member of the Privy Council, a role that further entangled him in political affairs. His support and protection of the royal prerogative helped him gain the position of Lord Keeper of the Great Seal in 1682, which put him in charge of the Court of Chancery.

HISTORICAL DOCUMENT

Habeas Corpus Act of the Restoration
Whereas great delays have been used by sheriffs, gaolers and other officers, to whose custody any of the King's subjects have been committed for criminal or supposed criminal matters, in making returns of writs of habeas corpus to them directed, by standing

out an alias and pluries habeas corpus, and sometimes more, and by other shifts to avoid their yielding obedience to such writs, contrary to their duty and the known laws of the land, whereby many of the King's subjects have been and hereafter may be long detained in prison, in such cases where by law they are bailable, to their great charges and vexation:

I. For the prevention whereof, and the more speedy relief of all persons imprisoned for any such criminal or supposed criminal matters; (2) be it enacted by the King's most excellent majesty, by and with the advice and consent of the lords spiritual and temporal, and commons, in this present parliament assembled, and by the authority thereof, That whensoever any person or persons shall bring any habeas corpus directed unto any sheriff or sheriffs, gaoler, minister or other person whatsoever, for any person in his or her custody, and the said writ shall be served upon the said officer, or left at the gaol or prison with any of the under-officers, under-keepers or deputy of the said officers or keepers, that the said officer or officers, his or their under-officers, under-keepers or deputies, shall within three days after the service thereof as aforesaid (unless the commitment aforesaid were for treason or felony, plainly and specially expressed in the warrant of commitment) upon payment or tender of the charges of bringing the said prisoner, to be ascertained by the judge or court that awarded the same, and endorsed upon the said writ, not exceeding twelve pence per mile, and upon security given by his own bond to pay the charges of carrying back the prisoner, if he shall be remanded by the court or judge to which he shall be brought according to the true intent of this present act, and that he will not make any escape by the way, make return of such writ; (3) and bring or cause to be brought the body of the party so committed or restrained, unto or before the lord chancellor, or lord keeper of the great seal of England for the time being, or the judges or barons of the said court from whence the said writ shall issue, or unto and before such other person or persons before whom the said writ is made returnable, according to the command thereof; (4) and shall then likewise certify the true causes of his detainer or imprisonment, unless the commitment of the said party be in any place beyond the distance of twenty miles from the place or places where such court or person is or shall be residing; and if beyond the distance of twenty miles, and not above one hundred miles, then within the space of ten days, and if beyond the distance of one hundred miles, then within the space of twenty days, after such delivery aforesaid, and not longer.

II. And to the intent that no sheriff, gaoler or other officer may pretend ignorance of the import of any such writ; (2) be it enacted by the authority aforesaid, That all such writs shall be marked in this manner, *Per statutum tricesimo primo Caroli secundi Regi*, and shall be signed by the person that awards the same; (3) and if any person or persons shall be or stand committed or detained as aforesaid, for any crime, unless for felony or treason plainly expressed in the warrant of commitment, in the vacation-time, and out of term, it shall and may be lawful to and for the person or persons so committed or detained (other than persons convict or in execution by legal process) or any one on his or their behalf, to appeal or complain to the lord chancellor or lord keeper, or any one of his Majesty's justices, either of the one bench or of the other, or the barons of the exchequer of the degree of the coif; (4) and the said lord chancellor, lord keeper, justices or barons or any of them, upon view of the copy or copies of the warrant or warrants of commitment and detainer, or otherwise upon oath made that such copy or copies were denied to be given by such person or persons in whose custody the prisoner or prisoners is or are detained, are hereby authorized and required, upon request made in writing by such person or persons, or any on his, her or their behalf, attested and subscribed by two witnesses who were present at the delivery of the same, to award and grant an habeas corpus under the seal of such court whereof he shall then be one of the judges, (5) to be directed to the officer or officers in whose custody the party so committed or detained shall be, returnable immediate before the said lord chancellor or lord keeper, or such justice, baron or any other justice or baron of the degree of the coif of any of the said courts; (6) and upon service thereof as aforesaid, the officer or officers, his or their under-officer or under-officers, under-keeper or under-keepers, or their deputy, in whose custody the party is so committed or detained, shall within the times respectively before limited, bring such prisoner or prisoners before the said lord chancellor or lord keeper, or such justices, barons or one of them, before whom the said writ is made returnable, and in case of his absence before any other of them, with the return of such writ, and the true causes of the commitment and detainer; (7) and thereupon within two days after the party shall be brought before them, the said lord chancellor or lord keeper, or such justice or baron before whom the prisoner shall be brought as aforesaid, shall discharge the said prisoner from his imprisonment, taking his or their recognizance, with one or more surety or sureties, in any sum according to their discretions, having regard to the quality of the prisoner and nature of the offence, for his or their appearance in the court of King's bench the term following, or at the next assizes, sessions or general gaol-delivery of and for such county, city or place where the commitment was, or where the offence was committed, or in such other court where the said offence is properly cognizable, as the case shall require, and then shall certify the said writ with the return thereof, and the said recognizance or recognizances into the said court where such appearance is to be made; (8) unless it shall appear unto the said lord chancellor or lord keeper, or justice or justices, or baron or barons, that the party so committed is detained upon a legal process, order or warrant, out of some court that hath jurisdiction of criminal matters, or by some warrant signed and sealed with the hand and seal of any of the said justices or barons, or some justice or justices of the peace, for such matters or offences for the which by the law the prisoner is not bailable.

III. Provided always, and be it enacted, That if any person shall have wilfully neglected by the space of two whole terms after his imprisonment, to pray a habeas corpus for his enlargement, such person so wilfully neglecting shall not have any habeas corpus to be granted in vacation-time, in pursuance of this act.

IV. And be it further enacted by the authority aforesaid, That if any officer or officers, his or their under-officer or under-officers, under-keeper or under-keepers, or deputy, shall neglect or refuse to make the returns aforesaid, or to bring the body or bodies of the prisoner or prisoners according to the command of the said writ, within the respective times aforesaid, or upon demand made by the prisoner or person in his behalf, shall refuse to deliver, or within the space of six hours after demand shall not deliver, to the person so demanding, a true copy of the warrant or warrants of commitment and detainer of such prisoner, which he and they are hereby required to deliver accordingly, all and every the head gaolers and keepers of such prisons, and such other person in whose custody the prisoner shall be detained, shall for the first offence forfeit to the prisoner or party grieved the sum of one hundred pounds; (2) and for the second offence the sum of two hundred pounds, and shall and is hereby made incapable to hold or execute his said office; (3) the said penalties to be recovered by the prisoner or party grieved, his executors or administrators, against such offender, his executors or administrators, by any action of debt, suit, bill, plaint or information, in any of the King's courts at Westminster, wherein no essoin, protection, privilege, injunction, wager of law, or stay of prosecution by *Non vult ulterius prosequi*, or otherwise, shall be admitted or allowed, or any more than one imparlance; (4) and any recovery or judgment at the suit of any party grieved, shall be a sufficient conviction for the first offence; and any after recovery or judgment at the suit of a party grieved for any offence after the first judgment, shall be a sufficient conviction to bring the officers or person within the said penalty for the second offence.

V. And for the prevention of unjust vexation by reiterated commitments for the same offence; (2) be it enacted by the authority aforesaid, That no person or persons which shall be delivered or set at large upon any habeas corpus, shall at any time hereafter be again imprisoned or committed for the same offence by any person or persons whatsoever, other than by the legal order and process of such court wherein he or they shall be bound by recognizance to appear, or other court having jurisdiction of the cause; (3) and if any other person or persons shall knowingly contrary to this act recommit or imprison, or knowingly procure or cause to be recommitted or imprisoned, for the same offence or pretended offence, any person or persons delivered or set at large as aforesaid, or be knowingly aiding or assisting therein, then he or they shall forfeit to the prisoner or party grieved the sum of five hundred pounds; any colourable pretence or variation in the warrant or warrants of commitment notwithstanding, to be recovered as aforesaid.

VI. Provided always, and be it further enacted, That if any person or persons shall be committed for high treason or felony, plainly and specially expressed in the warrant of commitment, upon his prayer or petition in open court the first week of the term, or first day of the sessions of oyer and terminer or general gaol-delivery, to be brought to his trial, shall not be indicted some time in the next term, sessions of oyer and terminer or general gaol-delivery, after such commitment; it shall and may be lawful to and for the judges of the court of King's bench and justices of oyer and terminer or general gaol-delivery, and they are hereby required, upon motion to them made in open court the last day of the term, sessions or gaol-delivery, either by the prisoner or any one in his behalf, to set at liberty the prisoner upon bail, unless it appear to the judges and justices upon oath made, that the witnesses for the King could not be produced the same term, sessions or general gaol-delivery; (2) and if any person or persons committed as aforesaid, upon his prayer or petition in open court the first week of the term or first day of the sessions of oyer and terminer and general gaol-delivery, to be brought to his trial, shall not be indicted and tried the second term, sessions of oyer and terminer or general gaol-delivery, after his commitment, or upon his trial shall be acquitted, he shall be discharged from his imprisonment.

VII. Provided always, That nothing in this act shall extend to discharge out of prison any person charged in debt, or other action, or with process in any civil cause, but that after he shall be discharged of his imprisonment for such his criminal offence, he shall be kept in custody according to the law, for such other suit.

VIII. Provided always, and be it enacted by the authority aforesaid, That if any person or persons, subjects of this realm, shall be committed to any prison or in custody of any officer or officers whatsoever, for any criminal or supposed criminal matter, that the said person shall not be removed from the said prison and custody into the custody of any other officer or officers; (2) unless it be by habeas corpus or some other legal writ; or where the prisoner is delivered to the constable or other inferior officer to carry such prisoner to some common gaol; (3) or where any person is sent by order of any judge or assize or justice of the peace, to any common workhouse or house of correction; (4) or where the prisoner is removed from one prison or place to another within the same county, in order to his or her trial or discharge in due course of law; (5) or in case of sudden fire or infection, or other necessity; (6) and if any person or persons shall after such commitment aforesaid make out and sign, or countersign any warrant or warrants for such removal aforesaid, contrary to this act; as well he that makes or signs, or countersigns such warrant or warrants, as the officer or officers that obey or execute the same, shall suffer and incur the pains and forfeitures in this act before mentioned, both for the first and second offence respectively, to be recovered in manner aforesaid by the party grieved.

IX. Provided also, and be it further enacted by the authority aforesaid, That it shall and may be lawful to and for any prisoner and prisoners as aforesaid, to move and obtain his or their habeas corpus as well out of the high court of chancery or court of exchequer, as out of the courts of King's bench or common pleas, or either of them; (2) and if the said lord chancellor or lord keeper, or any judge or judges, baron or barons for the time being, of the degree of the coif, of any of the courts aforesaid, in the vacation time, upon view of the copy or copies of the warrant or warrants of commitment or detainer, or upon oath made that such copy or copies were denied as aforesaid, shall deny any writ of habeas corpus by this act required to be granted, being moved for as aforesaid, they shall severally forfeit to the prisoner or party grieved the sum of five hundred pounds, to be recovered in manner aforesaid.

XI. And be it declared and enacted by the authority aforesaid, That an habeas corpus according to the true intent and meaning of this act, may be directed and run into any county palatine, the cinque-ports, or other privileged places within the kingdom of England, dominion of Wales, or town of Berwick upon Tweed, and the islands of Jersey or Guernsey; any law or usage to the contrary notwithstanding.

XII. And for preventing illegal imprisonments in prisons beyond the seas; (2) be it further enacted by the authority aforesaid, That no subject of this realm that now is, or hereafter shall be an inhabitant or resiant of this kingdom of England, dominion of Wales, or town of Berwick upon Tweed, shall or may be sent prisoner into Scotland, Ireland, Jersey, Guernsey, Tangier, or into parts, garrisons, islands or places beyond the seas, which are or at any time hereafter shall be within or without the dominions of his Majesty, his heirs or successors; (3) and that every such imprisonment is hereby enacted and adjudged to be illegal; (4) and that if any of the said subjects now is or hereafter shall be so imprisoned, every such person and persons so imprisoned, shall and may for every such imprisonment maintain by virtue of this act an action or actions of false imprisonment, in any of his Majesty's courts of record, against the person or persons by whom he or she shall be so committed, detained, imprisoned, sent prisoner or transported, contrary to the true meaning of this act, and against all or any person or persons that shall frame, contrive, write, seal or countersign any warrant or writing for such commitment, detainer, imprisonment or transportation, or shall be advising, aiding or assisting, in the same, or any of them; (5) and the plaintiff in every such action shall have judgment to recover his treble costs, besides damages, which damages so to be given, shall not be less than five hundred pounds; (6) in which action no delay stay or stop of proceeding by rule, order or command, nor no injunction, protection or privilege whatsoever, nor any more than one imparlance shall be allowed, excepting such rule of the court wherein the action shall depend, made in open court, as shall be thought in justice necessary, for special cause to be expressed in the said rule; (7) and the person or persons who shall knowingly frame, contrive, write, seal or countersign any warrant for such commitment, detainer or transportation, or shall so commit, detain, imprison or transport any person or persons contrary to this act, or be any ways advising, aiding or assisting therein, being lawfully convicted thereof, shall be disabled from thenceforth to bear any office of trust or profit within the said realm of England, dominion of Wales, or town of Berwick upon Tweed, or any of the islands, territories or dominions thereunto belonging; (8) and shall incur and sustain the pains, penalties and forfeitures limited, ordained and provided in and by the statute of provision and praemunire made in the sixteenth year of King Richard the Second; (9) and be incapable of any pardon from the King, his heirs or successors, of the said forfeitures, losses or disabilities, or any of them.

XIII. Provided always, That nothing in this act shall extend to give benefit to any person who shall by contract in writing agree with any merchant or owner of any plantation, or other person whatsoever, to be transported to any parts beyond the seas, and receive earnest upon such agreement, although that afterwards such person shall renounce such contract.

XIV. Provided always, and be it enacted, That if any person or persons lawfully convicted of any felony, shall in open court pray to be transported beyond the seas, and the court shall think fit to leave him or them in prison for that purpose, such person or persons may be transported into any parts beyond the seas, this act or any thing therein contained to the contrary notwithstanding.

XV. Provided also, and be it enacted, That nothing herein contained shall be deemed, construed or taken, to extend to the imprisonment of any person before the first day of June one thousand six hundred seventy and nine, or to any thing advised, procured, or otherwise done, relating to such imprisonment; any thing herein contained to the contrary notwithstanding.

XVI. Provided also, That if any person or persons at any time resident in this realm, shall have committed any capital offence in Scotland or Ireland, or any of the islands, or foreign plantations of the King, his heirs or successors, where he or she ought to be tried for such offence, such person or persons may be sent to such place, there to receive such trial, in such manner as the same might have been used before the making of this act; any thing herein contained to the contrary notwithstanding.

XVII. Provided also, and be it enacted, That no person or persons shall be sued, impleaded, molested, or troubled for any offence against this act, unless the party offending be sued or impleaded for the same within two years at the most after such time wherein the offence shall be committed, in case the party grieved shall not be then in prison; and if he shall be in prison, then within the space of two years after the decease of the person imprisoned, or his or her delivery out of prison, which shall first happen.

XVIII. And to the intent no person may avoid his trial at the assizes or general gaol-delivery, by procuring his removal before the assizes, at such time as he cannot be brought back to receive his trial there; (2) be it enacted, That after the assizes proclaimed for that county where the prisoner is detained, no person shall be removed from the common gaol upon any habeas corpus granted in pursuance of this act, but upon any such habeas corpus shall be brought before the judge of assize in open court, who is thereupon to do what to justice shall appertain.

XIX. Provided nevertheless, That after the assizes are ended, any person or persons detained, may have his or her habeas corpus according to the direction and intention of this act.

XX. And be it also enacted by the authority aforesaid, That if any information, suit or action shall be brought or exhibited against any person or persons for any offence committed or to be committed against the form of this law, it shall be lawful for such defendants to plead the general issue, that they are not guilty, or that they owe nothing, and to give such special matter in evidence to the jury that shall try the same, which matter being pleaded had been good and sufficient matter in law to have discharged the said defendant or defendants against the said information, suit or action, and the said matter shall be then as available to him or them, to all intents and purposes, as if he or they had sufficiently pleaded, set forth or alleged the same matter in bar or discharge of such information suit or action.

XXI. And because many times persons charged with petty treason or felony, or as accessories thereunto, are committed upon suspicion only, whereupon they are bailable, or not, according as the circumstances making out that suspicion are more or less weighty, which are best known to the justices of peace that committed the persons, and have the examinations before them, or to other justices of the peace in the county; (2) be it therefore enacted, That where any person shall appear to be committed by any judge or justice of the peace and charged as accessory before the fact, to any petty treason or felony, or upon suspicion thereof, or with suspicion of petty treason or felony, which petty treason or felony shall be plainly and specially expressed in the warrant of commitment, that such person shall not be removed or bailed by virtue of this act, or in any other manner than they might have been before the making of this act.

> **GLOSSARY**
>
> **Berwick upon Tweed:** the northernmost town in England, scene of many battles in the border wars between the kingdoms of England and Scotland
>
> **barons … degree of the coif:** relating to the Order of the Coif, a group of sergeants-at-law whose members became judges in the Court of Common Pleas and later the King's Bench
>
> **cinque ports:** originally, five (in the Plantagenet royal language of French, "cinque") ports in southeastern England (Dover, Sandwich, Romney, Hythe and Hastings) that were the first line of defense in case of an invasion of England, and were also the prime shipbuilding locations supplying the Royal Navy
>
> **colourable:** seemingly valid
>
> **enlargement:** setting free
>
> **general gaol-delivery:** a legal commission by which prisoners are quickly brought to trial before a court
>
> **lords spiritual and temporal, and commons:** members of Parliament. At the time of the act, the lords spiritual were bishops of the Church of England, and the lords temporal were members of the hereditary peerage; they comprised the House of Lords. "Commons," representatives of the towns and cities, sat in the House of Commons.
>
> *Non vult ulterius prosequi*: a plea of not wishing to pursue a prosecution further
>
> *Per statutum tricesimo primo Caroli secundi Regi*: in accordance with the thirty-first statute of the reign of King Charles the Second
>
> **returnable:** required by law to be delivered
>
> **vacation-time:** a parliamentary recess

Document Analysis

The final Habeas Corpus Act passed in 1679 contains twenty-one separate clauses. The clauses can be broadly grouped into three categories: those outlining the procedures, duties, and responsibilities for compliance with the act by all parties involved as well as penalties for noncompliance; those relating to the transportation of detainees pretrial or of those convicted of crimes after sentencing; and those supplied as amendments to the bill by the House of Lords.

Procedures, Duties, and Responsibilities and Penalties for Noncompliance

Since the purpose of giving statutory force to the pre-existing common-law writ was largely to ensure the establishment of clear procedures for observing habeas corpus, the most important clauses relate to duties of compliance, as well as to remedies for noncompliance with the measures of the act. The act stipulates in clause III that upon receiving a witnessed written request for the writ of habeas corpus by a detainee or his agents, judges are "authorized and required" to issue a writ of habeas corpus signed by them. From clause X, failure to comply with this clause during "vacation time" would result in a £500 fine. Detainees could request the writ at the High Court of Chancery, the Court of Exchequer, the King's Bench, or the Court of Common Pleas. The act requires in clause II that upon receiving the writ, the custodian or warder must bring the prisoner before the court within three days if he or she is held within twenty miles of the issuing court, within ten days if within one hundred miles, and within a maximum of twenty days for still greater distances.

Furthermore, as noted in clause V, the custodian or police officer to whom the request for a warrant of arrest was made had to issue one to the detainee within six hours of the request, and the custodian could not shift the custody of the prisoner. Failure to comply with this part of the act was punishable for the first offense by a £100 fine (payable to the detainee) and, for the second offense, by a £200 fine and ineligibility to hold "his said office" any longer. After the prisoner appeared before the court, the reason for his detention was to be considered by the judge if submitted by the custodian; otherwise the detainee had to be released. Where a warrant attended the prisoner, the judge had three options: to release the prisoner on the ground of insufficient cause, to bail the prisoner to appear at a later date, or to remand the prisoner in custody. If the custodian neglected or refused to bring the prisoner before the court, it was also punishable by a £100 fine. Clause VI adds that no person could be detained twice for the same offense, including through "colourable pretence or variation"—that is, slightly changing the charge to avoid the spirit of the act—with a breach punishable by a £500 fine. The penalties were, in general, considered by the Lords as harsh, but there is not much evidence of serious breaches of the act before its first suspension in 1689.

Transportation of Detainees and Prisoners
Clauses XI–XVI of the act relate to the practice of pretrial transportation of detainees to English colonies such as Jamaica or English territories such as Jersey and Guernsey in deliberate maneuvers to avoid the possibility of habeas corpus. Clauses XI, XII, and XIV had been the central features of the transportation bill that never passed separately. The practice of what amounted to extraterritorial rendition was notoriously highlighted by Edward Hyde, First Earl of Clarendon, who was impeached by the House of Commons in 1667 and forced to flee to France for flagrantly flouting the principle of habeas corpus by sending prisoners to Jersey and then to places farther afield. The problem was that the legal status of the common-law writ within Crown colonies was not altogether clear, and while it was thought to apply, the practical difficulties of applying for writs from afar and having them properly served effectively denied the detainees habeas corpus. It is important, however, to distinguish the illegal transportation of prisoners covered by the act from the legal transportation of those sentenced to penal servitude having been through the due process of law. For example, in 1686, 306 individuals who had taken part in the failed Monmouth Rebellion to overthrow James II were sent to Barbados, while another 159 were sent to Jamaica, all without infringing upon the provisions of the Habeas Corpus Act.

Clause XI declares that the act was to be enforceable in all places within the kingdom of England and the dominion of Wales, including places with unusual legal and constitutional statuses, "privileged places" such as the Cinque Ports, Berwick-upon-Tweed (for which English or Scottish jurisdiction had not been settled), and the Channel Islands of Jersey and Guernsey. Clause XII addresses the issue of unlawful transportation to and detention in places overseas, such as in the plantation colonies of the Caribbean. The act forbids all residents of England, Wales, and Berwick-upon-Tweed from being sent as prisoners to Scotland, Ireland, Jersey, Guernsey, or Tangier or any other of his majesty's dominions and territories. The act also states that breaches of the act would allow the plaintiff to bring an action of false imprisonment and to recover treble costs and at least £500 damages.

Clauses XIII (added by the Lords) and XIV protect against abuse of the act by detainees in the event that they consent to being sent to the colonies pretrial or after sentencing but then renege and try to bring an action of unlawful imprisonment under habeas corpus. Finally, clause XVI clarifies that the Habeas Corpus Act does not interfere with the ancient principle of judicial jurisdiction, by which any subject charged with a capital offense committed within the king's realm could be sent to the place where the crime was committed to face trial. This principle is still broadly in force.

Amendments by the House of Lords
During the Easter parliamentary recess of 1679, a small select committee of the House of Lords set to work drafting amendments to the habeas corpus bill. Lord North, long the most outspoken and eloquent opponent of the bill, was the motive force behind many of the amendments. The main revisions form the substantial parts of clauses IV, VIII, XIII, XVIII, XX, and XXI. It has been suggested that these clauses significantly weaken the act, but they mainly provide safeguards against abuse of the act by detainees or potential conflicts of interest with other laws and judicial proceedings.

Although ordinarily application for the writ of habeas corpus could be made at any time, including during vacation time or parliamentary recess, clause IV adds the caveat that if a prisoner had neglected to seek the writ within two terms of detention, habeas corpus would not be granted during vacation time. Clause VIII makes clear that the act only applied in criminal cases and could not be extended to civil cases or debtors, while the aforementioned clause XIII protects merchants who had contractual agreements for immigration.

Perhaps the most important amendment is clause XVIII, which anticipated potential abuse of the law by detainees seeking to use its provisions to evade or preempt trial at the scheduled assizes, The assizes were criminal courts that moved around the country periodically to try more serious cases referred to them by the Quarter Sessions. They were abolished along with the Quarter Sessions by the Courts Act of 1791. Once the date of the assizes was announced, no habeas corpus writs could be served, but the detainee could present the writ at the assizes when they were in session. This amendment solicited a further amendment by the House of Commons, clause XIX, which allowed habeas corpus to be served after the assizes, presumably if the assizes did not make the writ redundant.

The penultimate amendment, clause XX, secured the right of a general plea against any accusation of an infraction or breach of the act. This was a vital check on unwarranted accusations. The final amendment, clause XXI, relates to detentions based on the suspicion of felony or treason; it confirmed that these were still detainable offenses and that the act itself should not induce courts to release on bail such detainees who would not have been bailed prior to the act.

Essential Themes
The contemporary impact of the Habeas Corpus Act on English society has been considered by some historians to have been rather muted. Since it was first enacted, it has been suspended on several occasions, most notably in 1689, when the threat of Catholic-leaning counter-revolutionary forces loyal to James II threatened to destabilize the monarchy of the recently installed Protestant monarchs William III and Mary II. Another notable suspension was in the immediate aftermath of the French Revolution (1794–1795), when England was embroiled in a series of wars with France and concern about French spies was heightened by the activities of pro-revolutionary radical thinkers such as Thomas Paine. In 1817, the act was suspended to help control outbreaks of civil unrest caused by falling grain prices and unemployment following the end of the Napoleonic Wars in 1815.

However, the act's codification of the ancient common-law writ of habeas corpus had a significant impact on the expediency of justice and significantly curbed the royal prerogative. In combination with the English Bill of Rights, enacted a decade later, which curbed unreasonable bail demands and "cruel and unusual punishments," the right of individuals to be protected against procedural abuse and arbitrary interference with the administration of justice was supported as never before. The principle of habeas corpus was transposed to the American colonies and eventually enshrined in the U.S. Constitution; Article I, Section 9, significantly states that "the privilege of the writ of habeas corpus shall not be suspended" unless in times of rebellion or invasion, or to ensure public safety. The common-law concept of habeas corpus was adopted by many U.S. states in the framing of their individual constitutions. For example, Article LX of the Georgia Constitution of 1777 states, "The principles of the habeas-corpus act shall be a part of this constitution." In 2005, the United Kingdom's Prevention of Terrorism Act, passed in the wake of the attacks of September 11, 2001, allowed terror suspects to be detained without charge for a longer period than that stipulated in the 1984 Police and Criminal Evidence Act. This has been seen as an infringement on the principle of habeas corpus and proves the continuing relevance of the Habeas Corpus Act of 1679.

—*Peter Robinson*

Bibliography and Further Reading
Antieau, Chester J. *The Practice of Extraordinary Remedies: Habeas Corpus and the Other Common Law Writs*, vol. 1. Oceana Publications, 1987.
Care, Henry. *English Liberties; or, The Free-Born Subject's Inheritance*. G. Larkin, 1680.
Sharpe, Robert J. *The Law of Habeas Corpus*. Clarendon Press, 1989.

Websites
Blackstone, William. "Commentaries 3:129–37." *Commentaries on the Laws of England: A Facsimile of the First Edition of 1765–1769*. University of Chicago Press, 1979, *The Founders' Constitution* 3: Article 1, Section 9, Clause 2, Document 4, http://press-pubs.uchicago.edu/founders/documents/ a1_9_2s4.html. Accessed 6 Apr. 2017.
"Opinion on the Writ of Habeas Corpus." *The Founders' Constitution,* 3: Article 1, Section 9, Clause 2, Document 3. University of Chicago Press, 2000, http://press-pubs.uchicago.edu/founders/documents/a1_9_2s3.html. Accessed 6 Apr. 2017.

■ John Bunyan: *The Pilgrim's Progress*

Date: 1678
Author: John Bunyan
Genre: Book

Summary Overview

John Bunyan, a self-educated Puritan preacher, wrote his classic book *The Pilgrim's Progress from This World to That Which Is to Come* while he was in jail in 1675 for refusing to conform to the official Church of England. The book, an allegory describing the journey of a Christian from this world to the next, gives a vivid picture of the religious beliefs of Bunyan and other Nonconformists, who rejected the teaching of the State Church. In the first part of *The Pilgrim's Progress*, written originally to stand alone, Christian, the titular hero, becomes increasingly convinced that he and his community are under a sentence of judgment. Unable to persuade anyone else to flee destruction with him, he sets off alone on a journey to salvation. The second part tells the story of Christian's wife, Christiana, and their children on the same difficult journey.

The Pilgrim's Progress, first published in 1678, is a Puritan sermon in the form of a novel, using powerful and charming storytelling to teach the lesson that the world is the venue for the battle of spiritual forces and that victory comes only through denying the world to seek salvation. Bunyan's writings, of which *The Pilgrim's Progress* is far and away the best known, allowed him to reach a huge audience despite his incarceration. His account of a religious "everyman" made him a celebrity in his own day and has inspired countless people ever since.

Bunyan wrote for the sorts of people who attended or were likely to attend congregations not affiliated with the Church of England. Such Dissenters might lack formal education but often knew the Bible well and were familiar, through sermons, with many of the types of imagery Bunyan employed in *The Pilgrim's Progress*. The book was aimed both at those considering conversion and Christians who needed encouragement to remain faithful.

For many years *The Pilgrim's Progress* was appreciated as a classic work of English literature. Most English-language readers encounter it today only in the classroom, but Bunyan's work still reaches an audience through other authors who have incorporated his values and ideas. Today *The Pilgrim's Progress* remains widely read as a religious work, particularly by Protestants of almost all denominations. Modern Christians particularly appreciate Bunyan's theological understanding of discouragement as a natural part of faith. The text is also still used by Christian missionaries as a way to introduce Protestant beliefs about conversion and salvation.

Defining Moment

The English Civil War, a series of three armed conflicts (1641–1651), pitted not only Cavaliers (supporters of the king) against Roundheads (supporters of Parliament), or believers in absolutist monarchy by divine right against those who championed some form of constitutional government, it also pitted the official Anglican religious settlement against the religion of the Puritans (Protestants who preferred a more rigorous and Bible-centered faith). Nonconformists, or Dissenters, as Puritans who rejected the Anglican Church were known, formed the backbone of the parliamentary armies led by Oliver Cromwell, which eventually overthrew the monarchy. During the Commonwealth (1649–1660), while first Cromwell and then his son presided over the government, Dissenters were free to practice their religion as they chose.

Shortly after Cromwell's death, England welcomed back Charles II (r. 1660–1685) and with him a renewed Anglican settlement. The Restoration government moved quickly and severely against Dissenters, demanding full allegiance to the Church of England, or the Anglican Church. Official Anglicanism had wealth, resources, facilities, and educated clergy. Dissenting churches made do without any of these advantages, and the costs of resistance were high enough that most Dissenters were drawn from the uneducated and poor working classes. Some became involved in political schemes to overthrow Charles or, later, his brother James II (r. 1685–1688). Eventually, Dissenters would play a prominent role in ousting the Catholic James for the Protestant Mary and her Dutch Protestant husband William in the Glorious Revolution of 1688. Other Dissenters would leave England for places of refuge such

Burdened Christian flees from home. By Rachael Robinson Elmer, illustrator (died 12 February 1919) (archive.org) [Public domain], via Wikimedia Commons

as the New World (as the Pilgrims had done before the English Civil War). But most remained at home and avoided politics as best they could, worshiping according to their beliefs and living with the consequences.

John Bunyan participated personally in all the great happenings of his time. Although he was not yet a committed Puritan, as a teenager he served in the Parliamentary army toward the end of the English Civil War. Later, during the Commonwealth, he experienced his conversion and used the freedom of that era to become a Dissenting preacher. Like many other Nonconformists, he encountered persecution under the Restoration government. Bunyan spent more than twelve years in jail for preaching without a license. He died just before England's Glorious Revolution allowed some measure of freedom to those who shared his religious beliefs. Yet the ideas about faith he taught in *The Pilgrim's Progress*, along with the general English attitude on Nonconformity, would contribute toward shaping English views about freedom, government, and the intersection of Church and State, not only in Britain but in the United States as well.

Author Biography

The English writer and preacher John Bunyan was born in Harrowden in Bedfordshire on November 30, 1628, to an extremely poor family. He received only a minimal education and followed his father into trade as a brazier before he went on to serve in the Parliamentary army during the English Civil War. It was his marriage after the end of military service that changed Bunyan's life. His wife brought as her only dowry two religious texts. Reading those books focused Bunyan's thoughts increasingly on his own spiritual condition and eventually led to what he recognized as a conversion in 1653. A handful of other books, particularly the Bible, the Anglican Book of Common Prayer and John Foxe's account of the Christian martyrs through history, *Actes and Monuments* (more commonly known as *The Book of Martyrs*), played an important role in Bunyan's self-education. In 1655 he was baptized and received into the Baptist Church.

Bunyan's faith took a public role in religious matters when he began to dispute with local Quakers in 1656; this led to increasing involvement in ministry and finally a call to serve a local Independent congregation as pastor. Under the Commonwealth it was possible for self-proclaimed preachers to lead congregations. With the Restoration of both Charles II and the Anglican Church, however, the government began to move against unlicensed preachers. Bunyan refused to conform to the Church of England and was jailed in 1660. His first period of imprisonment lasted (with occasional interruptions) for twelve years. The confinement was lax, giving him opportunities to write. It was probably during this period that Bunyan began to plan *The Pilgrim's Progress*, though he did not begin the writing process until later—certainly he was busy enough turning out his autobiography (*Grace Abounding to the Chief of Sinners*) and other books, pamphlets, sermons, and poetry.

Upon release, Bunyan immediately renewed his career as a pastor, serving a congregation until he was arrested and jailed again in 1675. It was during the following brief stint in prison that he wrote the first part of *The Pilgrim's Progress*, although the work was not published for three more years. In 1684 he published the second half of the work. Bunyan's second jail term lasted only six months, and his increasing reputation and popularity protected him from further trouble. He was even offered royal patronage by James II, but Bunyan's religious convictions caused him to refuse the post. He continued writing and preaching until his death on August 31, 1688.

HISTORICAL DOCUMENT

Excerpts from Pilgrim's Progress by John Bunyan

The First Stage

As I walked through the wilderness of this world, I lighted on a certain place where was a den, and laid me down in that place to sleep; and as I slept, I dreamed a dream. I dreamed, and behold, I saw a man clothed with rags, standing in a certain place, with his face from his own house, a book in his hand, and a great burden upon his back. I looked and saw him open the book, and read therein; and as he read, he wept and trembled; and not being able longer to contain, he brake out with a lamentable cry, saying, "What shall I do?"

In this plight, therefore, he went home, and restrained himself as long as he could, that his wife and children should not perceive his distress; but he could not be silent long, because that his trouble increased. Wherefore at length he brake his mind to his wife and children; and thus he began to talk to them: "O, my dear wife," said he, "and you the children of my bowels, I, your dear friend, am in myself undone by reason of a burden that lieth hard upon me; moreover, I am certainly informed that this our city will be burnt with fire from heaven; in which fearful overthrow, both myself, with thee my wife, and you my sweet babes, shall miserably come to ruin, except (the which yet I see not) some way of escape can be found whereby we may be delivered." At this his relations were sore amazed; not for that they believed that what he had said to them was true, but because they thought that some frenzy distemper had got into his head; therefore, it drawing towards night, and they hoping that sleep might settle his brains, with all haste they got him to bed. But the night was as troublesome to him as the day; wherefore, instead of sleeping, he spent it in sighs and tears. So when the morning was come, they would know how he did. He told them, "Worse and worse": he also set to talking to them again; but they began to be hardened. They also thought to drive away his distemper by harsh and surly carriage to him; sometimes they would deride, sometimes they would chide, and sometimes they would quite neglect him. Wherefore he began to retire himself to his chamber to pray for and pity them, and also to condole his own misery; he would also walk solitarily in the fields, sometimes reading, and sometimes praying: and thus for some days he spent his time.

Now I saw, upon a time, when he was walking in the fields, that he was (as he was wont) reading in his book, and greatly distressed in his mind; and as he read, he burst out, as he had done before, crying, "What shall I do to be saved?"

I saw also that he looked this way, and that way, as if he would run; yet he stood still because (as I perceived) he could not tell which way to go. I looked then, and saw a man named Evangelist coming to him, and he asked, "Wherefore dost thou cry?"

He answered, "Sir, I perceive, by the book in my hand, that I am condemned to die, and after that to come to judgment; and I find that I am not willing to do the first, nor able to do the second."

Then said Evangelist, "Why not willing to die, since this life is attended with so many evils?" The man answered, "Because, I fear that this burden that is upon my back will sink me lower than the grave, and I shall fall into Tophet. And Sir, if I be not fit to go to prison, I am not fit to go to judgment, and from thence to execution; and the thoughts of these things make me cry."

Then said Evangelist, "If this be thy condition, why standest thou still?" He answered, "Because I know not whither to go." Then he gave him a parchment roll, and there was written within, "Fly from the wrath to come."

The man therefore read it, and looking upon Evangelist very carefully, said, "Whither must I fly?" Then said Evangelist, (pointing with his finger over a very wide field,) "Do you see yonder wicket-gate?" The man said, "No." Then said the other, "Do you see yonder shining light?" He said, "I think I do." Then said Evangelist, "Keep that light in your eye, and go up directly thereto, so shalt thou see the gate; at which, when thou knockest, it shall be told thee what thou shalt do." So I saw in my dream that the man began to run. Now he had not run far from his own door when his wife and children, perceiving it, began to cry after him to return; but the man put his fingers in his ears, and ran on crying, Life! life! eternal life! So he looked not behind him, but fled towards the middle of the plain.

The neighbors also came out to see him run, and as he ran, some mocked, others threatened, and some cried after him to return; and among those that did so, there were two that were resolved to fetch him back by force. The name of the one was Obstinate and the name of the other Pliable. Now by this time the man was got a good distance from them; but, however, they were resolved to pursue him, which they did, and in a little time they overtook him. Then said the man, "Neighbors, wherefore are you come?" They said, "To persuade you to go back with us." But he said, "That can by no means be: you dwell," said he, "in the city of Destruction, the place also where I was born: I see it to be so; and dying there, sooner or later, you will sink lower than the grave, into a place that burns with fire and brimstone: be content, good neighbors, and go along with me."

Obstinate: What, said Obstinate, and leave our friends and our comforts behind us!
Christian: Yes, said Christian, (for that was his name,) because that all which you forsake is not worthy to be compared with a little of that I am seeking to enjoy, and if you will go along with me, and hold it, you shall fare as I myself; for there, where I go, is enough and to spare. Come away, and prove my words.
Obstinate: What are the things you seek, since you leave all the world to find them?
Christian: I seek an inheritance incorruptible, undefiled, and that fadeth not away, and it is laid up in heaven, and safe there, to be bestowed, at the time appointed, on them that diligently seek it. Read it so, if you will, in my book.
Obstinate: Tush, said Obstinate, away with your book; will you go back with us or no?
Christian: No, not I, said the other, because I have laid my hand to the plough.
Obstinate: Come then, neighbor Pliable, let us turn again, and go home without him: there is a company of these crazy-headed coxcombs, that when they take a fancy by the end, are wiser in their own eyes than seven men that can render a reason.
Pliable: Then said Pliable, Don't revile; if what the good Christian says is true, the things he looks after are better than ours: my heart inclines to go with my neighbor.
Obstinate: What, more fools still! Be ruled by me, and go back; who knows whither such a brain-sick fellow will lead you? Go back, go back, and be wise.
Christian: Nay, but do thou come with thy neighbor Pliable; there are such things to be had which I spoke of, and many more glories besides. If you believe not me, read here in this book, and for the truth of what is expressed therein, behold, all is confirmed by the blood of Him that made it.

Pliable: Well, neighbor Obstinate, said Pliable, I begin to come to a point; I intend to go along with this good man, and to cast in my lot with him: but, my good companion, do you know the way to this desired place?
Christian: I am directed by a man whose name is Evangelist, to speed me to a little gate that is before us, where we shall receive instructions about the way.
Pliable: Come then, good neighbor, let us be going. Then they went both together.
Obstinate: And I will go back to my place, said Obstinate: I will be no companion of such misled, fantastical fellows.

Now I saw in my dream, that when Obstinate was gone back, Christian and Pliable went talking over the plain; and thus they began their discourse.

Christian: Come, neighbor Pliable, how do you do? I am glad you are persuaded to go along with me. Had even Obstinate himself but felt what I have felt of the powers and terrors of what is yet unseen, he would not thus lightly have given us the back.
Pliable: Come, neighbor Christian, since there are none but us two here, tell me now farther, what the things are, and how to be enjoyed, whither we are going.
Christian: I can better conceive of them with my mind, than speak of them with my tongue: but yet, since you are desirous to know, I will read of them in my book.
Pliable: And do you think that the words of your book are certainly true?
Christian: Yes, verily; for it was made by Him that cannot lie.
Pliable: Well said; what things are they?
Christian: There is an endless kingdom to be inhabited, and everlasting life to be given us, that we may inhabit that kingdom for ever.
Pliable: Well said; and what else?
Christian: There are crowns of glory to be given us; and garments that will make us shine like the sun in the firmament of heaven.
Pliable: This is very pleasant; and what else?

Christian: There shall be no more crying, nor sorrow; for he that is owner of the place will wipe all tears from our eyes.

Pliable: And what company shall we have there?

Christian: There we shall be with seraphims and cherubims, creatures that will dazzle your eyes to look on them. There also you shall meet with thousands and ten thousands that have gone before us to that place; none of them are hurtful, but loving and holy; every one walking in the sight of God, and standing in his presence with acceptance for ever. In a word, there we shall see the elders with their golden crowns, there we shall see the holy virgins with their golden harps, there we shall see men, that by the world were cut in pieces, burnt in flames, eaten of beasts, drowned in the seas, for the love they bare to the Lord of the place, all well, and clothed with immortality as with a garment.

Pliable: The hearing of this is enough to ravish one's heart. But are these things to be enjoyed? How shall we get to be sharers thereof?

Christian: The Lord, the governor of the country, hath recorded that in this book, the substance of which is, if we be truly willing to have it, he will bestow it upon us freely.

Pliable: Well, my good companion, glad am I to hear of these things: come on, let us mend our pace.

Christian: I cannot go as fast as I would, by reason of this burden that is on my back.

Now I saw in my dream, that just as they had ended this talk, they drew nigh to a very miry slough that was in the midst of the plain: and they being heedless, did both fall suddenly into the bog. The name of the slough was Despond. Here, therefore, they wallowed for a time, being grievously bedaubed with the dirt; and Christian, because of the burden that was on his back, began to sink in the mire.

Pliable: Then said Pliable, Ah, neighbor Christian, where are you now?

Christian: Truly, said Christian, I do not know.

Pliable: At this Pliable began to be offended, and angrily said to his fellow, Is this the happiness you have told me all this while of? If we have such ill speed at our first setting out, what may we expect between this and our journey's end? May I get out again with my life, you shall possess the brave country alone for me. And with that he gave a desperate struggle or two, and got out of the mire on that side of the slough which was next to his own house: so away he went, and Christian saw him no more.

Wherefore Christian was left to tumble in the Slough of Despond alone; but still he endeavored to struggle to that side of the slough that was farthest from his own house, and next to the wicket-gate; the which he did, but could not get out because of the burden that was upon his back: but I beheld in my dream, that a man came to him, whose name was Help, and asked him what he did there.

Christian: Sir, said Christian, I was bid to go this way by a man called Evangelist, who directed me also to yonder gate, that I might escape the wrath to come. And as I was going thither, I fell in here.

Help: But why did not you look for the steps?

Christian: Fear followed me so hard that I fled the next way, and fell in.

Help: Then, said he, Give me thine hand: so he gave him his hand, and he drew him out, and he set him upon sound ground, and bid him go on his way.

Then I stepped to him that plucked him out, and said, "Sir, wherefore, since over this place is the way from the city of Destruction to yonder gate, is it, that this plat is not mended, that poor travellers might go thither with more security?" And he said unto me, "This miry slough is such a place as cannot be mended: it is the descent whither the scum and filth that attends conviction for sin doth continually run, and therefore it is called the Slough of

Despond; for still, as the sinner is awakened about his lost condition, there arise in his soul many fears and doubts, and discouraging apprehensions, which all of them get together, and settle in this place: and this is the reason of the badness of this ground.

"It is not the pleasure of the King that this place should remain so bad. His laborers also have, by the direction of his Majesty's surveyors, been for above this sixteen hundred years employed about this patch of ground, if perhaps it might have been mended: yea, and to my knowledge," said he, "there have been swallowed up at least twenty thousand cart loads, yea, millions of wholesome instructions, that have at all seasons been brought from all places of the King's dominions, (and they that can tell, say, they are the best materials to make good ground of the place,) if so be it might have been mended; but it is the Slough of Despond still, and so will be when they have done what they can.

"True, there are, by the direction of the Lawgiver, certain good and substantial steps, placed even through the very midst of this slough; but at such time as this place doth much spew out its filth, as it doth against change of weather, these steps are hardly seen; or if they be, men, through the dizziness of their heads, step beside, and then they are bemired to purpose, notwithstanding the steps be there: but the ground is good when they are once got in at the gate."

Now I saw in my dream, that by this time Pliable was got home to his house. So his neighbors came to visit him; and some of them called him wise man for coming back, and some called him fool for hazarding himself with Christian: others again did mock at his cowardliness, saying, "Surely, since you began to venture, I would not have been so base as to have given out for a few difficulties," so Pliable sat sneaking among them. But at last he got more confidence, and then they all turned their tales, and began to deride poor Christian behind his back. And thus much concerning Pliable.

Now as Christian was walking solitary by himself, he espied one afar off come crossing over the field to meet him; and their hap was to meet just as they were crossing the way of each other. The gentleman's name that met him was Mr. Worldly Wiseman: he dwelt in the town of Carnal Policy, a very great town, and also hard by from whence Christian came. This man then, meeting with Christian, and having some inkling of him, (for Christian's setting forth from the city of Destruction was much noised abroad, not only in the town where he dwelt, but also it began to be the town-talk in some other places)—Mr. Worldly Wiseman, therefore, having some guess of him, by beholding his laborious going, by observing his sighs and groans, and the like, began thus to enter into some talk with Christian.

Mr. Worldly Wiseman: How now, good fellow, whither away after this burdened manner?
Christian: A burdened manner indeed, as ever I think poor creature had! And whereas you ask me, Whither away? I tell you, sir, I am going to yonder wicket-gate before me; for there, as I am informed, I shall be put into a way to be rid of my heavy burden.
Mr. Worldly Wiseman: Hast thou a wife and children?
Christian: Yes; but I am so laden with this burden, that I cannot take that pleasure in them as formerly: methinks I am as if I had none.
Mr. Worldly Wiseman: Wilt thou hearken to me, if I give thee counsel?
Christian: If it be good, I will; for I stand in need of good counsel.
Mr. Worldly Wiseman: I would advise thee, then, that thou with all speed get thyself rid of thy burden; for thou wilt never be settled in thy mind till then: nor canst thou enjoy the benefits of the blessings which God hath bestowed upon thee till then.
Christian: That is that which I seek for, even to be rid of this heavy burden: but get it off myself I cannot, nor is there any man in our country that can take it off my shoulders; therefore am I going this way, as I told you, that I may be rid of my burden.
Mr. Worldly Wiseman: Who bid thee go this way to be rid of thy burden?

Christian: A man that appeared to me to be a very great and honorable person: his name, as I remember, is Evangelist.

Mr. Worldly Wiseman: I beshrew him for his counsel! there is not a more dangerous and troublesome way in the world than is that into which he hath directed thee; and that thou shalt find, if thou wilt be ruled by his counsel. Thou hast met with something, as I perceive, already; for I see the dirt of the Slough of Despond is upon thee: but that slough is the beginning of the sorrows that do attend those that go on in that way. Hear me; I am older than thou: thou art like to meet with, in the way which thou goest, wearisomeness, painfulness, hunger, perils, nakedness, sword, lions, dragons, darkness, and, in a word, death, and what not. These things are certainly true, having been confirmed by many testimonies. And should a man so carelessly cast away himself, by giving heed to a stranger?

Christian: Why, sir, this burden on my back is more terrible to me than are all these things which you have mentioned: nay, methinks I care not what I meet with in the way, if so be I can also meet with deliverance from my burden.

Mr. Worldly Wiseman: How camest thou by thy burden at first?

Christian: By reading this book in my hand.

Mr. Worldly Wiseman: I thought so; and it has happened unto thee as to other weak men, who, meddling with things too high for them, do suddenly fall into thy distractions; which distractions do not only unman men, as thine I perceive have done thee, but they run them upon desperate ventures, to obtain they know not what.

Christian: I know what I would obtain; it is ease from my heavy burden.

Mr. Worldly Wiseman: But why wilt thou seek for ease this way, seeing so many dangers attend it? especially since (hadst thou but patience to hear me) I could direct thee to the obtaining of what thou desirest, without the dangers that thou in this way wilt run thyself into. Yea, and the remedy is at hand. Besides, I will add, that instead of those dangers, thou shalt meet with much safety, friendship, and content.

Christian: Sir, I pray open this secret to me.

Mr. Worldly Wiseman: Why, in yonder village (the village is named Morality) there dwells a gentleman whose name is Legality, a very judicious man, and a man of a very good name, that has skill to help men off with such burdens as thine is from their shoulders; yea to my knowledge, he hath done a great deal of good this way; aye, and besides, he hath skill to cure those that are somewhat crazed in their wits with their burdens. To him, as I said, thou mayest go, and be helped presently. His house is not quite a mile from this place; and if he should not be at home himself, he hath a pretty young man to his son, whose name is Civility, that can do it (to speak on) as well as the old gentleman himself: there, I say, thou mayest be eased of thy burden; and if thou art not minded to go back to thy former habitation, (as indeed I would not wish thee,) thou mayest send for thy wife and children to this village, where there are houses now standing empty, one of which thou mayest have at a reasonable rate: provision is there also cheap and good; and that which will make thy life the more happy is, to be sure there thou shalt live by honest neighbors, in credit and good fashion.

Now was Christian somewhat at a stand; but presently he concluded, If this be true which this gentleman hath said, my wisest course is to take his advice: and with that he thus farther spake.

Christian: Sir, which is my way to this honest man's house?

Mr. Worldly Wiseman: Do you see yonder high hill?

Christian: Yes, very well.

Mr. Worldly Wiseman: By that hill you must go, and the first house you come at is his.

So Christian turned out of his way to go to Mr. Legality's house for help: but, behold, when he was got now hard by the hill, it seemed so high, and also that side of it that was next the way-side did hang so much over, that Christian was afraid to venture further, lest the hill should fall on his head; wherefore there he stood still, and wotted not what to do. Also his burden now seemed heavier to him than while he was in his way. There came also flashes of fire, out of the hill, that made Christian afraid that he should be burnt: here therefore he did sweat and quake for fear. And now he began to be sorry that he had taken Mr. Worldly Wiseman's counsel; and with that he saw Evangelist coming to meet him, at the sight also of whom he began to blush for shame. So Evangelist drew nearer and nearer; and coming up to him, he looked upon him, with a severe and dreadful countenance, and thus began to reason with Christian.

Evangelist: What doest thou here, Christian? said he: at which words Christian knew not what to answer; wherefore at present he stood speechless before him. Then said Evangelist farther, Art not thou the man that I found crying without the walls of the city of Destruction?
Christian: Yes, dear sir, I am the man.
Evangelist: Did not I direct thee the way to the little wicket-gate?
Christian: Yes, dear sir, said Christian.
Evangelist: How is it then thou art so quickly turned aside? For thou art now out of the way.
Christian: I met with a gentleman so soon as I had got over the Slough of Despond, who persuaded me that I might, in the village before me, find a man that could take off my burden.
Evangelist: What was he?
Christian: He looked like a gentleman, and talked much to me, and got me at last to yield: so I came hither; but when I beheld this hill, and how it hangs over the way, I suddenly made a stand, lest it should fall on my head.
Evangelist: What said that gentleman to you?
Christian: Why, he asked me whither I was going; and I told him.
Evangelist: And what said he then?
Christian: He asked me if I had a family; and I told him. But, said I, I am so laden with the burden that is on my back, that I cannot take pleasure in them as formerly.
Evangelist: And what said he then?
Christian: He bid me with speed get rid of my burden; and I told him it was ease that I sought. And, said I, I am therefore going to yonder gate, to receive farther direction how I may get to the place of deliverance. So he said that he would show me a better way, and short, not so attended with difficulties as the way, sir, that you set me in; which way, said he, will direct you to a gentleman's house that hath skill to take off these burdens: so I believed him, and turned out of that way into this, if haply I might be soon eased of my burden. But when I came to this place, and beheld things as they are, I stopped, for fear (as I said) of danger: but I now know not what to do.

Then said Evangelist, Stand still a little, that I show thee the words of God.

So he stood trembling. Then said Evangelist, "See that ye refuse not Him that speaketh; for if they escaped not who refused him that spake on earth, much more shall not we escape, if we turn away from Him that speaketh from heaven." He said, moreover, "Now the just shall live by faith; but if any man draw back, my soul shall have no pleasure in him." He also did thus apply them: Thou art the man that art running into this misery; thou hast begun to reject the counsel of the Most High, and to draw back thy foot from the way of peace, even almost to the hazarding of thy perdition.

Then Christian fell down at his feet as dead, crying, Woe is me, for I am undone! At the sight of which Evangelist caught him by the right hand, saying, "All manner of sin and blasphemies shall be forgiven unto men." "Be not faithless, but believing." Then did Christian again a little revive, and stood up trembling, as at first, before Evangelist.

Then Evangelist proceeded, saying, Give more earnest heed to the things that I shall tell thee of. I will now show thee who it was that deluded thee, and who it was also to whom he sent thee. The man that met thee is one Worldly Wiseman, and rightly is he so called; partly because he savoreth only the doctrine of this world, (therefore he always goes to the town of Morality to church;) and partly because he loveth that doctrine best, for it saveth him best from the cross, and because he is of this carnal temper, therefore he seeketh to pervert my ways, though right. Now there are three things in this man's counsel that thou must utterly abhor.

1. His turning thee out of the way.
2. His laboring to render the cross odious to thee.
3. And his setting thy feet in that way that leadeth unto the administration of death.

First, Thou must abhor his turning thee out of the way; yea, and thine own consenting thereto; because this is to reject the counsel of God for the sake of the counsel of a Worldly Wiseman. The Lord says, "Strive to enter in at the straight gate," the gate to which I send thee; "for strait is the gate that leadeth unto life, and few there be that find it." From this little wicket-gate, and from the way thereto, hath this wicked man turned thee, to the bringing of thee almost to destruction: hate, therefore, his turning thee out of the way, and abhor thyself for hearkening to him.

Secondly, Thou must abhor his laboring to render the cross odious unto thee; for thou art to prefer it before the treasures of Egypt. Besides, the King of glory hath told thee, that he that will save his life shall lose it. And he that comes after him, and hates not his father, and mother, and wife, and children, and brethren, and sisters, yea, and his own life also, he cannot be his disciple. I say, therefore, for a man to labor to persuade thee that that shall be thy death, without which, the truth hath said, thou canst not have eternal life, this doctrine thou must abhor.

Thirdly, Thou must hate his setting of thy feet in the way that leadeth to the ministration of death. And for this thou must consider to whom he sent thee, and also how unable that person was to deliver thee from thy burden.

He to whom thou wast sent for ease, being by name Legality, is the son of the bond-woman which now is, and is in bondage with her children, and is, in a mystery, this Mount Sinai, which thou hast feared will fall on thy head. Now if she with her children are in bondage, how canst thou expect by them to be made free? This Legality, therefore, is not able to set thee free from thy burden. No man was as yet ever rid of his burden by him; no, nor ever is like to be: ye cannot be justified by the works of the law; for by the deeds of the law no man living can be rid of his burden: Therefore Mr. Worldly Wiseman is an alien, and Mr. Legality is a cheat; and for his son Civility, notwithstanding his simpering looks, he is but a hypocrite, and cannot help thee. Believe me, there is nothing in all this noise that thou hast heard of these sottish men, but a design to beguile thee of thy salvation, by turning thee from the way in which I had set thee. After this, Evangelist called aloud to the heavens for confirmation of what he had said; and with that there came words and fire out of the mountain under which poor Christian stood, which made the hair of his flesh stand up. The words were pronounced: "As many as are of the works of the law, are under the curse; for it is written, Cursed is every one that continueth not in all things which are written in the book of the law to do them."

Now Christian looked for nothing but death, and began to cry out lamentably; even cursing the time in which he met with Mr. Worldly Wiseman; still calling himself a thousand fools for hearkening to his counsel. He also was greatly ashamed to think that this gentleman's arguments, flowing only from the flesh, should have the prevalency with him so far as to cause him to forsake the right way. This done, he applied himself again to Evangelist in words and sense as follows.

Christian: Sir, what think you? Is there any hope? May I now go back, and go up to the wicket-gate? Shall I not be abandoned for this, and sent back from thence ashamed? I am sorry I have hearkened to this man's counsel; but may my sin be forgiven?

Evangelist: Then said Evangelist to him, Thy sin is very great, for by it thou hast committed two evils: thou hast forsaken the way that is good, to tread in forbidden paths. Yet will the man at the gate receive thee, for he has good-will for men; only, said he, take heed that thou turn not aside again, lest thou "perish from the way, when his wrath is kindled but a little."

GLOSSARY

beshrew: to curse, usually mildly

Mount Sinai: a mountain on the Sinai Peninsula of Egypt, by tradition the place where God gave the Ten Commandments to Moses

seraphims and cherubims: orders of angels

slough: any wet, muddy place; typically a stream or a canal in wet marshland or a side canal or inlet

Tophet: a place in a valley in ancient Jerusalem where human sacrifices were made

wicket-gate: any small opening or door, usually one that is part of a larger gate or door

Document Analysis

The first part of *The Pilgrim's Progress* tells the story of Christian's journey from his Native City of Destruction to the Heavenly City. Bunyan presents the trip, meant to represent the life of each Christian, as both ordinary and exciting. The pilgrim on life's journey will encounter fields and towns, friends and neighbors. The pilgrim will also encounter dangerous swamps, monsters, and wild animals. Since the world through which pilgrims travel is the meeting place of physical and supernatural life, both the ordinary elements of human experience and encounters with the extraordinary are normal parts of Christian's journey to salvation. The document produced here tells of the beginning of Christian's journey. The style, the imagery, and the constant biblical allusions in the text are typical of the whole work.

As I Walked through the Wilderness of This World

After an introduction in verse, Bunyan sets the stage for his story by describing it as the dream of the author; the author will not reawake until the final line of part 1. As a writer, Bunyan is known for his rich use of imagery—drawn heavily from the Authorized Version of the Bible. In this opening paragraph, for instance, the description of the future pilgrim is taken from scripture. "Filthy rags" are how the prophet Isaiah describes human attempts to please God; the Psalmist speaks of sins as a "heavy burden … too heavy for me." Similarly, the despairing cry, "What shall I do?" is an echo of several biblical passages. The sorrow, as the main character will soon relate, is a sense of impending judgment due for his own sins and the sins of his community. Such sorrow is a natural and appropriate response to encountering God's truth, as the future pilgrim does when he reads his book (the Bible).

In This Plight, Therefore, He Went Home

Bunyan's description of the future pilgrim's dilemma is a reflection of the differing understanding of salvation promoted by the state church (Church of England) and Bunyan's own beliefs. The Church of England did not see society itself under judgment, taught that salvation lay in taking one's appropriate place in society, and emphasized the communal rather than the individual aspects of salvation. Furthermore, the path to salvation offered through the Anglican Church was seen as the default position for any in the community that did not specifically reject it—no one need worry too much about being saved. Independents and other Puritans like Bunyan, however, understood society to be at odds with God. Salvation came only through rejecting society and its religious values and committing one's self entirely to God. Although Bunyan's version of Puritanism had strong communal implications (in part 2 of *The Pilgrim's Progress*, Christiana and her children travel together), there was an important individual component to religion. Underlying this stance was the assumption, in contrast to Anglicanism, that every person was lost *unless* he or she converted. The difference between the two positions is typical of a division in Western religiosity classified by sociologists as "church" versus "sect."

The mocking and derision the future pilgrim experienced would have been very familiar to Bunyan's audience. Bunyan was in jail when he wrote *The Pilgrim's Progress*, and all Nonconformists faced significant penalties—socially, economically, and legally—for rejecting the state church in favor of their own religious beliefs. Adherence to a Dissenting congregation might even mean alienation from family and friends. It was this contempt that Puritans received from the world for their beliefs that strengthened the Puritan notion that the world itself was lost. Certainly, the pressure to give up Dissenting beliefs and values taught the Puritans that the battles between good and evil over the destiny of souls were to be fought out in the world.

Bunyan has the first step in the journey to salvation begin with personal anguish. For Puritans, salvation required a strong sense of individual sin and unworthiness. Only those recognizing their sinfulness could turn to God for forgiveness and mercy. It was typical of Puritan values that a decision for conversion only followed many hours of reflection and consideration. While some of their modern-day heirs understand conversion as an instant, once-and-for-all occurrence, for Puritans it was a process involving time and multiple stages.

The phrase (odd to modern ears) "children of my bowels" reflects Bunyan's own familiarity with the Authorized Version of the Bible. The original Greek of the New Testament does indeed use the word correctly translated in the Authorized Version as "bowels" to describe what modern translations render in different places as "heart" or "feeling." Modern Western people usually make the heart the seat of human emotion. The ancients gave that role to the stomach. It is the stomach that receives the rush of acid, for instance, with some strong emotions or that churns with anxiety or hurts during times of stress. The main character is simply adapting a literary expression to describe how dear his children are to him.

Now I Saw ... [Him] Reading His Book, and Greatly Distressed in Mind

The importance of reading in the main character's conversion reflects Bunyan's own experience—his conversion was prompted by his wife's two books. Of course, the book here in the story later proves to be the Bible, the chief source of inspiration for Bunyan, as for all good Puritans. But even these Bible-centered Protestants did not reject the help of other forms of literature. *The Pilgrim's Progress* itself was meant to be one of the books that helped Pilgrims on their way.

Evangelist is the first character to be introduced by name. In Bunyan's story, the character of every person met in the pages is revealed by his or her name. Technically speaking, an Evangelist was one of the authors of the four Gospels (Matthew, Mark, Luke, and John), but Bunyan uses the name in the modern sense. Evangelist is someone who can tell the main character about salvation ("the Gospel" or "the Good News"). The future pilgrim has worked out his need for salvation on his own but requires someone to direct him on the path. Evangelist does not take him to salvation or plot the whole journey but merely points him in the right direction.

Notice that up to this point in the story the main character does not have a name. His character has not yet been defined. Only after he makes an important decision can his true nature be revealed by the name he is given. This encounter between Evangelist and the main character emphasizes the individualistic aspect of the Puritan understanding of salvation. To obtain eternal life, the pilgrim must be willing to leave other kinds of life (family life, public life) behind. Underlying Bunyan's beliefs was the conviction that "the world" (society, community, the established order) was opposed to God's will and a hindrance to salvation. One must choose between the world's way and God's way.

At the same time, Puritan religion was communal as well as individualistic. At some point each individual must make a personal decision, but such decisions are not made in isolation. There is no salvation for the main character with Evangelist to point the way. At critical times in the story other individuals appear or reappear to keep the pilgrim on the path. The corporate nature of pilgrim life is emphasized more strongly in the second part of the book, where the pilgrims travel in a group.

The description of the meeting between Evangelist and the main character is a classic depiction of Puritan values. Human sin and its deserved condemnation are self-evident, and many people in the course of life might become aware of them. However, some who recognize their own faults and know they need to be saved might, by society's pressure, decide to ignore their convictions. It is only when the sense of sin is too strong to ignore that the individual is willing to pursue relief. The main character is at this point not saved but a seeker after salvation. And to seek, he must leave his community behind.

The Neighbors Also Came Out
The decision to set out on the road to salvation is a momentous one. Only now can the pilgrim be called by his appropriate name, Christian. While the state church would have claimed that all those living in the city of Destruction (which Christian has just fled) were Christians, for the Puritans real Christians were those who were aware of their own sin and who turned to God for salvation.

The experience of opposition was an important part of Puritan self-understanding. Since the world was lost and under judgment, one could expect only opposition from those who lived in it. In the case of Christian, there is general contempt and specific opposition from the characters Obstinate and Pliable. Obstinate questions the pilgrim, allowing Christian to describe something of his hope for salvation, words that only bring derision on "the book." Obstinate calls for the pilgrim to give up his silliness and come home, while Pliable proves more open to the message. Ultimately Pliable resolves to travel with the pilgrim, while Obstinate turns back in disgust. It is probably not a good sign for Pliable's future as a pilgrim that he is more attracted to the journey by the joys of heaven than by the conviction of his own sin.

Bunyan's short description of the responses of Christian's neighbors hints at three types of opposition Nonconforming Christians experienced. The first was simple rejection, characterized by mockery—the sort of reaction Bunyan highlights in the story. The second, perhaps implied in the phrase "some cried after him to return," was a more serious effort to persuade Dissenters to abandon their peculiar religious ideas. Mr. Worldly Wiseman, who appears later in the reading, provides one example of this sort as he tries to talk Christian into losing his burden in Morality. The final type of opposition is implied in the attempt "to fetch him back by force." The state church possessed great power from the government to compel conformity. Bunyan himself, of course, wrote *The Pilgrim's Progress* while he was in jail for preaching without a license, a license that never would have been issued to him. The amount of legal trouble Dissenters faced varied from place to place and time to time. There were districts and periods where Nonconformists were generally ignored, while on other occasions they might face strict persecution. Even after 1688, though, when the freedom of Protestants to worship was generally allowed, Nonconformists faced severe legal limitations in terms of careers and education. When Bunyan describes the world as actively hostile to Puritan Christians, he is doing no more than recounting a reality he and most Nonconformists experienced.

Now I Saw in My Dream, That When Obstinate Was Gone Back
Christian and Pliable travel together while Christian gives more details about the glorious future awaiting believers in heaven. Their conversation demonstrates that the book Christian carries with him is indeed the Bible, a sure source of knowledge about spiritual realities. Although Christian is eager to hurry down the path to the Heavenly City, he finds himself slowed by the burden of sin he still carries on his back like a pack.

The "Slough of Despond" is one of Bunyan's most famous images. Like that of any good allegorical figure, its rich complexity defies simple characterization, but among other things it is a swamp that traps people who are beginning their pilgrimage to the Heavenly City. The Slough itself stains and defiles, and in it the weight of sin is even more burdensome. It is ultimately revealed that the swamp is created from the discouragement that attends an awareness of personal sin. Although it is a trap or hazard on the path to salvation, it is one that cannot be completely mended, because the sorrow and fear created by an awareness of sin is natural (and even necessary) for those seeking to escape judgment.

Even if the Slough cannot ever be entirely drained, it should not be the great obstacle that it is. Here Bunyan is making a typical Puritan complaint against both the Catholic Church and the Anglican Church. Like a monarch ordering his highways to be maintained, God had commanded the road through the Slough to be repaired and provided much teaching to help Christians avoid being caught in the swamp of discouragement and self-doubt, yet these lessons had been mishandled, leaving many stuck in the mire. With appropriate instruction, a believer should be able to find God's firm path through the dangerous slough. This is the fault of the state church, which neglects its essential functions and fails to teach important truths to its adherents, leaving pilgrims to find their own way down the difficult road to salvation.

Despite the hardships, Christian fights his way through the swamp, with the aid of the character Help—yet another reminder of the corporate aspect of Puritan faith. Christian needs others to give him a hand up from the swamp and to point him to the right path. But Pliable, who was so eager to experience the joys of the Heavenly City, is overwhelmed by the challenges of the journey and turns away. Christian continues on his way.

Now I Saw in My Dream That by This Time Pliable Was Got Home

Bunyan's audience would have been very familiar with individuals who had temporarily associated themselves with Dissenting congregations and then returned to the state church. The story of Pliable served as a cautionary tale. Those who went back to their old ways were likely to get just as much grief from their neighbors as if they had remained true, yet they would also miss out on heaven. In fact, since Pliable is around to be derided by his neighbors while Christian has moved on, Pliable may be even be worse off in the present life, just as he will certainly be worse off in the future one.

Now as Christian Was Walking Solitary

Christian continues on his journey and encounters a new figure, a man who has advice for him. The pilgrim has set out on the road to the Heavenly City in order to have the burden lifted from his back. Mr. Worldly Wiseman suggests that there are easier ways to remove the burden, ways that do not involve hardship, danger, or the loss of his family and community standing.

From a Puritan perspective, images of morality and civility promoted by society and the Church of England were traps. As Puritans understood the Bible, human effort ("keeping the law") could not save people from God's judgment. To them, much of what the state church offered was a reliance on human effort, helping people to feel better about themselves so that they no longer noticed their burden of sin but not actually providing salvation. The Puritans saw such teaching as a medicine that masked a patient's symptoms without curing the deadly disease. In rejecting "morality," the Puritans were not advocating wild, sinful lifestyles—after all, Puritanism today is a byword for ultra-strict conduct. Instead, they were rejecting "moralism," the idea that avoiding certain conspicuous sins was enough to please God. Civility was an even greater trap, elevating politeness and deference to society's ideals of appropriate public behavior as the ultimate standard of human conduct.

Mr. Worldly Wiseman mocks both the teaching of "the book" and Christian's efforts to understand it. The warning not to meddle in things too high for him was typical of the advice that often uneducated Dissenters might frequently receive. Many educated people believed that only the trained experts of the state church were competent to interpret the Bible and God's will and found it offensive that less-educated and less-qualified people would presume to do so. Although it was not necessarily true of the first generation of Puritans, there was an increasing element of class division between Dissenters and the supporters of the established church. This division would grow with time, so that most Nonconforming English groups (Congregationalists, Presbyterians, Baptists, and later Methodists), would be firmly working class in orientation.

For Bunyan, socially acceptable alternatives to fleeing the City of Destruction were foolish tricks. The burden of sin was a real problem pointing to a real solution, and any alleged "cure" that caused a would-be pilgrim to forsake the journey to salvation was a terrible lie. Christian is taken in and leaves the correct road for a dead-end path. Even though the difficult way of salvation is full of misleading tracks, it is always possible to get back on the right road.

So Christian Turned Out of His Way

Bunyan's phrase "so Christian turned out of his way" signals the gravity of Christian's mistake. To leave the path pointed out by Evangelist to seek a shortcut puts the whole pilgrimage at risk. Bunyan and his fellow Dissenters believed that the Church of England ignored biblical directives about the proper way to salvation and pointed the way instead to a path that led only to destruction.

There would be many false trails leading off the true road to the Heavenly City, but Bunyan highlights the path to morality and civility as being particularly dangerous. The way of morality and civility seemed to offer an attractive shortcut to relief from the burden of sin, yet as Christian tries to go in that direction, he finds the burden of sin growing and the path actually harder to follow. Trying to lead a genuinely moral life proves to be more difficult than it seemed initially and does not lead to salvation. Poor Christian despairs of ever reaching the Heavenly City. However, even though his sins are great, it is possible for him to return to the true path Fortunately, the pilgrim is not doomed by his misstep. It is possible for those who have gone astray to return to the right path. Bunyan provides Evangelist as the character who once again can point Christian in the right direction.

One of the ongoing debates within Christianity, going back to the time of Augustine and his opponents, is about the nature of the Christian life. Are pilgrims best represented as super-athletes, who need only an occasional spotter to remain pumped up, or are they more like patients in a hospital, weak and in constant need of medicine? Bunyan presents Christians in the mode of hospital patients. In life, pilgrims make mistakes. They take wrong turns; they fall into swamps; they are led astray and heed bad advice. It is because of human weakness that the journey is dangerous and full of pitfalls. Only by God's help, following the directions given in the Bible and with encouragement and assistance from God-given allies along the way, will Christian and other pilgrims arrive at the Heavenly City.

Evangelist's exhortation to Christian is very similar in form to a typical Puritan sermon. The introduction of headings (as with the "three things ... thou must utterly abhor") is still used in some traditions of preaching even today. Certainly the way in which Evangelist draws on complicated biblical imagery to provide a lesson about life would have been very familiar to anyone who attended a Dissenting congregation.

Essential Themes
It is often said that, after the Bible, *The Pilgrim's Progress* is the most printed, published, and translated book in the world. (It appeared in ninety different editions in the first hundred years after its publication and has been translated into more than two hundred languages.) Certainly it was the top bestseller in pre-modern England and enjoyed a similar popularity in colonial America. For generations Bunyan's allegory was the most popular religious text in the English-speaking world.

Although Bunyan's literary reputation has somewhat diminished in modern times, it was not only his religious views that were influential. Readers who passed over the spiritual message of *The Pilgrim's Progress* were often affected by Bunyan's powerful and creative literary style. Bunyan's influence extends even over those who reject his basic values or have never read his work—the popular magazine *Vanity Fair* takes its name from a large community's market in *The Pilgrim's Progress*, for Bunyan a place of temptation to avoid. Another of many of Bunyan's phrases to enter popular culture is "Slough of Despond."

As an author, Bunyan still continues to exert influence. C. S. Lewis, the author of the Narnia stories and a popular Christian writer, was inspired by Bunyan to write a modern Christian allegory, which he entitled *The Pilgrim's Regress*. *The Pilgrim's Progress* had a discernible impact on such classic literature as Charlotte Brontë's *Jane Eyre*, Louisa May Alcott's *Little Women*, Kurt Vonnegut's *Slaughterhouse-Five*, and, of course, William Makepeace Thackeray's *Vanity Fair*, as well as dozens of lesser-known modern works. It was made into an opera by Ralph Vaughan Williams and more recently into a rock opera.

More important to Bunyan would have been the religious legacy of his writing. When Bunyan wrote his classic work, he was expressing the values of a persecuted minority. With time, however, and certainly helped by the wide popularity of *The Pilgrim's Progress*, Puritan beliefs became more and more mainstream, until today many of their convictions are widely held in the Protestant community worldwide. Bunyan's understanding of conversion, of Christian mistrust of society, of the role of the individual, and of the authority of scripture are shared by the majority of Christians in Britain and the United States today. Perhaps the greatest testimony to how widely accepted *The Pilgrim's Progress* is by modern Christians is the inclusion of Christian's hymn "He Who Would Valiant Be" in the Church of England hymnal.

—Raymond A. Powell

Bibliography and Further Reading

Bunyan, John. *Grace Abounding to the Chief of Sinners.* Penguin, 1987.

Furlong, Monica. *Puritan's Progress: A Study of John Bunyan.* Hodder & Stoughton, 1975.

Greaves, Richard L. *Glimpses of Glory: John Bunyan and English Dissent.* Stanford University Press, 2002.

Hill, Christopher. *A Tinker and a Poor Man: John Bunyan and His Church, 1628–1688.* Knopf, 1988.

Mullett, Michael. *John Bunyan in Context.* Keele University Press, 1996.

The Pilgrim's Progress: Critical and Historical Views. Edited by Vincent Newey. University of Liverpool Press, 1980.

Winslow, Ola Elizabeth. *John Bunyan.* Macmillan, 1961.

Dutton, Richard A. "'Interesting, but Tough': Reading *The Pilgrim's Progress.*" *Studies in English Literature,* 18, no. 3 (Summer 1978, pp. 439–456).

Isaac Newton: *The Mathematical Principles of Natural Philosophy*

Date: 1687
Author: Isaac Newton
Genre: Treatise

Summary Overview
Possibly the most important document in the history of science, this is a summary of the laws of motion and the law of universal gravitation using the hypothetico-deductive method which assumes that the laws are valid and then works out their consequences, and compares those consequences with observation or experiment to test their validity. Absent from the discussion is any mention of purpose (teleology). Based on the success of the Newtonian method, Ernst Mach would later define science as "economy of thought."

In *Metaphysical Foundations of Modern Science*, E. A. Burtt considers Newton's role in replacing the traditional metaphysical categories—substance, essence, matter, form, quality, and quantity—by the more modern set—time, space, energy, and so on. The first list goes back to Aristotle and had been made acceptable to the late medieval world by the writings of Moses Maimonides (Jewish), Averroes (Muslim), and St. Thomas Aquinas (Christian). They placed man and the Earth at the center of the universe. More modern concepts arise in the works of Copernicus, Galileo, and Newton which are not so anthropocentric.

Prior to the modern synthesis, it would be sufficient to say that the universe was designed by an omniscient God to meet the needs of humankind. In the modern view humans are a happy accident in a universe that evolved obeying the natural laws that Newton discovered. Whether the modern synthesis provides the complete story or not is a matter of continuing debate.

Defining Moment
The critical year for Isaac Newton was the plague year of 1665, when Cambridge University had to close for fear of contagion. Newton had been accepted at Trinity College of Cambridge University as a sizar, or work-study student, in 1661, and graduated in 1665. Newly graduated, he undertook a period of intense mathematical work on his mother's farm during which he developed the basic principles of calculus. He returned to Cambridge in 1667 and was appointed Lucasian Professor of Mathematics in 1669.

The Royal Society of London was among the first scientific academies. It had begun about 1645 with the "Invisible College" of London and Oxford, and several smaller academies, when the newly restored Charles II granted it a Royal Charter in 1660. Isaac Newton was elected to the Society in 1671. Newton would become president of the Society in 1703 and was knighted by Queen Anne in 1705.

The immediate cause of the writing of *Principia Mathematica* was the arrival of Sir Edmund Halley in London in 1684. It was written, in Latin, over a period of three years and motivated by Newton's need to establish priority for his theory of universal gravitation under the inverse square force of gravity. Despite Newton's concern for priority, none of Newton's work was translated into English until after his death.

With the Royal Society established and norms of behavior not yet established, squabbles arose among prominent members. Robert Hooke, first experimental secretary, discovered the law of elasticity—stress is proportional to strain—but published it as an anagram, thus claiming priority without disclosing his discovery. Newton was no stranger to priority disputes, nor was he particularly respectful of the decision process.

Newton's proposal—that every part of any body exerted gravitational force on every other—was yet another argument that man was the center of the universe.

Author Biography
Isaac Newton was born on Christmas Day, 1642. His natural father was already dead. This left his mother with the task of finding another husband while raising young Isaac. Fortunately, the young child took to his studies. He was able to enter Cambridge University as a sizar, or work-study student. He graduated just as an outbreak of the plague forced Cambridge University to close for a time. He spent that time most profitably working at mathematics so that he could be appointed

PHILOSOPHIÆ NATURALIS PRINCIPIA MATHEMATICA.

Autore *JS. NEWTON*, *Trin. Coll. Cantab. Soc.* Matheseos Professore *Lucasiano*, & Societatis Regalis Sodali.

IMPRIMATUR·
S. PEPYS, *Reg. Soc.* PRÆSES.
Julii 5. 1686.

LONDINI,
Jussu *Societatis Regiæ* ac Typis *Josephi Streater*. Prostat apud plures Bibliopolas. *Anno* MDCLXXXVII.

Title page of *Principia*, first edition (1687). By The original uploader was Zhaladshar at English Wikisource (Transferred from en.wikisource to Commons.) [Public domain], via Wikimedia Commons

Lucasian Professor of Mathematics in 1669. He stayed at Cambridge until 1687.

As a professor, Newton had been uninspiring. Because his appointment required him to lecture for three hours per week, he did so, regardless of whether there was anyone to hear him.

Newton as a member of Parliament accomplished little. There is a story that once he stood up to speak, and the room silenced to hear what the great man had to say. But he just asked that the window be opened a bit.

Newton's politically powerful friends had him appointed Warden of the Mint in 1696 and 1699, There he showed his practical management skills and reorganized the minting process, making gold coins much harder to counterfeit. The knurled edges found on United States silver coins are a legacy from Isaac Newton.

Newton died on March 20, 1737 (according to the Gregorian calendar in use in England at the time). He was afforded a state funeral and lies interred in Westminster Abbey.

HISTORICAL DOCUMENT

Excerpt from *The Mathematical Principles of Natural Philosophy* by Isaac Newton
Beginning of Book III: System of the World
Rules of Reasoning in Philosophy
RULE I.

We are to admit no more causes of natural things than such as are both time and sufficient to explain their appearances.

To this purpose the philosophers say that Nature does nothing in vain, and more is in vain when less will serve; for Nature is pleased with simplicity, and affects not the pomp of superfluous causes.

RULE II.

Therefore to the same natural effects we must, as far as possible, assign the same causes.

As to respiration in a man and in a beast; the descent of stones in *Europe* and in *America*; the light of our culinary fire and of the sun; the reflection of light in the earth, and in the planets.

RULE III.

The qualities of bodies, which admit neither intension nor remission of degrees, and which are found to belong to all bodies within the reach of our experiments, are to be esteemed the universal qualities of all bodies whatsoever.

For since the qualities of bodies are only known to us by experiments, we are to hold for universal all such as universally agree with experiments; and such as are not liable to diminution can never be quite taken away. We are certainly not to relinquish the evidence of experiments for the sake of dreams and vain fictions of our own devising; nor are we to recede from the analogy of Nature, which uses to be simple, and always consonant to itself. We no other way know the extension of bodies than by our senses, nor do these reach it in all bodies; but because we perceive extension in all that are sensible, therefore we ascribe it universally to all others also. That abundance of bodies are hard, we learn by experience; and because the hardness of the whole arises from the hardness of the parts, we therefore justly infer the hardness of the undivided particles not only of the bodies we feel but of all others. That all bodies are impenetrable, we gather not from reason, but from sensation. The bodies which we handle we find impenetrable, and thence conclude impenetrability to be an universal property of all bodies whatsoever. That all bodies are moveable, and endowed with certain powers (which we call the *vires inertiae*) of persevering in their motion, or in their rest, we only infer from the like properties observed in the bodies which we have seen. The extension, hardness, impenetrability, mobility, and *vis inertiae* of the whole, result from the extension, hardness, impenetrability, mobility, and *vires inertiae* of the parts; and thence we conclude the least particles of all bodies to be also all extended, and hard and impenetrable, and moveable, and endowed with their proper *vires inertia*. And this is the foundation of all philosophy. Moreover, that the divided but contiguous particles of bodies may be separated from one another, is matter of observation; and, in the particles that remain undivided, our minds are able to distinguish yet lesser parts, as is mathematically demonstrated. But whether the parts so distinguished, and not yet divided, may, by the powers of Nature, be actually divided and separated from one an other, we cannot certainly determine. Yet, had we the proof of but one experiment that any undivided particle, in breaking a hard and solid body, suffered a division, we might by virtue of this rule conclude that the undivided as well as the divided particles may be divided and actually separated to infinity.

Lastly, if it universally appears, by experiments and astronomical observations, that all bodies about the earth gravitate towards the earth, and that in proportion to the quantity of matter which they severally contain; that the moon likewise, according to the quantity of its matter, gravitates towards the earth; that, on the other hand, our sea gravitates towards the moon; and all the planets mutually one towards another; and the comets in like manner towards the sun; we must, in consequence of this rule, universally allow that all bodies whatsoever are endowed with a principle of mutual gravitation. For the argument from the appearances concludes with more force for the universal gravitation of all bodies than for their impenetrability; of which, among those in the celestial regions, we have no experiments, nor any manner of observation. Not that I affirm gravity to be essential to bodies: by their *vis insita* I mean nothing but their *vis inertiae*. This is immutable. Their gravity is diminished as they recede from the earth.

RULE IV.

In experimental philosophy we are to look upon propositions collected by general induction from phaenomena as accurately or very nearly true, notwithstanding any contrary hypotheses that may be imagined, till such time as other phaenomena occur, by which they may either be made more accurate, or liable to exceptions.

This rule we must follow, that the argument of induction may not be evaded by hypotheses.

...

Conclusion of Book III
General Scholium

The hypothesis of vortices is pressed with many difficulties. That every planet by a radius drawn to the sun may describe areas proportional to the times of description, the periodic times of the several parts of the vortices should observe the duplicate proportion of their distances from the sun; but that the periodic times of the planets may obtain the sesquiplicate proportion of their distances from the sun, the periodic times of the parts of the vortex ought to be in the sesquiplicate proportion of their distances. That the smaller vortices may maintain their lesser revolutions about Saturn, Jupiter, and other planets, and swim quietly and undisturbed in the greater vortex of the sun, the periodic times of the parts of the sun's vortex should be equal; but the rotation of the sun and planets about their axes, which ought to correspond with the motions of their vortices, recede far from all these proportions. The motions of the comets are exceedingly regular, are governed by the same laws with the motions of the planets, and can by no means be accounted for by the hypothesis of vortices; for comets are carried with very eccentric motions through all parts of the heavens indifferently, with a freedom that is incompatible with the notion of a vortex.

Bodies projected in our air suffer no resistance but from the air. Withdraw the air, as is done in Mr. Boyle's vacuum, and the resistance ceases; for in this void a bit of line down and a piece of solid gold descend with equal velocity. And the parity of reason must take place in the celestial spaces above the earth's atmosphere; in which spaces, where there is no air to resist their motions, all bodies will move with the greatest freedom; and the planets and comets will constantly pursue their revolutions in orbits given in kind and position, according to the laws above explained; but though these bodies may, indeed, persevere in their orbits by the mere laws of gravity, yet they could by no means have at first derived the regular position of the orbits themselves from those laws.

The six primary planets are revolved about the sun in circles concentric with the sun, and with motions directed towards the same parts, and almost in the same plane. Ten moons are revolved about the earth, Jupiter and Saturn, in circles concentric with them, with the same direction of motion, and nearly in the planes of the orbits of those planets; but it is not to be conceived that mere mechanical causes could give birth to so many regular motions, since the comets range over all parts of the heavens in very eccentric orbits; for by that kind of motion they pass easily through the orbs of the planets, and with great rapidity; and in their aphelions, where they move the slowest, and are detained the longest, they recede to the greatest distances from each other, and thence suffer the least disturbance from their mutual attractions. This most beautiful system of the sun, planets, and comets, could only proceed from the counsel and dominion of an intelligent and powerful Being. And if the fixed stars are the centres of other like systems, these, being formed by the like wise counsel, must be all subject to the dominion of One; especially since the light of the fixed stars is of the same nature with the light of the sun, and from every system light passes into all the other systems: and lest the systems of the fixed stars should, by their gravity, fall on each other mutually, he hath placed those systems at immense distances one from another.

This Being governs all things, not as the soul of the world, but as Lord over all; and on account of his dominion he is wont to be called Lord God παντοκράτωρ, or Universal Ruler; for God is a relative word, and has a respect to servants; and Deity is the dominion of God not over his own body, as those imagine who fancy God to be the soul of the world, but over servants. The Supreme God is a Being eternal, infinite, absolutely perfect; but a being, however perfect, without dominion, cannot be said to be Lord God; for we say, my God, your God, the God of Israel, the God of Gods, and Lord of Lords; but we do not say, my Eternal, your Eternal, the Eternal of Israel, the Eternal of Gods; we do not say, my Infinite, or my Perfect: these are titles which have no respect to servants. The word God usually signifies Lord; but every lord is not a God. It is the dominion of a spiritual being which constitutes a God: a true, supreme, or imaginary dominion makes a true, supreme, or imaginary God. And from his true dominion it follows that the true God is a living, intelligent, and powerful Being; and, from his other perfections, that he is supreme, or most perfect. He is eternal and infinite, omnipotent and omniscient; that is, his duration reaches from eternity to eternity; his presence from infinity to infinity; he governs all things, and knows all things that are or can be done. He is not eternity or infinity, but eternal and infinite; he is not duration or space, but he endures and is present. He endures for ever, and is every where present; and by existing always and every where, he constitutes duration and space. Since every particle of space is always, and every indivisible moment of duration is every where, certainly the Maker and Lord of all things cannot be never and no where. Every soul that has perception is, though in different times and in different organs of sense and motion, still the same indivisible person. There are given successive parts in duration, co-existent parts in space, but neither the one nor the other in the person of a man, or his thinking principle; and much less can they be found in the thinking substance of God. Every man, so far as he is a thing that has perception, is one and the same man during his whole life, in all and each of his organs of sense. God is the same God, always and every where. He is omnipresent not virtually only, but also substantially; for virtue cannot subsist without substance. In him are all things contained and moved; yet neither affects the other: God suffers nothing from the motion of bodies; bodies find no resistance from the omnipresence of God. It is allowed by all that the Supreme God exists necessarily; and by the same necessity he exists always and every where. Whence also he is all similar, all eye, all ear, all brain, all arm, all power to perceive, to understand, and to act; but in a manner not at all human, in a manner not at all corporeal, in a manner utterly unknown to us. As a blind mail has no idea of colours, so have we no idea of the manner by which the all-wise God perceives and understands all things. He is utterly void of all body and bodily figure, and can therefore neither be seen, nor heard, nor touched; nor ought he to be worshipped under the representation of any corporeal thing. We have ideas of his attributes, but what the real substance of any thing is we know not. In bodies, we see only their figures and colours, we hear only the sounds, we touch only their outward surfaces, we smell only the smells, and taste the savours; but their inward substances are not to be known either by our senses, or by any reflex act of our minds: much less, then, have we any idea of the substance of God. We know him only by his most wise and excellent contrivances of things, and final causes: we admire him for his perfections; but we reverence and adore him on account of his dominion: for we adore him as his servants; and a god without dominion, providence, and final causes, is nothing else but Fate and Nature. Blind metaphysical necessity, which is certainly the same always and every where, could produce no variety of things. All that diversity of natural things which we find suited to different times and places could arise from nothing but the ideas and will of a Being necessarily existing. But, by way of allegory, God is said to see, to speak, to laugh, to love, to hate, to desire, to give, to receive, to rejoice, to be angry, to fight, to frame, to work, to build; for all our notions of God are taken from the ways of mankind by a certain similitude, which, though not perfect, has some likeness, however. And thus much concerning God; to discourse of whom from the appearances of things, does certainly belong to Natural Philosophy.

Hitherto we have explained the phenomena of the heavens and of our sea by the power of gravity, but have not yet assigned the cause of this power. This is certain, that it must proceed from a cause that penetrates to the very centres of the sun and planets, without suffering the least diminution of its force; that operates not according to the quantity of the surfaces of the particles upon which it acts (as mechanical causes use to do), but according to the quantity of the solid matter which they contain, and propagates its virtue on all sides to immense distances, decreasing always in the duplicate proportion of the distances. Gravitation towards the sun is made up out of the gravitations towards the several particles of which the body of the sun is composed; and in receding from the sun decreases accurately in the duplicate proportion of the distances as far as the orb of Saturn, as evidently appears from the quiescence of the aphelions of the planets; nay, and even to the remotest aphelions of the comets, if those aphelions are also quiescent. But hitherto I have not been able to discover the cause of those properties of gravity from phaenomena, and I frame no hypotheses; for whatever is not deduced from the phaenomena is to be called an hypothesis; and hypotheses, whether metaphysical or physical, whether of occult qualities or mechanical, have no place in experimental philosophy. In this philosophy particular propositions are inferred from the phenomena, and afterwards rendered general by induction. Thus it was that the impenetrability, the mobility, and the impulsive force of bodies, and the laws of motion and of gravitation, were discovered. And to us it is enough that gravity does really exist, and act according to the laws which we have explained, and abundantly serves to account for all the motions of the celestial bodies, and of our sea.

And now we might add something concerning a certain most subtle Spirit which pervades and lies hid in all gross bodies; by the force and action of which Spirit the particles of bodies mutually attract one another at near distances, and cohere, if contiguous; and electric bodies operate to greater distances, as well repelling as attracting the neighbouring corpuscles; and light is emitted, reflected, refracted, inflected, and heats bodies; and all sensation is excited, and the members of animal bodies move at the command of the will, namely, by the vibrations of this Spirit, mutually propagated along the solid filaments of the nerves, from the outward organs of sense to the brain, and from the brain into the muscles. But these are things that cannot be explained in few words, nor are we furnished with that sufficiency of experiments which is required to an accurate determination and demonstration of the laws by which this electric and elastic Spirit operates.

Source: Newton, Isaac. Newton's Principia. Translated by Andrew Motte. New York: Daniel Adee, 1846.

GLOSSARY

aphelion: in a planetary or cometary orbit, the point farthest from the sun

hypothetico-deductive method: the method used in modern physics where one assumes a mathematical model and then tests it by comparing its predictions with experiment or observation

teleology: the notion that the behavior of objects is purposeful, e.g,. heavy objects fall because they "want" to be on the Earth's surface

vortex: an alternative way of envisioning gravitation, now obsolete

Document Analysis

The sections reproduced here are the beginning and end of Book III.

Rule I. This is familiar to philosophers as Ockham's razor, an argument against making unnecessary assumptions. While this basic principle was known to Aristotle, it was discarded in favor of mysterious essences that made all motion depend on God.

Rule II. This is a corollary to Rule I. It is an argument against vitalism, though few before the current epoch would see it as such.

Rule III is awkward because it is stated in the language made obsolete by modern chemistry. In Newton's time philosophers still found the notion of a vacuum problematic. The precise nature of gases had yet to be worked out, and the only matter that the philosophers could be sure of was composed of rigid spheres. The inertia of solid bodies is seen as resulting from their composition. The section concludes by hinting at Newton's Third Law of Motion: For every action, there is an equal and opposite reaction.

Rule IV is that we must respect the conclusions of inductive logic.

The General Scholium that follows the text of Book II is an argument against the theory of vortices. In this, Newton argues that something far less complicated is needed. He concludes his work with some observations about God. It must be remembered that Newton took religion very seriously and that he had devoted much of his younger life to alchemy. Newton is forced to make a distinction between God as universal ruler and the Christian Lord who responds to worship by humanity.

Essential Theme

The essential theme here is that one must respect Ockham's razor in theorizing about nature. Such a conclusion would be cited by Stephen Hawking, who held the same academic appointment as Newton, as reason for dispensing entirely the hypothesis of a god behind nature. But clearly, Newton is not willing to go that far.

—*Donald R. Franceschetti, PhD*

Bibliography and Further Reading

Burtt, Edwin A. *The Metaphysical Foundations of Modern Physical Science: A Historical and Critical Essay.* London: K. Paul, Trench, Trubner, 1925. Print.

Dobbs, B.J.T. *The Foundations of Newton's Alchemy, Or, "the Hunting of the Greene Lyon".* Cambridge: Cambridge University Press, 1975. Print.

Gleick, James. *Isaac Newton.* Vintage, 2007. Internet resource.

Hawking, Stephen, ed. *On the Shoulders of Giants: The Great Works of Physics and Astronomy.* Philadelphia, PA: Running, 2004. Print.

Westfall, Richard S. *Never at Rest: A Biography of Isaac Newton.* Cambridge: Cambridge University Press, 2010. Print.

White, Michael. *Isaac Newton: The Last Sorcerer.* Reading, Mass: Perseus Books, 1999. Print.

English Bill of Rights

Date: 1689
Authors: Convention Parliament
Genre: Constitution

Summary Overview

The English Bill of Rights is a statute law that was passed by Parliament and given royal assent on December 16, 1689. Along with the Magna Carta (1215), the Petition of Right (1628), the Act of Habeas Corpus (1679), and the Act of Settlement (1701), the English Bill of Rights is considered one of the most important documents that make up the uncodified constitution of England. The constitution is said to be uncodified because it is not recorded in a single document but is rather a collection of documents written at different times. Developments in the late twentieth century, such as the United Kingdom's entry into the European Union and the process of devolution in Scotland and Wales, have cast doubt on the continuing relevance of the Bill of Rights. However, its passage into law is still regarded as a significant legal and constitutional watershed.

The English Bill of Rights was closely modeled on the Declaration of Rights, to which William and Mary, Prince and Princess of Orange, assented on February 13, 1689, before their declaration as King William III and Queen Mary II. The bill defined the relationship between the English monarch and Parliament, consisting of the House of Commons and House of Lords, and it firmly placed sovereignty with Parliament and by extension the people of England. Whether the bill technically constituted the establishment of a constitutional monarchy is debatable. At the very least, it formally heralded the end in England of the "divine right of kings." It also halted the drift toward absolutism that had been characteristic of the Stuart dynasty, in particular King Charles I (r. 1625–1649) and King James II (r. 1685–1688). In short, the bill provided the framework for establishing a constitutional monarchy, and that framework consisted of wide-ranging provisions pertaining to three main concerns: defining the relationship between Parliament and the Crown, clarifying the rules of royal succession, and giving statutory protection to the rights of individuals.

The English Bill of Rights was composed amid the turbulence of the Glorious Revolution of 1688–1689, during which James II fled to France and the throne was offered to William and Mary. Many of the bill's provisions were left deliberately and necessarily vague; the intention was that they would be "worked up" in subsequent decades. In fact, many were, most notably as the Triennial Act (1694), which ensured regular parliamentary meetings and elections; the Civil List Act (1697), which made Parliament, rather than the king, directly responsible for the payment of people on the Civil List (made up of officials charged with carrying out duties associated with the maintenance of the royal household); and the Act of Settlement (1701), which settled the succession to the English throne.

Defining Moment

The English Bill of Rights owes its existence to events that led up to the Glorious Revolution, also known as the English Revolution. Many of the bill's provisions directly address contentious political issues of this tumultuous period.

Following the death of King Charles II on February 6, 1685, his brother, James, a staunch but converted Catholic, ascended the British throne and became James II of England and Ireland as well as James VII of Scotland. James's Catholicism immediately posed several problems, since England had been confirmed as a Protestant Anglican nation over a century earlier by the Second Act of Supremacy and the Act of Uniformity. These acts formed the basis of the Elizabethan Religious Settlement of 1559, which established the sovereign as "supreme governor" of the Anglican Church and compelled the English people to attend Anglican Sunday services. However, despite England's Anglicanism, James was crowned amid objections that were muted for a number of reasons. First, only twenty-five years had passed since the English monarchy had been restored in 1660 after the collapse of the Protectorate, the period of Oliver Cromwell's direct personal rule as lord protector. Supporters of the monarchy and royal prerogative feared that the legitimacy of the Restoration itself might be threatened if James were denied the throne. Second, aristocratic families, notably Tory, held sacrosanct the principles of lineage and hereditary suc-

An 18th-century engraving, based on a drawing by Samuel Wale, of the Bill of Rights being presented to William and Mary. Samuel Wale [Public domain], via Wikimedia Commons

cession because they supported their own hereditary titles. Third, widespread aversion to reviving the turmoil associated with the English Civil War (1642–1651), which for many English was still within living memory, restrained the likelihood of dissent.

Perhaps those memories were stirred during the summer of 1685, less than five months after James became king, when the illegitimate Protestant son of Charles II, the Duke of Monmouth, James Scott, failed in his violent attempt to usurp the throne. Therefore, initial reticence toward challenging James's succession was not altogether surprising, despite worries that he might later use his royal prerogative to grant greater tolerance to Catholics and reintegrate them into civic life in defiance of the Corporation Act of 1661, which made membership of town corporations dependent upon taking of the sacrament according to the rites of the Church of England, and the Test Act of 1673, which imposed a similar test on public and military officeholders.

In addition to signaling the possibility of religious strife, the reign of James II commenced amid profound constitutional debate regarding the precise status of the monarch in relation to Parliament and the people whom its members represented. The supremacy of Parliament as the sovereign decision-making body over the king had been debated during the reign of Charles I. Some members of Parliament, especially those who were Whigs, had already detected absolutist traits in James II's behavior and wanted to safeguard the sovereignty of Parliament with statutory force. Initially, though, most members of Parliament and leading lights of the aristocracy adopted a wait-and-see policy, provided that James would not overstep his powers as king. Also, James did not yet have a male heir, and many believed that the Crown would eventually revert to a Protestant, in particular, James's oldest daughter, Anne, who had been raised as an Anglican rather than a Catholic.

A number of James's actions, however, soon showed that he shared the Stuart penchant for absolutist rule—in particular, by using his dispensing power to exempt subjects from the force of statute laws. He also actively promoted Catholic participation in civil life, which could have led to a "Catholic Restoration." He began filling his court with Catholics, including his private Jesuit confessor, Sir Edward Petre, and a representative from the papacy, Cardinal Ferdinando d'Adda. Further, on April 4, 1687, James exercised his dispensing power by issuing the Declaration of Indulgence, which circumvented penal laws against Catholics and Protestant dissenters. James then issued a revised Declaration of Indulgence on April 27, 1688, and ordered Anglican clergymen to read it aloud in their churches. William Sancroft, the Archbishop of Canterbury, and six other bishops—together known as the "Seven Bishops"—refused to read the declaration to their congregations. Because they petitioned the king to rescind the order to have the declaration read, they were quickly arrested and tried for seditious libel. In June they were acquitted to rapturous celebration by largely Anglican crowds.

The "Seven Bishops" case alienated James's Tory supporters, who came to fear a Catholic rebellion, especially in light of the fact that the hysteria surrounding false allegations of a "Popish plot" in 1678 to assassinate Charles II, involving Jesuit priests and numerous Catholic nobles, had still not fully subsided. Furthermore, the effects of King Louis XIV's revocation of the Edict of Nantes in 1685, ending toleration of French Protestants in his kingdom, added to the climate of suspicion and fear. Thus, James's use of his dispensing power to promote Catholics against existing statutory law, his persecution of prominent Anglican clergymen, and his desire for a large standing army, combined with events abroad, united two opposing political factions, the Whigs and the Tories, against him. The spark that triggered the sequence of events culminating in the deposal of James and the installation of William and Mary came on June 10, 1688, when James's wife, Mary of Modena, gave birth to a male heir, James Edward. The possibility of a Catholic succession to the British throne was, for most English Protestants, simply untenable.

In response to the threat of a Catholic royal succession, seven representatives of England's leading Protestant families, nicknamed the "Immortal Seven," with tacit support from the Anglican Church, made a direct appeal to Prince William of Orange. William was James II's Protestant son-in-law; he was married to James's younger daughter, Mary, who, like her sister, Anne, had been raised a Protestant. Mary was also William's cousin, since William's mother was the daughter of Charles I. The letter, dated June 30, 1688, signaled the beginning of a new chapter in English political history. As stadtholder ("head of state") of five of the United Provinces of the Netherlands, William of Orange was fiercely Protestant and keenly interested in maintaining war with the absolutist Catholic French monarch, Louis XIV, in order to defend Dutch interests.

On November 5, 1688, William landed at Brixham on Tor Bay in southwestern England with a vast armada of ships. Ahead of his arrival, he had dispatched agents to distribute leaflets written in English that stated his intention to rescue England for the Protestant cause. Bad weather had impeded James II's fleet in the Thames estuary, and after the defection to William of several high-profile commanders, James's army gradually lost confidence. William's forces proceeded toward London with little resistance; meanwhile, James himself was captured. On December 23, 1688, James was allowed to flee to France. The peers of the realm suggested recalling all members of Parliament from the reign of Charles II to decide how to deal with what amounted to an interregnum. On February 13, 1689, the Declaration of Rights was read aloud to William and Mary, who swore oaths in support of it, and they were crowned King William III and Queen Mary II on April 11, 1689. Following the coronation, the declaration was reworked and renamed the Bill of Rights. Finally, after much negotiation in the House of Commons and the House of Lords, especially over the monarch's dispensing power, the bill was given royal assent on December 16, 1689.

Author Biographies
The Bill of Rights was by its very nature a collectively authored document. Since it was based on the Declaration of Rights, authorship can be attributed to the Convention Parliament, which was the first parliament convened following the arrival of William of Orange in England. The Convention Parliament comprised members who had been in Charles II's last Parliament, which he had dissolved in 1681. A small commission made up of Convention Parliament members drafted the declaration. Individual contributions of commission members, however, are difficult to determine. Many constitutional historians have argued that the political philosophy of John Locke was the intellectual foundation of the Bill of Rights. Locke had been in exile in Holland throughout much of James II's reign and had returned to England with William of Orange's wife, Queen Mary II, in 1688. However, only an indirect connection can be made, since most of Locke's important works, such as *Two Treatises of Government*, which emphasized the concept of a separation of powers, were published after his return to England.

HISTORICAL DOCUMENT

English Bill of Rights: An Act Declaring the Rights and Liberties of the Subject and Settling the Succession of the Crown
Whereas the Lords Spiritual and Temporal and Commons assembled at Westminster, lawfully, fully and freely representing all the estates of the people of this realm, did upon the thirteenth day of February in the year of our Lord one thousand six hundred eighty-eight present unto their Majesties, then called and known by the names and style of William and Mary, prince and princess of Orange, being present in their proper persons, a certain declaration in writing made by the said Lords and Commons in the words following, viz.:

Whereas the late King James the Second, by the assistance of divers evil counselors, judges and ministers employed by him, did endeavour to subvert and extirpate the Protestant religion and the laws and liberties of this kingdom;

I. By assuming and exercising a power of dispensing with and suspending of laws and the execution of laws without consent of Parliament;

II. By committing and prosecuting divers worthy prelates for humbly petitioning to be excused from concurring to the said assumed power;

III. By issuing and causing to be executed a commission under the great seal for erecting a court called the Court of Commissioners for Ecclesiastical Causes;

IV. By levying money for and to the use of the Crown by pretence of prerogative for other time and in other manner than the same was granted by Parliament;

V. By raising and keeping a standing army within this kingdom in time of peace without consent of Parliament, and quartering soldiers contrary to law;

VI. By causing several good subjects being Protestants to be disarmed at the same time when papists were both armed and employed contrary to law;

VII. By violating the freedom of election of members to serve in Parliament;

VIII. By prosecutions in the Court of King's Bench for matters and causes cognizable only in Parliament, and by divers other arbitrary and illegal courses;

IX. And whereas of late years partial corrupt and unqualified persons have been returned and served on juries in trials, and particularly divers jurors in trials for high treason which were not freeholders;

X. And excessive bail hath been required of persons committed in criminal cases to elude the benefit of the laws made for the liberty of the subjects;

XI. And excessive fines have been imposed; And illegal and cruel punishments inflicted;

XII. And several grants and promises made of fines and forfeitures before any conviction or judgment against the persons upon whom the same were to be levied;

All which are utterly and directly contrary to the known laws and statutes and freedom of this realm;

And whereas the said late King James the Second having abdicated the government and the throne being thereby vacant, his Highness the prince of Orange (whom it hath pleased Almighty God to make the glorious instrument of delivering this kingdom from popery and arbitrary power) did (by the advice of the Lords Spiritual and Temporal and divers principal persons of the Commons) cause letters to be written to the Lords Spiritual and Temporal being Protestants, and other letters to the several counties, cities, universities, boroughs and cinque ports, for the choosing of such persons to represent them as were of right to be sent to Parliament, to meet and sit at Westminster upon the two and twentieth day of January in this year one thousand six hundred eighty and eight [old style date], in order to such an establishment as that their religion, laws and liberties might not again be in danger of being subverted, upon which letters elections having been accordingly made;

And thereupon the said Lords Spiritual and Temporal and Commons, pursuant to their respective letters and elections, being now assembled in a full and free representative of this nation, taking into their most serious consideration the best means for attaining the ends aforesaid, do in the first place (as their ancestors in like case have usually done) for the vindicating and asserting their ancient rights and liberties declare:

I. That the pretended power of suspending the laws or the execution of laws by regal authority without consent of Parliament is illegal;

II. That the pretended power of dispensing with laws or the execution of laws by regal authority, as it hath been assumed and exercised of late, is illegal;

III. That the commission for erecting the late Court of Commissioners for Ecclesiastical Causes, and all other commissions and courts of like nature, are illegal and pernicious;

IV. That levying money for or to the use of the Crown by pretence of prerogative, without grant of Parliament, for longer time, or in other manner than the same is or shall be granted, is illegal;

V. That it is the right of the subjects to petition the king, and all commitments and prosecutions for such petitioning are illegal;

VI. That the raising or keeping a standing army within the kingdom in time of peace, unless it be with consent of Parliament, is against law;

VII. That the subjects which are Protestants may have arms for their defence suitable to their conditions and as allowed by law;

VIII. That election of members of Parliament ought to be free;

IX. That the freedom of speech and debates or proceedings in Parliament ought not to be impeached or questioned in any court or place out of Parliament;

X. That excessive bail ought not to be required, nor excessive fines imposed, nor cruel and unusual punishments inflicted;

XI. That jurors ought to be duly impaneled and returned, and jurors which pass upon men in trials for high treason ought to be freeholders;

XII. That all grants and promises of fines and forfeitures of particular persons before conviction are illegal and void;

XIII. And that for redress of all grievances, and for the amending, strengthening and preserving of the laws, Parliaments ought to be held frequently. And they do claim, demand and insist upon all and singular the premises as their undoubted rights and liberties, and that no declarations, judgments, doings or proceedings to the prejudice of the people in any of the said premises ought in any wise to be drawn hereafter into consequence or example.

I. To which demand of their rights they are particularly encouraged by the declaration of his Highness the prince of Orange as being the only means for obtaining a full redress and remedy therein. Having therefore an entire confidence that his said Highness the prince of Orange will perfect the deliverance so far advanced by him, and will still preserve them from the violation of their rights which they have here asserted, and from all other attempts upon their religion, rights and liberties:

II. The said Lords Spiritual and Temporal and Commons assembled at Westminster do resolve that William and Mary, prince and princess of Orange, be and be declared king and queen of England, France and Ireland and the dominions thereunto belonging, to hold the crown and royal dignity of the said kingdoms and dominions to them, the said prince and princess, during their lives and the life of the survivor to them, and that the sole and full exercise of the regal power be only in and executed by the said prince of Orange in the names of the said prince and princess during their joint lives, and after their deceases the said crown and royal dignity of the same kingdoms and dominions to be to the heirs of the body of the said princess, and for default of such issue to the Princess Anne of Denmark and the heirs of her body, and for default of such issue to the heirs of the body of the said prince of Orange. And the Lords Spiritual and Temporal and Commons do pray the said prince and princess to accept the same accordingly.

III. And that the oaths hereafter mentioned be taken by all persons of whom the oaths have allegiance and supremacy might be required by law, instead of them; and that the said oaths of allegiance and supremacy be abrogated.

I, A.B., do sincerely promise and swear that I will be faithful and bear true allegiance to their Majesties King William and Queen Mary. So help me God.

I, A.B., do swear that I do from my heart abhor, detest and abjure as impious and heretical this damnable doctrine and position, that princes excommunicated or deprived by the Pope or any authority of the see of Rome may be deposed or murdered by their subjects or any other whatsoever. And I do declare that no foreign prince, person, prelate, state or potentate hath or ought to have any jurisdiction, power, superiority, pre-eminence or authority, ecclesiastical or spiritual, within this realm. So help me God.

I. Upon which their said Majesties did accept the crown and royal dignity of the kingdoms of England, France and Ireland, and the dominions thereunto belonging, according to the resolution and desire of the said Lords and Commons contained in the said declaration.

II. And thereupon their Majesties were pleased that the said Lords Spiritual and Temporal and Commons, being the two Houses of Parliament, should continue to sit, and with their Majesties' royal concurrence make effectual provision for the settlement of the religion, laws and liberties of this kingdom, so that the same for the future might not be in danger again of being subverted, to which the said Lords Spiritual and Temporal and Commons did agree, and proceed to act accordingly.

III. Now in pursuance of the premises the said Lords Spiritual and Temporal and Commons in Parliament assembled, for the ratifying, confirming and establishing the said declaration and the articles, clauses, matters and things therein contained by the force of law made in due form by authority of Parliament, do pray that it may be declared and enacted that all and singular the rights and liberties asserted and claimed in the said declaration are the true, ancient and indubitable rights and liberties of the people of this kingdom, and so shall be esteemed, allowed, adjudged, deemed and taken to be; and that all and every the particulars aforesaid shall be firmly and strictly holden and observed as they are expressed in the said declaration, and all officers and ministers whatsoever shall serve their Majesties and their successors according to the same in all time to come.

IV. And the said Lords Spiritual and Temporal and Commons, seriously considering how it hath pleased Almighty God in his marvelous providence and merciful goodness to this nation to provide and preserve their said Majesties' royal persons most happily to reign over us upon the throne of their ancestors, for which they render unto him from the bottom of their hearts their humblest thanks and praises, do truly, firmly, assuredly and in the sincerity of their hearts think, and do hereby recognize, acknowledge and declare, that King James the Second having abdicated the government, and their Majesties having accepted the crown and royal dignity as aforesaid, their said Majesties did become, were, are and of right ought to be by the laws of this realm our sovereign liege lord and lady, king and queen of England, France and Ireland and the dominions thereunto belonging, in and to whose princely persons the royal state, crown and dignity of the said realms with all honours, styles, titles, regalities, prerogatives, powers, jurisdictions and authorities to the same belonging and appertaining are most fully, rightfully and entirely invested and incorporated, united and annexed.

V. And for preventing all questions and divisions in this realm by reason of any pretended titles to the crown, and for preserving a certainty in the succession thereof, in and upon which the unity, peace, tranquility and safety of this nation doth under God wholly consist and depend, the said Lords Spiritual and Temporal and Commons do beseech their Majesties that it may be enacted, established and declared, that the crown and regal government of the said kingdoms and dominions, with all and singular the premises thereunto belonging and appertaining, shall be and continue to their said Majesties and the survivor of them during their lives and the life of the survivor of them, and that the entire, perfect and full exercise of the regal power and government be only in and executed by his Majesty in the names of both their Majesties during their joint lives; and after their deceases the said crown and premises shall be and remain to the heirs of the body of her Majesty, and for default of such issue to her Royal Highness the Princess Anne of Denmark and the heirs of the body of his said Majesty; and thereunto the said Lords Spiritual and Temporal and Commons do in the name of all the people aforesaid most humbly and faithfully submit themselves, their heirs and posterities for ever, and do faithfully promise that they will stand to, maintain and defend their said Majesties, and also the limitation and succession of the crown herein specified and contained, to the utmost of their powers with their lives and estates against all persons whatsoever that shall attempt anything to the contrary.

VI. And whereas it hath been found by experience that it is inconsistent with the safety and welfare of this Protestant kingdom to be governed by a popish prince, or by any king or queen marrying a papist, the said Lords Spiritual and Temporal and Commons do further pray that it may be enacted, that all and every person and persons that is, are or shall be reconciled to or shall hold communion with the see or Church of Rome, or shall profess the popish religion, or shall marry a papist, shall be excluded and be for ever incapable to inherit, possess or enjoy the crown and government of this realm and Ireland and the dominions thereunto belonging or any part of the same, or to have, use or exercise any regal power, authority or jurisdiction within the same; and in all and every such case or cases the people of these realms shall be and are hereby absolved of their allegiance; and the said crown and government shall from time to time descend to and be enjoyed by such person or persons being Protestants as should have inherited and enjoyed the same in case the said person or persons so reconciled, holding communion or professing or marrying as aforesaid were naturally dead.

VII. And that every king and queen of this realm who at any time hereafter shall come to and succeed in the imperial crown of this kingdom shall on the first day of the meeting of the first Parliament next after his or her coming to the crown, sitting in his or her throne in the House of Peers in the presence of the Lords and Commons therein assembled, or at his or her coronation before such person or persons who shall administer the coronation oath to him or her at the time of his or her taking the said oath (which shall first happen), make, subscribe and audibly repeat the declaration mentioned in the statute made in the thirtieth year of the reign of King Charles the Second entitled, "An Act for the more effectual preserving the king's person and government by disabling papists from sitting in either House of Parliament." But if it shall happen that such king or queen upon his or her succession to the crown of this realm shall be under the age of twelve years, then every such king or queen shall make, subscribe and audibly repeat the same declaration at his or her coronation or the first day of the meeting of the first Parliament as aforesaid which shall first happen after such king or queen shall have attained the said age of twelve years.

VIII. All which their Majesties are contented and pleased shall be declared, enacted and established by authority of this present Parliament, and shall stand, remain and be the law of this realm for ever; and the same are by their said Majesties, by and with the advice and consent of the Lords Spiritual and Temporal and Commons in Parliament assembled and by the authority of the same, declared, enacted and established accordingly.

IX. And be it further declared and enacted by the authority aforesaid, that from and after this present session of Parliament no dispensation by *non obstante* of or to any statute or any part thereof shall be allowed, but that the same shall be held void and of no effect, except a dispensation be allowed of in such statute, and except in such cases as shall be specially provided for by one or more bill or bills to be passed during this present session of Parliament.

X. Provided that no charter or grant or pardon granted before the three and twentieth day of October in the year of our Lord one thousand six hundred eighty-nine shall be any ways impeached or invalidated by this Act, but that the same shall be and remain of the same force and effect in law and no other than as if this Act had never been made.

GLOSSARY

cinque ports: originally, five (in the Plantagenet royal language of French, "cinque") ports in southeastern England (Dover, Sandwich, Romney, Hythe, and Hastings) that were the first line of defense in case of an invasion of England, and were also the prime shipbuilding locations supplying the Royal Navy. By William and Mary's time, there were actually thirty such ports, but their status was largely ceremonial.

Lords Spiritual and Temporal, and Commons: members of Parliament. At the time of the act, the Lords Spiritual were bishops of the Church of England, and the Lords Temporal were members of the hereditary peerage; they comprised the House of Lords. "Commons," representatives of the towns and cities, sat in the House of Commons.

Document Analysis

The Bill of Rights can be broken into two distinct parts. The first part contains a list of "abuses" committed by James II, which are then followed by articles that restate the substance of each of these abuses in the negative and declare each of them either "illegal," "pernicious," "against law," or "void." The second part comprises thirteen articles designed to safeguard the Protestant succession to the throne, to establish that both Houses of Parliament give their assent to the succession and bill, and, finally, to secure the permanence of the document.

First Part: Abuses and Restatements

James's twelve abuses are restated as thirteen articles declaring what are more accurately described as wrongs rather than rights. This was a rhetorical ploy by the framers of the bill to secure its passage in Parliament. By reviewing and assenting to the criminality of James II's actions, it was difficult to deny the correctness of the subsequent generalized restatements, which were more controversial. For example, the second abuse, regarding the prosecution of "worthy prelates" for petitioning the king, is restated as "it is the right of the subjects to petition the king." The preamble is important in determining the bill's legality and emphasizes the lawful, full, and free nature of the Convention Parliament and the circumstances under which the Declaration of Rights, on which the Bill of Rights was based, was read aloud.

The twelve abuses of James II and the articles restating them are separated by an important passage that is a de facto declaration that James II had abdicated and placed himself in exile in France. By contrast, in the same paragraph, William of Orange is praised as "the glorious instrument of delivering this kingdom from popery and arbitrary power." It is made clear that a Convention Parliament was lawfully convened upon the advice and consent of "the Lords Spiritual and Temporal" and leaders in the House of Commons and that it was entrusted with the task of ensuring that "laws and liberties might not again be in danger of being subverted."

The first and second articles, which refer to the first abuse of James II, deal with the king's power to suspend or temporarily dispense with the law, or the execution of the law, without prior approval of Parliament. In reality, kings had seldom invoked the so-called suspending power. The first article, therefore, found broad agreement within the Convention Parliament. The second article, relating to the dispensing power of the Crown, was far more controversial. This concerned the monarch's ability to exempt people or groups from laws under certain conditions. Both Charles II and James II had regularly invoked the dispensing power to give greater freedom to Catholics and Protestant dissenters. The phrase "of late" makes explicit reference to the actions of James II; it was designed to circumvent claims of historical precedent for monarchs using the dispensing power. Historical precedent, however, was not so easily dismissed. The concept of dispensing power had existed since the thirteenth century, when Henry II had used it in imitation of papal dispensations. Elizabeth I also widely used the dispensing power, though seldom controversially. Many Tories argued that the monarch's dispensing power was necessary because laws were seldom revised and often became outdated. The clause was left in the bill anyway because the majority of Convention Parliament members felt that the dispensing power was a major hurdle to the establishment of a constitutional monarchy.

The second and third abuses also had direct relevance to the events preceding the Glorious Revolution. The second abuse, corresponding to the fifth restatement, mentions "worthy prelates" who had petitioned the king. These were the "Seven Bishops" who had been prosecuted for having petitioned James II, after they had refused to read the Declaration of Indulgence aloud in their churches. The right to petition the king originated in Saxon times and has since been considered one of the ancient rights of English subjects. The third abuse corresponds to the third restatement, which outlaws the Court of Commissioners for Ecclesiastical Causes. James II had established this court in 1686 to assist Catholics and to monitor universities and the Anglican Church. The measure was deeply unpopular, especially because such commissions had been outlawed in 1661.

Rising levels of taxation, which also related to control over revenue, had long created conflict between Parliament and the monarchy. According to the fourth charge of abuse, James II had levied money for use by the Crown in ways other than those stipulated by Parliament. Charles I had also antagonized Parliament with his unsanctioned revival of the ship tax and other ancient laws. Revenue was important for the monarch for three main reasons: first, for maintaining the Civil List and his own court; second, to pay for a standing army and defense of the realm; and third, to bribe secret service agents, influence elections, and secure loyalty. The bill covers all three of these reasons and limits the monarch's power to raise revenue.

The Civil List was of great importance, since it funded officials working for the royal family, offices known as sinecures (which required little or no real work but which were often accompanied by titles and salaries and were designed as a way of distributing royal patronage), and the pensions of courtiers and servants of the Crown upon retirement from active service. All were skillfully distributed to ensure support for the king. If Parliament could not control the revenue used for these purposes, then it would be ineffective and cede more power to the king. The fourth article states that revenue may not be collected for use of the Crown "without grant of Parliament." However, control over revenue would remain a source of contention during William III's rule. In the early years of his reign, William frequently tussled with Parliament over revenue for the Civil List and payment for the war with France. Gradually, later Parliaments took greater control over revenue.

The sixth article, corresponding to the fifth abuse of James II, bans the king from keeping a standing army without the support of Parliament. James's decision to maintain a standing army in times of peace without the consent of Parliament not only had drained revenue but also had been extremely menacing and against English tradition. Furthermore, the armies of Charles II and James II were composed mainly of Catholics, and many leading generals were Catholic. Debates about a standing army would resurface in the late eighteenth century during the American Revolution. In James's time, it is unlikely that Parliament would have endorsed the creation of a standing army. The Catholic threat is also reflected in the seventh article (corresponding to the sixth abuse), which states that Protestants are allowed to bear arms. This article has relevance to the Second Amendment to the U.S. Constitution, where the right to bear arms is guaranteed in the context of maintaining the security of the state. Significantly, however, the English Bill of Rights does not justify this right.

The eighth, ninth, and thirteenth articles concern elections and parliamentary procedure. The eighth article, corresponding to the seventh abuse, declares that elections should be free. This was a direct attack on royal interference in elections in ways that had included designating candidates, excluding people from office, and voiding election results. It is important to note, however, that this provision focuses on the candidates, not the voters. The ninth article (corresponding to the eighth abuse) requires that speech in Parliament be free and that verbal exchanges among members of Parliament shall not be subject to court proceedings. This basic tenet of parliamentary privilege is still practiced today. The thirteenth and final article, without a directly corresponding abuse, maintains that Parliament shall be convened frequently. In the seventeenth century, the king's prerogative to govern without Parliament sitting—a prorogued Parliament—had been invoked several times, most notably by Charles I in 1629 in what became known as the Eleven Years' Tyranny. The frequency of parliamentary gathering was also related to counteracting a strong argument in favor of the monarch's dispensing power: the need to amend and update legislation.

The tenth, eleventh, and twelfth articles (corresponding to the ninth through twelfth abuses) all focus on judicial procedure and the rights of individuals. The tenth clause has perhaps the most contemporary significance, since it limits excessive bail, fines, and "cruel and unusual punishments." Judicial discretion was considerable during this period, and this article sought to prevent arbitrary abuse by judges. While judges rarely issued punishments outside the bounds of the law, they often set disproportionate and prohibitive bail, an amount of money paid as a guarantee of returning to court for judgment. This article was designed to ensure that all subjects had the same standing before the court. The words "cruel and unusual punishments" have a somewhat different meaning than what normally would be assumed today. In Restoration England, cruelty was defined not in terms of suffering but whether the punishment was commensurate with the crime. The eleventh article describes the process for selecting jury panels and specifies that a jury for a treason trial must be composed of "freeholders," subjects who owned land or property. This meant that juries were composed of wealthier members of society and excluded leaseholders or people who rented land and dwellings. The twelfth article, corresponding to the twelfth abuse of James II, prohibits the practice of promising to others the fines and lands of defendants prior to trial, which blatantly presupposed guilt and was contrary to the basic tenets of jurisprudence.

Second Part: Safeguarding the Succession and the Bill of Rights

The second part of the Bill of Rights is more typical of a seventeenth-century legal document, both in style and language. The three most important features include a precise description of the royal succession (covered by articles II, VIII, IX, and X), a determination that there shall not be a Catholic monarch or a monarch married to a Catholic (Article IX), and a provision that safeguarded the bill and subsequent acts passed by the Convention Parliament from being dispensed *non obstante*—dispensed by the monarch, that is—unless a particular act itself would allow dispensation (the substance of articles XI and XII). The bill further emphasizes that the enthronement of William and Mary has the authority and support of both Houses of Parliament (articles I, II, VI, and VIII), that James II abdicated his throne (Article VII), and that with their majesties' consent, Parliament participates in the governance of the realm (Article V). Article IV is a statement of William and Mary's acceptance of the crown, while Article III contains oaths of allegiance to the crown.

Guaranteeing the royal succession is a problem for all monarchies. Indeed, the establishment of the Church of England had stemmed from Henry VIII's desire for a male heir. The unexpected birth of a male heir to James II and Mary of Modena had triggered the Glorious Revolution. The Bill of Rights established the following succession: William III and Mary II were to continue as lawful king and queen during their lifetimes. Upon the death of either one, the other would become sole ruler. After the deaths of both monarchs, the rightful line of kingship would pass to the "heirs of the body" of Mary II. If for any reason there was no royal issue, the throne would revert to Queen Anne of Denmark, Mary II's sister, and in the event of her death, to her progeny. If none of these successions were possible, then the heirs of William III would have the royal title. The framers of the bill were anxious to settle the succession quickly, although further stipulations would have to be made in the Act of Settlement of 1701. In the end, Queen Anne outlived her only progeny, Prince William, Duke of Gloucester, who died of smallpox in July 1700 at the age of eleven. This tested the new rules of succession and reset the line to the Hanoverian descendants of King James I, the heirs of Sophia, Duchess of Hanover. Sophia was the daughter of the German Elector Palatine Frederick V and Princess Elizabeth, who was the daughter of King James I. Her son was the first Hanoverian English king, George I.

The succession was drawn up to ensure a Protestant successor. The bill states that henceforth there shall be no Catholic monarch of England nor any monarch married to a Catholic. This law is still in force today, and the rationale behind this determination is obvious. A Catholic monarch such as James II could have sought rapprochement with the pontiff in Rome, interfered with the Anglican Church, or otherwise compromised the "safety and welfare" of Protestant England.

Essential Themes

The Bill of Rights has had a lasting impact on England's constitutional development and political history as well as on the formulation of comprehensive bills of rights in other countries. Much of its content was the product of its time, especially of the political upheaval and dramatic events of the Glorious Revolution. As a testament to the bill's definitive nature, however, it is still widely cited today, and it retains statutory force and is considered a pillar of the Revolution Settlement, encompassing a series of acts beginning with the Bill of Rights (1689) and ending with the Act of Settlement (1701), which secured a Protestant succession to the English throne.

The importance of the Bill of Rights as a focal point for individual rights and free and fair government reemerged in the late eighteenth century, when it was widely discussed during the American and French revolutions. The Revolution Society, founded to celebrate the Glorious Revolution of 1688 and chaired by Charles Stanhope, Third Earl Stanhope, reprinted the Bill of Rights in its entirety to raise awareness of its constitutional importance and as an example of English liberties during the formulation of a new French Constitution in the early 1790s. However, interpretations of the process that led up to the bill's enactment have been continually debated. The conservative historian J. C. D. Clark has argued that the significance of the bill has been exaggerated and that it did little more than put rights and freedoms that had long existed into written form. Nonetheless, in its historical context the Bill of Rights represented a decisive step in favor of parliamentary sovereignty. The sections on cruel and unusual punishment and free and fair elections anticipate many of the key legal documents of the twentieth century.

In addition to its historical importance, the bill has had a huge political, philosophical, and linguistic influence worldwide by setting forth a precedent upon which framers of later constitutions and declarations have drawn. Most notably, the U.S. Bill of Rights and the United Nation's Universal Declaration of Human Rights, while different in scope and tenor, are clearly indebted to the English Bill of Rights.

—*Peter Robinson*

Bibliography and Further Reading

Clark, J.C.D. *English Society, 1660–1832: Religion, Ideology, and Politics during the Ancien Régime.* Cambridge University Press, 2000.

Conceptual Change and the Constitution. Edited by Terence Ball and J.G.A. Pocock. University of Kansas Press, 1988.

Liberty Secured? Britain before and after 1688. Edited by J.R. Jones. Stanford University Press, 1992.

Pincus, C.A. *England's Glorious Revolution, 1688–1689: A Brief History with Documents.* Palgrave Macmillan, 2006.

Pocock, J.G.A. *The Ancient Constitution and the Feudal Law: A Study of English Historical Thought in the Seventeenth Century.* Cambridge University Press, 1987.

Websites

Nurmayani, H.E.N.R. Dewi. "Bill of Rights 1688." *Global Ethics Network*, 7 Mar. 2013, Carnegie Council, http://www.globalethicsnetwork.org/profiles/blogs/bill-of-rights-1688. Accessed 27 Mar. 2017.

Walker, Aileen, Oonagh Gay and Lucinda Maer. "Bill of Rights 1689." U.K. Parliament, House of Commons Library, 5 Oct. 2009, http://researchbriefings.parliament.uk/ResearchBriefing/Summary/SN00293. Accessed 27 Mar. 2017.

John Locke: *Second Treatise on Civil Government*

Date: 1690
Author: John Locke
Genre: Treatise

Summary Overview

John Locke's *Second Treatise on Civil Government*, part of the larger work *Two Treatises of Government*, which Locke published anonymously in 1690, is an important text in the history of theories of natural law and the social contract, and thus stands as a key document in the history of Western political thought. In fact, the *Second Treatise on Civil Government* provided an intellectual foundation for the future rejection of absolute monarchies—a process that began in Western culture in the eighteenth century, most notably with the French and American revolutions, and continued into the nineteenth century.

John Locke was one of the most influential philosophers and political theorists of seventeenth-century England. In the first of his *Two Treatises of Government*, Locke refuted the views that had been published by another political theorist, Robert Filmer, who argued that monarchs had a divine right to rule. The second, and more famous, treatise was identified on the volume's cover as "an Essay Concerning the True Original, Extent, and End of Civil Government." Thus it came to be called the *Second Treatise on Civil Government*.

The *Second Treatise on Civil Government* was written with two purposes in mind. The first was to justify resistance to King Charles II, who proved unpopular after being restored to the British throne in 1660 because of his Catholic leanings. The second purpose was to justify the so-called Glorious Revolution, which brought William of Orange and Mary II from Holland to England in 1688 to claim the throne, and in the process driving Charles II's successor (and Mary's father), James II, into exile—although Locke had been at work on the treatise years before the Glorious Revolution took place. The corpus of Locke's work, including the *Second Treatise on Civil Government*, was crucial in the history of rationalism, itself a key component of the eighteenth century's Enlightenment. The views expressed by Locke found their way into such pivotal documents as the American Declaration of Independence.

Locke's intended audience for the *Two Treatises of Government* has been a matter of considerable scholarly debate. The orthodox view is that his primary audience was the aristocracy of England, which had been the motivating force behind the Glorious Revolution, and the views expressed in the *Second Treatise* seem to provide a justification for that revolution. However, the aristocracy never really accepted Locke's views, regarding them as too radical. Other scholars have argued that Locke's primary audience was the landed gentry, yet this class also regarded Locke as too radical, even though Locke was outlining a theory of government that would have provided stability for the landed class, particularly in his defense of private property. Still other scholars contend that Locke's true audience consisted of such people as city merchants, tradespeople, artisans, and minor gentry. These classes would have found Locke's views congenial, for his essential argument is that people possess natural rights as free men and women regardless of the amount of property they own. Locke effectively advocates the inclusion of these classes in the process of choosing a nation's leaders and form of government.

Defining Moment

The context of the *Second Treatise on Civil Government* was the Glorious Revolution of 1688, an event whose roots stretched back at least to the reign of King Henry VIII in the early sixteenth century. Henry's rejection of Roman Catholicism and his reformation of the Church in England coincided with the greater Protestant Reformation, launched by Martin Luther in Germany in 1517 with the publication of his *Ninety-five Theses*. Henry's reforms, however, did not go far enough for those who wanted to see the church fully purified. Out of this discontent rose the Puritans, who became the party of radical reform. Pitted against them was the Church of England (Anglican) establishment, which sought to impose national unity of religion in England. The ensuing struggle reached a climax of armed conflict in the mid-seventeenth century under King Charles I: The three-stage English Civil War took place through the 1640s between the Royalists (supporters of

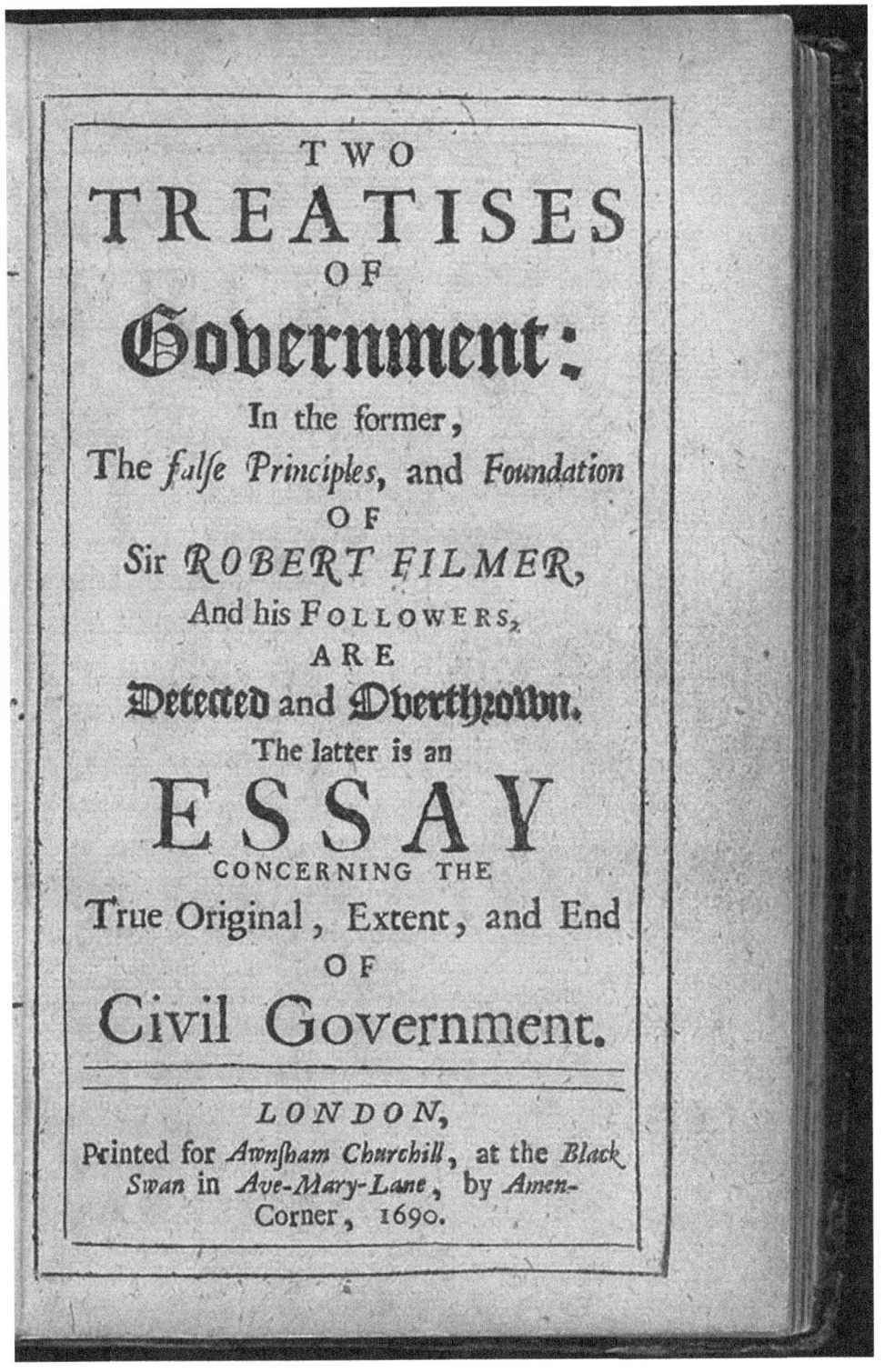

Title page of Locke's *Two Treatises of Government* (1690). [Public domain], via Wikimedia Commons

the king) and a Parliament dominated by Puritans. In 1649 the defeated Charles I was convicted of treason by Parliament and executed.

The Puritans, led by Oliver Cromwell and later his son Richard, ruled England for about seven years; during this period, called the Interregnum, the state was variously called the Commonwealth or the Protectorate. Under the Puritans, strict standards of morality were enforced, with holidays, the theater, gambling, and other amusements suppressed. Richard succeeded his father to the position of Lord Protector on the latter's death, but after Richard abdicated in 1659, the monarchy was restored, and Charles II was crowned in 1660, an event called the Restoration. The Restoration was a period of reaction to the strict morality enforced during the Commonwealth, as people indulged their pent-up desires for theater, art, fashion, and pleasure. Charles's own hedonistic way of life was almost a relief to the English people. At the same time, efforts were made to impose religious uniformity in England. The Anglicans were able to expel Presbyterian and other "dissenting" Protestant ministers from their pulpits, pushing them to the fringes of society along with Catholics. Charles II, though, was sympathetic to Catholicism and sought to grant legal relief to Catholics, as well as to Dissenters.

Charles personally favored a policy of religious tolerance, but he bowed to Parliament's desire to restore the supremacy of the Church of England by agreeing to the Clarendon Code, a series of laws that enforced religious conformity and made "meeting houses" and dissenting or nonconformist worship illegal. Yet in 1672 he issued the Royal Declaration of Indulgence, which extended tolerance to Nonconformists and Catholics. Later, though, he rescinded the declaration under pressure from Parliament. Then, in the late 1670s, the purported "Popish plot" provoked fear after it was revealed that Charles's brother and heir, James, was a Catholic. This discovery led to a split between the Whig Party, which advocated the exclusion of Catholics and Dissenters from public office, and the Tory Party, which opposed exclusion. When a 1683 plot to assassinate both Charles and James, the Rye House Plot, was exposed, numerous Whig leaders were forced into exile or killed.

Charles meanwhile had dissolved Parliament in 1679 when it attempted to remove James from the line of succession, and he ruled without Parliament until he died in 1685—on his deathbed converting to Catholicism.

When the Catholic James II's wife Mary of Modena gave birth to a son, the nobility decided that the time had come to extirpate Catholic rule once and for all by inviting William, Prince of Orange, a Protestant, to assume the throne of England. (Orange was a principality in Holland; it is now part of France.) William had some legitimate claim to the throne as the husband of James II's daughter, Mary, by his deceased first wife, Anne Hyde. William invaded England in 1688, met with no meaningful resistance, and was crowned on April 11, 1689. With James II in exile, the establishment of Protestantism in England was made permanent. This change in the monarchy was named the Glorious Revolution because in the main it was accomplished without bloodshed. Such a major step, however, required justification. John Locke provided that justification in his *Second Treatise*, at the same time outlining a theory and philosophy of government. It is believed, too, that a goal of his was to refute the views of Thomas Hobbes's influential book *Leviathan*, an argument in favor of absolutist governments published in 1651 and translated into Latin in 1668.

Author Biography

John Locke was born in Wrington, England, on August 29, 1632, to Puritan parents. During the English Civil War in the 1640s his father fought for the Parliamentarians. He attended the Westminster School in London and was made a King's Scholar. In 1652 he entered the Christ Church college at Oxford University, earning a bachelor's degree in 1656 and a master's in 1658. He discovered, however, that his interest lay less with the classical subjects taught at Oxford and more with newly emerging experimental sciences and medicine. Inspired by the empirical views of such thinkers as Sir Francis Bacon and René Descartes, he began to investigate natural science subjects, eventually joining England's Royal Society in 1668. In the 1660s he collaborated on experiments with Robert Boyle, considered the father of modern chemistry. In Locke's journals and correspondence between 1656 and 1666 are repeated references to his interests in natural science and in the study of society, politics, and moral philosophy.

In 1666 Locke met Lord Anthony Ashley Cooper and became his personal adviser on general affairs—an important relationship because Baron Ashley was an active politician who supported a constitutional monarchy, Protestant succession, civil liberties, toleration of religion, the rule of Parliament, and the expansion of the

British Empire for trade. Ashley, later the First Earl of Shaftesbury, was one of the sponsors of the bill to exclude James II from succeeding to the throne, and in the aftermath he was tried for treason but was acquitted. After the Rye House Plot was uncovered, Locke fled to Holland, fearing that he would be tainted by his association with Lord Shaftesbury. Meanwhile, throughout the late 1660s and 1670s he was intimately involved with issues of trade and colonization while continuing his studies and gathering ideas for one of his most famous works, *An Essay Concerning Human Understanding*. This book, published in 1689, proved to be a cornerstone of Enlightenment views about perception, sensation, reason, knowledge, and the relationship between knowledge and faith. In 1690 he published his political masterpiece, *Two Treatises of Government*. After a stint at the newly created Board of Trade, he retired to a country estate in Essex called Oates, where he died on October 28, 1704.

HISTORICAL DOCUMENT

**Excerpt from *Second Treatise on Civil Government*
by John Locke
Chapter II. Of the State of Nature.**

I. Sect. 4. To understand political power right, and derive it from its original, we must consider, what state all men are naturally in, and that is, a state of perfect freedom to order their actions, and dispose of their possessions and persons, as they think fit, within the bounds of the law of nature, without asking leave, or depending upon the will of any other man.—A state also of equality wherein all the power and jurisdiction is reciprocal, no one having more than another; there being nothing more evident, than that the creatures of the same species and rank, promiscuously born to all the same advantages of nature, and the use of the same faculties, should also be equal one amongst another without subordination or subjection, unless the lord and master of them all should, by any manifest declaration of his will, set one above another, and confer on him, by an evident and clear appointment, an undoubted right to dominion and sovereignty.

II. Sect. 5. This equality of men by nature, the judicious Hooker looks upon as so evident in itself, and beyond all question, that he makes it the foundation of that obligation to mutual love amongst men, on which he builds the duties they owe one another, and from whence he derives the great maxims of justice and charity. His words are, The like natural inducement hath brought men to know that it is no less their duty, to love others than themselves; for seeing those things which are equal, must needs all have one measure; if I cannot but wish to receive good, even as much at every man's hands, as any man can wish unto his own soul, how should I look to have any part of my desire herein satisfied, unless myself be careful to satisfy the like desire, which is undoubtedly in other men, being of one and the same nature? To have any thing offered them repugnant to this desire, must needs in all respects grieve them as much as me; so that if I do harm, I must look to suffer, there being no reason that others should shew greater measure of love to me, than they have by me shewed unto them: my desire therefore to be loved of my equals in nature as much as possible may be, imposeth upon me a natural duty of bearing to them-ward fully the like affection; from which relation of equality between ourselves and them that are as ourselves, what several rules and canons natural reason hath drawn, for direction of life, no man is ignorant. Eccl. Pol. lib. i.

III. Sect. 6. But though this be a state of liberty, yet it is not a state of licence: though man in that state have an uncontrolable liberty to dispose of his person or possessions, yet he has not liberty to destroy himself, or so much as any creature in his possession, but where some nobler use than its bare preservation calls for it. The state of nature has a law of nature to govern it, which obliges every one: and reason, which is that law, teaches all mankind, who will but consult it, that being all equal and independent, no one ought to harm another in his life, health, liberty, or possessions: for men being all the workmanship of one omnipotent, and infinitely wise maker; all the servants of one sovereign master, sent into the world by his order, and about his business; they are his property, whose workmanship they are, made to last during his, not one another's pleasure: and being furnished with like faculties, sharing all in one community of nature, there cannot be supposed any such subordination among us, that may authorize us to destroy one another, as if we were made for one another's uses, as the inferior ranks of creatures are for our's. Every one, as he is bound to preserve himself, and not to quit his station wilfully, so by the like reason, when his own preservation comes not in competition, ought he, as much as he can, to preserve the rest of mankind, and may not, unless it be to do justice on an offender, take away, or impair the life, or what tends to the preservation of the life, the liberty, health, limb, or goods of another.

IV. Sect. 7. And that all men may be restrained from invading others rights, and from doing hurt to one another, and the law of nature be observed, which willeth the peace and preservation of all mankind, the execution of the law of nature is, in that state, put into every man's hands, whereby every one has a right to punish the transgressors of that law to such a degree, as may hinder its violation: for the law of nature would, as all other laws that concern men in this world be in vain, if there were no body that in the state of nature had a power to execute that law, and thereby preserve the innocent and restrain offenders. And if any one in the state of nature may punish another for any evil he has done, every one may do so: for in that state of perfect equality, where naturally there is no superiority or jurisdiction of one over another, what any may do in prosecution of that law, every one must needs have a right to do.

V. Sect. 8. And thus, in the state of nature, one man comes by a power over another; but yet no absolute or arbitrary power, to use a criminal, when he has got him in his hands, according to the passionate heats, or boundless extravagancy of his own will; but only to retribute to him, so far as calm reason and conscience dictate, what is proportionate to his transgression, which is so much as may serve for reparation and restraint: for these two are the only reasons, why one man may lawfully do harm to another, which is that we call punishment. In transgressing the law of nature, the offender declares himself to live by another rule than that of reason and common equity, which is that measure God has set to the actions of men, for their mutual security; and so he becomes dangerous to mankind, the tye, which is to secure them from injury and violence, being slighted and broken by him. Which being a trespass against the whole species, and the peace and safety of it, provided for by the law of nature, every man upon this score, by the right he hath to preserve mankind in general, may restrain, or where it is necessary, destroy things noxious to them, and so may bring such evil on any one, who hath transgressed that law, as may make him repent the doing of it, and thereby deter him, and by his example others, from doing the like mischief. And in the case, and upon this ground, every man hath a right to punish the offender, and be executioner of the law of nature.

VI. Sect. 9. 1 doubt not but this will seem a very strange doctrine to some men: but before they condemn it, I desire them to resolve me, by what right any prince or state can put to death, or punish an alien, for any crime he commits in their country. It is certain their laws, by virtue of any sanction they receive from the promulgated will of the legislative, reach not a stranger: they speak not to him, nor, if they did, is he bound to hearken to them. The legislative authority, by which they are in force over the subjects of that commonwealth, hath no power over him. Those who have the supreme power of making laws in England, France or Holland, are to an Indian, but like the rest of the world, men without authority: and therefore, if by the law of nature every man hath not a power to punish offences against it, as he soberly judges the case to require, I see not how the magistrates of any community can punish an alien of another country; since, in reference to him, they can have no more power than what every man naturally may have over another.

VII. Sect. 10. Besides the crime which consists in violating the law, and varying from the right rule of reason, whereby a man so far becomes degenerate, and declares himself to quit the principles of human nature, and to be a noxious creature, there is commonly injury done to some person or other, and some other man receives damage by his transgression: in which case he who hath received any damage, has, besides the right of punishment common to him with other men, a particular right to seek reparation from him that has done it: and any other person, who finds it just, may also join with him that is injured, and assist him in recovering from the offender so much as may make satisfaction for the harm he has suffered.

VIII. Sect. 11. From these two distinct rights, the one of punishing the crime for restraint, and preventing the like offence, which right of punishing is in every body; the other of taking reparation, which belongs only to the injured party, comes it to pass that the magistrate, who by being magistrate hath the common right of punishing put into his hands, can often, where the public good demands not the execution of the law, remit the punishment of criminal offences by his own authority, but yet cannot remit the satisfaction due to any private man for the damage he has received. That, he who has suffered the damage has a right to demand in his own name, and he alone can remit: the damnified person has this power of appropriating to himself the goods or service of the offender, by right of self-preservation, as every man has a power to punish the crime, to prevent its being committed again, by the right he has of preserving all mankind, and doing all reasonable things he can in order to that end: and thus it is, that every man, in the state of nature, has a power to kill a murderer, both to deter others from doing the like injury, which no reparation can compensate, by the example of the punishment that attends it from every body, and also to secure men from the attempts of a criminal, who having renounced reason, the common rule and measure God hath given to mankind, hath, by the unjust violence and slaughter he hath committed upon one, declared war against all mankind, and therefore may be destroyed as a lion or a tyger, one of those wild savage beasts, with whom men can have no society nor security: and upon this is grounded that great law of nature, Whoso sheddeth man's blood, by man shall his blood be shed. And Cain was so fully convinced, that every one had a right to destroy such a criminal, that after the murder of his brother, he cries out, Every one that findeth me, shall slay me; so plain was it writ in the hearts of all mankind.

IX. Sect. 12. By the same reason may a man in the state of nature punish the lesser breaches of that law. It will perhaps be demanded, with death? I answer, each transgression may be punished to that degree, and with so much severity, as will suffice to make it an ill bargain to the offender, give him cause to repent, and terrify others from doing the like. Every offence, that can be committed in the state of nature, may in the state of nature be also punished equally, and as far forth as it may, in a commonwealth: for though it would be besides my present purpose, to enter here into the particulars of the law of nature, or its measures of punishment; yet, it is certain there is such a law, and that too, as intelligible and plain to a rational creature, and a studier of that law, as the positive laws of commonwealths; nay, possibly plainer; as much as reason is easier to be understood, than the fancies and intricate contrivances of men, following contrary and hidden interests put into words; for so truly are a great part of the municipal laws of countries, which are only so far right, as they are founded on the law of nature, by which they are to be regulated and interpreted.

X. Sect. 13. To this strange doctrine, viz. That in the state of nature every one has the executive power of the law of nature, I doubt not but it will be objected, that it is unreasonable for men to be judges in their own cases, that self-love will make men partial to themselves and their friends: and on the other side, that ill nature, passion and revenge will carry them too far in punishing others; and hence nothing but confusion and disorder will follow, and that therefore God hath certainly appointed government to restrain the partiality and violence of men. I easily grant, that civil government is the proper remedy for the inconveniencies of the state of nature, which must certainly be great, where men may be judges in their own case, since it is easy to be imagined, that he who was so unjust as to do his brother an injury, will scarce be so just as to condemn himself for it: but I shall desire those who make this objection, to remember, that absolute monarchs are but men; and if government is to be the remedy of those evils, which necessarily follow from men's being judges in their own cases, and the state of nature is therefore not to be endured, I desire to know how much better it is than the state of nature, where one man, commanding a multitude, has the liberty to be judge in his own case, and may do to all his subjects whatever he pleases, without the least liberty to any one to question or controul those who execute his pleasure? and in whatsoever he doth, whether led by reason, mistake or passion, must be submitted to? much better it is in the state of nature, wherein men are not bound to submit to the unjust will of another: and if he that judges, judges amiss in his own, or any other case, he is answerable for it to the rest of mankind.

XI. Sect. 14. It is often asked as a mighty objection, where are, or ever were there any men in such a state of nature? To which it may suffice as an answer at present, that since all princes and rulers of independent governments all through the world, are in a state of nature, it is plain the world never was, nor ever will be, without numbers of men in that state. I have named all governors of independent communities, whether they are, or are not, in league with others: for it is not every compact that puts an end to the state of nature between men, but only this one of agreeing together mutually to enter into one community, and make one body politic; other promises, and compacts, men may make one with another, and yet still be in the state of nature. The promises and bargains for truck, &c; between the two men in the desert island, mentioned by Garcilasso de la Vega, in his history of Peru; or between a Swiss and an Indian, in the woods of America, are binding to them, though they are perfectly in a state of nature, in reference to one another: for truth and keeping of faith belongs to men, as men, and not as members of society.

XII. Sect. 15. To those that say, there were never any men in the state of nature, I will not only oppose the authority of the judicious Hooker, Eccl. Pol. lib. i. sect. 10, where he says, The laws which have been hitherto mentioned, i.e. the laws of nature, do bind men absolutely, even as they are men, although they have never any settled fellowship, never any solemn agreement amongst themselves what to do, or not to do: but forasmuch as we are not by ourselves sufficient to furnish ourselves with competent store of things, needful for such a life as our nature doth desire, a life fit for the dignity of man; therefore to supply those defects and imperfections which are in us, as living single and solely by ourselves, we are naturally induced to seek communion and fellowship with others: this was the cause of men's uniting themselves at first in politic societies. But I moreover affirm, that all men are naturally in that state, and remain so, till by their own consents they make themselves members of some politic society; and I doubt not in the sequel of this discourse, to make it very clear.

Chapter III. Of the State of War.

I. Sect. 16. THE state of war is a state of enmity and destruction: and therefore declaring by word or action, not a passionate and hasty, but a sedate settled design upon another man's life, puts him in a state of war with him against whom he has declared such an intention, and so has exposed his life to the other's power to be taken away by him, or any one that joins with him in his defence, and espouses his quarrel; it being reasonable and just, I should have a right to destroy that which threatens me with destruction: for, by the fundamental law of nature, man being to be preserved as much as possible, when all cannot be preserved, the safety of the innocent is to be preferred: and one may destroy a man who makes war upon him, or has discovered an enmity to his being, for the same reason that he may kill a wolf or a lion; because such men are not under the ties of the commonlaw of reason, have no other rule, but that of force and violence, and so may be treated as beasts of prey, those dangerous and noxious creatures, that will be sure to destroy him whenever he falls into their power.

II. Sect. 17. And hence it is, that he who attempts to get another man into his absolute power, does thereby put himself into a state of war with him; it being to be understood as a declaration of a design upon his life: for I have reason to conclude, that he who would get me into his power without my consent, would use me as he pleased when he had got me there, and destroy me too when he had a fancy to it; for no body can desire to have me in his absolute power, unless it be to compel me by force to that which is against the right of my freedom, i.e. make me a slave. To be free from such force is the only security of my preservation; and reason bids me look on him, as an enemy to my preservation, who would take away that freedom which is the fence to it; so that he who makes an attempt to enslave me, thereby puts himself into a state of war with me. He that, in the state of nature, would take away the freedom that belongs to any one in that state, must necessarily be supposed to have a design to take away everything else, that freedom being the foundation of all the rest; as he that, in the state of society, would take away the freedom belonging to those of that society or commonwealth, must be supposed to design to take away from them every thing else, and so be looked on as in a state of war.

III. Sect. 18. This makes it lawful for a man to kill a thief, who has not in the least hurt him, nor declared any design upon his life, any farther than, by the use of force, so to get him in his power, as to take away his money, or what he pleases, from him; because using force, where he has no right, to get me into his power, let his pretence be what it will, I have no reason to suppose, that he, who would take away my liberty, would not, when he had me in his power, take away every thing else. And therefore it is lawful for me to treat him as one who has put himself into a state of war with me, i.e. kill him if I can; for to that hazard does he justly expose himself, whoever introduces a state of war, and is aggressor in it.

IV. Sect. 19. And here we have the plain difference between the state of nature and the state of war, which however some men have confounded, are as far distant, as a state of peace, good will, mutual assistance and preservation, and a state of enmity, malice, violence and mutual destruction, are one from another. Men living together according to reason, without a common superior on earth, with authority to judge between them, is properly the state of nature. But force, or a declared design of force, upon the person of another, where there is no common superior on earth to appeal to for relief, is the state of war: and it is the want of such an appeal gives a man the right of war even against an aggressor, tho' he be in society and a fellow subject. Thus a thief, whom I cannot harm, but by appeal to the law, for having stolen all that I am worth, I may kill, when he sets on me to rob me but of my horse or coat; because the law, which was made for my preservation, where it cannot interpose to secure my life from present force, which, if lost, is capable of no reparation, permits me my own defence, and the right of war, a liberty to kill the aggressor, because the aggressor allows not time to appeal to our common judge, nor the decision of the law, for remedy in a case where the mischief may be irreparable. Want of a common judge with authority, puts all men in a state of nature: force without right, upon a man's person, makes a state of war, both where there is, and is not, a common judge.

V. Sect. 20. But when the actual force is over, the state of war ceases between those that are in society, and are equally on both sides subjected to the fair determination of the law; because then there lies open the remedy of appeal for the past injury, and to prevent future harm: but where no such appeal is, as in the state of nature, for want of positive laws, and judges with authority to appeal to, the state of war once begun, continues, with a right to the innocent party to destroy the other whenever he can, until the aggressor offers peace, and desires reconciliation on such terms as may repair any wrongs he has already done, and secure the innocent for the future; nay, where an appeal to the law, and constituted judges, lies open, but the remedy is denied by a manifest perverting of justice, and a barefaced wresting of the laws to protect or indemnify the violence or injuries of some men, or party of men, there it is hard to imagine any thing but a state of war: for wherever violence is used, and injury done, though by hands appointed to administer justice, it is still violence and injury, however coloured with the name, pretences, or forms of law, the end whereof being to protect and redress the innocent, by an unbiassed application of it, to all who are under it; wherever that is not bona fide done, war is made upon the sufferers, who having no appeal on earth to right them, they are left to the only remedy in such cases, an appeal to heaven.

VI. Sect. 21. To avoid this state of war (wherein there is no appeal but to heaven, and wherein every the least difference is apt to end, where there is no authority to decide between the contenders) is one great reason of men's putting themselves into society, and quitting the state of nature: for where there is an authority, a power on earth, from which relief can be had by appeal, there the continuance of the state of war is excluded, and the controversy is decided by that power. Had there been any such court, any superior jurisdiction on earth, to determine the right between Jephtha and the Ammonites, they had never come to a state of war: but we see he was forced to appeal to heaven. The Lord the Judge (says he) be judge this day between the children of Israel and the children of Ammon, Judg. xi. 27. and then prosecuting, and relying on his appeal, he leads out his army to battle: and therefore in such controversies, where the question is put, who shall be judge? It cannot be meant, who shall decide the controversy; every one knows what Jephtha here tells us, that the Lord the Judge shall judge. Where there is no judge on earth, the appeal lies to God in heaven. That question then cannot mean, who shall judge, whether another hath put himself in a state of war with me, and whether I may, as Jephtha did, appeal to heaven in it? of that I myself can only be judge in my own conscience, as I will answer it, at the great day, to the supreme judge of all men.

Chapter IV. Of Slavery.
Sect. 22. The natural liberty of man is to be free from any superior power on earth, and not to be under the will or legislative authority of man, but to have only the law of nature for his rule. The liberty of man, in society, is to be under no other legislative power, but that established, by consent, in the commonwealth; nor under the dominion of any will, or restraint of any law, but what that legislative shall enact, according to the trust put in it. Freedom then is not what Sir Robert Filmer tells us, Observations, A. 55. a liberty for every one to do what he lists, to live as he pleases, and not to be tied by any laws: but freedom of men under government is, to have a standing rule to live by, common to every one of that society, and made by the legislative power erected in it; a liberty to follow my own will in all things, where the rule prescribes not; and not to be subject to the inconstant, uncertain, unknown, arbitrary will of another man: as freedom of nature is, to be under no other restraint but the law of nature.

Sect. 23. This freedom from absolute, arbitrary power, is so necessary to, and closely joined with a man's preservation, that he cannot part with it, but by what forfeits his preservation and life together: for a man, not having the power of his own life, cannot, by compact, or his own consent, enslave himself to any one, nor put himself under the absolute, arbitrary power of another, to take away his life, when he pleases. No body can give more power than he has himself; and he that cannot take away his own life, cannot give another power over it. Indeed, having by his fault forfeited his own life, by some act that deserves death; he, to whom he has forfeited it, may (when he has him in his power) delay to take it, and make use of him to his own service, and he does him no injury by it: for, whenever he finds the hardship of his slavery outweigh the value of his life, it is in his power, by resisting the will of his master, to draw on himself the death he desires.

Sect. 24. This is the perfect condition of slavery, which is nothing else, but the state of war continued, between a lawful conqueror and a captive: for, if once compact enter between them, and make an agreement for a limited power on the one side, and obedience on the other, the state of war and slavery ceases, as long as the compact endures: for, as has been said, no man can, by agreement, pass over to another that which he hath not in himself, a power over his own life. I confess, we find among the Jews, as well as other nations, that men did sell themselves; but, it is plain, this was only to drudgery, not to slavery: for, it is evident, the person sold was not under an absolute, arbitrary, despotical power: for the master could not have power to kill him, at any time, whom, at a certain time, he was obliged to let go free out of his service; and the master of such a servant was so far from having an arbitrary power over his life, that he could not, at pleasure, so much as maim him, but the loss of an eye, or tooth, set him free, Exod. xxi.

Chapter V. Of Property.

Sect. 25. Whether we consider natural reason, which tells us, that men, being once born, have a right to their preservation, and consequently to meat and drink, and such other things as nature affords for their subsistence: or revelation, which gives us an account of those grants God made of the world to Adam, and to Noah, and his sons, it is very clear, that God, as king David says, Psal. cxv. 16. has given the earth to the children of men; given it to mankind in common. But this being supposed, it seems to some a very great difficulty, how any one should ever come to have a property in any thing: I will not content myself to answer, that if it be difficult to make out property, upon a supposition that God gave the world to Adam, and his posterity in common, it is impossible that any man, but one universal monarch, should have any property upon a supposition, that God gave the world to Adam, and his heirs in succession, exclusive of all the rest of his posterity. But I shall endeavour to shew, how men might come to have a property in several parts of that which God gave to mankind in common, and that without any express compact of all the commoners.

Sect. 26. God, who hath given the world to men in common, hath also given them reason to make use of it to the best advantage of life, and convenience. The earth, and all that is therein, is given to men for the support and comfort of their being. And tho' all the fruits it naturally produces, and beasts it feeds, belong to mankind in common, as they are produced by the spontaneous hand of nature; and no body has originally a private dominion, exclusive of the rest of mankind, in any of them, as they are thus in their natural state: yet being given for the use of men, there must of necessity be a means to appropriate them some way or other, before they can be of any use, or at all beneficial to any particular man. The fruit, or venison, which nourishes the wild Indian, who knows no enclosure, and is still a tenant in common, must be his, and so his, i.e. a part of him, that another can no longer have any right to it, before it can do him any good for the support of his life.

Sect. 27. Though the earth, and all inferior creatures, be common to all men, yet every man has a property in his own person: this no body has any right to but himself. The labour of his body, and the work of his hands, we may say, are properly his. Whatsoever then he removes out of the state that nature hath provided, and left it in, he hath mixed his labour with, and joined to it something that is his own, and thereby makes it his property. It being by him removed from the common state nature hath placed it in, it hath by this labour something annexed to it, that excludes the common right of other men: for this labour being the unquestionable property of the labourer, no man but he can have a right to what that is once joined to, at least where there is enough, and as good, left in common for others.

Sect. 28. He that is nourished by the acorns he picked up under an oak, or the apples he gathered from the trees in the wood, has certainly appropriated them to himself. No body can deny but the nourishment is his. I ask then, when did they begin to be his? when he digested? or when he eat? or when he boiled? or when he brought them home? or when he picked them up? and it is plain, if the first gathering made them not his, nothing else could. That labour put a distinction between them and common: that added something to them more than nature, the common mother of all, had done; and so they became his private right. And will any one say, he had no right to those acorns or apples, he thus appropriated, because he had not the consent of all mankind to make them his? Was it a robbery thus to assume to himself what belonged to all in common? If such a consent as that was necessary, man had starved, notwithstanding the plenty God had given him. We see in commons, which remain so by compact, that it is the taking any part of what is common, and removing it out of the state nature leaves it in, which begins the property; without which the common is of no use. And the taking of this or that part, does not depend on the express consent of all the commoners. Thus the grass my horse has bit; the turfs my servant has cut; and the ore I have digged in any place, where I have a right to them in common with others, become my property, without the assignation or consent of any body. The labour that was mine, removing them out of that common state they were in, hath fixed my property in them.

Sect. 29. By making an explicit consent of every commoner, necessary to any one's appropriating to himself any part of what is given in common, children or servants could not cut the meat, which their father or master had provided for them in common, without assigning to every one his peculiar part. Though the water running in the fountain be every one's, yet who can doubt, but that in the pitcher is his only who drew it out? His labour hath taken it out of the hands of nature, where it was common, and belonged equally to all her children, and hath thereby appropriated it to himself.

Sect. 30. Thus this law of reason makes the deer that Indian's who hath killed it; it is allowed to be his goods, who hath bestowed his labour upon it, though before it was the common right of every one. And amongst those who are counted the civilized part of mankind, who have made and multiplied positive laws to determine property, this original law of nature, for the beginning of property, in what was before common, still takes place; and by virtue thereof, what fish any one catches in the ocean, that great and still remaining common of mankind; or what ambergrise any one takes up here, is by the labour that removes it out of that common state nature left it in, made his property, who takes that pains about it. And even amongst us, the hare that any one is hunting, is thought his who pursues her during the chase: for being a beast that is still looked upon as common, and no man's private possession; whoever has employed so much labour about any of that kind, as to find and pursue her, has thereby removed her from the state of nature, wherein she was common, and hath begun a property.

Source: Locke, John. *The Works of John Locke*, vol. 5. London: 1801.

GLOSSARY

Eccl. Pol. lib. i: a reference to Volume 1 of Richard Hooker's *Of the Lawes of Ecclesiastical Politie*

Document Analysis

The excerpts from the *Second Treatise on Civil Government* are taken from four chapters: Chapter II, "Of the State of Nature"; Chapter III, "Of the State of War"; Chapter IV, "Of Slavery"; and Chapter V, "Of Property." These excerpts deal with fundamental questions about government, including the origin of government and what makes the authority of government legitimate.

Chapter II: "Of the State of Nature."

Locke's *Second Treatise* argues that governments originated from a primal social contract. Locke, like other social contract theorists, posited a fictive political environment called the "state of nature," a kind of theoretical state in which people enjoy absolute freedom, without the constraints of society and government. He begins with the premise that originally people lived in a primitive state of nature without any government and in accordance with the "law of nature." In support of his view he quotes Richard Hooker, an Anglican theologian and the author of the multivolume work *Of the Lawes of Ecclesiastical Politie*, first published in the 1590s. The essence of Hooker's view, according to Locke, is that equality is "the foundation of that obligation to mutual love amongst men." Freedom, however, does not mean unfettered license—that is, license for people to do wrong or to do whatever they want. While people live in a state of nature, they are obligated to follow the law of nature, which dictates that a person may not "take away, or impair the life, or what tends to the preservation of the life, the liberty, health, limb, or goods of another." Still, in the state of nature some people violate the natural rights of others. Thus, to protect their rights, people join together to create government. This is accomplished by means of a "social contract" by which each person agrees to give up certain rights, such as the right to exact vengeance, in order to better protect the more fundamental rights of life, liberty, and property.

Much of the discussion in this chapter is given over to such matters as vengeance, criminals, and violations of natural law. Locke argues that if there are no means of enforcing natural law, then people can violate it at will. In a pure state of nature, an individual who has been harmed by another possesses a natural right to seek retribution. In so doing, that person achieves power over another, and this power is essentially the beginnings of government. The person who has harmed another has broken the tie ("tye," as Locke spells it) that binds people to one another. In breaking the tie, the offender has harmed not just an individual but, indeed, the entire human species. The social contract creates a government that is assigned the duty of protecting natural rights. Laws are made legitimate by the fact that the government is created by the will of the people; by consenting to the social contract, each person is obeying himself or herself, because the law is really each person's will. This is the case even if someone has not expressly agreed to the social contract. By staying within a society, a person tacitly accepts the terms of the social contract. The social contract then makes government legitimate; its laws are morally binding because they are the laws created by the personal consent of the governed.

Locke goes into some detail in discussing particular instances. He argues that a national government does not have jurisdiction over aliens. More important, he takes up the issues of punishment, deterrence of crime, and retribution. Again, in a state of nature, people are executors of their right to self-preservation and therefore of the right to seek retribution against a criminal. The problem, of course, noted in section 13, is that in the state of nature, every person is, in effect, prosecutor, judge, jury, and potential executioner with respect to his or her own concerns and grievances. Nevertheless, a person in a state of nature at least has the right to seek justice when the laws of nature have been violated—and as a check, that person's justice is then subject to the sense of justice of "the rest of mankind" and to potential further retribution. A larger problem is that a king or prince as head of a government, "commanding a multitude," can likewise function as prosecutor, judge, jury, and executioner, but without any means of retribution available to the masses in the case of royal injustice. The paradox for Locke is that government, while restraining vengeance and retribution, can be yet another form of subjecting people to the potentially unjust will of another.

Chapter III: "Of the State of War."
Locke begins this chapter by defining war—which in this discussion is considered more in the context of conflict between individuals—as a state of "enmity and destruction" that comes about when one person makes a premeditated assault on another's life. But a crucial part of the law of self-preservation is that one person may take another's life in self-defense, since any aggression on the part of one person challenges the victim's essential freedom. In the author's words, "I should have a right to destroy that which threatens me with destruction: for, by the fundamental law of nature, man being to be preserved as much as possible, when all cannot be preserved, the safety of the innocent is to be preferred." From this premise Locke argues that one can kill a thief because any attack on a person's property is an attack on his or her freedom. Further, anyone who attempts to put himself in a position of absolute power over another is essentially making war—clearly an argument against absolute monarchies and the presumed divine right of monarchs to rule.

Locke proceeds by delineating how the state of war and the state of nature are not the same. In the state of nature, people live together and are governed by reason. They have no common superiors in the form of persons. War, on the other hand, is a state in which people exert force on others. Facing force or the threat of force, a person under attack has the right to fight back—to make war. The defining characteristic of the state of nature, Locke argues, is the lack of a common judge or authority. By reason rather than through any personal authority, then, force directed against a person is considered a violation of the natural law that prevails in the state of nature and thus forms a sufficient basis for waging war.

War, however, can take place both in the state of nature and in society. The difference between the two, noted in section 19, has to do with the conclusion of the conflict. In the state of nature, war does not come to an end unless the aggressor makes peace and offers reparations for any damage done. Until that time comes, the injured party has the right to try to destroy his adversary. In society, on the other hand, both the aggressor and the victim can appeal to authority to resolve the conflict. A chief problem that can occur is that the authorities can fail to act with justice. When such is the case, the state of war will persist, for "wherever violence is used, and injury done, though by hands appointed to administer justice, it is still violence and injury, however coloured with the name, pretences, or forms of law" (section 20).

Again, such passages can be viewed as offering justification not only for the regicide of 1649 but also for the Glorious Revolution. Other writers, such as Robert Filmer (whose arguments are addressed by Locke primarily in the *First Treatise*) and Thomas Hobbes (in *Leviathan*) had argued that monarchs held supreme authority; in Filmer's view, they have a divine right to rule, while in Hobbes's view, supreme monarchs are necessary to protect people from their own baseness and destructiveness. The essence of Locke's argument is that people have the same right to oppose unjust leadership as they do to oppose attacks on their persons or property in a state of nature. Locke concludes the discussion by maintaining that people enter into society principally to avoid the state of war, for the existence of authority increases stability and personal security and reduces the need for war.

Chapter IV: "Of Slavery."

This chapter does not deal with slavery as the word is traditionally understood. Rather, it deals more generally with the concept of one person having absolute power over another. Thus, a person under a despotic government is just as much a slave as someone engaged in forced labor for another. Locke states his fundamental view in the chapter's opening sentence: "The natural liberty of man is to be free from any superior power on earth, and not to be under the will or legislative authority of man, but to have only the law of nature for his rule." He goes on to distinguish natural liberty from social liberty. Natural liberty is a state in which one is guided by the law of nature; social liberty is a state in which people have the right to be subject to no legislative power other than that created by the consent of the governed. A commonwealth is established only "by consent." The commonwealth's authorities can act only "according to the trust" put in them.

Locke's view is that freedom from power that is absolute or arbitrary is fundamental—so much so that a person cannot give it up, even if one wanted to do so. Further, slavery represents an extension of the state of war discussed in Chapter III. In Section 24, Locke cites the example of the Jews in the Old Testament Book of Exodus, who sold themselves not into slavery but into drudgery, for their conquerors did not have absolute power over them.

Chapter V: "Of Property."

A central portion of the *Second Treatise* is Locke's discussion of property. He begins with the notion that both the Bible and natural reason sanction the right of people to use the Earth for their survival and comfort. The important question is that if the Earth exists for humankind in general, how does one acquire individual property? Locke's answer is to begin by noting that one's body is property. But a person owns not only the physical object of one's body but also the labor one performs with that body. Labor, then, is a type of property, so when people add their labor to some item, they now own the item (or at least a share of the item). Locke provides a simple example in Section 28: An apple on a tree exists for the benefit of humankind. However, when the apple is picked, a person has added labor to the apple, and the apple now belongs to the person. A person can do this without obtaining the consent of humankind.

Locke argues, however, that this type of economic activity has boundaries. People can fairly acquire only as many goods as they can reasonably use. If a person picks more apples than needed, the surplus will rot and go to waste. Similarly, in the case of land, people are entitled only to as much land as they can reasonably use—to build a house on, for example, or to farm. In summary, what determines the value of a commodity is the labor invested in it, and it is labor that people use to make their world inhabitable.

Essential Themes

Locke's influence on thinkers and political actors in the eighteenth century was varied. Often that influence was indirect, as those who followed him, rather than forming a cohesive group of philosophical disciples, were attracted to different aspects of his views. Some built upon his epistemology, the philosophical line of inquiry that examines what can be known and the process of knowing. Others were attracted to his advocacy of religious toleration, while still others saw his quiet reasoning style as a model for thinking in the Age of Reason and the Enlightenment.

What can be said with some assurance is that Locke in general and the *Second Treatise on Civil Government* in particular had a profound impact on the American colonists—although a minority of scholars dispute this view. The Declaration of Independence, which Thomas Jefferson said was an expression of American sentiment, is a very Lockean document, for the principles embodied in the declaration can trace their origins back to the *Second Treatise* and its treatment of the inalienable natural rights of the people. Indeed, in the preamble to the Declaration of Independence, the authors refer to the "the separate and equal station to which the laws of nature and of nature's God entitle them." The document famously goes on to state, "We hold these truths to be self-evident, that all men are created equal, that they are endowed by their Creator with certain unalienable rights, that among these are life, liberty, and the pursuit of happiness." These are words that could almost have been written by Locke himself. Later, after the American Revolution, the delegates to the Constitutional Convention in 1787 demonstrated knowledge of Locke's philosophy and embodied his principle of political compacts in such documents as the Federalist Papers. The Fifth Amendment and Fourteenth Amendment to the Constitution derive from Locke, and his *Second Treatise* is quoted directly where it says that no one shall be deprived of "life, liberty, or property" without due process of law.

Ironically—given that Locke is now considered a major Enlightenment thinker—the *Second Treatise* was not widely read in the eighteenth and nineteenth centuries, and while many intellectuals saw his theories as important, many others dismissed them. Only in the twentieth century did interest in Locke revive, and his work is now considered foundational in the history of constitutional government.

—Andrew J. Waskey

Bibliography and Further Reading

Aaron, Richard I. *John Locke*. 2nd ed. Oxford University Press, 1955.

Cranston, Maurice W. *John Locke: A Biography*. Oxford University Press, 1985.

Czajkowski, Casimir J. *The Theory of Private Property in John Locke's Political Philosophy*. University of Notre Dame Press, 1941.

Johnson, Merwyn S. *Locke on Freedom: An Incisive Study of the Thought of John Locke*. Best Printing, 1978.

Sabine, George H. *A History of Political Theory*. 3rd ed. Holt, Rinehart and Winston, 1961.

The Cambridge Companion to Locke. Edited by Vere Chappell. Cambridge University Press, 1994.

Yolton, John W. *John Locke: An Introduction*. Oxford University Press, 1985.

Websites

"The Digital Locke Project." Digital Locke Project, http://www.digitallockeproject.nl/.

"Timeline: The Life and Work of John Locke (1632–1704)." The Forum at the Online Library of Liberty, http://oll.libertyfund.org/index.php?option=com_content&task=view&id=1181&Itemid=273.

CHRISTIANITY AND SOCIETY IN THE EAST

The East Asian world was in transition in the seventeenth century, as were other parts of the world. The Japanese Tokugawa Shogunate had come to power after a civil war in the previous century; the Manchurian Qing Dynasty had replaced the Ming Dynasty in China. Both the Shogunate and the Qing Dynasty need to impose some sort of order in their societies if they were to establish their new authority; both were also required to confront and address the challenge that Christianity posed to that order and authority. While one society embraced Christianity, at least for a while, the other rejected it out of hand.

Japan's story unfolded in this manner: In 1603, after failing to secure Korea as a colony, the shogun Tokugawa Ieyasu came home to defeat his rivals and establish the Tokugawa Shogunate (1600-1868), with its new capital at Edo (Tokyo). The Japanese economy stabilized in the Tokugawa era as powerful landlords, the daimyo, were defeated and settled in peace. Merchants sold silks, sake, fans, porcelain, books, and other goods to markets all over the world, and as a result, they came into contact with Portuguese missionaries operating in the region. The Jesuits made a few converts in southern Japan, most of them rebellious daimyo looking for reasons to revolt again against the Tokugawa. In the 1630s, during an era of economic prosperity, a revolt against the high costs of rent and taxes began in the same southern Japanese provinces where the Christians had some influence. Convinced that Christianity was to blame, the shogunate decided to ban Christianity in Japan. Followers of the Christian faith were crucified, and it was declared that foreigners could not enter or leave Japan with impunity. For the two centuries that followed, the Tokugawa Shogunate managed Japan as an isolated, hermit-like island nation, cut off from most of the world.

In 1600, China was a land of 130 million people with a booming economy based on the development of new textiles, industrial inventions and techniques for production. A wealthy population that was not attached to the land like aristocrats began to burgeon. Some of these people, such as Li Yü (author of *Meritorious Deeds at No Cost*), looked to cement their social status producing *shanshu*, a type of self-help book that would help individuals apply Confucian principles to their daily lives. Yet there was corruption and apathy in the centers of government—the Ming emperors were largely decadent and uninvolved in taking care of their people. It seemed clear that there was a need for a change of dynasty.

The source of that change came as a shock. The Manchurians, the old Jurchen Jin of the Mongol era, invaded China led by their chieftain, Nurhachi, and in 1644 they established the Qing or "pure" Dynasty. Despite the fact that the transition from one dynasty to another did not send shock waves throughout the Chinese economy, many Chinese considered the Qing Dynasty a mistake—one being made for the second time in three centuries—that would allow China to be ruled by barbarians from outside the country. Many Chinese called for the immediate overthrow of the Qing and so, in order to identify those loyal to the dynasty and rebels who would work to overthrow it, the regent for the first Qing emperor issued an edict demanding that all Chinese men wear their hair in a queue. Those who refused to comply would be executed. From that point onward, the relationship between the Qing Dynasty and its people only got more complicated.

Despite this harsh behavior, the Qing Dynasty can also be seen as far more dynamic at its center, in part due to having emperors with scholarly inclinations and who were inspired by the Jesuit missionaries Jesuits arrived in the late sixteenth century, bringing with them both a zeal for religious conversions and scientific knowledge. Though Christianity never became a state religion as a result of the emperors' contact with Jesuits, a growing interest in western science and technology, especially astronomy, did take hold. Instead of banishing visitors from the west as Japan had chosen to do, wealthy and educated Chinese embraced the travelers from the west. The Emperor Kangxi even made an official declaration stating that Jesuit missionaries meant no harm to Chinese society and thus were free to practice their religion. In a relatively short time, however, the Qing emperors came to regret their connection to the west, as more and more Europeans infiltrated their growing economy and began to assert their demands to access it.

Tokugawa Ieyasu: Laws Governing Military Households

Date: 1615
Author: Tokugawa Ieyasu
Genre: State edict

Summary Overview

In 1615 Tokugawa Hidetada, the second shogun of Japan's Tokugawa *bakufu*, or military government, promulgated the Laws Governing Military Households, or Buke Shohatto, a set of instructions or rules for members of Japan's large military class. The Laws Governing Military Households were meant to maintain peace and regulate all aspects of the behavior of warriors, extending from the lords of domains to the lesser samurai who served them. Although they are correctly interpreted as a set of laws, only a few of the stipulations laid out in the thirteen Articles of this document were meant to be enforced in the sense that a law governing the crime of murder or burglary would be. Instead, most of the Laws Governing Military Households were broadly prohibitive or hortatory in nature; they were meant to give general guidelines for behavior rather than proscribe specific acts.

The significance of the Laws Governing Military Households lay in the new standards set forth for military rule in Japan's early-modern era, also known as the Tokugawa Period (1600–1868). The laws in the document essentially had four aims. First, they signified the determination of the Tokugawa government to enforce the peace, to ensure that Japan would not return again to the warfare and decentralized rule that had characterized it in the preceding century. Second, they set forth the importance of Confucian social and political ideals at the same time that they stressed the need to maintain distinctions of rank and status; in this manner, the document was conservative in nature. Third, in an indirect but powerful way, they contributed to the rapid urbanization of Japan that took place in the seventeenth century. And, finally, they played a role in the eventual demise of the samurai, or warrior, class as a whole. Few of these effects were immediately realized, and few of them would have occurred without other policies or practices enacted either by the *bakufu* or the great lords (daimyo), but the Laws Governing Military Households was at the same time the basis for all of them.

Defining Moment

Between 1467 and 1477 war between two factions of the largely defunct Ashikaga *bakufu* took place within the boundaries of Kyoto, the capital (and only major city) in Japan at the time. Besides decimating much of the capital, the war ushered in the so-called Warring States Period, a century-long period of upheaval in which Japan was ruled piecemeal by feudal lords, approximately two hundred in number. Given Japan's relatively small size (an area equivalent to the state of Montana, though the northernmost island of Japan, Hokkaido, was largely uninhabited at the time and outside of Japanese control), these two hundred domains were small in area. The lords of these domains were spoken of as *daimyo*, meaning literally, "great name," and they established their authority by means of military prowess.

The Warring States Period was a transitional time in Japanese history, dividing the medieval and early-modern worlds, and it was unique in several distinguishing ways. Accordingly, the establishment of Tokugawa rule in the seventeenth century, and the accompanying practices, policies, and laws—such as Laws Governing Military Households—can be understood only in the context of developments during this critical era. Four developments were particularly significant.

First, prior to the Warring States Period, Japan was ruled by an aristocratic elite that included Kyoto courtiers (among them, the hereditary emperor), powerful temples and clerics of the Buddhist and Shinto faiths, and the upper echelon of the warrior class. Although the balance of power between these three blocs changed over the centuries, its members had long been the dominant players in the world of politics and economics. That changed after 1467. With full-scale warfare throughout the land, traditional distinctions of hereditary status and rank lost much of their importance. Instead, military might came to define both political power and social influence as never before, and, of course, it was the warriors alone who wielded the sword. Never before had an individual's genealogy or hereditary status meant so little in Japan. People of the time recognized this shift and coined a new word, *gekokujo*, meaning "the low overthrowing the high," reflecting the radical changes they were seeing. Whereas in the past, warriors of influence were men with distinguished pedigrees, linked back to elite families, now many of the greatest warriors were upstarts, individuals whose immediate ancestors may have been farmers or minor warriors serving greater lords.

Second, prior to the Warring States Period, much of the land in the country was held in the form of private estates by courtier families and temples. Many warriors held extensive fiefs, too, but the proportion of land under their control increased dramatically in the century after the civil war began in 1467, as they confiscated estates and incorporated them within their domains. In short, by 1568 most of the land and its economic capacity were in the hands of warriors.

Third, despite the growth of warrior power, the position of the great lords (daimyo) was by no means secure. They were, of course, often at war with neighboring daimyo; were at pains to maintain the loyalty of their vassals, who were not against seeking a new lord if it was to their advantage; and were challenged, and in some cases threatened, by the rise of leagues of commoners, who likewise sought expanded influence in this period of upheaval. More than a few daimyo lost their heads at the hands of one of their own men (or sons), others were overthrown or defeated, and some daimyo families survived much of the century of warfare only to be destroyed near its end. Instability and insecurity were watchwords of the period.

Fourth, despite the upheaval of the century, it was also a time of economic and population growth and technological progress. This was possible because war was not going on everywhere all the time. Many regions went decades with little or no fighting, and much of the fighting that did occur, at least until late in the period, was small in scale and limited in destruction. This allowed some daimyo to extend and build their economic and political bases. In the process, local economies grew, and new technologies led to increased prosperity. In this manner the Warring States Period provided a solid foundation for the remarkable growth in these areas that would take place in the seventeenth century.

In 1568 Oda Nobunaga, having established a sizable domain in central Japan, marched his army into Kyoto, making it known that he intended to once again bring Japan under single rule. He is known as the first of the "three unifiers." By the time of his death in 1582, Nobunaga controlled more than two-thirds of the country, but he was stopped short by one of his own vassals, who attacked him while he was staying the night at a Kyoto temple. His successor, the second unifier, was Toyotomi Hideyoshi, another of Nobunaga's vassals. Hideyoshi was able to grasp power and eventually unify all Japan under a system that has been defined as "federal," in that he held a major portion of power but allowed daimyo to maintain their domains as long as they pledged loyalty to him. Tokugawa Ieyasu, the third unifier, continued this approach after grasping power in 1600. The result was that the early-modern system of government consisted of a shogun at its head (though nominally under the authority of the hereditary emperor in Kyoto), with approximately two hundred daimyo beneath him, each of whom controlled his own domain, which varied in size depending on his status and the goodwill of the shogun. It was a rather odd system, structured largely upon military ideals and organization, with the shogun serving as "the greatest among equals."

The more immediate context of the promulgation of Laws Governing Military Households was Tokugawa Ieyasu's assertion of unchallenged control after defeating the armies of Toyotomi Hideyori in the summer of 1615. Hideyori, the heir of the second unifier, Hideyoshi, was just five years of age when his father died in 1598. In the battles for supremacy that ended in Tokugawa Ieyasu's victory in 1600, the great warriors sidestepped Hideyori and the question of his legitimacy as Hideyoshi's political heir. He was allowed to continue to reside in his castle in Osaka, and it was there that he eventually reached adulthood. But by 1614 he had become a potential threat, and Ieyasu decided that he must be destroyed. With that accomplished by mid-year of 1615, the Tokugawa *bakufu* was finally in a position to promulgate laws governing the behavior of the military houses.

Author Biography

Although they were issued by the Tokugawa government when Hidetada was shogun, the Laws Governing Military Households was a product of Ieyasu's efforts. This is not surprising, since Ieyasu, even though he was formally retired, continued to rule the country and shape and define the new political system. Ieyasu did not actually draft the laws. Instead, drafting was the work of Ishin Suden (1569–1633), a Zen monk and close adviser to Ieyasu. Suden spent several decades of his early life in the Kyoto temple Nanzenji but from 1608 formed ties with Ieyasu and was used in various capacities by the shogun in the years that followed. Like many others within the Buddhist priesthood, Suden was highly educated and thus was in a position to assist Ieyasu in preparing laws. It would be wrong, however, to speak of Suden as the author, because ultimately these were Ieyasu's laws, put into written form by Suden after much discussion with and instruction from Ieyasu.

HISTORICAL DOCUMENT

An Excerpt from Laws Governing Military Households

1. The study of literature and the practice of the military arts, including archery and horsemanship, must be cultivated diligently.

    "On the left hand literature, on the right hand use of arms" was the rule of the ancients. Both must be pursued concurrently. Archery and horsemanship are essential skills for military men. It is said that war is a curse. However, it is resorted to only when it is inevitable. In time of peace, do not forget the possibility of disturbances. Train yourselves and be prepared.

2. Avoid group drinking and wild parties.
    The existing codes strictly forbid these matters. Especially, when one indulges in licentious sex, or becomes addicted to gambling, it creates a cause for the destruction of one's own domain.

3. Anyone who violates the law must not be harbored in any domain.

    Law is the foundation of social order. Reason may be violated in the name of law, but law may not be violated in the name of reason. Anyone who violates the law must be severely punished.

4. The daimyo, the lesser lords (shomyo), and those who hold land under them (kyunin) must at once expel from their domains any of their own retainers or soldiers who are charged with treason or murder.

    Anyone who entertains a treasonous design can become an instrument for destroying the nation and a deadly sword to annihilate the people. How can this be tolerated?

5. Hereafter, do not allow people from other domains to mingle or reside in your own domain. This ban does not apply to people from your own domain.

    Each domain has its own customs different from others. If someone wishes to divulge his own domain's secrets to people of another domain, or to report the secrets of another domain to people of his own domain, he is showing a sign of his intent to curry favors.

6. The castles in various domains may be repaired, provided the matter is reported without fail. New construction of any kind is strictly forbidden.

    A castle with a parapet exceeding ten feet in height and 3,000 feet in length is injurious to the domain. Steep breastworks and deep moats are causes of a great rebellion.

7. If innovations are being made or factions are being formed in a neighboring domain, it must be reported immediately.

    Men have a proclivity toward forming factions, but seldom do they attain their goals. There are some who [on account of their factions] disobey their masters and fathers, and feud with their neighboring villages. Why must one engage in [meaningless] innovations, instead of obeying old examples?

8. Marriage must not be contracted in private [without approval from the bakufu].

    Marriage is the union symbolizing the harmony of yin and yang, and it cannot be entered into lightly. The thirty-eighth hexagram kuei [in the Book of Changes], says, "Marriage is not to be contracted to create disturbance. Let the longing of male and female for each other be satisfied. If disturbance is to take hold, then the proper time will slip by." The "Peach Young" poem of the Book of Odes says, "When men and women observe what is correct, and marry at the proper time, there will be no unattached women in the land." To form a factional alliance through marriage is the root of treason.

9. The daimyo's visits (sankin) to Edo must follow the following regulations:

    The Shoku Nihongi [Chronicles of Japan] contains a regulation saying that "Unless entrusted with some official duty, no one is permitted to assemble his clansmen at his own pleasure. Furthermore no one is to have more than twenty horsemen as his escort within the limits of the capital. ..." Hence it is not permissible to be accompanied by a large force of soldiers. For the daimyo whose revenues range from 1,000,000 koku down to 200,000 koku of rice, not more than twenty horsemen may accompany them. For those whose revenues are 100,000 koku or less, the number is to be proportionate to their incomes. On official business, however, the number of persons accompanying him can be proportionate to the rank of each daimyo.

10. The regulations with regard to dress materials must not be breached.

    Lords and vassals, superiors and inferiors, must observe what is proper within their positions in life. Without authorization, no retainer may indiscriminately wear fine white damask, white wadded silk garments, purple silk kimono, purple silk linings, and kimono sleeves which bear no family crest. Lately retainers and soldiers have taken to wearing rich damask and silk brocade. This was not sanctioned by the old laws, and must now be kept within bounds.

11. Persons without rank are not to ride in palanquins.

    Traditionally there have been certain families entitled to ride palanquins without permission, and there have been others receiving such permission. Lately ordinary retainers and soldiers have taken to riding in palanquins, which is a wanton act. Hereafter, the daimyo of various domains, their close relatives, and their distinguished officials may ride palanquins without special permission. In addition, briefly, doctors and astrologers, persons over sixty years of age, and those who are sick or invalid may ride palanquins after securing necessary permission. If retainers and soldiers wantonly ride palanquins, their masters shall be held responsible. The above restrictions do not apply to court nobles, Buddhist prelates, and those who have taken the tonsure.

12. The samurai of all domains must practice frugality.

    When the rich proudly display their wealth, the poor are ashamed of not being on a par with them. There is nothing which will corrupt public morality more than this, and therefore it must be severely restricted.

13. The lords of all domains must select as their officials men of administrative ability.

    The way of governing a country is to get the right men. If the lord clearly discerns between the merits and faults of his retainers, he can administer due rewards and punishments. If the domain has good men, it flourishes more than ever. If it has no good men, it is doomed to perish. This is an admonition which the wise men of old bequeathed to us.

Take heed and observe the purport of the foregoing rules.
First year of Genna [1615], seventh month.

GLOSSARY

bakufu: the central Japanese state, located in Edo (today renamed Tokyo)

Book of Changes: *Yi Jin* or *I Ching*, one of the Confucian Five Classics, also called the Classic of Changes

Book of Odes: *Shi Jing*, one of the Confucian Five Classics, also called the Classic of Poetry

Daimyo: a businessman prosperous enough to afford the trappings of aristocracy

First year of Genna, seventh month: The Japanese dating system does not correspond to Western dating methods. "Genna" refers to the era, and the month can be construed as August.

yin and yang: Taoist conception of the balance of the universe, symbolized by an S shape in a circle, the left colored and the right blank, with circles of the opposite shade in each side

Document Analysis

The Laws Governing Military Households was promulgated by being formally read to a gathering of two hundred of Japan's most important daimyo at Fushimi Castle, outside Kyoto, on July 7, 1615. The audience were the sort of people who could have constituted a serious threat to the *bakufu*. In addition to having heard the laws read, the daimyo also received written copies of the laws either at that time or shortly thereafter, as did daimyo who were not in attendance.

The document consists of thirteen articles. Each begins with a statement of exhortation or prohibition. There then follows a brief explanatory section, often drawing upon classical sources (both Chinese and Japanese) or traditional principles to support the argument. This was to be expected. In the year previous to the laws' issuance, Suden and numerous associates among the Buddhist priesthood and Kyoto nobility had been busily engaged in copying and studying such classical sources from the country's libraries, all at Ieyasu's behest. Close analysis also reveals that precedents for most of the articles can be found in previous law codes; many, in fact, originated with the daimyo "house codes" (laws governing the behavior of a daimyo's retainers or vassals) of the Warring States Period, evidence that the Tokugawa were confronted with many of the same issues as their daimyo predecessors, particularly when it came to the control and management of vassals.

In brief, the laws' thirteen articles stipulated the following: (1) Warriors were to study both literary and military arts; (2) excessive drinking and partying were forbidden; (3) criminals were not to be sheltered in any domain; (4) warrior lords had to expel from their domains any warriors charged with treason or murder; (5) outsiders to the domains were not to be allowed to fraternize or reside therein; (6) castles could be repaired, if reported, but new construction was forbidden; (7) warrior factions of any type were forbidden; (8) marriages could not be arranged without *bakufu* approval; (9) daimyo had to follow regulations when calling on the shogun; (10) one's dress had to accord with one's status; (11) only those of appropriate rank were allowed to ride in palanquins; (12) samurai of the various domains had to be frugal; and (13) lords of domains should select men of talent as their officials.

Articles 1 and 13 address the question of wise rule and how to accomplish it. Article 1 is justifiably considered the most important article of the laws. The approach to rulership that it lays out can be interpreted both as a standard that the Tokugawa expected the daimyo to uphold and as a declaration of the intentions of the central holders of power, the Tokugawa shoguns themselves. The declaration of the need not just for literary arts but for military arts as well provides a clear signal that the Tokugawa expected that the existing governmental system of 1615, structured largely upon a military organization with which all daimyo were familiar, would continue. In other words, the Tokugawa foresaw neither themselves nor the daimyo abandoning their weapons or martial attitude and training. The system was to remain military at heart. In this sense, the Tokugawa affirmed the position of the warrior class.

And although this affirmation might not have seemed significant at the time, it became so during the next two centuries, as Japan enjoyed a period of remarkable peace, free of war, from the late 1630s until the 1850s. During these years the samurai and their institutions became rusty and antiquated and in many ways irrelevant to the early modern society that developed. Nonetheless, their position was confirmed and bolstered by the sort of ideals expressed in Article 1 of the laws.

At the same time that it confirms the military arts, Article 1 also stresses the literary arts as crucial to good rulership. Another way to put this, commonly used at the time, was that one came to power by the sword but then ruled (if he was wise) with the brush (that is to say, the pen). As defined by Confucian philosophy, wise rulers were cultivated and educated, characteristics that allowed them to draw on past examples to meet the challenges of the present, understand the needs of the people, and show compassion to their subjects. In Article 1, the Tokugawa assert that they intend to be rulers of this type. It was an assertion they needed to make because, in contrast to the Kyoto courtiers, Japan's warriors were often seen as boorish and uncultivated. It was a stigma that was not easily overcome, particularly as the court, with emperor and courtiers, continued to exist (supported, in fact, by the *bakufu*), a symbol of the height of cultivation.

Articles 2 and 12 are concerned with the proper behavior of individuals. Although exhortations to avoid drinking and gambling or to live frugally might seem petty or overly intrusive into the private affairs of individuals, they were not viewed as such at the time. According to Confucian teachings, moral behavior is at the heart of good government, and Ieyasu was determined that his rule, and that of the daimyo beneath him, follow that model.

In light of the stable, peaceful, and prosperous society that was well in place by the middle of the seventeenth century, the stipulations in Articles 3 through 8 can appear quaint or archaic to historians. But it is important to keep in mind that warriors in 1615 had lived lives in which warfare was the norm, intrigue and treason against one's lord were common occurrences, and peace was as fleeting as the clouds of autumn. Accordingly, the Tokugawa issued these grave warnings and severe decrees to counteract such tendencies. By all measures, the results were positive and impressive.

Article 3 provides a powerful philosophical background to the specific stipulations that follow in later articles. The assertions that "law is the foundation of social order" and "reason may be violated in the name of law, but law may not be violated in the name of reason" reveal the overriding concern for peace and stability. In essence, the author of the statement acknowledges that law is not perfect, that at times reason might suggest that the law could be ignored or sidestepped. Yet that is unacceptable. Imperfect though it may be, law, if followed, would ensure stability in society.

Articles 6 and 8 are the two laws in this section that had the most practical significance. Article 6, with its restrictions on new castle construction by daimyo, is best understood in conjunction with another law, known as the One Domain, One Castle Decree, issued under the name of the shogun's three top advisers less than a month before the issuance of Laws Governing Military Households. That edict explicitly decreed that within each domain all castles except that in which the daimyo resided were to be destroyed. The purpose was clear: to limit the military capabilities of daimyo, ensuring that they did not establish fortified states capable of challenging the Tokugawa *bakufu*. The need for this limitation was a reflection of developments in the Warring States Period, during which time castles became fort-like structures, used as much for fortifications for troops on the offensive as for defensive bulwarks.

The intent of Article 8, with its regulation of marriages among daimyo, is clear, given the common practice in earlier centuries and in many places around the world of forging political and military alliances through the means of matrimony. No alliances could be made without the consent of the *bakufu*.

Articles 9–11 deal with questions of status. Simply put, they require all warriors, from daimyo to foot soldiers, to act in accordance with their position in society. The specific examples given—concerning the number of attendants a daimyo might employ when calling on the shogun, the quality and luxuriousness of one's dress, and the privilege of riding in a palanquin (in short, being carried by menials rather than riding a horse or moving under one's own power)—were surely not meant to be exclusive. The quality of food one ate and the entertainment one engaged in were also governed by one's status, as was the privilege of taking additional wives. Moreover, similar, but more restrictive laws of this nature regulated the manners of merchants and others of means, extending to the size and style of their residences. It was believed in Japan at the time, and backed by Confucian ideology, that in a well-ordered society people knew their place and acted accordingly. To fail to do so would invite commotion and disharmony. Moreover, as these three articles suggest, distinctions in status existed *within* classes as much as *between* classes. In other words, although class could be an important marker in distinguishing groups and individuals, in many cases the divisions between individuals of different statuses within a class were sharper than those between individuals of different classes. Low-level samurai, for instance, were much closer in status to commoners, such as merchants, than they were to their own daimyo or to the shogun, neither of whom they could have ever had the opportunity of meeting.

Essential Themes
Many of the articles in Laws Governing Military Households are moralistic and hortatory in nature. Did warriors take it to heart to follow both literary and military arts, as stipulated in Article 1? Did they avoid heavy drinking and wild parties, as laid out in Article 2? And were they frugal in their daily lives, as decreed in Article 12? In short, did members of the warrior class follow Confucian political and social ideals, as interpreted by Tokugawa Ieyasu and his associates, as seen in these articles? There are no simple answers to these questions, but there is good evidence that Confucian ideology, thus defined, played a prominent role in shaping the lives and ideals of the warrior class in Tokugawa Japan. As early as 1651, for example, a warrior named Yui Shosetsu planned and undertook a rebellion against the *bakufu* because its contemporary leaders failed, he claimed, to follow the high ideals laid out by Ieyasu. Of course, the Laws Governing Military Households was just one among many forums in which Confucian ideals were expressed at the time; nonetheless, the document was part of a larger and influential discourse.

In a more practical sense, the 1615 Laws Governing Military Households (along with those for emperor and courtiers and for religious institutions) laid the foundation for Tokugawa rule. With their regulation of inter-daimyo relations, castle building, and marriage, the laws severely limited the potential of any lords to challenge the *bakufu*. And none did, for more than 250 years. Viewed in this manner, the laws summarized in the document were stunningly successful.

The Laws Governing Military Households also provided an important model for later laws. In fact, each of the succeeding fourteen Tokugawa shoguns (excepting two whose rule was very brief) reissued the Laws Governing Military Households, with fewer or more changes depending upon the needs of the time. During the first half of the period, this was done in Edo Castle with daimyo in attendance; later that was seen as unnecessary. Nonetheless, the Laws Governing Military Households remained a standard for the age, a set of rules and instructions by which warriors of all ranks were to gauge their actions.

Some of the effects of the Laws Governing Military Households were surely unexpected, at least to Tokugawa Ieyasu and his associates who drafted them. Article 6 is striking in this regard. By restricting new castle construction—and limiting castles to one per domain, as decreed in the earlier law of 1615—the *bakufu* set in motion developments that would dramatically change the makeup of Japanese society. Each limited to one castle within his domain, daimyo began to build large and sumptuous edifices, hardly the sort of fortified structures from which they could carry out military offensives. At the same time, daimyo worked to ensure that their own vassals did not become a threat, by removing them from lands in the countryside to the castle towns, in exchange for stipends. The result was rapid urbanization as castle towns became cities virtually overnight, replete with new commercial goods, new forms of culture, and large warrior and merchant classes. This was an unintended, yet unmistakable result of a seemingly straightforward law. The largest castle town, by the way, was the shogun's headquarters at Edo (present-day Tokyo), which by 1700 was home to more than one million inhabitants.

Another unexpected effect, which by no means can be attributed solely to the laws, was the eventual demise of the warrior class. Despite the warrior ideals of "military arts" seen in Article 1, the overall thrust of the Laws Governing Military Households (coupled with the more general policies and practices of the Tokugawa *bakufu*) was to make the warrior class anachronistic. Law and order and absolute loyalty to one's lord were the ideals of the new age, and there was no room for those who thought or acted otherwise. Everything that had made the Warring States Period one of continual upheaval was now outlawed: treasonous plans, murder, lawlessness, questionable associations, excessive numbers of castles, "innovations," factions, and marriage alliances. Most of all, hierarchy and status differentiations were to be maintained. By no means could *gekokujo* ("the low overthrowing the high") be tolerated. The result was a warrior class that became increasingly unnecessary and obsolete. The very success of the Tokugawa *bakufu*, and in a sense the Laws Governing Military Households, meant the inevitable end of Japan's warring class.

—Lee Butler, PhD

Bibliography and Further Reading

Bowring, Richard. *In Search of the Way: Thought and Religion in Early-Modern Japan, 1582–1860*. Oxford University Press, 2017

Gordon, Andrew. *A Modern History of Japan: From Tokugawa Times to the Present*. Oxford University Press, 2014.

Hall, John Whitney. *Cambridge History of Japan*. Volume 4: *Early Modern Japan*. Cambridge University Press, 1991.

Yonemoto, Marcia. *Mapping Early Modern Japan: Space, Place, and Culture in the Tokugawa Period, 1603–1868*. University of California Press, 2003.

Websites

"Edo Period 1603–1868." *Encyclopedia Japan,* https://doyouknowjapan.com/history/edo/. Accessed 6 Apr. 2017].

"The Minor Daimyo." *Nakasendo Way: A Journey to the Heart of Japan*. Walk Japan (2017), https://doyouknowjapan.com/history/edo/. Accessed 6 Apr. 2017.

Japan's Closed Country Edict

Date: 1635
Authors: Various
Genre: State directive

Summary Overview

In 1635 the Tokugawa Shogunate, Japan's military government at that time, issued a regulatory code known as the Closed Country Edict. This was one of several sets of laws issued during the 1630s that caused Japan to become largely closed off from the rest of the world for more than two centuries. During the sixteenth and seventeenth centuries, European exploration had begun to radically alter both the shape of the world and relations between peoples from different parts of the globe. Accordingly, the fact that Japan's rulers took steps to halt those developments as they affected Japan was significant.

The Closed Country Edict of 1635 was one of several codes that led to Japan's status as a "closed country." Although historians have long debated the impetus behind the Closed Country Edict and its effectiveness and results, they are nonetheless in agreement that its impact was immense. Without it, Japan's early modern history might have developed in a dramatically different manner. Among the edict's effects were the following: (1) It limited Japan's relations with other nations and peoples from 1635 until the 1850s; (2) it forced the country as a whole to focus on internal developments during these centuries; (3) it added to the country's stability, since it was one of a number of measures that gave the Tokugawa increased control over the Japanese people; (4) it gave the government power to regulate all aspects of foreign relations, which it did to its advantage (and to the detriment of the great lords).

Defining Moment

In the autumn of 1543 a Portuguese ship arrived in southern Japan; it was the first Western vessel to reach that land. Lacking a central government at the time, Japan conducted no formal foreign relations. However, there was much international activity in the area, and the Japanese were part of it. A number of the *daimyo*, particularly those in southwestern Japan, were active in overseas trade. Many Japanese pirates (and pirates of other nationalities) plied the waters of Southeast Asia and East Asia, and there were a number of small Japanese colonies established by traders at ports throughout the region. The arrival of the Westerners saw the emergence of a robust intra-Asian trade network, in which goods and precious metals moved between China, Japan, South Asia, and Southeast Asia on boats of many nationalities. This trade would thrive for another century, with the Portuguese and later the Dutch acquiring most of their wealth in Asia by becoming major trade participants in the region, rather than by sending spices and other luxury items back to Europe.

Christian missionaries—members of the Society of Jesus, or Jesuits—first came to Japan in 1549, only six years after the first Portuguese ship arrived. The Jesuits were part of the Counter-Reformation, the Catholic Church's effort to regain Europe from the Protestants and spread the Gospel to the far reaches of the Earth. They were learned and devout, dedicated to the cause they had joined. And they were supported in their efforts by the Portuguese traders, who gave them passage and donated funds to their work. Thus, as the Portuguese traders worked to enlarge their portion of trade with Japan, their Jesuit associates worked to convert the Japanese to Christianity.

Because the Portuguese brought wealth to the regions in which they stopped, the *daimya* of southwestern Japan were anxious that the traders make use of their harbors. Some, like Omura Sumitada, who controlled Nagasaki, even donated lands and harbors, which, in effect, allowed the Portuguese to establish foreign enclaves within the country. Some *daimyo* also converted to Christianity and encouraged (occasionally with a heavy hand) their subjects to do likewise. The result was that by 1580 there may have been as many as one hundred thousand Japanese Christians, and by 1600 as many as three hundred thousand, though what percentage of those were committed to the faith is difficult to say. Nonetheless, Christianity and the foreigners who brought it began to have an impact upon Japan.

Politically, Japan began to change during this time as well. In 1600, Tokugawa Ieyasu was the last of three great generals to unite Japan's warring factions around his leadership. Ieyasu's heirs followed in his footsteps for the next 250 years as the Tokugawa Shogunate. To

Toyotomi Hideyori (1593 - June 5, 1615) was the son and designated successor of Toyotomi Hideyoshi, the general who first united all of Japan. [Public domain], via Wikimedia Commons

bring lasting stability to Japan, the shogunate needed steady sources of revenue, the *daimyo* needed to be controlled, lawlessness needed to be brought to an end, and foreign affairs and foreign trade needed to be regulated. A major concern was the foreign trade activity of the southwestern *daimyo*, men with large domains and large armies; their ability to dominate foreign trade added to the threat they posed to the central regime. The fact that so many of the *daimyo* had converted to Christianity also warranted careful consideration.

Around the turn of the century other Westerners arrived in Japanese ports: Spanish (both traders and Franciscan missionaries), Dutch, and English. The Franciscans and Jesuits were soon at odds, and there was evidence to suggest that many of the foreigners presented a threat to the peace—a threat that needed to be addressed. In 1614 Ieyasu finally issued an edict banning Christianity and expelling all missionaries. With the death of Ieyasu in 1616, persecution of Christians began in earnest, carried out under the direction of Tokugawa Hidetada and Tokugawa Iemitsu, the second and third Tokugawa shoguns. Particularly noteworthy was the "Great Martyrdom" of 1622, in which 132 Christians, both Jesuits and Japanese converts, were executed in Nagasaki.

One reason the Tokugawa shoguns were willing to undertake such harsh measures is that foreign trade was unlikely to be hurt, since the Dutch had begun to supplant the Iberian powers on the seas. And whereas the Portuguese and Spanish were zealous in their religion, the Dutch were not. Moreover, in order to solidify their position, the Dutch took steps to undermine their European rivals, playing off Tokugawa fears of Christianity.

From an economic standpoint, a key aspect of Tokugawa policy in these early decades was the regulation of the silk trade under *ito wappu*, or the "raw silk apportionment" system. Because the Portuguese had been able to gain restricted access to trade with China in the late sixteenth century, they were the sole purveyors of raw silk to Japan, the most highly prized and profitable of goods in this market. Stiff competition for silk among Japanese merchants led to steep prices and enormous profits for the Portuguese. In order to change this situation and regulate the import silk market, in 1604 the Tokugawa established the *ito wappu* system, which took control away from the Portuguese and gave it to powerful Japanese merchants from several of the large cities (at first Kyoto, Nagasaki, and Sakai, to which were shortly added Osaka and Edo: thus the "five trading cities" referred to in Article 12 of the edict). These merchants negotiated terms, set prices, and allocated goods both to their benefit and the benefit of the government. The Portuguese continued to make a profit from the silk trade, but it was much reduced.

This was the general context in which the Closed Country Edict was issued in 1635. Its issuance (as well as those edicts that preceded and followed it in the same decade) was not immediately precipitated by a particular incident or crisis, involving, for example, foreign affairs, Christianity, or international commerce—suggesting that these laws reflected a set of policies that had been many years in the making, here at last put into final form.

Author Biographies

Just who the author or authors of this document were is hard to know. The edict was issued under the rule of the third shogun, Tokugawa Iemitsu (1604–1651). Although it is highly unlikely that he wrote it (common practice was to have learned advisers or high officials draft edicts), he no doubt had a large say in what was in it. Like the other early Tokugawa shoguns, Iemitsu was a personal ruler who took an active role in establishing policy and laying down laws. Iemitsu differed from his two predecessors, however, in that he was the first shogun to have no experience in battle. Probably for this reason he did much to establish the bureaucratic structure of the shogunate, shifting it away from the military organization that had characterized it under his father and grandfather. In this sense, the Closed Country Edict was appropriate to him. Accordingly, it is fair to say that the content reflected Iemitsu's concerns and ideas and that it had been worked out in conjunction with his advisers.

As for the five individuals who signed the edict of 1635—Hotta Masamori, Abe Tadaaki, Matsudaira Nobutsuna, Sakai Tadakatsu (1587–1662), and Doi Toshikatsu (1573–1644)—we must be careful not to ascribe authorship to them without appropriate caveats. In the first place, since most of the 1635 edict had already appeared in a decree of 1633, the authorship of the earlier document must also be considered. At that time, only two of these men (Sakai and Doi) were serving as senior councilors (the council being the governmental body that issued these edicts). Sakai and Doi may, in fact, have been the principal authors, as they were influential *daimyo* (wealthy landowners or businessmen) with close ties to the Tokugawa. Moreover, both were longtime appointees, having served as senior councilors for more than a decade. Sakai Tadakatsu had established his worth to the Tokugawa in 1600 when he fought with Tokugawa Ieyasu in the battle that brought Ieyasu to power. Doi Toshikatsu had even longer and closer connections to the Tokugawa, having become a powerful retainer to Tokugawa Hidetada in 1579. Both men were rewarded with large fiefs and eventually important positions in the shogunate.

HISTORICAL DOCUMENT

Japan's Closed Country Edict
Items: for Nagasaki

1. Japanese ships are strictly forbidden to leave for foreign countries.

2. No Japanese is permitted to go abroad. If there is anyone who attempts to do so secretly, he must be executed. The ship so involved must be impounded and its owner arrested, and the matter must be reported to the higher authority.

3. If any Japanese returns from overseas after residing there, he must be put to death.

4. If there is any place where the teachings of padres (Christianity) is practiced, the two of you must order a thorough investigation.

5. Any informer revealing the whereabouts of the followers of padres (Christians) must be rewarded accordingly. If anyone reveals the whereabouts of a high ranking padre, he must be given one hundred pieces of silver. For those of lower ranks, depending on the deed, the reward must be set accordingly.

6. If a foreign ship has an objection [to the measures adopted] and it becomes necessary to report the matter to Edo, you may ask the Omura domain to provide ships to guard the foreign ship, as was done previously.

7. If there are any Southern Barbarians (Westerners) who propagate the teachings of padres, or otherwise commit crimes, they may be incarcerated in the prison maintained by the Omura domain, as was done previously.

8. All incoming ships must be carefully searched for the followers of padres.

9. No single trading city shall be permitted to purchase all the merchandise brought by foreign ships.

10. Samurai are not permitted to purchase any goods originating from foreign ships directly from Chinese merchants in Nagasaki.

11. After a list of merchandise brought by foreign ships is sent to Edo, as before you may order that commercial dealings may take place without waiting for a reply from Edo.

12. After settling the price, all white yarns (raw silk) brought by foreign ships shall be allocated to the five trading cities and other quarters as stipulated.

13. After settling the price of white yarns (raw silk), other merchandise [brought by foreign ships] may be traded freely between the [licensed] dealers. However, in view of the fact that Chinese ships are small and cannot bring large consignments, you may issue orders of sale at your discretion. Additionally, payment for goods purchased must be made within twenty days after the price is set.

14. The date of departure homeward of foreign ships shall not be later than the twentieth day of the ninth month. Any ships arriving in Japan later than usual shall depart within fifty days of their arrival. As to the departure of Chinese ships, you may use your discretion to order their departure after the departure of the Portuguese *galeota*.

15. The goods brought by foreign ships which remained unsold may not be deposited or accepted for deposit.

16. The arrival in Nagasaki of representatives of the five trading cities shall not be later than the fifth day of the seventh month. Anyone arriving later than that date shall lose the quota assigned to his city.

17. Ships arriving in Hirado must sell their raw silk at the price set in Nagasaki, and are not permitted to engage in business transactions until after the price is established in Nagasaki.

You are hereby required to act in accordance with the provisions set above. It is so ordered.

From:
Lord of Kaga, seal [Hotta Masamori]
Lord of Bungo, seal [Abe Tadaaki]
Lord of Izu, seal [Matsudaira Nobutsuna]
Lord of Sanuki, seal [Sakai Tadakatsu]
Lord of Oi, seal [Doi Toshikatsu]

To:
Sakakibara, Lord of Hida [Motonao]
Sengoku, Lord of Yamato [Hisataka]

GLOSSARY

fifth day of the seventh month: The Japanese dating system is not equivalent to Western dating. This date can be construed as sometime in the summer.

***galeota*:** galleon

twentieth day of the ninth month: The Japanese dating system is not equivalent to Western dating. This date can be pinpointed to the autumn.

Document Analysis

The Closed Country Edict of 1635 consists of seventeen articles and can be roughly divided into three sections. Understanding these divisions provides a key to understanding the concerns and intent of the Tokugawa leadership that produced the document. Three articles address the question of Japanese travel and trade abroad, both of which are prohibited, five articles deal with Christian missionaries and their teachings, and the remaining nine articles are directed at foreign trade and the protocols and requirements associated with it.

It is important to note that the title given the document, Closed Country Edict, was a later addition ascribed by historians as they attempted to classify it. To call this document the Closed Country Edict suggests an interpretation that the authors may not have expected or desired, and this is something that must be kept in mind. The edict, in fact, had no title beyond the simple "Items: for Nagasaki," meaning a list of articles or instructions. Considered in that light, we might also ask which of the seventeen articles actually established policy that led to Japan's becoming a closed country.

Articles 1–3

The first three articles, those that address Japanese travel and trade abroad, clearly do establish policy leading to a closed country. By restricting both Japanese ships and individuals of Japanese birth from traveling to foreign countries, or returning from foreign countries after having resided there, the Tokugawa government made it clear that if foreign relations and trade were maintained, they would be conducted by foreigners *in their ships*, not by Japanese in Japanese vessels. In this sense, the edict did indeed define one type of closed country, a country in which resident nationals must remain. Leaving for any purpose, long-term or short-term, was unacceptable. It also put an end to (or at least cut off irrevocably) the several small Japanese colonies in the Southeast Asian coastal region, which meant that Japan would remain limited in size and space to more traditional borders.

Beyond the first three articles, there is very little in this edict that specifies or decrees, implicitly or explicitly, that Japan is to be a closed country. Only Article 14 hints at this; it stipulates that foreign vessels must depart for home by the autumn, unless they reached Japan late, in which case they must leave within fifty days of arrival. From this alone, it is difficult to know just when in a given year foreign vessels arrived in Japan, but it must have been during the first week or so of the seventh month (as the Japanese dated it), since Article 16 states that Japanese merchants are to arrive in Nagasaki by the summer. Taken together, these two articles suggest that foreign trading vessels were probably allowed in Japan for approximately two months each summer, but the edict says nothing further about foreign relations or foreign residents except where Christianity is at issue.

Articles 4–8

The five articles that deal with Christianity are not the harsh, strongly prohibitive declarations about the religion or threats against missionaries and believers that one might expect. Article 4, for example, requires the two Nagasaki commissioners (to whom the Closed Country Edict is addressed) to carry out investigations into suspected gatherings of believers, while Article 5 notes that those who inform on Christians should be given rewards, and Article 6 suggests that precedence be followed in having the Omura domain guard any foreign ship that has an objection to Tokugawa policy (usually related to Christianity, the reason the article is placed here). Finally, Article 7 concerns the protocol surrounding the incarceration of Christians and instructs the commissioners to have suspects placed in the prison of the Omura domain. In short, these articles deal with secondary or administrative matters. Prohibitions against Christianity, missionaries, and Japanese Christian believers had all been explicitly stated in earlier edicts, beginning with that of Ieyasu in 1613. The authors of the 1635 edict saw no need to reiterate those prohibitions.

Articles 9–17

The remaining nine articles deal with foreign trade. The detailed stipulations suggest that much here is new or at least had not already been made explicit in edict form, and that was in fact the case. Officials could turn back to earlier laws and edicts to chart policies that regulated and prohibited Christianity, but that was not true of the *ito wappu* system, which had been laid out in rudimentary form in 1604 but lacked specific prohibitions and regulations until the five edicts of the 1630s.

Closer examination of these nine articles reveals that three are directed at Japanese merchants, three at foreign merchants (those who brought the goods in their ships), and three at both groups. Articles 9 and 16 define acceptable behavior for Japanese merchants, ensuring that no merchants from one city monopolize trade, and require Japanese merchants to arrive in Nagasaki by a certain day (in the summer) in order to be able to purchase goods. As the Tokugawa stipulate here and elsewhere, things are to be done with order. Those who failed to do so would inevitably lose their privileges. Article 10 is likewise directed at Japanese merchants, though it is more difficult to understand. It prohibits samurai from purchasing goods from Chinese vessels, suggesting that at least some warriors in the new and peaceful world of Tokugawa Japan were engaged in commerce, an activity the Tokugawa shoguns did not look highly upon. The reason was that trade and commercial activities were regarded as unbefitting the warrior (that is, gentlemanly) class, whose work was to be noble and uplifting.

The three articles directed at foreign merchants are Article 14, which sets the date of departure for foreign ships; Article 15, which prohibits the deposit of unsold goods in Nagasaki; and Article 17, which requires traders on foreign ships arriving in Hirado (another port in southwestern Japan) to sell their silk at the price established in Nagasaki. At this point in time, given the extent of state control over the sale of raw silk, none of these articles was particularly onerous; they merely ensured that no irregularities would occur in the system as already established. Also, as suggested in Article 17, foreign trade in Japan was becoming limited in location; no longer could traders on a foreign vessel arrive at any harbor that they wished and there carry out trade with local inhabitants.

The articles that are relevant to both foreign and Japanese merchants are articles 11–13; they all deal with the protocols of foreign trade regarding silk and other commodities. Article 11 confirms an earlier practice regarding permission to engage in buying and selling, while Article 12 reiterates the privileged position of the "five trading cities" in the silk market. Article 13 states that non-silk merchandise may be traded after the price on raw silk is set. It also provides two caveats: It gives the local commissioners discretion to regulate the quantity of goods brought for sale in Chinese ships, since the vessels are small and can carry only limited loads, and it requires purchasers to pay for their goods within twenty days of the date when the price for the item is set.

Essential Themes
Without the Closed Country Edict (and accompanying policies such as the ban on Christianity), early modern Japan might have developed in radically different ways than it did. For example, Christianity might have become an influential religious and social force, altering Japan's culture in fundamental ways. Likewise, relations with foreign peoples might have increased in extent and depth, with Japanese travelers journeying frequently to other parts of Asia, the Near East, and even Europe. Another possibility is that an open Japan would have been less internally stable than it was. Those were all possibilities, but they did not occur. Instead, Japan was closed (if imperfectly), and it followed a distinct path largely unshaped by foreign intercourse for more than two hundred years.

Although the Tokugawa leadership may have considered its policy of prohibiting foreign travel by Japanese vessels and individuals merely a matter of security, there is no question that the impact of these articles was considerable. The measures forced the Japanese to turn inward, to consider first themselves and their world rather than the broader world beyond their borders. As a result, the rich and unique early-modern culture of Tokugawa Japan—with its kabuki theater, ukiyo-e woodblock prints, and distinctive crafts—developed within a closed country, a land in which foreign ideas and habits had limited influence.

Although the Closed Country Edict was effective at "keeping Japanese in," it was less effective at "keeping foreigners out," primarily because that was not its intent. Nonetheless, there was constriction over time, some of it brought about by decree and some the result of external factors. Important factors included the state's decision to ban entry to all Europeans of the Catholic faith; the English decision early in the seventeenth century to abandon Japan as unprofitable, which left only the Dutch on the European side and the Chinese among the Asians; and a Tokugawa decree of 1639, which restricted the Dutch and Chinese to the harbor of Nagasaki, where small numbers of them resided in foreign enclaves and carried out trade annually when their ships arrived from abroad. The only other foreign intercourse the shogunate allowed was trade between the *daimyo* of Tsushima and Korea (which faced each other across the straits of Japan) and trade between the *daimyo* of Satsuma and the Kingdom of the Ryukyus (islands to the south of Japan, the most prominent being Okinawa). Despite these annual contacts, Japan was indeed a land that saw and housed very few foreigners during the Tokugawa era. Native Japanese could not help but feel that the rest of the world was far away and its peoples very different.

Because Japan became largely closed off to outsiders, by the late eighteenth century the idea of *sakoku*, or "Japan as a closed country," had become accepted policy, despite the fact that no formal declaration of closure had ever been made. This was a case in which a practice had become doctrine over time, a tradition shaped by years of acceptance.

For the Tokugawa, the Closed Country Edict was one of a handful of critical policies that gave the shoguns firm control over the country. Peace reigned for 250 years, during which time Japan experienced unprecedented population growth and commercial activity. The Tokugawa Period was not without problems, some of them severe, but it was also a remarkable period, a time when Japan moved from having been a medieval society to being an early-modern one, and at least some of the credit for that must go to the influence of the Closed Country Edict.

Finally, it is important to note that Japan's closed country policy led to confrontations with the West in the early and middle nineteenth century. These confrontations nearly resulted in Japan's subjugation, as it stubbornly held to a practice that was shortsighted and impractical, at least by the 1850s. Nonetheless, Japan emerged independent and largely unscathed, though the Tokugawa government and the old military order collapsed in the process.

—*Lee Butler, PhD*

Bibliography and Further Reading
Tashiro, Kazui. "Foreign Relations during the Edo Period: Sakoku Reexamined." *Journal of Japanese Studies,* vol. 8, no. 2 (1982): 283–306.

Toby, Ronald. "Reopening the Question of Sakoku: Diplomacy in the Legitimation of the Tokugawa Bakufu." *Journal of Japanese Studies,* vol. 3, no. 2 (1977): 323–364.

Boxer, Charles. *The Christian Century in Japan, 1549–1650.* University of California Press, 1951.

Elison, George. *Deus Destroyed: The Image of Christianity in Early Modern Japan*. Harvard University Asia Center, 1988.

Hall, John Whitney. *The Cambridge History of Japan*. Volume 4: *Early Modern Japan*. Cambridge University Press, 1991.

Sansom, George. *A History of Japan, 1615–1867*. Stanford University Press, 1963.

Toby, Ronald. *State and Diplomacy in Early Modern Japan: Asia in the Development of the Tokugawa Bakufu*. Princeton University Press, 1984.

Matteo Ricci: "Religious Sects among the Chinese"

Date: 1615
Author: Matteo Ricci
Genres: Memoir, travelogue

Summary Overview

"Religious Sects among the Chinese" was written by Matteo (Matthew) Ricci (1552–1610), an Italian Roman Catholic priest and member of the Society of Jesus, who was among the first Europeans to travel to China in the pre-modern period. Although Europeans had interacted with Chinese officials and traders since the early decades of the sixteenth century, their comprehension of Chinese culture, political thought, religion, and society was impeded by a formidable language barrier. When Ricci was sent to southern China in 1582 to join a fledgling Jesuit mission, he made the mastery of spoken and written Mandarin his primary task. He was the first European to study the canon of classical Chinese thought and one of the first Westerners to communicate what he had learned back to Europe.

Defining Moment

In 1534, a former Spanish soldier named Ignatius de Loyola founded the Society of Jesus, a Roman Catholic missionary order meant to spread Catholicism around the world to counter the spread of Protestantism. The Jesuits, as the order's members were called, were motivated to spread the religion through missionary work and education, usually combining the two by traveling to new places in the world and establishing religious schools. The sixteenth century was also Europe's Age of Exploration, and Jesuits ended up traveling all over the world. In some places, Jesuits were attacked and killed; in others, they were recognized as men of science and learning. One of the latter places was China.

In the late sixteenth and early seventeenth centuries, numerous Jesuit missionaries came to China to spread belief in Catholicism. One of these missionaries was Matteo Ricci, an Italian Jesuit with a strong educational background in science. Ricci was fast accepted into the life of the Ming dynasty, coming to know and teach the Ming emperor and creating some conversions. Ricci's acceptance was helped along by his open-minded attitude toward Chinese religion and philosophy—he generally believed that Confucian doctrine was derived from some sort of exotic Christian revelation in China and that it was thus possible to reconcile Confucianism and Christianity in the effort to win conversions.

Jesuits took up Ricci's vision of Confucianism as a translated version of Christianity, and worked to convert the higher levels of Ming Chinese society as a result, since Confucianism dictated that social inferiors were to show deference to their superiors. The accommodation of Confucianism was useful in that it allowed Catholic missionaries to gain acceptance in Ming educated society and the missionaries gained many converts, especially in the imperial court in Beijing. Christianity spread into the coastal cities and the countryside through networks of Jesuit missionaries and Ming imperial officials schooled in Confucianism. Eventually, the success of Jesuit missionaries led to other Catholic orders, the Dominicans and Franciscans, sending missionaries to China.

Matteo Ricci's description of the different forms of indigenous religious practice found in China comes from an unfinished memoir, *The Journals of Matthew Ricci*, that he wrote at the end of his life in Beijing. Like other travel narratives, this book begins with an overview of the pertinent aspects of Chinese culture before relating the progress of its protagonists. Seeking to garner support for the missionary effort, Ricci's junior colleague, Nicolas Trigault (1577–1628), completed the narrative, translated it from Italian into Latin, and oversaw its publication as *De Christiana expeditione apud Sinas* (*The Christian Expedition among the Chinese*) in 1615 at Augsburg, Germany. The book went through several editions and was translated either partly or wholly several times during the seventeenth century, fixing a durable image of China in the minds of European readers.

Author Biography

Matteo Ricci was born in Macerata, Italy, in 1552. He joined the Society of Jesus in 1571 and was assigned as a missionary to go to the Portuguese trade colony at Macao in China, where he arrived in 1582. He was very well educated, studying philosophy, theology, mathematics, cosmology, and astronomy, all subjects that would prove

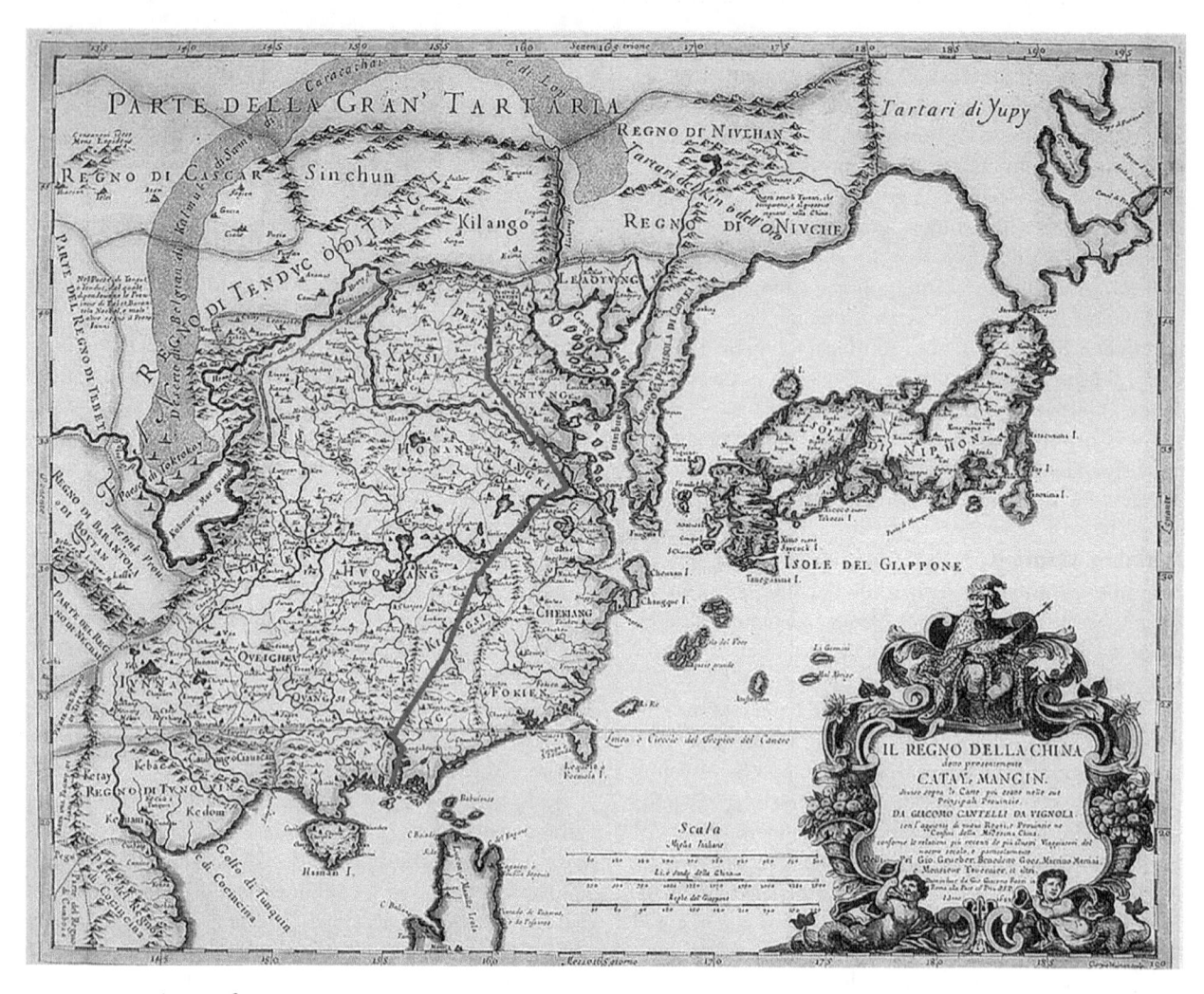

Matteo Ricci's way from Macau to Beijing. By Giacomo Cantelli (1643-1695), Giovanni Giacomo de Rossi (17th century) [Public domain], via Wikimedia Commons

useful in the future. He believed that the best means to convert Chinese people to Christianity was by trying to understand their culture and adopting it himself. Thus, he learned Mandarin, dressed first as a Buddhist monk and later like a Confucian scholar, assumed the Chinese name Li Madou and adapted to Chinese customs. Meanwhile, he also brought with him the skills to make clocks, musical instruments, telescopes and astrolabes, maps, and architectural drawings. He was also well versed in several languages besides Mandarin. As he expected, these skills attracted an audience, and was soon a popular figure in southern China.

In 1601 Ricci met the Ming emperor Wanli, beginning a decade-long relationship with the imperial court. His knowledge of mathematics and astronomy impressed the Confucian scholars, who were surprised to discover that Ricci's knowledge of the stars was superior to their own. Ricci often made sundials, astrolabes and celestial globes to present as gifts to his Chinese friends. His scientific knowledge was critical in his acceptance among them, as knowledge was prized as virtuous in the Confucian world. Ricci became an ambassador not just for Christianity but for Western civilization in general, providing a means for the Chinese to respect the learning acquired in other parts of the world. Likewise, Ricci was able to integrate himself into Chinese court life, coming to understand the Chinese way of life while trying to recognize its similarities to the Catholic culture he wanted to advance in China itself. Ricci's fondest goal was to convert the emperor to Christianity, under the assumption that the Chinese people would follow their emperor in worship.

Over the course of his time in China, Ricci wrote several books in Chinese and Latin, including *The True Meaning of the Lord of Heaven*, *On Friendship*, and *Ten Discourses by a Paradoxical Man*. He also produced a translation of Euclid's *Geometry* into Mandarin, and drew up several maps of the world, which also impressed his Chinese hosts, whose maps were not nearly so detailed or accurate. He was so renowned that students preparing to take the examinations to allow them to join the imperial bureaucracy came to speak with him to hone their knowledge. Ricci died in 1610, and was buried in Beijing. Soon after his death, his memoirs were published, from which "Religious Sects Among the Chinese" was taken.

HISTORICAL DOCUMENT

"Religious Sects among the Chinese" by Matteo Ricci

Of all the pagan sects known to Europe, I know of no people who fell into fewer errors in the early ages of their antiquity than did the Chinese. From the very beginning of their history it is recorded in their writings that they recognized and worshipped one supreme being whom they called the King of Heaven, or designated by some other name indicating his rule over heaven and Earth. It would appear that the ancient Chinese considered heaven and Earth to be animated things and that their common soul was worshipped as a supreme deity. As subject to this spirit, they also worshipped the different spirits of the mountains and rivers, and of the four corners of the Earth. They also taught that the light of reason came from heaven and that the dictates of reason should be hearkened to in every human action. Nowhere do we read that the Chinese created monsters of vice out of this supreme being or from his ministering deities, such as the Romans, the Greeks, and the Egyptians evolved into gods or patrons of the vices.

One can confidently hope that in the mercy of God, many of the ancient Chinese found salvation in the natural law, assisted as they must have been by that special help which, as the theologians teach, is denied to no one who does what he can toward salvation, according to the light of his conscience. That they endeavored to do this is readily determined from their history of more than four thousand years, which really is a record of good deeds done on behalf of their country and for the common good. The same conclusion might also be drawn from the books of rare wisdom of their ancient philosophers. These books are still extant and are filled with most salutary advice on training men to be virtuous. In this particular respect, they seem to be quite the equals of our own most distinguished philosophers. Just as fallen human nature continues to degenerate without the help of divine grace, so, too, primitive ideas of religion become so obscure with the passing of time, that there are very few who do not descend to the worse error of atheism when they abandon the cult of inanimate gods.

In this chapter, we shall treat only of the triple cult of the Chinese as distinguished from all other pagan sects. The traces of Saracen, Judaic, and of Christian worship evident in China we shall leave for later consideration. Chinese books enumerate only three cults or systems of religious observance for the whole world and this people knows of no others. These are the Literati, the Sciequia, and the Laucu. All Chinese and all people of the surrounding nations who make use of Chinese writing—the Japanese, the Koreans, the Leuquici or Formosans, and the Cochin Chinese—belong to one or other of these three sects.

The sect of the Literati is proper to China and is the most ancient in the kingdom. They rule the country, have an extensive literature, and are far more celebrated than the others. Individually, the Chinese do not choose this sect; they rather imbibe the doctrine of it in the study of letters. No one who attains honors in the study of letters or who even undertakes the study would belong to any other sect. Confucius is their Prince of Philosophers, and according to them, it was he who discovered the art of philosophy. They do not believe in idol worship. In fact they have no idols. They do, however, believe in one deity who preserves and governs all things on earth. Other spirits they admit, but these are of less restricted domination and receive only minor honors. The real Literati teach nothing relative to the time, the manner, or the author of the creation of the world. We use the word real, or true, because there are some of them, less celebrated, who interpret dreams, but not much faith is placed in them as they deal mostly with trifles and improbable things. Their law contains a doctrine of reward for good done and of punishment for evil, but they seem to limit it to the present life and to apply it to the evil-doer and to his descendants, according to their merits. The ancients scarcely seem to doubt about the immortality of the soul because, for a long time after a death, they make frequent reference to the departed as dwelling in heaven. They say nothing, however, about punishment for the wicked in hell. The more recent Literati teach that the soul ceases to exist when the body does, or a short time after it. They, therefore, make no mention of heaven or of hell. To some of them this seems to be rather a severe doctrine and so this school teaches that only the souls of the just survive. They say that the soul of a man is strengthened by virtue and solidified to endure, and since this is not true of the wicked, their souls vanish, like thin smoke, immediately after leaving the body.

The doctrine most commonly held among the Literati at present seems to me to have been taken from the sect of idols, as promulgated about five centuries ago. This doctrine asserts that the entire universe is composed of a common substance; that the creator of the universe is one in a continuous body, a corpus continuum as it were, together with heaven and earth, men and beasts, trees and plants, and the four elements, and that each individual thing is a member of this body. From this unity of substance they reason to the love that should unite the individual constituents and also that man can become like unto God because he is created one with God. This philosophy we endeavor to refute, not only from reason but also from the testimony of their own ancient philosophers to whom they are indebted for all the philosophy they have.

Although the Literati, as they are called, do recognize one supreme deity, they erect no temples in his honor. No special places are assigned for his worship, consequently no priests or ministers are designated to direct that worship. We do not find any special rites to be observed by all, or precepts to be followed, nor any supreme authority to explain or promulgate laws or to punish violations of laws pertaining to a supreme being. Neither are there any public or private prayers or hymns to be said or sung in honor of a supreme deity. The duty of sacrifice and the rites of worship for this supreme being belong to the imperial majesty alone. This is so true that if anyone else should offer such a sacrifice in usurpation of this right, he would be punished as an intruder upon the duty of the King and as a public enemy. ...So, too, only ranking magistrates and the highest officers in the realm are permitted to sacrifice to the spirits of the mountains, or the rivers, or of the four sections of the universe. Such religious ceremonies are strictly forbidden to private individuals. The precepts of this law are contained in the Tetrabiblion and in the five books of doctrine. Other than these books, there are no legal codes, excepting certain commentaries on these same volumes.

The most common ceremony practiced by all the Literati, from the King down to the very lowest of them, is that of the annual funeral rites, which we have already described. As they themselves say, they consider this ceremony as an honor bestowed upon their departed ancestors, just as they might honor them if they were living. They do not really believe that the dead actually need the victuals which are placed upon their graves, but they say that they observe the custom of placing them there because it seems to be the best way of testifying their love for their dear departed. Indeed, it is asserted by many that this particular rite was first instituted for the benefit of the living rather than for that of the dead. In this way it was hoped that children, and unlearned adults as well, might learn how to respect and to support their parents who were living, when they saw that parents departed were so highly honored by those who were educated and prominent. This practice of placing food upon the graves of the dead seems to be beyond any charge of sacrilege and perhaps also free from any taint of superstition, because they do not in any respect consider their ancestors to be gods, nor do they petition them for anything or hope for anything from them. However, for those who have accepted the teachings of Christianity, it would seem much better to replace this custom with alms for the poor and for the salvation of souls.

The Temple of Confucius is really the cathedral of the upper lettered and exclusive class of the Literati. The law demands that a temple be built to the Prince of Chinese Philosophers in every city, and in that particular part of the city which has been described as the center of learning. These temples are sumptuously built and adjoining them is the palace of the magistrate who presides over those who have acquired their first literary degree. In the most conspicuous place in the temple there will be a statue of Confucius, or if not a statue, a plaque with his name carved in large letters of gold. Near to this are placed the statues of certain of his disciples whom the Chinese revere as saints, but of an inferior order.

With the coming of each new moon and also at the time of the full moon, the magistrates congregate in this temple, together with those of the baccalaureate order, to do honor to their great master. The ritual in this instance is made up of bowing and of bending the knees, of the lighting of candles, and the burning of incense. Each year on his birthday and at other times fixed by custom, they offer him dishes of food elaborately prepared and assert their thanks for the doctrines contained in his writings. This they do because by means of these doctrines they acquired their literary degrees, and the country acquired the excellent public civil authority invested in the magistracy. They do not recite prayers to Confucius nor do they ask favors of him or expect help from him. They honor him only in the manner mentioned of honoring their respected dead. …

The ultimate purpose and the general intention of this sect, the Literati, is public peace and order in the kingdom. They likewise look toward the economic security of the family and the virtuous training of the individual. The precepts they formulate are certainly directive to such ends and quite in conformity with the light of conscience and with Christian truth. They make capital of five different combinations, making up the entire gamut of human relations; namely, the relations of father and son, husband and wife, master and servants, older and younger brothers, and finally, of companions and equals. According to their belief, they alone know how to respect these relationships, which are supposed to be wholly unknown to foreigners, or if known, wholly neglected. Celibacy is not approved of and polygamy is permitted. Their writings explain at length the second precept of charity: "Do not do unto others what you would not wish others to do unto you." It really is remarkable how highly they esteem the respect and obedience of children toward parents, the fidelity of servants to a master, and devotion of the young to their elders.

Because of the fact that they neither prohibit nor command anything relative to what should be believed regarding a future life, many who belong to this caste identify the other two cults with their own. They really believe that they are practicing a high form of religion if they are tolerant of falsehood and do not openly spurn or disapprove of an untruth. The Literati deny that they belong to a sect and claim that their class or society is rather an academy instituted for the proper government and general good of the kingdom. One might say in truth that the teachings of this academy, save in some few instances, are so far from being contrary to Christian principles, that such an institution could derive great benefit from Christianity and might be developed and perfected by it.

The second important sect among the Chinese is known as Sciequia or Omitose. The Japanese call it Sciacca and Amidabu, the sect being quite similar in character in both countries. The Japanese also call it the Lex Totoqui. This code of law was brought to China from the West, in the year sixty-five of the Christian era. It was imported from the region of Thiencio, also called Shinto, which was formerly two kingdoms but today is known by the single title of Hindustan, lying between the rivers Indus and Ganges. A written record is extant that the King of China sent legates to this country, after being enlightened in a dream to do so. These messengers brought back the books of the laws and also interpreters to translate them into Chinese. The founders of the sect had died before the doctrine found its way into China. From this it would appear quite evident that this doctrine passed from the Chinese to the Japanese…

It would seem that the original authors of the teachings of this second sect had drawn certain of their ideas from our philosophers of the West. For example, they recognize only four elements, to which the Chinese, rather foolishly, add a fifth. According to the latter, the entire material world—men, beasts, plants, and mixed bodies—is composed of the elements of fire, water, earth, metal, and wood. With Democritus and his school, they believe in a multiplicity of worlds. Their doctrine of the transmigration of souls sounds like that of Pythagoras, except that they have added much commentary and produced something still more hazy and obscure. This philosophy seems not only to have borrowed from the West but to have actually caught a glimpse of light from the Christian Gospels. The doctrine of this second sect mentions a certain trinity in which three different gods are fused into one deity, and it teaches reward for the good in heaven and punishment for the wicked in hell. They make so much of celibacy that they seem to reject marriage entirely and it is a common custom with them to abandon their homes and families and to go on pilgrimage to beg alms. In some respects their profane rites resemble our own ecclesiastical ceremonies, as for instance their recitation in chant which hardly differs from our Gregorian. There are statues in their temples and the vestments worn by those offering a sacrifice are not unlike our copes. In reciting prayers they frequently repeat a certain name, which they pronounce Tolome but which they themselves do not understand. …

Whatever ray of truth there may be in their doctrine is, however, unfortunately obscured by clouds of noisome mendacity. Heaven and earth are quite confused in their ideas, as are also a place of reward and one of punishment, in neither of which do they look for an eternity for souls departed. These souls are supposed to be reborn after a certain number of years in some one of the many worlds which they postulate. There they may do penance for their crimes if they wish to make amends for them. This is only one of the many nonsensical doctrines with which they have afflicted the unfortunate country.

Neither meat nor any living thing should be eaten, according to the doctrine of this sect, but very few of its adherents observe this regulation. This violation of a rule and other faults as well can be readily atoned for by almsgiving, and, more than that, they can redeem any soul at all from eternal punishment by means of prayers.

…Despite such beginnings and down to the present time, this sect has increased and decreased according to the varying fervor of the years. The continual multiplication of its books, whether currently introduced from the West or made in China, which is more probable, is the fuel that keeps its ardor ablaze with a popularity that seems impossible to extinguish. The very number and variety of its writings has resulted in such a complicated mixture of doctrine and of nonsensical trifles that even those who profess to believe in it cannot riddle it out.

Traces of the antiquity of this sect are evident today in the great number of its temples, which are usually very ornate in decorations. In these temples one sees enormous and monstrous idols of brass and marble, of wood and of yellow clay. Adjoining the temples there are high towers, built of stone or of brick tile, in which huge bells and other ornaments of great value are preserved. The sacrificing priests of this cult are called Osciami. Their faces and their heads are kept clean shaven, contrary to the custom of the country. Some of them are on a continual pilgrimage; others lead a very trying life in caves in the mountains. The greater part of them, numbering as one might figure about two or three millions, live in the numerous cloisters of the temples. These latter are supported by alms and by revenues formerly established for that purpose, though they also provide for their keep by personal labor. ...

This second sect is acquiring a new impetus, even now in our own times, building many temples and restoring others. Its followers for the most part are women and eunuchs and the common horde, and particularly a certain class who claim to be the more religious followers of the cult, who call themselves Ciaicum, or the observers of the fast. They abstain at all times from meat and fish, and in their homes they venerate a whole collection of idols with frequent praying. So as not to be wholly lacking of some means of livelihood, they answer invitations to recite prayers in the homes of others. Women are not excluded from residence in these religious centers, but they live apart from the men, shave their heads, and do not get married. They are known to the Chinese as Nicu and are not nearly as numerous as the men.

The third religious sect is called Lauzu, and had its origin with a philosopher who was contemporaneous with Confucius. The period of gestation anticipating his birth is supposed to have lasted for eighty years and so he is called Lauzu, or the Old Man Philosopher. He left no writings of his doctrine, nor does it appear that he desired to institute a new or separate cult. After his death, however, certain sectaries, called the Taufu, named him as the head of their sect and compiled various books and commentaries from other religions, and these were written in rather elegant literary style. These enthusiasts, too, have their own religious houses and live as celibates. They buy in their disciples and are as low and dishonest a class as those already described. They do not cut their hair but rather wear it as do the people in general, but they are easily distinguished by the custom of wearing a wooden skullcap on the knot or cluster of hair worn on the top of the head. Some of the followers of this creed, who are married, profess a more religious observance in their homes, where they recite set prayers for themselves and for others. ...They also talk of places of punishment and of reward, but their ideas of such places differ not a little from those of the sectaries already mentioned. This group favors a paradise of body and of soul for its members, and in their temples they have pictures of those who have been taken bodily up into heaven. Certain exercises are prescribed in order to accomplish this phenomenon, such as definite sitting positions accompanied with particular prayers and medicines, by use of which they promise their followers the favor of the gods and eternal life in heaven, or at least a longer life on earth. From such nonsense as this one can easily conclude as to the deceit injected into their delirium.

The special duty of the ministers of this group is to drive demons from homes by means of incantations. This is done in two different ways; by covering the walls of the house with pictures of horrid monsters drawn in ink on yellow paper and by filling the house with a bedlam of uncanny yelling and screaming and in this manner making demons of themselves. Bringing down rain from heaven in time of drought, stopping it when rain is too abundant, and preventing public and private calamities in general are some of the powers they claim to possess. If what is promised really came to pass, then those who permit themselves to be attracted by the promises would have a reason for their interest. Since, however, these impostors are invariably wrong in everything they foretell, it is difficult to understand what excuse of pretext can be alleged for following them, by men who otherwise are sufficiently intelligent. ...

The ministers of this sect live in the royal temples of heaven and earth, and it is part of their office to be present at all sacrifices made in these temples either by the King himself or by a magistrate representing him. This, of course, serves to increase their prestige and their authority. The orchestra for such occasions is also composed of the ministers. Every musical instrument known to the Chinese will be included in this assembly, but the music they produce sounds decidedly off key to European ears. These same musicians are frequently invited to funeral services which they attend in ornate vestments, playing upon flutes and other musical instruments. The consecration of new temples and the direction of public processions of supplicants through the streets also come within their jurisdiction. These processions are ordered by the civil authorities of the towns, at stated times, and at the expense of the local neighborhood. ...

These three sects embrace about all the capital superstitions of this pagan people, but the vanity of their human folly does not cease here. As time goes on, through the influence of their leaders, each of these sources of superstition gives rise to so many streams of deceit and deception that under these three captions, one could number nearer to three hundred different and disparate religious sects. The frequent innovations go from bad to worse by the daily augmentation of corrupt practices and rules, of which the members of the sects take advantage for loose and licentious living.

Humvu, the founder of the present reigning family, ordained that these three laws, namely the sects, should be preserved for the good of the kingdom. This he did in order to conciliate the followers of each sect. In legislating for their continuance, however, he made it of strict legal requirement that the cult of the Literati should have preference over the others, and that they alone should be entrusted with the administration of public affairs. Thus it happens that no sect is allowed to work for the extinction of another. The rulers make it a practice to cultivate the devotion of all three of them, using them in their own interest when need be, and conciliating each in turn by renovating their old temples or by building new ones. The wives of the King are usually more devoted to the sect of the idols, conferring alms upon the ministers and even supporting a whole institution of them, beyond the palace walls, in order to profit by their prayers.

The number of idols in evidence throughout the kingdom of China is simply incredible. Not only are they on exhibition in the temples, where a single temple might contain thousands of them, but in nearly every private dwelling. Idols are assigned a definite place in a private home, according to the custom of the locality. In public squares, in villages, on boats, and through the public buildings, this common abomination is the first thing to strike the attention of a spectator. Yet, it is quite certain that comparatively few of these people have any faith in this unnatural and hideous fiction of idol worship. The only thing they are persuaded of in this respect is, that if their external devotion to idols brings them no good, at least it can do them no harm.

In conclusion to our consideration of the religious sects, at the present time, the most commonly accepted opinion of those who are at all educated among the Chinese is, that these three laws or cults really coalesce into one creed and that all of them can and should be believed. In such a judgment, of course, they are leading themselves and others into the very distracting error of believing that the more different ways there are of talking about religious questions, the more beneficial it will be for the public good. In reality they finally end up by accomplishing something altogether different from what they expected. In believing that they can honor all three laws at the same time, they find themselves without any law at all, because they do not sincerely follow any one of them. Most of them openly admit that they have no religion, and so by deceiving themselves in pretending to believe, they generally fall into the deepest depths of utter atheism.

> **GLOSSARY**
>
> **the Literati:** followers of Confucian philosophy
>
> **the Leuquici or Formosans:** the indigenous people of Taiwan
>
> **Cochin Chinese:** the Vietnamese
>
> **Tetrabiblion:** Ricci's term for the Four Books of the classic Confucian philosophical system; Ricci uses a term for them that is similar to a Latin series on astronomy from the third century CE
>
> **Sciequia or Omitose:** Buddhism
>
> **Hindustan:** India; in this case, northern India where Buddhism originated
>
> **cope:** a long, cowled cape worn by priests
>
> **Lauzu:** Taoism
>
> **Humvu:** the Ming emperor Hongwu, founder of the dynasty

Document Analysis

Ricci's understanding of Chinese religion was derived from his observations traveling from southern China to the imperial capital over the course of three decades. He learned much from the study of Chinese texts but also from his preferred interlocutors: State officials, called mandarins or literati, whose primary intellectual frame of reference was derived from the Confucian canon. Ricci viewed the religious panorama of China through a Christian lens, seeing various forms of belief and behavior that were either indifferent or at odds with what he considered orthodoxy. Beyond this specific religious frame, he also viewed Chinese religion in the light of the ancient Greek and Roman culture that he knew from his studies in Europe. Classical antiquity, it seemed to Ricci, offered a ready point of comparison for contemporary Western readers: Like the Greeks, the Chinese were polytheistic, and, like the Romans, they had an elaborate political system based on important moral principles. So moral philosophy and paganism were intertwined in China, as they had once been in Europe; the addition of Christian revelation might potentially transform the Ming realm into another Rome.

Before describing how he executed this ambitious apostolic charge, Ricci offers a panorama of the main schools of thought in China. He was convinced that what he called the Sect of the Literati (Confucianism) was fundamentally different from its counterparts, Buddhism and Daoism. The literati were scholar-officials whose career progression was rooted in the study of the Four Books and the Five Classics of Confucianism and whose positions within the Chinese state obliged them to perform certain annual rituals. Here Ricci describes them as skeptical toward other religious traditions, prizing only moral precepts such as loyalty to the state and filial piety. He is keen to assert that their "sect" is a respectable philosophical system, which, at its core, was not offensive to Christian doctrine—indeed, Confucianism could complement Christianity, just as Greek philosophy complemented Christian theology. Confucian ritual behaviors and non-Christian edifices, Ricci makes clear, are not signs of paganism and are, in any case, reserved for only the highest ranks of the imperial hierarchy. Fortunately for the Jesuit missionaries, the literati held the keys to the social and political acceptance of their Western religion in China.

Buddhism and Daoism are not treated with the same degree of respect in this selection. Ricci's views were clearly influenced by those literati who dismissed these other religions as distractions for rustics or charlatans, but the fact that the contemporary Buddhist (and, to a lesser extent, Daoist) clergy had inspired a surge in popular piety in the early seventeenth century meant that the Jesuit properly identified his competition. Ricci paints a picture of Daoism as a complex of absurd, incoherent teachings, but he views Buddhism as a corruption of true religion, that is, Christianity, which the righteous Chinese had attempted to get from India. In contrast to the Sect of the Literati, both Buddhism and Daoism are marked by dubious practices, such as excessive fasting, and by confused logic, which led them to believe in magic and reincarnation.

Essential Themes
By the time Ricci died in 1610, there were about 2,500 Catholics in China. Matteo Ricci remains a renowned figure in Chinese history, the man who introduced the Chinese (peaceably) to Western knowledge. Yet his methods were questioned after his death. While the Jesuits remained popular and connected to the imperial court in China after the succession of the Qing dynasty in 1644, the Dominican and Franciscan orders also sent missionaries, who were appalled at Ricci's accommodations of Chinese theology into Christian practice. They argued against Jesuit methods to the pope, and in 1705 Pope Clement XI declared the Dominican ban on ancestor worship to be more correct and the sanctioned practice of Christianity in China. As a result, in 1721 the Qing Emperor Kangxi banned Christianity in the "Chinese rites controversy."

—*Liam Matthew Brockey*

Bibliography and Further Reading
Cronin, Vincent. *The Wise Man from the West: Matteo Ricci and His Mission to China*. Ignatius Press, 2016.
Hart, Roger. *Imagined Civilizations: China, The West, and Their First Encounter*. Johns Hopkins University Press, 2013.
Hsia, R. Po-Chia. *Matteo Ricci and the Catholic Mission to China, 1583-1610: A Short History with Documents*. Hackett Publishing Company, Inc., 2016.
Laven, Mary. *Mission to China: Matteo Ricci and the Jesuit Encounter with the East*. Faber, 2011.
Spence, Jonathan D. *The Memory Palace of Matteo Ricci*. Penguin Books, 1984.

Websites
Brucker, Joseph. "Matteo Ricci." *The Catholic Encyclopedia,* http://www.newadvent.org/cathen/13034a.htm. Accessed 29 Apr. 2017.
Bruno, Debra. "Can Matteo Ricci's Beatification Mend China's Rift with the Catholic Church?" *The Atlantic* (November 13, 2013), https://www.theatlantic.com/china/archive/2013/11/can-matteo-ricci-s-beatification-mend-china-s-rift-with-the-catholic-church/281405/. Accessed 29 Apr. 2017.
"Matteo Ricci and the Ming Dynasty." *In Our Time*, 16 April 2015. BBC Radio 4, http://www.bbc.co.uk/programmes/b05qjq67. Accessed 29 Apr. 2017.
O'Connor, J and E. F. Robertson. "Matteo Ricci." University of St. Andrews Scotland (1997), http://www-history.mcs.st-andrews.ac.uk/Biographies/Ricci_Matteo.html. Accessed 29 Apr. 2017.

Li Yü: "On Being Happy Though Poor"

Date: 1671
Author: Li Yü (Li Liweng)
Genre: Essay

Summary Overview

The Chinese playwright and novelist Li Yü was one of many wealthy men in early Qing dynasty China who decided to enlighten people with his notions of how one should live "the good life." Unlike most of his contemporaries, Li had a sense of humor about the enterprise, as he showed in "On Being Happy Though Poor." The more important point of the work was that it was indicative of the prosperity of China in the era when the Ming dynasty ended and the Qing dynasty began. China was able to feed and maintain a vast population, had begun to build trade contacts with the west through Catholic missionaries, and its government improved dramatically with the collapse of the corrupt Ming emperors and their advisors. When a civilization is able to feed itself, indulge in the arts, prosper beneath an efficient governmental administration, and maintain control over its relations with the rest of the world, it is easy for its people to philosophize about the best means to achieve a happy life. Educated Chinese men regularly published works like *Casual Notes in a Leisurely Mood* (1671), the book from which "On Being Happy Though Poor" is extracted. It is a sign of the affluence of Chinese society in the mid-seventeenth century.

Defining Moment

China was a land of 130 million people by the year 1600. Simply by dint of its sheer demographic and geographic size, the Chinese Ming empire entered a period of positive economic development, where trade and artisanal production picked up to supply this teeming population. Mongol invasions had petered out; northeastern China, an area known as Manchuria, had opened up to agriculture. Rice flowed out of the Yangtze River valley, and trade connections extended to SouthEast Asia and India. Chinese manufacturers perfected porcelain making for export—the product euphemistically known as "china"—which was renowned in Europe for its fine construction.

In the production of textiles, Chinese manufacturers learned about cotton from Korean traders, and began building mills to create cotton cloth. The silk industry also made massive profits, particularly overseas in Japan, and Chinese silks sold in Europe at six times their prices in China. To produce both textiles, Chinese manufacturers invented looms and spinning machines to speed up the production process. In other industries, printers came up with new printing block techniques, banking financed economic development, engineers came up with the world's first suspension bridges; Chinese farmers even came up with a prototype for a tractor. China was on the verge of an industrial revolution.

At this very point, Ming economic prosperity started to decline. Bad winters and bad harvests hit Manchuria, and people there, many of them still nomads, migrated south to find food, past the Great Wall into China proper. Manchurian warriors under a khan named Nurhachi had helped Chinese armies drive the Japanese off the Korean peninsula in the late sixteenth century; now those same nomads sought to end Ming dynasty decadence and corruption, and replace the Ming on the imperial throne. Nurhachi's sons and grandsons eventually drove the Ming out of the Forbidden City and inaugurated the Qing dynasty in 1644.

The Qing emperors were never popular due to their "foreign" origins; as with the Mongols, Mandarin-speaking Chinese saw the Qing dynasty as a political humiliation. However, social and economic development returned to its previously high levels—China prospered once again under the Qing.

The seventeenth century, then, was an era of political instability and social and economic riches. Being a Confucian civilization that prized knowledge, order and decorum above all things, the Chinese people were inclined to behave themselves well during this period. This was in part due to the growing popularity of "morality books," or shanshu, popularly published manuscripts that purported to tell the reader how to live a positive life. Shanshu first began to be published during the Song dynasty (960-1279), but the advent of the printing press and the prosperity of the times made many wealthy men eager to promote their own spiritual values as the key to material improvement. Shanshu combined Confucian, Taoist and Buddhist principles, usually telling parables that told the reader

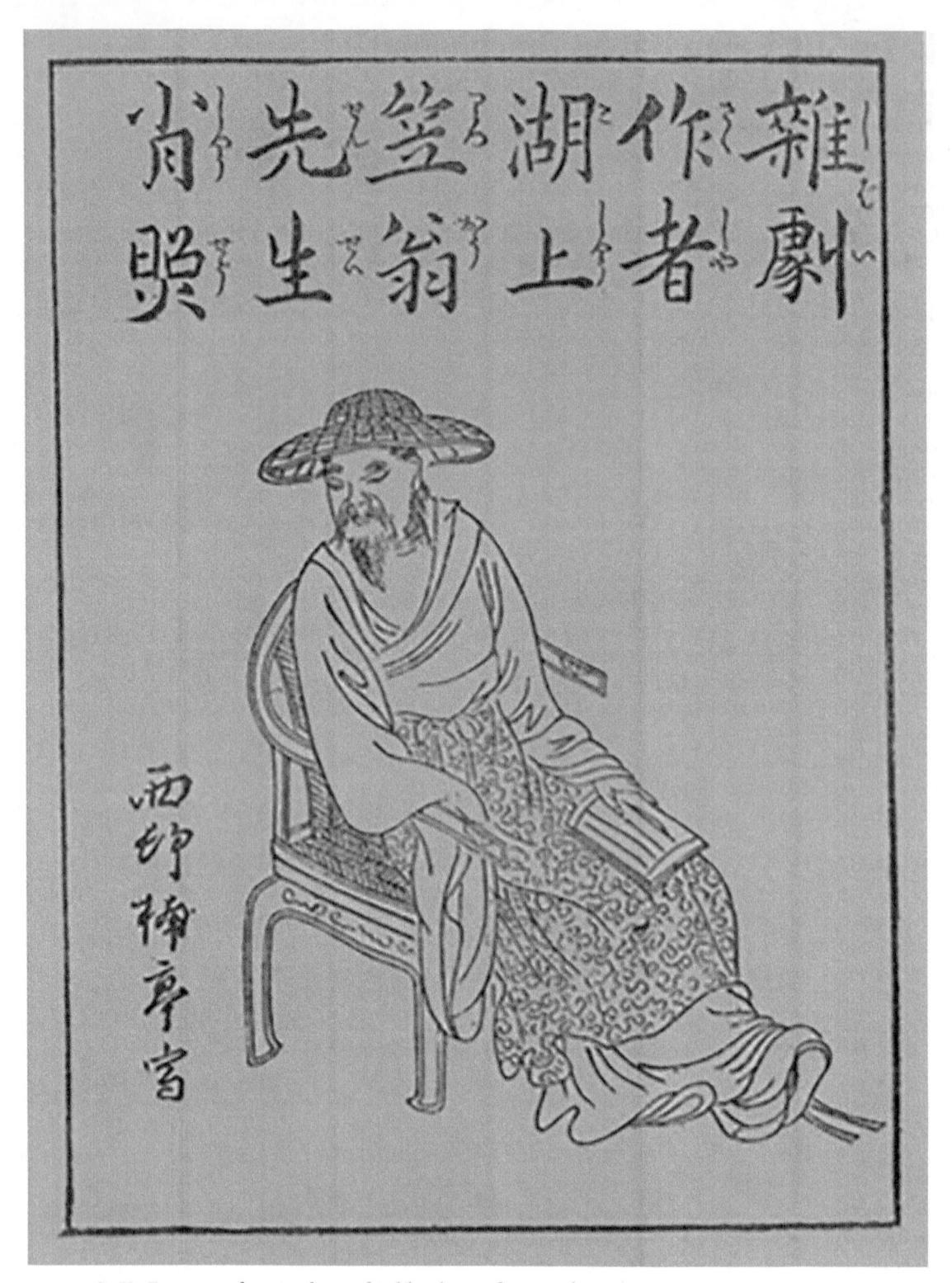

Li Yü By ismeretlen, Közkincs, [Public domain], via Wikimedia Commons

how to live a positive moral existence that was within natural boundaries and which would accumulate good karma for the future. One such work was Li Yu's *Casual Notes in a Leisurely Mood* (1671), and one of its most popular chapters was the amusing parable "On Being Happy Though Poor."

Author Biography
Li Yü (1610–78) was perhaps the most talented literary figure in seventeenth-century China, renowned as a playwright, novelist and essayist. He published his own and other people's works and owned his own theatrical troupe, for which he occasionally acted parts. He was also well versed in landscape architecture and gourmet eating.

Li was originally a Confucian scholar. He did not pass the civil service examination to attain a job in the Ming Chinese state, but that turned out to be fortuitous when the dynasty collapsed to Manchurian invaders in 1644. Instead, Li gave himself the alias Li Liweng, in order to avoid trouble with the new Qing dynasty, and in 1651, he moved to the city of Hangzhou and decided to use his Confucian education to become a playwright. He became one of the most successful playwrights and storytellers in Chinese history, producing a series of erotic works and satirical commentary on Chinese life at the time. Often his works included anecdotes about city life and folk customs which made them popular with ordinary people. To stimulate sales of his work, Li opened up a bookstore in Beijing; to be assured that his plays would be performed, he started his theatrical troupe. Obviously a born promoter, Li Yü was the best-selling writer of his time in China.

Like many wealthy men, Li Yü decided to publicize his experiences in life as he got older, for the benefit of his readers. The most popular of these works was *Xianqing Ouji* (1671), translated in many ways but best rendered as *Casual Thoughts in a Leisurely Mood*. It was divided into eight parts with 234 different topics, including chapters on writing, acting, architecture, gardening, food, sex and clothing. One of its topics was a matching satirical essay called "On Being Happy Though Rich." Another section of the book was on Li's thoughts on the production of theater, for which it is most often read today; in general, though, it is a work on "the art of living."

Toward the end of his life, Li fell afoul of Qing dynasty authorities and had to move back to the city of Hangzhou and go into hiding. He died in 1678.

HISTORICAL DOCUMENT

Excerpt from "On Being Happy Though Poor" by Li Yü
The recipe for being happy when one is poor contains nothing more arcane than the simple prescription, "one step back." I may consider myself poor; but there will be other men poorer than I. I may count myself lowly; but there will be other men lowlier than I. I may regard my wife as an encumbrance; but there are widows and widowers, orphans, and childless folk who strive in vain to acquire just such an encumbrance. I may deplore the calluses on my hands; but there are men in the jails and in the wild lands who long without prospect for a livelihood with plough or shovel.

Rest in such thoughts as these, and the sea of sorrows gives place to a land of joy; but if all your reckoning is in a forward direction, weighing yourself against your betters, then you will know not a moment's peace but live fettered forever in a prison cell.

A man of substance once spent the night in a courier station. The humid summer was at its height and his bed-curtains admitted swarms of mosquitoes which would not be driven off. He fell prey to reminiscences of home, of a lofty hall arching like the sky itself over him, of bamboo matting cool as ice, and a whole bevy of fan-wielding concubines. There he would hardly be aware of summer's presence; how had he ever managed to get himself into his present predicament? Thoughts of bliss increased his frustrations, and the upshot was a night of total sleeplessness.

The station sergeant had lain down on the steps outside where clouds of mosquitoes gnawed at him until it seemed his bones must be exposed. In desperation at last he began running up and down the yard, his arms and legs ceaselessly flailing so as to afford no foothold to his attackers. His movements back and forth were those of a man bothered and annoyed, yet the sighs he gave were sighs of relief and satisfaction, as though he had found a source of pleasure in the midst of his misery.

The rich man was puzzled, and called him over to question him. "Your sufferings," he said, "are a dozen or a hundred times more severe than mine, yet I am miserable and you seem to be enjoying yourself. Can you explain this?"

"I was just remembering," said the sergeant, "the time some years ago when an enemy of mine brought charges against me and had me thrown into jail. That was summer too, and the jailor to prevent my running away bound my wrists and ankles every night so that I could not move. There were more mosquitoes then than tonight, and they bit me at will, for however I longed to dodge and hide I could make no effort to do so. But see how tonight I can run up and down, moving my arms and legs just as I wish—it's like I'm comparing a living man with a devil in hell. Thinking of the past I realize how pleasant things are now, and I can ignore whatever sufferings there might be."

His words roused the rich man to the understanding of his own error; for what he had heard was the secret of being happy though poor.

Document Analysis

Li's thesis in "On Being Happy Though Poor" is to recognize that someone always has it worse than you do. This is a very Confucian prescription for living a good life. Confucianism is especially concerned with one's responsibilities in life—to be deferential to one's superiors, to be indulgent and protective of one's inferiors. It is also reminiscent of Buddhism, by the seventeenth century a very popular foreign religion that had spread throughout the entire empire. Buddhism calls on its adherents to ignore the material life for the salvation of one's spirit, and when people can recognize themselves as being lucky to have more wealth than others, more social status, a better family life, a better working life, this proves to be the key to happiness. Li counters that "…if all your reckoning is in a forward direction, weighing yourself against your betters, then you will know not a moment's peace but live fettered forever in a prison cell."

As with many stories in morality books, this one concludes with a parable. The story is of a wealthy man staying in a hostel during a sweltering summer, who cannot get the mosquitoes to leave his bedroom. His thoughts drift off to his home, where he would be much happier than in the nasty confines of his room at the inn, and he spends a sleepless night in his bed. Then he notes that the innkeeper, or station sergeant, is similarly flailing his arms and legs to get rid of mosquitoes, but with a smile and sighs "as though he had found a source of pleasure in the midst of his misery." When the wealthy man asks him how he can be enjoying himself when being harassed by mosquitoes, the sergeant tells him he had once been bound at the wrists and ankles when being attacked by mosquitoes, and he had had no way to defend himself. Therefore, the ability to run about like a crazy man swatting at bugs was a positive pleasure in comparison to his memories of the past. Thus, the rich man recognized that "what he had heard was the secret of being happy though poor." The image of a man wildly waving at bugs and laughing about it cannot help but bring a smile to the reader's face, but the point is still made: To be happy, count your blessings.

Essential Themes

When Li Yü died, China was in the beginnings of the reign of the Kangxi emperor (1661-1722), the longest reigning emperor in Chinese history. Kangxi was a Confucian scholar and poet, who ruled firmly and fairly, exercising tolerance to everyone within his purview. In the midst of his emperorship, he even came close to accepting Christianity and converting to the religion, in part due to the excellent trade connections represented by the European presence in China. His grandson, the Qianlong emperor (1736-1795), was just as effective, making the eighteenth century a high point in the history of the dynasty and in Chinese history in general. Accordingly, scholarly productions like morality books increased during the early Qing dynasty, along with dictionaries, encyclopedias and histories.

Li Yü himself has long remained recognized as China's seventeenth-century version of Shakespeare, a man of letters. His works were widely published, and eventually translated into several languages, including English, by the philosopher and scholar Lin Yutang (1895-1976). Using some of Li's writings as guidance, Lin published his own shanshu in 1937, *The Importance of Living*.

—David Simonelli

Bibliography and Further Reading

Brokaw, Cynthia Joanne. *The Ledgers of Merit and Demerit: Social Change and Moral Order in Late Imperial China*. Princeton University Press, 1991.

Chun-shu Chang and Shelley Hsueh-lun Chang. *Crisis and Transformation in Seventeenth-Century China: Society, Culture, and Modernity in Li Yü's World*. University of Michigan Press, 1992.

Hanan, Patrick. *The Invention of Li Yu*. Harvard University Press, 1988.

Porter, Jonathan. *Imperial China, 1350-1900*. Rowman & Littlefield, 2016.

Regent Dorgon: Edict to the Board of War and Imperial Edict to the Board of Rites

Date: 1644–1645
Author: Dorgon, regent for the Qing Shunzhi Emperor
Genre: State edict

Summary Overview

In 1644, a Manchurian army—considered hillbilly foreigners in Mandarin-speaking Han China—overran Beijing and drove out the Ming dynasty's armies, starting a new dynasty in China's history. After some minor power struggles at the center of the new dynasty, the new Shunzhi Emperor was placed on the throne as the head of the Qing, or "pure" dynasty. As perceived foreigners, however, the Qing were perceived as a humiliation equivalent to the Mongol conquest of three hundred years earlier, and many Chinese were determined to resist their domination, deviously and violently if necessary.

The Shunzhi Emperor was only six when the dynasty was established, and his rule was taken over, by regents, as has been customary in world history—proxy rulers who managed the state until the emperor came of age. Regent Dorgon was a clever man, whose followers had primed him to be the emperor himself before he refused the throne in favor of his nephew, for family dynastic purposes. To assure himself and his administration of the loyalty of the Chinese people, Dorgon issued these edicts, the second building on the first, to get Chinese men to cut their hair in the same fashion as Manchurians. Dorgon saw this physical manifestation of Qing law as a way of marking out those people around the emperor's territories who did not intend to acquiesce to Manchurian rule. Indeed, many Chinese men resisted the hairstyle; later, however, the wearing of queues behind a shaved forehead became the standard Chinese style, a sign that people had resigned themselves to Qing rule, however reluctantly.

Defining Moment

The second half of the Ming dynasty was marked by absentee imperial government and egregious corruption, especially in its final decades. The Ming emperor Wanli reigned for 48 years (1572-1620), and virtually the entire time, he left rule over the Chinese empire to his eunuchs while he indulged himself in food, spending and luxuries. The eunuchs were inefficient and corrupt, and cruel to anyone who challenged their authority or called them on their failures. While the wealthy in China withdrew into their educations and businesses, the vast poor population suffered from famines and high taxes to support the imperial bureaucracy. While Chinese economics actually benefited from imperial neglect, most Chinese suffered from it.

In 1592, Japanese shoguns invaded Korea; the indigenous Joseon dynasty begged Wanli for help, resulting in the Imjin War. Chinese armies eventually drove the Japanese off the peninsula, but the war weakened the Ming military and its treasury. The result was that when northern peoples made incursions into China, the Ming armies offered little resistance. By the time Wanli died, the most insistent of these northerners were the Jurchen peoples of what is today Manchuria, led by the chieftain Nurhaci. In 1625, Nurhaci conquered the northern city of Mukden (Shenyang today) and made it the capital of a new Manchurian dynasty. His conquest was made easier by the fact that many Chinese themselves had risen in rebellion against the dynasty, while the dynasty did not pay its armies. In 1644, the last Ming emperor hung himself in the Forbidden City as Manchurian armies swept into Beijing, and over the next decade, the Manchurians asserted themselves as the next dynasty in China, the Qing or "pure" dynasty.

A year earlier, Nurhaci's designated successor, Hong Taiji, had died before the capture of Beijing. By consensus, he was succeeded by his six year-old son Fu-lin, called the Shenzhi Emperor. As he was not of age, Shenzhi's rule was given over to Hong Taiji's brother and greatest general, who took the name Dorgon, or "badger," as regent.

To maintain consistency and experience in government, Dorgon reappointed a number of Ming officials to the new Qing administration. Some chose suicide rather than serve a people they considered to be bar-

A late Qing dynasty woodblock print representing the Yangzhou massacre of May 1645. Dorgon's brother, Dodo, ordered this massacre to scare other southern Chinese cities into submission. By the late 19th century, the massacre was used by anti-Qing revolutionaries to arouse anti-Manchu sentiment among the Han Chinese population. [Public domain], via Wikimedia Commons

barians, but other Chinese stepped up into positions within the bureaucracy. This encouraged Dorgon to believe that Manchurian rule over China was possible. Manchurians amounted to a grand total of 2 percent of the population of the empire, but they could succeed through principles of good administration—the Qing emperors would generally be scholarly and attentive—and so long as it was possible to identify resistance to the Qing administration.

Manchurian men had long worn their hair in a specific style: Shaved all the way around except for two long braids, a smaller one in width at the nape of the neck and a larger one off the back of the head, called a queue. When Nurhaci had conquered Mukden and northern China, the easiest way for him to identify the loyal Manchurians in his midst was through their hairstyles. He therefore demanded that anyone loyal to his rule adopt the hairstyle—the queue became a symbol of submission. Dorgon decided to apply this rule to the whole of China in a pair of edicts, one applied in a gentler fashion, one more forceful, in 1644 and 1645.

Author Biography
The Regent Dorgon was born in 1612 as the fourteenth son of the Manchurian chieftain Nurhaci, the recognized founder of the Qing dynasty. As a son of a king, he was originally known as Prince Rui. He became a successful general in the years after his father's death, assuming leadership of the family as they closed in on the Ming capital of Beijing. He fought in the name of his brother Hong Taiji, and upon Hong Taiji's death, Prince Rui was considered one of the obvious people in the family with a claim to be the next emperor. He battled with his nephew Hooge to determine which of them would take the throne. Instead, at Prince Rui's suggestion, they compromised on Hong Taiji's ninth son, the six year old Fulin, and put him on the throne as the Shunzhi Emperor. Prince Rui was acclaimed regent; he took the name Dorgon, meaning "badger." Under Regent Dorgon, the Qing armies completed the conquest of China from the previous Ming dynasty's armies. He died in 1650 during a hunting trip and was declared an emperor after his death, in honor of his earlier sacrifice of the throne and service as regent.

HISTORICAL DOCUMENT

Regent Dorgon's Edict to the Board of War and Imperial Edict to the Board of Rites (1644-1645)

Edict to the Board of War
Now that our dynasty has established its authority in Peking, the soldiers and common people who endured recent calamities are all our children. We will save them from disasters and give them security. Send messengers to cities and forts of all regions requesting their surrender. If, on the day this message arrives, their inhabitants shave their heads and submit, all local officials shall be promoted one rank. Soldiers and common people will be exempt from deportation. Leading civil and military officials should personally collect tax registers and army rosters and immediately bring them to the capital for imperial audience. Those who claim to submit but do not shave their heads are hesitant and watchful. They should be given a deadline for compliance based on their distance from the capital and rewarded accordingly when they arrive in Peking. If they do not meet the deadline, it is clear that they are resisting and definitely should be punished; troops are to be sent to suppress them. Princes with the surname Zhu [members of the Ming imperial family] who conform to this order shall not be deprived of their titles and will continue to enjoy imperial grace.

Imperial Edict to the Board of Rites
In the past the system of dressing the hair in a queue was not uniformly enforced. People were allowed to do as they pleased because we wanted to wait until the whole country was pacified before putting into force this system. Now, within and without, we are one family. The Emperor is like the father and the people are like his sons. The father and sons are of the same body; how can they be different from one another? If they are not as one then it will be as if they had two hearts and would they then not be like the people of different countries? We do not need to mention this because we believe all subjects under Heaven must be aware of it themselves. All residents of the capital and its vicinity will fulfill the order to shave their heads within ten days of this proclama-

tion. For Zhili and other provinces, compliance must take place within ten days of receipt of the order from the Board of Rites. Those who follow this order belong to our country; those who hesitate will be considered treasonous bandits and will be heavily penalized. Anyone who attempts to evade this order to protect his hair or who uses cunning language to argue against it will not be lightly dealt with. All officials in regions that we have already pacified who insultingly advance a memorial related to this matter arguing for the continuation of the Ming system and not following the system of our dynasty will be executed without possibility of pardon. As for other apparel, unhurried change is permitted, but it cannot differ from the system of our dynasty. The aforementioned Board will immediately dispatch this message to the capital and its vicinity and to the provincial, prefectural, sub-prefectural, and county yamen and garrisons of Zhili and other provinces. Civil and military yamen officials, clerks, scholars, students, and all members of military and civilian households shall carry this out without exception.

GLOSSARY

yamen: the administrative office/residence of a local bureaucrat in imperial China

Zhili: the province surrounding the capital of Beijing—ruled directly from the Forbidden City

Document Analysis

The two edicts here presented are evidence of the Qing dynasty's need to assert itself as having the "mandate of heaven"—the favor of the ancestors toward bearing the responsibilities of the imperial throne. Certainly those Chinese who knew of the Ming dynasty's excesses were happy to see it go, but the idea of handing over the empire to another set of northern "foreigners" made many Chinese uncomfortable. The tone of the two edicts relays how that lack of comfort had an impact on Regent Dorgon and his efforts to get the Han Chinese people to submit to his authority. It also shows the two sides of Qing authority as they would reveal themselves over the next 275 years: As tolerance, patience and the pursuit of knowledge, and as sternness, righteousness and violence.

Edict to the Board of War

The Edict to the Board of War was issued in 1644, as Qing armies had captured Beijing (Peking). The Regent Dorgon starts off immediately with a tone of benevolence—"the soldiers and common people who endured recent calamities are all our children." Dorgon wanted to end the warfare around China, to allow the Ming armies to surrender peaceably and assert Qing authority and legitimacy as soon as possible. Yet he also wanted some sign that a peaceful surrender was real, that he would not have to endure a surprise rebellion as his managed the affairs of the Shunzhi Emperor. The hair-braiding order was an obvious way of accomplishing this; anyone who submitted immediately and shaved his head was amenable to the new dynasty, and anyone who did not shave was a potential enemy within.

A critical point about the adoption of the Manchurian queue was that it was anti-Confucian. Confucius had asserted that everything on one's body had been inherited from your parents, and it was a necessary sign of respect to them to avoid damaging or removing any part of one's body in any way. Most Chinese men therefore wore their hair like Taoist monks, tied up in a bun on top of their heads. Dorgon's edict called on them to violate this principle, something he apparently recognized. Dorgon offered incentives for compliance—promotion for local officials who got their charges to comply, exemption from deportation to other parts of the empire for people who adopted the queue, maintenance of privileges for the Ming imperial family if they agreed to go along and shave their heads. Those who did not comply were "hesitant and watchful," which was understandable for a while; but if they did not comply eventually, they would be punished, in some vague and unspecified fashion.

Nevertheless, compliance was not as forthcoming as Dorgon wanted. Han Chinese men considered the hairstyle humiliating, particularly in its purposeful implication of submission to a foreign dynasty. In particular, former Ming officials whom Dorgon was counting on to help streamline his administration claimed that the "queue order," as it was referred to, violated the Ming dynasty's "System of Rites and Music"—the former dynasty's ceremonial practices. This infuriated Dorgon, who was specifically trying to assert his own rules within the new Qing dynasty—it implied that these administrators did not believe the Qing dynasty would or should last. Therefore, he issued another edict, this one far more strict.

Imperial Edict to the Board of Rites

It was not a mistake that Dorgon handed this edict to the Qing dynasty's own Board of Rites, to assert that there was to be a new set of ceremonial values and all Chinese would have to assimilate into them.

He stated that the "queue order" had not been enforced while the empire was still in the last stages of the war with the Ming; by now, 1645, that war was basically over and the Chinese people were again "one family." Tellingly, Regent Dorgon uses Confucian concepts of the family to demand that the Chinese people follow the emperor as their father—"how can they be different from one another?"—and then he gets very specific: People of the capital and its province of Zhili must comply within ten days. Anyone who defies the order "will be considered treasonous bandits and will be heavily penalized"; former Ming officials who try to write memorials (memorandums) arguing against the order will be executed.

The famous Chinese summary of this edict was "Keep your hair, lose your head; keep your head, lose your hair." Over the course of a decade, Qing officials and armies traveled throughout China, demanding compliance with the queue order and executing those who refused to cooperate. Notorious massacres took place as a result of resistance, and though no one knows how many men refused to adopt the Manchurian hairstyle, estimates range in the hundreds of thousands for the number of people killed by order of Regent Dorgon's edicts.

Essential Themes

Despite the excesses of the imposition of the queue order, the early Qing emperors were renowned for their fair and enlightened rule. The emperors worked with Manchurian officials, whom they trusted, keeping themselves separate from the Han Chinese population. But they also welcomed contact with foreigners early on, particularly European traders and the Catholic missionaries who came with them. The Chinese economy supported the empire's vast population, and the Qing dynasty gradually settled in to a positive role in China.

Two hundred years later, in the 1840s, China's fortunes reversed dramatically. The Opium War (1839-1842) with Britain was humiliating, and inspired rebellions on the part of the Han Chinese people. The prime way to identify rebels was that they tended to grow out their hair and abandon the queue—if the queue was the symbol of the dynasty's power, a growing head of hair meant opposition to that power. After the Chinese Revolution of 1911, the last emperor, Puyi, abdicated his throne, and Chinese everywhere—including Puyi himself—cut off their queues and began to grow out their hair.

—David Simonelli

Bibliography and Further Reading

Kuhn, Phillip A. *Soulstealers: The Chinese Sorcery Scare of 1768*. Harvard University Press, 1990.

The Oxford Illustrated History of Modern China. Edited by Jeffrey Wasserstrom. Oxford University Press, 2016.

Wakeman, Frederic E. *The Great Enterprise: The Manchu Reconstruction of Imperial Order in Seventeenth-Century China*. University of California Press, 1985.

Websites

"The Queue Order in the Early Qing dynasty." *Cultural China*, http://history.cultural-china.com /en/34History5603.html. Accessed 20 Apr. 2017.

Meritorious Deeds at No Cost

Date: 1650
Author: Unknown
Genre: Essay

Summary Overview
Meritorious Deeds at No Cost is a seventeenth-century Chinese "morality book," or *shanshu*, one of many works published in the era that applied Confucian principles to everyday life. Most morality books were written by wealthy men who studied Confucianism and, in line with Confucian principles, felt a responsibility to enlighten and better their social inferiors. Their publication and popularity were a function of China's prosperity at the end of the Ming and the beginning of the Qing dynasties, the period in which *Meritorious Deeds at No Cost* originated.

Defining Moment
Kong Fuzi (551-479 BCE) was a Chinese philosopher, alive during the chaotic Eastern Zhou dynasty in ancient Chinese history; his name was Latinized by the Jesuit missionary Matteo Ricci as "Confucius," which is the name by which most Westerners know him today. Confucius was a wandering teacher who collected an estimated 3,000 students in his own lifetime, who recorded his many sayings and lessons in a book called the *Analects*. As a teacher, he responded to the greed, corruption and violence of the period in China; as a philosopher, he could perhaps be said to puts the Chinese way of life into words. Even today, Chinese children learn to print ideograms by printing sayings from the *Analects*.

Confucius's most important principle was decorum, for one to know one's place in their family and in society, to take care of their younger relatives and social inferiors, and show respect and deference to their older relatives, their ancestors and their social superiors. One of his most famous sayings in the *Analects* was that "if there is a good emperor on the throne, and every son listens to his father, all is well." Confucianism was fundamentally conservative in orientation; the best way to revere one's elders and ancestors was to study them and do as they did, in the pursuit of knowledge. Knowledge was virtuous, and allowed one to achieve *ren*, the virtues of goodness and community. Critical was the fact that Confucianism proved to be more than simply a method of systematizing the world—it was adopted by the Han dynasty as the philosophy of Chinese empire. Government officials all were required to attend one of many Confucian universities to study Confucianism, and only when they passed an exam on Confucian principles could they be placed in the imperial hierarchy.

Confucian scholars had revisited Confucius's ideas several times over two millennia, applying the philosopher's ideas to the times to maintain its relevance. In general, Confucianism was elitist: Since study at a Confucian university was expensive, the official philosophy of China supported the current social order, men over women, age over youth, wealth over poverty. During the Ming dynasty (1368-1644), however, a period of economic and population growth, Chinese society gained more and more people whose wealth was tied up in trade, commerce and finance as opposed to land—it was becoming more equalized. Appropriately, a scholar and Ming official named Wang Yangming taught that anyone could achieve *ren*, that knowledge was not exclusive to expensive books, and that morality could and should be practiced by anyone, not just those who might study Confucianism.

Wang's ideas were popular, especially in a time when books were becoming less expensive. In fact, many newly wealthy people who wanted to assert their education and refinement took up Wang's ideas by writing and publishing "morality books," a genre established during the old Song dynasty and revived in the sixteenth and seventeenth centuries. Essentially, morality books were the equivalent of today's Western "self-help" books, texts designed to teach the reader how to lead a good life and contribute positively to the society around them. The example here, *Meritorious Deeds at No Cost*, was published anonymously, and was particularly popular because its list of positive actions emphasized doing good without laying out any money—decency was a province for everyone, and not just the rich. Reading the text gives some idea about the nature of Chinese society in the seventeenth century.

Author Biography

The author of *Meritorious Deeds at No Cost* is unknown. Likely, the author was comparatively wealthy; the publication of morality books were a sign of status in Ming and Qing society. The printing press was invented in Korea and transported to China a few centuries earlier, and China's long-time use of paper to make books meant that books became cheaper as more printing presses were created.

HISTORICAL DOCUMENT

Excerpt from *Meritorious Deeds at No Cost*

1. Local Gentry

Take the lead in charitable donations.

Rectify your own conduct and transform the common people.

Make a sincere effort to inform the authorities of what would be beneficial to the people of your locality.

Make every effort to dissuade the local authorities from doing what would be detrimental to the people of your locality.

If people have suffered a grave injustice, expose and correct it.

Settle disputes among your neighbors fairly.

When villagers commit misdeeds, admonish them boldly and persuade them to desist.

Do not let yourself be blinded by emotion and personal prejudice.

Be tolerant of the mistakes of others.

Be willing to listen to that which is displeasing to your ears.

Do not make remarks about women's sexiness.

Do not harbor resentment when you are censured.

Protect virtuous people.

Hold up for public admiration women who are faithful to their husbands and children who are obedient to their parents.

Restrain those who are stubborn and [disrespectful].

Prevent plotting and intrigue.

Endeavor to improve manners and customs.

Encourage fair and open discussion.

Prevent your household slaves and servants from causing trouble by relying on your influence.

Try not to arouse the resentment of others by showing partiality to the younger members of your own family.

Do not provoke incidents that result in harm or loss to others.

Do not be arrogant, on account of your own power and wealth, toward relatives who are poor or of low status.

Persuade others not to seek gain through oppression or honors through intrigue.

Do not encroach on others' lands and dispossess them.

Do not scheme to buy up others' property.

Do not mix debased silver with good.

Do not ignore your own relatives and treat others as if they were your kin.

Influence other families to cherish good deeds.

Do not officiously take charge of the affairs of those outside your own household.

Do not disport yourself with lewd friends.

Do not look for pretexts to injure others.

Do not allow yourself to be overcome by personal feelings and therefore treat others unjustly.

Do not let your feelings of pleasure and displeasure influence others or suggest to them how they can benefit themselves.

Restrain others from arranging lewd theater performances.

Do not scheme to seize geomantic advantages (*fengshui*) for yourself or deceitfully deprive others of them.

Instruct your children, grandchildren, and nephews to be humane and compassionate toward all and to avoid anger and self-indulgence.

Do not deceive or oppress younger brothers or cousins.

Do not force others off the road by dropping stones in dangerous places.

Do not scheme to deprive others of some advantage in order to suit your own convenience.

Encourage others to read and study without minding the difficulties.

Urge others to esteem charity and disdain personal gain.

Do not underestimate the value of others [or underpay them].
Do not let what you hear from servants and slaves cause you to turn against relatives and friends.
Persuade others to settle lawsuits through conciliation.
Try to settle complaints and grievances among others.
Do not force others to lend you their property.
Do not force others to enter into deals on credit.
Curb the strong and protect the weak.
Show respect to the aged and compassion for the poor.
Do not keep too many concubines.
Do not keep catamites.
Do not marry off household slaves to wicked men or cripples for your own selfish gain.
Choose a favorable time for marrying off household slaves.
Do not force "good" people to become base [i.e., lose their freedom].

...

2. Scholars

Be loyal to the emperor and filial to your parents.
Honor your elder brothers and be faithful to your friends.
Establish yourself in life by cleaving to honor and fidelity.
Instruct the common people in the virtues of loyalty and filial piety.
Respect the writings of sages and worthies.
Be wholehearted in inspiring your students to study.
Show respect to paper on which characters are written.
Try to improve your speech and behavior.
Teach your students also to be mindful of their speech and behavior.
Do not neglect your studies without reason.
Do not despise others or regard them as unworthy of your instruction.
Be patient in educating the younger members of poor families.
If you find yourself with smart boys, teach them sincerity, and with children of the rich and noble, teach them decorum and duty.
Exhort and admonish the ignorant by lecturing to them on the provisions of the community compact and the public laws.

Do not speak or write thoughtlessly of what concerns the women's quarters.
Do not expose the private affairs of others or harbor evil suspicions about them.
Do not write or post notices that defame other people.
Do not write petitions or accusations to higher authorities.
Do not write bills of divorce or separation.
Do not let your feelings blind you in defending your friends and relatives.
Do not incite gangs (bang) to raid others' homes and knock them down.
Do not encourage the spread of immoral and lewd novels [by writing, reprinting, expanding, and so on].
Do not call other people names or compose songs making fun of them.
Publish morality books in which are compiled things that are useful and beneficial to all.
Do not attack or vilify commoners; do not oppress ignorant villagers.
Do not deceive the ignorant by marking texts in such a way as to overawe and mislead them.
Do not show contempt for fellow students by boasting of your own abilities.
Do not ridicule other people's handwriting.
Do not destroy or lose to books of others.

...

3. Agriculturalists

Do not miss the proper times for farmwork.
Have regard for [the lives of] insects.
When fertilizing the fields, do not harm living creatures.
Do not obstruct or cut off paths. Fill up holes that might give trouble to passersby.
Do not instigate landlords to buy up lands.
Do not steal and sell your master's grain in connivance with his servants.
Do not damage crops in your neighbors' fields by leaving animals to roam at large, relying on your landlord's power and influence to protect you.
Do not encroach [on others' property] beyond the boundaries of your own fields and watercourses, thinking to ingratiate yourself with your landlord.
Do not disturb others' graves or interfere with the geomantic advantages of others.

In plowing, do not infringe on graves or make them hard to find.

Do not suggest to your master that he willfully cut off watercourses and extort payments from neighbors.

Do not take your landlord's seed crop for your own benefit.

Do not damage the crops in neighboring fields out of envy because they are so flourishing.

Do not instigate your landlord to take revenge on a neighbor on the pretext that the neighbor's animals have damaged your crops.

Do not through negligence in your work do damage to the fields of others.

Do not become lazy and cease being conscientious because you think your landlord does not provide enough food and wine or fails to pay you enough.

Fill up holes in graves.

Take good care of others' carts and tools.

Do not kill mules and cattle, pigs and sheep, even if they eat your crops.

Keep carts and cattle from trampling down others' crops.

Do not desecrate the gods of the soil by plowing or hoeing the land or irrigating or spreading manure on days of abstention [*wu*, i.e., the fifth day of each ten-day cycle, which is the first of two days identified with wood in the Five-Phases cycle].

...

5. Dealers and Merchants

Do not deceive ignorant villagers when fixing the price of goods.

Do not raise the price of fuel and rice too high.

When the poor buy rice, do not give them short measure.

Sell only genuine articles.

Do not use short measure when selling and long measure when buying.

Do not deceitfully serve unclean dishes or leftover food to customers who are unaware of the fact.

Do not dispossess or deprive others of their business by devious means.

Do not envy the prosperity of others' business and speak ill of them wherever you go.

Be fair in your dealings.

Treat the young and the aged on the same terms as the able-bodied.

When people come in the middle of the night with an urgent need to buy something, do not refuse them on the ground that it is too cold [for you to get up and serve them].

Pawnshops should lend money at low interest.

Give fair value when you exchange silver for copper coins. Especially when changing money for the poor, be generous to them.

When a debtor owes you a small sum but is short of money, have mercy and forget about the difference. Do not bring him to bankruptcy and hatred by refusing to come to terms.

When the poor want to buy such things as mosquito nets, wadded clothing, and quilts, have pity on them and reduce the price. Do not refuse to come to terms.

Document Analysis

Meritorious Deeds at No Cost is divided up into sections based on the social status or occupation of the reader. It is organized to be read from the wealthiest people to the poorest. Many of its prescriptions reveal how social status worked at different level in the hierarchical structure—what would be considered "meritorious" and what would be considered rude or inconsiderate, and thus anti-Confucian.

The first section is on "Local Gentry," people who lacked an aristocratic pedigree but had strong name recognition locally and were likely somehow involved in imperial administration. The text calls on them to be generous, upstanding, involved in local governance and justice, impartial and open-minded, considerate and appreciative. The text in particular notes that gentry have a certain power over local people's lives—including their own slaves and servants—and need to exercise that power with discretion, maintaining a humble demeanor. The powerful should not be devious, gobbling up land opportunities, debasing currencies or indulging their own sexual pleasure publicly. An unusual concept is that one should "not force others off the road by dropping stones in dangerous places," perhaps a reference to an actual incident from the time now lost to history.

The second section is on "Scholars," meaning Confucian scholars, both in government and working as teachers. Their inclusion below gentry displays their status in China—education gave one a social status above that of the average person. Here, the author expects a Confucian-educated figure to be loyal, to pursue responsibility toward the emperor, his administration, and one's family and society. One should be an instructor in both word and deed, teaching positive values and inhabiting them in daily life. Books are particularly to be revered as sources of knowledge—"Show respect to paper on which characters are written." It is interesting how many of these statements deal with tempering one's expectations for change—one should not disobey or complain to higher authorities, for example. Scholars appear to have been rather mischievous in the era as well—the author exhorts them not to incite gangs, write "immoral and lewd novels," make fun of people in any way, or lead them down a deliberately false path of learning.

"Agriculturalists," or farmers, occupy the third section. Largely, the peasant should know their place not just in society—avoid stealing grain from your landlords—but also in the universe: "Have regard for [the lives of] insects." One should be conscientious and not envious toward one's neighbors. Farming often required disturbing the earth, and in particular, a peasant should avoid disturbing the remains of the ancestors in graves.

The last section is on "Dealers and Merchants." Here, people dealing in commerce and money should not take advantage of the poor, either by deceiving them or exploiting their needs, for example for fuel and rice. One should be honest and above-board at all times; "do not deceitfully serve unclean dishes or leftover food to customers who are unaware of the fact." Like agriculturalists, dealers and merchants should not be envious and should always deal fairly. It is interesting that peasants are listed before people working in commerce, giving a sense that the making of money was frowned upon in Chinese society and placed one lower in the social scale as a result.

Essential Themes

Morality books were largely a revelation of the nature of a Confucian society; while these books' popularity waned by the eighteenth century, China has remained a Confucian society all the way to the present day. Two of the emperors of the Qing dynasty would be Confucian scholars, Kangxi and Qianlong. However, the scholars themselves always represented reactionary conservative values at the emperor's court, and therefore were a hindrance to modernization once Europeans with imperialist aims imposed themselves on China in the nineteenth century. With the coming of a communist state in 1949, the regime of Mao Zedong condemned Confucianism as a relic of the past, and some effort was made to break down the philosophy's hold on Chinese society. Upon Mao's death, however, realism prevailed, and today Confucius is still revered as China's greatest philosopher.

—David Simonelli

Bibliography and Further Reading

Brokaw, Cynthia Joanne. *The Ledgers of Merit and Demerit: Social Change and Moral Order in Late Imperial China.* Princeton University Press, 1991.

Porter, Jonathan. *Imperial China, 1350-1900.* Rowman & Littlefield, 2016.

Websites

Richey, Jeff. "Confucius (551-479 BCE)." *Internet Encyclopedia of Philosophy.* University of Tennessee at Martin, http://www.iep.utm.edu/confuciu/. Accessed 5 May. 2017.

Yang Guangxian: *I Cannot Do Otherwise (Budeyi)*

Date: 1664
Author: Yang Guangxian
Genre: Essay

Summary Overview

European exploration in East Asia brought merchants and traders to China; it also brought Christianity, in the form of Catholic missionaries. Behind the Jesuit Matteo Ricci, these priests often used the Chinese esteem for science to their advantage, displaying Western knowledge of astronomy, firearms, mathematics and physics to entice their hosts into accepting Christianity as the truest root source of knowledge. They made few converts, but the Jesuits were still accepted and revered at the highest levels of Chinese society as learned men, and came to occupy important positions in imperial government. The usurpation of their traditional positions upset many Confucian scholars, one of whom was Yang Guangxian (1597-1669). Yang was an astronomer who believed that the Jesuit Johann Adam Schall von Bell, the Qing Shunzhi Emperor's favored astronomer, was perpetuating numerous falsehoods about the similarities between Christianity and Confucianism that occasionally had dire consequences. In the following essay, he suggested that Schall's poor calculations of the stars had cost the Shunzhi Emperor his life; the charge was taken seriously enough to put Schall and his followers on trial at the Qing court.

Defining Moment

By the time the Qing dynasty began in 1644, Christian missionaries had occupied place at the previous Ming dynasty's court over the course of four decades. The Jesuits were so respected that they were simply accepted into the new dynasty as advisors and considered just as reliable as the Confucian scholars that traditionally advised emperors over the course of Chinese history. The Jesuits' expertise in the sciences made them valued counselors, but they were not nearly as successful with conversions. It helped that they were inclined to show respect for traditional Chinese beliefs in ancestor worship and Confucianism; it made many Confucians welcome the Christians as like-minded figures, believing in an afterlife and a similar responsibility of one person to another.

But not all. Many Confucian scholars were threatened by the presence of other educated counselors in the imperial state, and they were capable of finding just as many contradictions between Confucian principles and Christian theology. One of these scholars was Yang Guangxian, a trained astronomer. At the Qing court, the Shunzhi Emperor (1644-1661) employed a Jesuit, Johann Adam Schall von Bell, as the head of his Imperial Astronomical Bureau. The emperor and the astronomer had a good relationship, and his employment had lasted at court since the emperor attained the throne at the age of six. Yet Schall's job involved reading the stars to find auspicious times for imperial events to take place—a thorough contradiction of Christian principles in its consulting of ancestors and gods as opposed to praying to the Christian God for answers. This contradiction did not seem to bother Schall; it led Yang to try to have Schall ousted in what came to be called "the Calendar Controversy."

Yang believed that Christianity and the emperor's relationship with Schall were a threat to the Confucian values at the center of court life, and Chinese life in general. He wrote a series of essays over the course of two decades, the most important of which were written and compiled between 1659 and 1664 in a book he published himself, called *I Cannot Do Otherwise* (in pinyin, *Budeyi*).

By that time, the Shunzhi Emperor was three years dead, having died young of measles. The emperor had an infant son, Prince Rong, who had died in 1658; one of Schall's jobs as court astronomer was to read the stars to determine the most auspicious time to bury the boy and gain the favor of the emperor's ancestors toward another birth. Yang claimed that Schall had read the stars incorrectly, that his calendrical measurements in general were faulty due to his belief in Christianity, and that the Shunzhi Emperor had therefore been punished by the ancestors with his own death at age twenty-three. *I Cannot Do Otherwise* is focused mostly around the science behind this accusation. It tries to find evidence by exposing the allegedly faulty scientific reasoning of the Jesuits, including their notions of how the heavens work and that the Earth is a globe in space as opposed to a block floating in water. In this essay,

Yang was most polemical about the damning distinctions he saw between the alleged dishonesty and falsehoods at the center of Christianity versus the truths inherent in Confucianism.

Author Biography
Yang Guangxian was born in the late Ming dynasty in 1597. He became a Confucian scholar and started out as a soldier, but various personal indiscretions saw him internally exiled when the dynasty came to an end in 1644. He learned astronomy, and expected to use the skill to work his way up in the imperial hierarchy; instead, he found many government positions occupied by European Jesuit missionaries, to which he took offense. He believed that Christianity was a deviant religion that weakened the imperial state—a serious charge to the Qing dynasty's officials, who were eager to assert their legitimacy as Manchurians governing the Mandarin Chinese empire.

Yang wrote a pair of books criticizing Western astronomy (*On Collecting Errors*) and Christianity (*On Exposing Heterodoxy*) but neither gained much of an audience. When he chose a target, the Jesuit astronomer Adam Schall, he attracted more attention. Immediately after the emperor's son Prince Rong died as an infant, Yang accused Schall of misinterpreting the stars to determine the boy's burial. He also argued that the Jesuits wanted to change the Chinese calendar to match that of Christian Europe's Gregorian calendar. The imperial administration's Board of Rites rejected the charges, until the emperor himself died in 1661. When Yang then published *I Cannot Do Otherwise* in 1664, attacking Christianity as an "evil religion," the Board of Rites took his accusations seriously. In 1665, Schall and seven of his Chinese converts were put on trial for their alleged failure to protect the Qing dynasty's mandate of heaven; they were found guilty, and five of the converts were executed. Schall himself was removed from his commission at court; having already suffered a stroke, he was not subject to execution, and died in 1666.

Yang Guangxian took over as head of the Imperial Astronomy Bureau, but his own failures as an astronomer were exposed right away. The new Kangxi emperor held a contest in 1668 and 1669 between several astronomers to see whose calendrical system of measuring the stars was the best; Schall's assistant, Frederick Verbiest, proved successful in every contest. Yang was removed from his post in disgrace, and the Kangxi emperor reversed the verdict of the Board of Rites, reinstating the Jesuits and pardoning Schall after his death. Yang, on the other hand, was sentenced to be executed, but his advanced age allowed him to merely be sent home. He died in 1669.

HISTORICAL DOCUMENT

Excerpt from *I Cannot Do Otherwise (Budeyi)*
In [the Jesuit Father] Adam Schall's own preface one can read that [the Christian scholars] Xu Guangqi and Li Zhizao both understood that they could not dare publicly to give offense to Confucian norms. Adam Schall's work says that one man and one woman were created as the first ancestors of all humankind. He was not actually so bold as to make the contemptuous assertion that all the peoples in the world are offshoots of his teaching, but according to a book by [the Christian scholar] Li Zubo, the Qing dynasty is nothing but an offshoot of Judea; our ancient Chinese rulers, sages, and teachers were but the offshoots of a heterodox sect; and our classics and the teachings of the sages propounded generation after generation are no more than the remnants of a heterodox teaching. How can we abide these calumnies! They really aim to inveigle the people of the Qing into rebelling against the Qing and following this heterodox sect, which would lead all-under-Heaven to abandon respect for rulers and fathers. …

Our Confucian teaching is based on the Five Relationships (between parent and child, ruler and minister, husband and wife, older and younger brothers, and friends), whilst the Lord of Heaven Jesus was crucified because he plotted against his own country, showing that he did not recognize the relationship between ruler and subject. Mary, the mother of Jesus, had a husband named Joseph, but she said Jesus was not conceived by him.

Those who follow this teaching [Christianity] are not allowed to worship their ancestors and ancestral tablets. They do not recognize the relationship of parent and child. Their teachers oppose the Buddhists and Daoists, who do recognize the relationship between ruler and subject and father and son. Jesus did not recognize the relationship between ruler and subject and parent and child, and yet the Christians speak of him as recognizing these relationships. What arrant nonsense! ...

[The Jesuit Father] M. Ricci wished to honor Jesus as the Lord of Heaven (Tianzhu) who leads the multitude of nations and sages from above, and he particularly honored him by citing references to the Lord-on-High (Shangdi) in the Six Classics of China, quoting passages out of context to prove that Jesus was the Lord of Heaven. He said that the Lord of Heaven was referred to in the ancient classical works as the Lord-on-High, and what we in the west call "the Lord of Heaven" is what the Chinese have spoken of as "the Lord-on-High." [According to Ricci] the Heaven (Tian) of the blue sky functions as a servant of the Lord-on-High, which is located neither in the east nor in the west, lacks a head or stomach, has no hands or feet, and is unable to be honored. How much less would earth-bound land, which a multitude of feet trample and defile, be considered something to be revered? Thus Heaven and Earth are not at all to be revered. Those who argue like this are no more than beasts able to speak a human language.

Heaven is the great origin of all events, things, and principles. When principles (li) are established, material-force (qi) comes into existence. Then, in turn, numbers are created and from these numbers, images begin to take form. Heaven is Principle within form, and Principle is Heaven without form. When shape comes in to its utmost form, then Principle appears therein; this is why Heaven is Principle. Heaven contains all events and things, while Principle also contains all events and things and, as a result, when one seeks the origin of things in the Supreme Ultimate (Taiji) it is only what we call Principle. Beyond principle there is no other principle, and beyond Heaven there is no other Heaven [i.e., Lord of Heaven].

GLOSSARY

heterodox: in this context, meaning out of the normal or official doctrine—unorthodox, or heretic

Document Analysis

Yang Guangxian wrote twenty-two different essays over five years for *I Cannot Do Otherwise*. Most of the excerpt here comes from a central essay criticizing Christianity, but there are several other essays that attack Western science as well—for Yang, the most effective criticism of the religion was to describe the errors in which it led men in their scientific studies and understanding of the universe. The book is named after a famous defense made by the Confucian scholar Mencius in response to a pair of popular philosophers he did not agree with—"I, too, wish to follow in the footsteps of the three sages in rectifying the hearts of men, laying heresies to rest, opposing extreme actions, and banishing excessive views. I am not fond of disputation; I cannot do otherwise. Whoever can, with words, combat [the popular philosophers] is a true disciple of the sages." By titling his book after this famous quote, yang is positing himself in the same position as Mencius, countering a popular but false religion because it is the right thing to do.

Most of Yang's criticisms of Christianity come from his study of one of Schall's books published in China, *Jin cheng shu xiang* (*Images in a booklet presented to his majesty*), which was given to the Ming emperor Chongzhen in 1640. It included printed reproductions of engravings of Jesus' life and crucifixion, with text describing the action. Yang begins by accusing Schall and two other Chinese Christian officials, Xu Guangqi and Li Zhizao, of being devious in trying to shape their visions of Christianity to avoid giving offense to the Confucian norms of Chinese society. He then criticizes the story of Adam and Eve as being impossible—the Qing dynasty is not derived from people who lived in the Roman Empire province of Judea 1600 years earlier. Even more, Confucianism and its famous classic works are not a different version of Christianity, "a heterodox sect" in Yang's formulation of heresy. He believes the goal of the Jesuits is to lead a Christian rebellion against the dynasty, an electric charge in an era when the dynasty's legitimacy was in question due to its Manchurian origins.

Yang describes that rebellion as representing the "abandon[ment of] respect for rulers and fathers." In Chinese life, there are Five Relationships as defined by Confucius—between parent and child, ruler and minister, husband and wife, older and younger brothers, and friends. Jesus, in yang's opinion, is the antithesis of all of these relationships—he was crucified on a charge of sedition, plotting against the Roman state in Judea, and thus disrespectful of the emperor. Furthermore, Yang casts aspersions on Jesus' alleged origins as the son of God, treating Joseph as a foolish cuckold and Mary as a loose woman. Christians do not worship ancestors; even Buddhists and Daoists, who have been traditional rivals of Confucians in Chinese life, have respect for betters, elders and ancestors. "Jesus did not recognize the relationship between ruler and subject and parent and child, and yet the Christians speak of him as recognizing these relationships. What arrant nonsense! …"

Yang then discusses the revered Matteo Ricci, who described Jesus as the "Lord of Heaven," saying that he was the equivalent of the Lord-on-High as described in the Six Classics of China, six major works of literature defining Chinese life in the formative period of Chinese civilization. He ridicules the idea that an unknowable, unseeable God lives in the sky, with no reverence whatsoever for the Earth that gives strength to ancestor worship—"Those who argue like this are no more than beasts able to speak a human language."

Finally, Yang launches into a heartfelt defense of the Chinese conception of the universe, as defined by Confucius. Heaven is the origin of principles; without principles, there can be no knowledge, life or Earth as it is known—"Heaven is Principle within form, and Principle is Heaven without form." Effectively, what yang is trying to argue is that any afterlife or god which exists must be one and the same with the basic ethical relationships men have with themselves and the universe; there is no separation, as the Christians claim, between a God and a Heaven.

Yang's arguments in *I Cannot do Otherwise* met with critical approval by the Kangxi emperor's Board of Rites. Schall and his counterparts were put on trial, and for a brief period of time Christianity was out of favor at the imperial court. All Christians were banished to the Portuguese trading port in China, Macao, except for four Jesuits who remained at court.

Essential Themes

Ironically, Yang Guangxian actually had no desire to become the head of the Imperial Astronomy Bureau; he made his arguments out of an honest desire to expose what he believed were the heresies in Christianity. When the Kangxi emperor chose him to succeed Schall, he was 68 years old; he also openly admitted that, while he could read stars, he did not understand the mathematics necessary to plot a calendar appropriately, and that others could do a better job. Despite writing four memorials to the emperor begging not to take the position, Qing Kangxi insisted he take the position; as he must have dreaded, he was fast exposed as a poor astronomer in the contests with Frederick Verbiest, and deposed to be sent home and die in disgrace.

Christianity, meanwhile, flourished under the Kangxi emperor for another four decades—there seemed some possibility that the emperor might convert. However, the assertions of Schall and Ricci of the coordination between Confucianism and Christianity came into question, this time from the west as opposed to the east. Pope Clement XI declared ancestor worship to be heresy, and papal delegations arrived at Kangxi's court to demand compliance. Instead, Qing Kangxi turned against Christianity for its lack of tolerance, and the Jesuit effort to bring Christianity to China through science fizzled out.

—David Simonelli

Bibliography and Further Reading

Jami, Catherine. *The Emperor's New Mathematics: Western Learning and Imperial Authority during the Kangxi Reign (1662-1722)*. Oxford University Press, 2012.

Menegon, Eugenio. "Yang Guangxian's Opposition to Johann Adam Schall: Christianity and Western Science in His Work *Budeyi*." *Western Learning and Christianity in China: The Contribution and Impact of Johann Adam Schall von Bell, S.J. (1592-1666)*. Edited by Roman Malek, S.V.D. China-Zentrum with Monumenta Serica Institute, 1998.

Smith, Richard J. *The Qing Dynasty and Traditional Chinese Culture*. Lanham MD: Rowman & Littlefield, 2015.

Spence, Jonathan D. *Emperor of China: Self Portrait of K'ang Hsi*. Knopf, 1974.

Wu, Silas H. L. *Passage to 'Power: K'Ang-Hsi and His Heir Apparent, 1661-1722*. Harvard University Press, 1979.

Websites

Cordier, Henri. "The Church in China." *The Catholic Encyclopedia*, volume 3. New York: Robert Appleton Company, 1908, http://www.newadvent.org/cathen/03669a.htm. Accessed 9 Apr. 2017.

Melvin, Sheila. "A Jesuit Astronomer in a Qing Emperor's Court." *ChinaFile* (2014). Center for US-China Relations, http://www.chinafile.com/reporting-opinion/caixin-media/jesuit-astronomer-qing-emperors-court. Accessed 7 May 2017.

Kangxi Emperor: Edict of Toleration

Date: 1692
Author: Qing emperor Kangxi
Genre: State edict

Summary Overview

In the late seventeenth century, European influence grew in China to the point where Christianity made a small but widespread mark on Chinese life. This was most pronounced because of the emperor Kangxi's fascination with the religion and the sacrificial figure of Jesus at its center. In 1692, he issued the following edict declaring that Christians in China meant no harm to the dynasty and brought modernization with them, and would therefore be allowed to last and prosper. In the decades to follow, however, conflict between different Catholic sects and the pope over allowing Chinese practices into Christian worship turned the Kangxi emperor against Catholicism—if not Catholics and their purest beliefs—and he reversed this edict. After his reign, China retreated into its normal isolation and opposition to Western influence, which would be forcefully broken in the nineteenth century.

Defining Moment

Christianity's history in China has been tumultuous. The first missionaries to China came from Syria during the Tang dynasty in 635, and were allowed to build churches; by the end of the dynasty, the emperor Tang Wuzong declared all foreign religions illegal and Christianity died out. The Mongols accepted more Christians coming along the Silk Road trade routes at the end of the thirteenth century. Estimated converts numbered about 6,000, and Pope Clement V even named an Archbishop of Beijing. But the decline of the Mongol Yuan dynasty brought a decline in Christian practice too as the Chinese people considered any foreign institution as being associated with the barbarian Mongols. Ming dynasty Emperor Hongwu expelled all Christians in 1368, the first year of his reign.

Two centuries later, Christian missionaries once again arrived in China, and this time, the establishment of overseas trade routes meant there would be many more of them. The Society of Jesus sent the Portuguese Jesuit Matteo Ricci, who arrived in Macao in 1582. Ricci admired the Chinese and translated many of their texts into Portuguese, while producing studies of their state, culture and language, including a translating dictionary. He also came to understand and accommodate Confucianism, Taoism, Buddhism, ancestor worship and their practices into Christian worship, to make Christianity more appealing. By the time of his death in 1610, he may have had five thousand converts, and as Ricci had moved to Beijing, many of them were members of the imperial court. Other Catholic missionaries streamed into China, and Christian networks flourished, for the first time without much fear of being cut off by the dynasty in power. By the end of the seventeenth century, there were more than a hundred missionaries working in China with an estimated 200,000 baptized converts.

In 1644, the Ming dynasty fell to conquest by Manchurian tribes led by their chieftain Nurhachi, who became the first emperor of the new Qing dynasty. As ethnic peoples from outside of the traditional homelands of mandarin-speaking Chinese, the Qing emperors were seen as outsiders, a perception that would last all the way until the last emperor abdicated in 1911. This drove the early Qing emperors to assert themselves as fair and worthy rulers of the Middle Kingdom, as China was referred to, which meant showing tolerance, learning and appreciation for new ideas that would benefit the Chinese people as a whole. Christianity—the religion of a people who came to China bearing scientific knowledge that surpassed that of the Chinese at the time—fit right in with this mandate on new ideas.

The most enlightened of these emperors in the early Qing dynasty was Kangxi (1661–1722), whose dynasty name meant "peaceful harmony." His father, the emperor Shunzi, left the Forbidden City to visit churches in Beijing, which had a profound influence on his son. The Kangxi emperor was fascinated by foreign missionaries and the philosophy of Christianity, and he invited Jesuits to speak with him at his court. Jesuits taught Kangxi about astronomy, mathematics, and music—they imported a piano and taught the emperor to play it. The emperor wrote poems on Christianity and there was some speculation that he might convert to the religion.

The Kangxi Emperor at the age of 45, painted in 1699. By Unknown court artist [Public domain], via Wikimedia Commons

While Christianity had royal patrons, it also had its enemies in China, particularly Confucian scholars who were traditionally reactionary and saw the religion as a threat. Christian missionaries were accused of heresy and the destruction of religious statues, and numerous tracts circulated exposing the dangers of the new religion. The most telling Confucian criticism of the missionaries was that they occasionally objected to the practices of Chinese ancestor worship, practices as old as Chinese civilization itself. While the original Jesuit missionaries accommodated the veneration of Confucius and the traditional rites of communicating with the ancestors, incoming Dominican and Franciscan missionaries took exception to these practices as evidence of a lack of piety and forbade them in Catholic ceremonies.

Jesuits, Dominicans and Franciscans all sent emissaries to Rome to ask for the pope's opinion on the issue. So did the Kangxi emperor—he saw the benefits of connection with the materially-advanced Westerners and wanted to keep the connection alive. As a part of this policy, the emperor issued an "Edict of Toleration" in 1692 which officially recognized Catholic missionary activity and allowed the religion to propagate in China.

Author Biography

The Qing emperor Kangxi (1654–1722) was the longest reigning emperor in Chinese history, at sixty-one years. He is generally considered by historians to be one of China's greatest emperors as well. His reign was prosperous and expansive, and as a person he was scholarly and inclined to tolerance and benevolence. He did much to accommodate the Chinese people to rule by a dynasty of foreigners, as the Manchurian Qings were viewed.

Kangxi assumed the throne at the age of eight; after much squabbling and violent court disputes between his four regents, he came of age and assumed the throne before he was twenty. He stabilized the Manchurian hierarchy and suppressed rebellions by former Ming dynasty subordinates and other rebels opposed to Manchurian rule. He also established a trusted group of court advisors whom he used to bypass other, more corrupt figures at court and assure that his dictates were obeyed to the letter of the law. Territorially, he expanded China's rule into Tibet and lower Mongolia, strengthened tributary relationships with Taiwan and Vietnam, and settled border disputes with the Russian empire of Peter the Great—he essentially drew the borders of the Chinese state as it still exists today.

The emperor showed an unusually sensitive concern for his people's welfare in a civilization where emperors believed they had a responsibility to the ancestors in heaven to rule fairly. Kangxi was renowned as a scholar and poet who had a dictionary drawn up to standardize the Chinese language, and he also sponsored a fair-minded history of the Ming dynasty that preceded the Qing, looking for reasons as to why the dynasty had failed. He toured his empire regularly, compiling notes on his inspection tours that he used to address local problems, and patronized culture and the arts as well. He had his minions keep meticulous records on the royal treasury, and trebled its income in forty years, to the point where he canceled taxes for his people in four different years because he believed he had enough money to run the government successfully. (Later, he would write a memo to his son and successor, advising him to root out corruption amongst the Confucian officials and eunuchs at court.)

Kangxi's reign coincided with the height of Europe's commercial revolution, when western and southern European traders crisscrossed the globe searching for resources to carve a section out of a mercantile world economy. While the emperor obviously prized Catholic Christianity, he was careful to keep European trade and economic missions at arm's length, while simultaneously promoting and monopolizing internal Chinese industry and commerce. Europeans brought with them guns and cannon, which the Kangxi emperor used to modernize his military forces. They also brought new foodstuffs such as maize, peanuts and potatoes, which helped provide for a growing population.

Toward the end of the emperor's reign, rivalries grew between Jesuits, Dominicans and Franciscans over whether ancestor worship could be accommodated into Christian worship. The Kangxi emperor, being inclined to tolerance, agreed with his Jesuit advisors that honoring one's ancestors did not conflict with worship of God. When a papal declaration denied that this was acceptable, the emperor was clearly pained and aggravated, and he turned on Dominican and Franciscan missions in China, closing their churches. Still, though he was never baptized, there is some question as to whether he had adopted Christian doctrine as his own by the time of his death in 1722.

HISTORICAL DOCUMENT

Emperor Kangxi: Edict of Toleration

The Europeans admired our sacred culture when they sailed to [our land] from ten thousand li away. They have offered many services to this nation.... The Europeans are very quiet; they do not excite any disturbances in the provinces, they do no harm to anyone, they commit no crimes, and their doctrine has nothing in common with that of the false sects in the empire, nor has it any tendency to excite sedition. ... We decide therefore that all temples dedicated to the Lord of heaven, in whatever place they may be found, ought to be preserved, and that it may be permitted to all who wish to worship this God to enter these temples, offer him incense, and perform the ceremonies practiced according to ancient customs by the Christians. Therefore let no one henceforth offer them any opposition.

GLOSSARY

li: Chinese unit for measuring sizeable distances; a *li* is about a third of a mile long, or 500 meters—here the emperor merely uses the term to describe a long distance away

Document Analysis

The Kangxi emperor's Edict of Toleration is simple, though in some ways oblique. Most of the edict, in fact, is a direct answer to Confucian accusations against Christianity, which the emperor likely heard often from the many Confucian scholars who served as advisors in his court. The edict says that the Christian missionaries revere Chinese culture—true of the Jesuits he consorted with, less so of Dominicans and Franciscans who banned ancestor worship amongst their converts in southern China. He adds that the European missionaries have brought "many services" to China, likely meaning the material knowledge they bestowed upon the emperor and his court. Interpreted this way, the emperor was likely trying to appeal to his scholars to be more open-minded on the religion, as there is nothing Confucians revered more than the acquisition of knowledge as a means of being virtuous.

The Kangxi emperor adds that the Catholic missionaries have committed no crimes, have not disturbed anyone with their religion, and that there are other (likely now forgotten) religious sects in China that did challenge the dynasty's imperial rule. Therefore, Christianity was to be accepted as a tolerated religion, and Christian converts were free to "perform the ceremonies practiced according to ancient customs," an interesting play comparing Christianity's ancient rites to the ancient rites of ancestor worship.

Essential Themes

As if in purposeful defiance of the emperor's edict, Pope Clement XI took office in the Vatican in 1700, and immediately declared the Dominican ban on ancestor worship to be more correct and the sanctioned practice of Christianity in China. Papal delegations arrived at Kangxi's court, contradicting the Jesuit inclination to tolerance—and the emperor's inclination to tolerance. Kangxi was by no means used to having his edicts contradicted by anyone, particularly in favor of religious rigidity. He rejected the pope's orders and turned out the pope's emissaries, seeing them as lacking in respect for Chinese traditions and culture. Starting in 1706, Christian missionaries in China now had to register with the dynasty and declare their adherence to Jesuit principles, what came to be called the "Chinese rites controversy."

The curtailing of missionary activity was never truly carried out under Kangxi. Emissaries made their way back and forth from China to Europe, and Clement XI's successor established a "Chinese Institute" in Naples dedicated to furthering the spread of Catholicism in China. Yet the Kangxi emperor's successors and their advisors were not nearly as lenient as he had been. A dispute over the Qing dynastic succession after Kangxi's death pitted a converted Christian son of Kangxi against the eventual Yongzheng emperor; Yongzheng took his vengeance by banning Christianity in

1724. China's three hundred churches were destroyed or confiscated, and the number of Christians in China dropped dramatically in the eighteenth century. By the time the next great Qing emperor, Qianlong, took the throne, few Chinese would willingly admit that they were Christians, for fear of ostracism or punishment. Christianity was considered a barbarian religion propagated by a barbarian people.

In the nineteenth century, China fought and lost the Opium Wars to Britain between 1839 and 1842. Hong Kong became a British protectorate, and through Hong Kong, Protestant missionaries arrived in China from Britain and the United States for the first time. Their most important convert was a former Confucian scholar named Hong Xiuquan, who led the Taiping Rebellion from 1850 to 1864. The rebellion cost the Qing dynasty all of the goodwill it had built up in the seventeenth and eighteenth centuries; worse, it could only be put down with the help of British and French mercenary armies, exposing the weakness of the dynasty before European military power. The more the dynasty struggled to maintain its legitimacy, the further inroads that Protestant missionaries made into Chinese life. Eventually, the Qing dynasty finally abdicated in favor of a republic in 1911, during the Chinese Revolution, whose leader, Sun Yat-sen, was a Chinese Christian.

—*David Simonelli*

Bibliography and Further Reading

Hibbert, Eloise Talcott. *Jesuit Adventure in China during the Reign of K'ang Hsi*. E. P. Dutton, 1941.

Jami, Catherine. *The Emperor's New Mathematics: Western Learning and Imperial Authority during the Kangxi Reign (1662-1722)*. Oxford University Press, 2012.

Smith, Richard J. *The Qing Dynasty and Traditional Chinese Culture*. Rowman & Littlefield, 2015.

Spence, Jonathan D. *Emperor of China: Self Portrait of K'ang Hsi*. Knopf, 1974.

Wu, Silas H. L. *Passage to Power: K'Ang-Hsi and His Heir Apparent, 1661-1722*. Harvard University Press, 1979.

Websites

Hearn, Maxwell K. and Madeleine Zelin, consultants. "The Kangxi and Qianlong Emperors." *Recording the Grandeur of the Qing: The Southern Inspection Tour Scrolls of the Kangxi and Qianlong Emperors*. Asian Topics in World History: Asia for Educators, Columbia University (2005), http://www.learn.columbia.edu/nanxuntu/html/emperors/index.html. Accessed 9 Apr. 2017.

Cordier, Henri. "The Church in China." *The Catholic Encyclopedia*, volume 3. New York: Robert Appleton Company, 1908, http://www.newadvent.org/cathen/03669a.htm. Accessed 9 Apr. 2017.